# DEIFICATION IN THE LATIN PATRISTIC TRADITION

# CUA STUDIES IN EARLY CHRISTIANITY

**GENERAL EDITOR**
Philip Rousseau, *Andrew W. Mellon Distinguished Professor*

**EDITORIAL BOARD**
Katherine L. Jansen, *Department of History*
William E. Klingshirn, *Department of Greek and Latin*
Trevor C. Lipscombe, *The Catholic University of America Press*
Frank J. Matera, *School of Theology and Religious Studies*
Timothy Noone, *School of Philosophy*
Sidney H. Griffith, *Department of Semitic and Egyptian Languages and Literatures*

**INTERNATIONAL EDITORIAL BOARD**
Pauline Allen, *Australian Catholic University*
Lewis Ayres, *Durham University*
Daniel Boyarin, *University of California, Berkeley*
Gillian Clark, *University of Bristol*
Angelo di Berardino, OSA, *Istituto Patristico Augustinianum, Rome*
Hubertus R. Drobner, *Theologische Fakultät, Paderborn*
David W. Johnson, SJ, *Jesuit School of Theology, Berkeley*
Judith Lieu, *University of Cambridge*
Éric Rebillard, *Cornell University*
John M. Rist, *University of Toronto*
Linda Safran, *University of Toronto*
Susan T. Stevens, *Randolph-Macon College*
Rita Lizzi Testa, *Università degli Studi di Perugia*
Michael A. Williams, *University of Washington, Seattle*

# DEIFICATION IN THE LATIN PATRISTIC TRADITION

EDITED BY
*Jared Ortiz*

The Catholic University of America Press
Washington, D.C.

Copyright © 2019
The Catholic University of America Press
All rights reserved

Library of Congress Cataloging-in-Publication Data
Names: Ortiz, Jared, author.
Title: Deification in the Latin patristic tradition /
edited by Jared Ortiz.
Description: Washington, D.C. : The Catholic University
of America Press, [2019] | Series: CUA studies in early Christianity |
Includes bibliographical references and index.
Identifiers: LCCN 2018047198 | ISBN 9780813237831
(pbk)
Subjects: LCSH: Deification (Christianity) | Christian literature,
Early—Latin authors—History and criticism.
Classification: LCC BT767.8 .D45 2019 | DDC 234—dc23
LC record available at https://lccn.loc.gov/2018047198

CONTENTS

Acknowledgments vii
List of Abbreviations ix

Introduction 1

1. Making Worshipers into Gods: Deification in the Latin Liturgy 9
   *Jared Ortiz*

2. Dying to Become Gods: Deification in the *Passion of Perpetua and Felicity* 30
   *Thomas Heffernan*

3. Sequestered in Christ: Deification in Tertullian 54
   *Mark A. Frisius*

4. After the Fashion of God: Deification in Cyprian 75
   *Benjamin Safranski*

5. Loaning and Borrowing: Deification in Novatian 94
   *James L. Papandrea*

6. Making Man Manifest: Deification in Hilary of Poitiers 111
   *Janet Sidaway*

7. Beyond Carnal Cogitations: Deification in Ambrose of Milan 132
   *Fr. Brian Dunkle, SJ*

8. Rebirth into a New Man: Deification in Jerome 153
   *Vít Hušek*

9. "We Shall Be That Seventh Day": Deification in Augustine        169
    *Ron Haflidson*

10. Between Empire and *Ecclesia*: Deification in
    Peter Chrysologus                                               190
    *Fr. David Meconi, SJ*

11. The Wonderful Exchange: Deification in Leo the Great           208
    *Daniel Keating*

12. Every Happy Man Is a God: Deification in Boethius              231
    *Michael Wiitala*

13. Beholding Christ in the Other and in the Self: Deification
    in Benedict of Nursia and Gregory the Great                    253
    *Fr. Luke Dysinger, OSB*

14. A Common Christian Tradition: Deification in the
    Greek and Latin Fathers                                        272
    *Norman Russell*

    Selected Bibliography                                          295
    Contributors                                                   309
    Index                                                          311

ACKNOWLEDGMENTS

This volume began as a three-day workshop at the 2015 Oxford Patristic Conference. I am grateful to Gillian Clark, who helped with the logistics, as well as all those who participated. The ready friendship, good will, and thoughtfulness of Fr. Brian Dunkle, Fr. Luke Dysinger, Mark Frisius, Tom Heffernan, Vít Hušek, Dan Keating, Fr. David Meconi, Jim Papandrea, Norman Russell, and Janet Sidaway made that conference both deeply edifying and very enjoyable. I am thankful for Ben Safranski and Michael Wiitala, who joined the project as we expanded its scope. I want to thank Andrew Peecher, who did yeoman's work as everything was getting off the ground, as well as Andrea Antenan Peecher, who read through every essay with me, offered astute suggestions, and was an incredibly perceptive interlocutor throughout the editing process. Robin Jensen provided her characteristic insight into our cover art and saved us from some embarrassing mistakes. Lastly, I wish to thank Hope College and the Harry A. and Margaret D. Towsley Foundation for providing an early sabbatical, which allowed me to complete the manuscript.

# ABBREVIATIONS

| | |
|---|---|
| ACW | Ancient Christian Writers |
| ANF | Ante-Nicene Fathers (ed. Roberts et al.) |
| CCL | Corpus Christianorum: Series Latina |
| CCCM | Corpus Christianorum: Continuatio Mediaevalis |
| CSCO | Corpus Scriptorum Christianorum Orientalium |
| CSEL | Corpus Scriptorium Ecclesiasticorum Latinorum |
| FOTC | Fathers of the Church (The Catholic University of America Press) |
| GCS | Die griechische christliche Schriftsteller der ersten Jahrhunderte |
| *GeV* | *Sacramentarium Gelasianum* |
| *JECS* | *Journal of Early Christian Studies* |
| *JTS* | *Journal of Theological Studies* |
| NIV | New International Version (Holy Bible) |
| NPNF | Nicene and Post-Nicene Fathers (ed. Schaff) |
| NRSV | New Revised Standard Version (Holy Bible) |
| PG | Patrologia Graeca (ed. Migne) |
| PL | Patrologia Latina (ed. Migne) |
| RB | *Rule of Benedict* (St. Benedict) |
| RM | *Rule of the Master* (Anon.) |
| *SAEMO* | *Sancti Ambrosii Episcopi Mediolanensis Opera* |
| SC | Sources Chrétiennes |
| *VC* | *Vigiliae Christianae* |
| *Ve* | *Sacramentarium Veronense* |
| *ZKT* | *Zeitschrift für Katholische Theologie* |

# DEIFICATION IN THE LATIN PATRISTIC TRADITION

*Jared Ortiz*

# INTRODUCTION

The seed for this book was planted several years ago when I was asked to write a survey article on deification in the Latin Fathers and was told by several scholars that due to the thin fare offered by the Latin Fathers, my essay was due to be rather thin itself.[1] This seemed to be confirmed by the paucity of secondary material available on the Latin tradition: Norman Russell had devoted seven pages to the Latin Fathers in an appendix, there was an old dissertation on Hilary of Poitiers, and a few scattered articles on Augustine, but not much else.[2] In the only other survey of deification in the Latin Fathers, written in 1957, Gustave Bardy asserts from the outset, "Latin theology has always insisted much less than Greek theology on the divinization of man," and later adds, "It is easy to write on *The Divinization of the Christian according to the Greek Fathers*, as Jules Gross has done (Paris, 1938). One could not, though, compose a parallel work on divinization among the Fathers of the Latin Church."[3] Perhaps comments

---

1. This essay appeared as "Deification in the Latin Fathers" in *Called to Be the Children of God: The Catholic Theology of Human Deification*, ed. Fr. David Meconi, SJ, and Carl E. Olson (San Francisco: Ignatius Press, 2016), 59–81.

2. See Norman Russell, *The Doctrine of Deification in the Greek Patristic Tradition* (Oxford: Oxford University Press, 2009), 325–32; Philip Wild, *The Divinization of Man according to St. Hilary* (PhD diss., Mundelein Seminary, 1950); Victorino Capánaga, "La deificación en la soteriología agustiniana," *Augustinus Magister* 2 (1954): 745–54; Gerald Bonner, "Augustine's Concept of Deification," *Journal of Theological Studies* 37 (1986): 369–86; Robert Puchniak, "Augustine's Conception of Deification, Revisited," in *Theosis: Deification in Christian Theology*, ed. Stephen Finlan and Vladimir Kharlamov (Eugene, Ore.: Pickwick, 2006), 122–33. Daniel Keating, in his *The Appropriation of Divine Life in Cyril of Alexandria* (Oxford: Oxford University Press, 2004), includes a chapter comparing the Latin Fathers Augustine and Leo to Cyril, as well as a thoughtful assessment of the "perceived East-West differences" on deification (227–93).

3. Gustave Bardy, "Divinisation: Chez les Pères Latins," in *Dictionnaire de Spiritualité, ascétique et*

like these simply ruffled my Western pride, but I had a feeling that there was more to the story. So, I spent a long summer in the wonderful library of Mount Angel Abbey pouring over the Latin corpus and, to my delight, was able to gather dozens upon dozens of pages of deification material from the Latin tradition.

With all the material available, I knew, *pace* Bardy, there was a book to be written, a long-overdue companion to Norman Russell's magisterial *The Doctrine of Deification in the Greek Patristic Tradition*. The current volume is not yet that companion, but is a first step along the way. I decided to invite a talented team of senior and junior scholars to contribute to a workshop on deification in the Latin tradition at Oxford's XVII International Conference on Patristic Studies. In August 2015, a dozen of us spent three happy afternoons in an upper room at Merton College working through the Latin tradition of deification together. In addition to the warm sense of collegiality, there was also a palpable sense of excitement and discovery. We knew we were discovering—or rediscovering—something beautiful and important. We found that each of our Latin authors had deeply engaged deification in unique and interesting ways, ways that enriched their theology and our understanding of deification. Each of those papers at Oxford has been developed, expanded to twice the length, and included in this volume. Two essays—the ones on Cyprian and Boethius—were solicited after the Oxford conference to fill in certain lacunae.

The difficulty for thinking about deification in the Latin tradition was well articulated by the ninth-century theologian John Scotus Eriugena, who also suggested a way forward: "While the use of the term deification is very rare in Latin books, we certainly find the meaning [*intellectus*] in many of them."[4]

---

*mystique doctrine et histoire*, ed. Charles Baumgartner (Paris: Beauchesne, 1957), 1390; author's translation. Comments like these have been common since the turn of the twentieth century. For the reasons why, see Carl Mosser, "An Exotic Flower? Calvin and the Patristic Doctrine of Deification," in *Reformation Faith: Exegesis and Theology in the Protestant Reformations*, ed. Michael Parsons (Milton Keynes: Paternoster, 2014), 38–56, at 40–48. Even in the deification renaissance of the past thirty years, the Latin Fathers are given scant treatment. Aside from Puchniak's essay on Augustine in the Finlan/Kharlomov volume, none of the collections about deification in the Christian tradition treat the Latin Fathers in any substantial way. Fortunately, the tide is turning and there is a slowly growing body of literature on deification in the Latin patristic tradition: see, for example, David Vincent Meconi, SJ, *The One Christ: St. Augustine's Theology of Deification* (Washington, D.C.: The Catholic University of America Press, 2013); Ellen Scully, *Physicalist Soteriology in Hilary of Poitiers* (Leiden: Brill, 2015); Alexey Fokin, "The Doctrine of Deification in Western Fathers of the Church: A Reconsideration," in *Für uns und für unser Heil. Soteriologie in Ost und West*, ed. Theresia Hainthaler et al. (Innsbruck-Wien: Tyrolia Verlag, 2014), 207–20.

4. Eriugena, *Periphyseon* 5 (Corpus Christianorum: Continuatio Mediaevalis [hereafter "CCCM"] 165:217), author's translation: "Sed huius nominis (deificationis dico) in latinis codicibus rarissimus est usus, intellectum uero eius apud multos."

Indeed, the term *deificatio* is coined by Eriugena himself in his translation of Pseudo-Dionysius, while other words with the root *deif-* are relatively sparse before then. A search in the Brepolis Library of Latin Texts Database yields only seventy-three occurrences of *deif-* words from the second to seventh century.[5] Eriugena, like many of us who study this topic, admits that he does not understand why this is the case, though he suggests that one cause might be the *disciplina arcana*: "to those who are not strong enough to ascend beyond fleshly thoughts it seems too lofty, incomprehensible, and incredible and on account of this not to be proclaimed in public."[6] Whatever the reason, it is clear that the Latin Fathers do not extensively employ the technical terminology for deification. This has led many scholars to conclude that the Latin tradition is largely bereft of a theology of deification, but, as Eriugena reminds us, this is not a necessary conclusion. The *intellectus* can be present, even if the terms are not. Even many of the Greek Fathers whom we associate with the doctrine of deification—Irenaeus, for example—do not use a technical vocabulary to discuss it.[7]

To think about deification in the Latin Patristic tradition, then, we must not confine our study to the terminology, useful and interesting as it is, but look to the "meaning" and, what Andrew Louth calls "the pattern of theology" our authors display.[8] How does the *intellectus* of deification appear in the constellation of their thought? Does their vision contain the key elements of a theology of deification? In short, do Latin Christians of the patristic period hold a full understanding of salvation as participation in God and the communication

---

5. This database is large, but by no means complete. One missing piece is the Latin translation of Athanasius's *Life of Anthony*, which contains several instances of *deif-* words (often in places where the Greek does not use the term). If one extends the search through the ninth century, the number of uses of the root *deif-* increases to 643 total. The majority of these uses come from Eriugena and his translations of Dionysius the Areopagite and Maximus the Confessor. Paschasius Radbertus is also a prominent user of *deif-* words in the ninth century. Interestingly, after a bit of a lull, there is a rise in the twelfth century with 243 more uses and an explosion in the thirteenth with more than 800 additional uses. It seems as though many of our common assumptions about deification in the *whole* Latin tradition need to be rethought.

6. Eriugena, *Periphyseon* 5 (CCCM 165:217), author's translation: "altus nimium uisus est ultraque carnales cogitationes ascendere non ualentibus incomprehensibilis et incredibilis, ac per hoc non publice praedicandus." See Brian Dunkle's essay in this volume for an exploration of Eriugena's claim in the preaching and writing of Ambrose.

7. Russell, *Doctrine of Deification*, 105. See Daniel Keating, *Deification and Grace* (Naples, Fla.: Sapientia Press, 2007), 8–9, for a concise but properly nuanced discussion of the content and terminology of deification. Also helpful is Keating's "Typologies of Deification," *International Journal of Systematic Theology* 17, no. 3 (July 2015): 274–75.

8. Andrew Louth, "The Place of *Theosis* in Orthodox Theology," in *Partakers of the Divine Nature: The Historical Development of Deification in the Christian Tradition* (Grand Rapids, Mich.: Baker Academic, 2007), 33.

of his divine life to us? The consistently surprising evidence of the essays below would argue that many Latin authors do hold deification as an integral part of their theological vision, have deeply engaged it, and have done so by drawing on a common Christian tradition which they developed in unique ways.[9] For these Latin authors, deification holds a place of "structural significance" in their theology, entailing a vision of our glorious destiny in Christ through the Spirit, a belief in the real transformation of the Christian, which, moreover, calls for our graced participation.[10] While rarely if ever an independent locus of reflection, deification is an integral and uplifting part of their theological vision.

The volume begins with the liturgy, with the cult within which all of our authors were formed, and within which most of them, as bishops, priests, or abbots, formed others. In "Making Worshipers into Gods: Deification in the Latin Liturgy," I show that the rich and varied presence of deification language and images in the liturgical literature of the second to seventh century means that the Latin church of the patristic period certainly believed in deification: *lex orandi, lex credendi*. But more than this, the prayers and mystagogical teaching around the sacraments—especially of the baptism liturgy—offer a coherent theology of deification which every Latin Christian would have encountered at some time in some form.

In the next essay, "Dying to Become Gods: Deification in the *Passion of Perpetua and Felicity*," Thomas Heffernan takes us to the first Latin Christian

---

9. The first Latin Christian literature appears around the turn of the second century. These Latin-speaking Christians did not have to discover deification, but were drawing on biblical and traditional modes of speaking about salvation. Latin Christians received a Christianity that had first been articulated in a Greek context or, at least, a Greek language, in which the *intellectus* of deification was already a constitutive part. For helpful discussions of the biblical roots of deification, see Norman Russell, *Fellow Workers with God: Orthodox Thinking of Theosis* (Crestwood, N.Y.: St. Vladimir's Seminary Press, 2009), 55–72; Russell, *The Doctrine of Deification*, 53–89; Keating, *Deification and Grace*, 16–21, 48–55, 100–104, 116–18; Gregory Glasov, "Theosis, Judaism, and Old Testament Anthropology," 16–31; Stephen Finlan, "Second Peter's Notion of Divine Participation," 32–50, in *Theosis* (ed. Finlan).

10. Andrew Louth lists these three elements as necessary for there to be a "doctrine" of deification rather than merely a "theme." See Louth, "The Place of *Theosis* in Orthodox Theology," 43, and "Deification" in *The New Westminster Dictionary of Christian Spirituality*, ed. Philip Sheldrake (Louisville, Ky.: Westminster John Knox Press, 2005), 230. He borrows this distinction from Gösta Hallonsten, "*Theosis* in Recent Research: A Renewal of Interest and a Need for Clarity," in Michael J. Christensen and Jeffrey A. Wittung (eds.), *Partakers of the Divine Nature: The History and Development of Deification in the Christian Traditions* (Madison, N.J.: Fairleigh Dickenson University Press, 2007), 281. I do not think the distinction between a doctrine and theme of deification is particularly useful (see Keating, "Typologies," 274, for a brief critique), but Louth's list of elements is helpful for showing that the Latin Fathers teach deification in a way that even their critics would recognize.

literature, the late second-century martyr accounts of North Africa. Heffernan shows how Perpetua becomes a prophet, speaking God's word and doing God's deeds. In the early Latin martyr literature, deification is expressed through powerful stories of transcendence, incorruptibility, the gift of healing, revivifying the dead, and an intimate union with God reserved for the martyr alone.

Mark Frisius's "Sequestered in Christ: Deification in Tertullian" shows us one of the more unique approaches to deification in the Latin tradition. Frisius examines the way in which Tertullian's incarnational and eschatological thought are connected with an understanding of deification. In particular, Tertullian applies the legal concept of the sequester to establish the unity between divinity and human flesh. Through this incarnational activity, the perfection of the flesh becomes an eschatological possibility and the believer, whose soul has been purified by the Holy Spirit, is able to receive the divine attributes. In this way, Tertullian uniquely approaches the concept of deification while remaining faithful to his rigoristic approach to the Christian life.

Cyprian is a close reader of Tertullian, but he takes a different approach on deification. In "After the Fashion of God: Deification in Cyprian," Benjamin Safranski argues that Cyprian develops a theology of deification by drawing on his own experience of being reborn as a new man. Employing the complementary terms "adoption" and "sonship," Cyprian says that the basis for deification is found in our baptism and brought to fruition through the imitation of Christ, especially in the mercy shown in almsgiving. Incorporated into Christ and living up to the dignity of our baptismal rebirth, we receive the increase of grace that ultimately results in being taken to the Father.

James Papandrea takes us on a tour of pre-Latin-speaking Rome to show how deification is present in the heart of the West from early on, before focusing on the theology of Novatian and his unique appropriation of the exchange formula. In "Loaning and Borrowing: Deification in Novatian," Papandrea argues that Novatian is a pioneer of the doctrine of the *communicatio idiomatum*, who uses the language of "loaning" and "borrowing" to preserve the immutability of the divine, while still allowing for the divine nature of Christ to experience the human condition. Papandrea outlines Novatian's understanding of the *communicatio idiomatum* and demonstrates how he believed that it led to a conferral of divinity on humanity.

Hilary of Poitiers was familiar with theological developments in the East as well as the West. Janet Sidaway's "Making Man Manifest: Deification in Hilary of Poitiers" focuses on Hilary's theology of the full humanity of the incarnate Christ as the means whereby humankind attains the glory originally planned for it. She explores his novel interpretation of the transfiguration as "anthropophany," his exegesis of the kenotic text of Philippians 2:6–8 and the eschatological text of 1 Corinthians 15:24–28 to argue that God becomes "all in all" because Christ's brotherhood with us enables us to share his glory.

Fr. Brian Dunkle, SJ, follows Eriugena who not only says that the *intellectus* of deification is found in many Latin authors, "but above all in Ambrose." In "Beyond Carnal Cogitations: Deification in Ambrose of Milan," Dunkle argues that Ambrose is committed to a robust vision of deification that is nevertheless expressed in terms accessible to a broad audience. Dunkle shows how Ambrose tends to employ the strong tropes of deification—in particular, the exchange formula and 2 Peter 1:4—in his doctrinal and ascetical works, writings, that is, aimed at a more mature Christian audience. But Ambrose also uses the more accessible language of image and likeness as well as the *natura/gratia* pair to articulate an account of deification for mixed audiences which, Dunkle suggests, demonstrates Eriugena's point that certain forms of deification language are only proper to the spiritually advanced.

Vít Hušek's "Rebirth into a New Man: Deification in Jerome" shows Jerome to be an able representative of the deification tradition. Conversant in Greek and Latin theology, Jerome discusses deification as participation in divine life, adoptive sonship, and grace and its special gifts, in particular the life of virginity which, when lived rightly, is a process of angelification. Hušek also treats Jerome's adaptation of other important themes, such as the inequality of divine gifts and the interplay between divine grace and human agency.

Ron Haflidson discusses deification in Augustine's eschatology by returning to the beginning. In "'We Shall Be That Seventh Day': Deification in Augustine," Haflidson focuses on Augustine's Genesis commentaries to show how, for Augustine, God's declaration that the light is good on the first day of creation (Gn 1:4) and God's rest on the seventh day (Gn 2:2) reveal features of redeemed human beings' participation in God's nature by the sanctifying work of the Holy Spirit. Haflidson takes up the neglected idea of deification as rest—that we shall become the Sabbath where God is fully present in us. Haflidson also takes up an important dimension of deification in discussing the continuity between our sanctified knowledge while on earth with our heavenly knowledge in our deified resurrected state.

In the next essay, "Between Empire and *Ecclesia*: Deification in Peter Chrysologus," Fr. David Meconi, SJ, immerses us in the bustling city of Ravenna with its important and sorely understudied bishop, Peter Chrysologus. Meconi argues that Peter's sermons offer a triadic theology of deification, combining a rich and creative use of the "great exchange" with the Pauline doctrine of divine adoption and a unique understanding of our participation in the divine nature. What makes Peter's sermons particularly striking, Meconi argues, is how he delivers them with all the realities of Ravenna's imperial court in mind, where deification language would have been more readily associated with the imperial cult and not the salvation of the average citizen.

Daniel Keating highlights how the "fundamental tenet" of a theology of deification, the "formula of exchange,"[11] is fundamental to the thought of Leo the Great, one of the great synthesizers of the Latin tradition. In "The Wonderful Exchange: Deification in Leo the Great" he shows how Leo consistently and with creative variation casts human salvation in terms of the "exchange formula" to communicate that Christ became fully what we are so that we might become what he is and might partake of the riches of his divine life and power. For Leo, the ultimate goal of salvation is that we might be united to Christ and experience the fruits of his divinity in our transformed and glorified humanity. Leo's Christology is at the service of a soteriology centered on human participation in the divine life.

Boethius is unique among the other figures considered in this volume in that his account of deification makes no explicit reference to Christ. In "Every Happy Man Is a God: Deification in Boethius," Michael Wiitala shows how Boethius develops in his *Consolation of Philosophy* a distinctly Neo-Platonic notion of deification, in which human beings are made divine through participation in God, who is understood as happiness itself, goodness itself, and unity itself. This account is, Wiitala argues, compatible with Boethius's Catholic Christianity, even if Boethius does not fully integrate it. Philosophy can see the goal, Boethius seems to say, but cannot show the way. Boethius is an important witness to the Neo-Platonic background that influenced many of our Latin authors.

In Fr. Luke Dysinger's essay, we turn to the monastery and the ascetic and contemplative dimensions of deification. In "Beholding Christ in the Other

---

11. See Russell, *Doctrine of Deification*, 321.

and in the Self: Deification in Benedict of Nursia and Gregory the Great," Dysinger argues that Benedict and Gregory both depict contexts in which the Christian is able to recover and manifest to others aspects of primordial glory. The Rule of St. Benedict presumes an anticipation of eschatological renewal and transformation that occurs within the Christian community. In Gregory, the "uncircumscribed light of God" transforms the Christian ascetic into a contemplative who helps others to behold transcendent realities in ordinary circumstances. Dysinger also deftly, and delightfully, shows how these two Latin authors became models for the Byzantine tradition of *theosis*.

Finally, Norman Russell concludes the collection with an essay comparing the contribution of the Latin Fathers with that of the Greek Fathers. In "A Common Christian Tradition: Deification in the Greek and Latin Fathers," Russell argues that these two distinct linguistic cultures share a commitment to the basic tenets of deification. By looking at the broader theological structures in which "deification" is embedded, Russell finds a number of common characteristics between the Latin and Greek understanding of deification: it is Christologically driven, ecclesial in nature, eschatological in orientation, and, finally, draws on similar Platonic themes, such as participation, the soul's ascent to God, and becoming like God through moral and ascetical discipline. The difference between the Latin and Greek Fathers on deification is not one of absence and presence, but rather a matter of emphasis.

It is often suggested that deification is something foreign to the Western mind and would have to be "grafted" onto it or "imported" from the East. But the essays presented here tell a different story. Deification is native to the Latin confession of faith, integral to Latin worship and praxis, and a common teaching that is found in creative and interesting ways in all of the major figures of the Latin tradition. My hope is that this volume will be the first of many more studies of the Latin understanding of deification. But, more importantly, my hope is that this volume will demonstrate that East and West are not as divided—at least on this point—as we are sometimes led to believe. Perhaps the witness of the Latin authors here might make it a little easier to see that all Christians are inheritors of a beautiful tradition which teaches that even now, together, "we all, with unveiled face, beholding the glory of the Lord, are being changed into his likeness from one degree of glory to another" (2 Cor 3:18).

*Jared Ortiz*

# 1. MAKING WORSHIPERS INTO GODS
*Deification in the Latin Liturgy*

Latin Christians of the patristic period were regularly being deified. They were often reminded of this fact in their liturgies and they often reflected upon it in their writings. Deification was not the esoteric teaching of a few superior theologians, but a popular teaching that was written into the very art and architecture of Latin churches and baptisteries. It was part of the meaning and symbolism of the rites of initiation, a recurring theme in sermons and catechesis, and a topic of the formularies, that is, the prayers of the liturgy which changed from week to week and were used for instruction throughout the year. Latin Christians who had eyes to see and ears to hear would have known that their destiny was to be deified and that this process began the moment they were called to be baptized and lasted throughout their life as they progressed in virtue with the help of the sacraments. They would have known, as Augustine strikingly says, that God "makes his worshipers into gods."[1]

It has become common to assert that the Latin Fathers did not seriously hold a teaching about deification. But a fair and open reading of the liturgies, sacramentaries, and mystagogies of the Latin church reveals that deification

---

1. Augustine, *City of God* 10.1: "facitque suos cultores deos" (Corpus Christianorum: Series Latina [hereafter, CCL] 47); author's translation. For Augustine, this occurs through true worship of the one true God. For the most recent studies of deification in Augustine, see J.-C. Byeon, "La deificatio hominis in sant' Agostino" (PhD diss., Institutum Patristicum Augustinianum, 2008); David Meconi, *The One Christ: St. Augustine's Theology of Deification* (Washington, D.C.: The Catholic University of America Press, 2013); and Ron Haflidson, "'We Shall Be That Seventh Day': Deification in Augustine," in this volume.

is woven into the fabric of Latin thought. In the available Latin liturgies, *deif-* words do not appear (nor do they appear in the Greek ones either), though the content of deification is alluded to throughout in both metaphysical and poetic language.[2] It is one of the many themes in the liturgical literature, but, I will argue, not simply one among other themes. Rather, it is a kind of crowning theme that brings coherence to the others and has the power to integrate them.[3]

In this essay, I want to begin to draw together the many allusions to deification in the Latin liturgical literature in order to show two things. One, I wish to demonstrate that, contrary to the widespread assertion that the Latins did not hold deification in any serious way, the presence of deification themes in the liturgical literature is evidence that the Latin church of the patristic period certainly believed and taught deification.[4] But more than this, I would like to sketch a theology of deification as it emerges from the prayers of the Latin church and the mystagogical reflections of the Latin Fathers.

In broad strokes, the theology of deification that we discover in these texts looks something like this: for the Latins, Christ is the new man whose newness consists in uniting divinity and humanity. Through the sacraments, this newness is re-presented to believers who are invited to enter into union with Christ's humanity which unites them to his divinity. Through baptism, believers begin to partake of Christ's divine nature, which means that the baptized have arrived at the end times; they are new creations living in the old creation; they are restored to their original innocence and therefore the gates of paradise are no longer barred to them; they have arrived at the Promised Land flowing with milk and honey. The "confirmation" rite—including anointing

---

2. On this point, see Gerhart Ladner, *The Idea of Reform: Its Impact on Christian Thought and Action in the Age of the Fathers* (Cambridge, Mass.: Harvard University Press, 1959), 294. A search of the *Corpus Orationum* turns up only one reference to a word with the root *deif-* and this from a medieval Dominican prayer.

3. See G. M. Lukken, *Original Sin in the Roman Liturgy: Research into the Theology of Original Sin in the Roman Sacramentaria and the Early Baptismal Liturgy* (Leiden: Brill, 1973), 373–74, for a brief but compelling account of the Latin initiation rites in a deification key.

4. Most recent scholars of the liturgy argue that the principle *lex orandi, lex credendi* works both ways: praying informs believing, while beliefs shape and refine what and how a community prays. See Maxwell E. Johnson, *Praying and Believing in Early Christianity: The Interplay between Christian Worship and Doctrine* (Collegeville, Minn.: Liturgical Press, 2013); Paul Bradshaw, "Difficulties in Doing Liturgical Theology," *Pacifica* 11 (June 1998): 181–94; Edward Kilmartin, *Christian Liturgy: Theology and Practice*, vol. 1: *Systematic Theology* (Kansas City, Mo.: Sheed and Ward, 1988), 96–99. In this essay, I do not intend to argue that any particular prayers informed any particular theology (or vice versa), though they may very well have. Rather, I argue that there is a pattern of deification ideas present in the liturgical literature which shows that there was a common belief in deification.

and the imposition of hands—configures the newly baptized to Christ's kingly and priestly glory, confirms their divine filiation, and bestows the Holy Spirit on them, by which their participation in the divine nature is augmented. The eucharist transforms them into what they eat, namely, the Word of God, advancing their likeness to God, continually reforming and conforming them to the heavenly image. These sacraments call them to a new way of life which is a life where their actions become God's actions in them. Through participation in the sacraments, meditation on scripture, and the practice of virtue, believers grow in union with and likeness to God.[5]

## *Admirabile Commercium*

In many of the Latin liturgical prayers, the incarnation of Christ is understood as the foundation of our deification through the sacraments: through the Son of God's assumption of a human nature, we are enabled to partake of his divine things. There is a "magnificent exchange" wherein Christ receives our human things and we receive his divine ones. The following Christmas Preface to the Eucharistic prayer from the *Verona Sacramentary* (ca. 560) shows a series of creative uses of this "formula of exchange":

> Since the magnificent exchange [*magnificum commercium*] of our reparation has shone forth—that is, since out of the old man a new man stood forth—mortality was cured by mortality. When the human condition is healed by the created medicine of the human condition itself, and an offspring ignorant of all sin arises from the guilty, sinful generation, then not only does our frailty, taken up by your Word, receive perpetual honor [*perpetui honoris*], but also by this marvelous sharing [*mirando consortio*], our frailty is made eternal.[6]

---

5. It should go without saying that not every particular Latin figure or set of liturgical texts discussed below conforms to this generalized picture and I occasionally point out some divergent traditions. Still, there are enough similarities in their thought to warrant calling it a pattern.

6. *Sacramentarium Veronense* (hereafter, *Ve*) 1260. The critical edition is *Sacramentarium Veronense* (*Cod. Bibl. Capit. Veron. LXXXV [80]*), ed. L. C. Mohlberg (Rome: Herder, 1955). The text has been turned into a searchable concordance at liturgia.it. All translations of *Ve* are my own based on the texts found there. For other prayers that employ the exchange formula, see *Ve* 176, 1115, 1239, 1269, 1357. See also *Sacramentarium Gelasianum* (hereafter, *GeV*) 7, 27, 48, 129, 398. The critical edition is *Liber Sacramentorum Romanae Aeclesiae Ordinis Anni Circuli* (*Cod. Vat. Reg. lat. 316/Paris Bibl. Nat. 7193, 41/56*) (*Sacramentarium Gelasianum*), ed. L. C. Mohlberg (Rome: Herder, 1960). This text is also available at liturgia. it. All translations of the *GeV* are my own based on the texts found there. According to Eric Palazzo, the *Verona* was compiled around 560 and the *Gelasian* around 650: see *A History of Liturgical Books from the Beginning to the Thirteenth Century* (Collegeville, Minn.: Liturgical Press, 1998), 35. Both contain prayers that were in use long before the time of their compilation.

The exchange formula alerts us that we are in a deification context: God unites himself to our human weakness and repairs it by the power of his divinity. Out of the old comes a new man who still bears the marks of the old—mortality, the human condition, frailty—but instead of dragging him down, he uses this oldness to heal us. It becomes the soil from which springs new life. Our weakness, now united to his strength, becomes medicine for us, which not only restores us, but gives us a new and divine quality: eternal life.

The preface draws on Paul's discussion of Christ as the new Adam.[7] From the context, it seems that what is "new" about Christ is that he unites the divine and the human. Christ is "ignorant of all sin" just like the first Adam, but in the incarnation Christ does not simply assume the status of Edenic humanity. Rather, he has taken up "our frailty" and bestowed on it a "perpetual honor." "Honor," in this context, is the equivalent of the Greek *doxa*, "glory," a sign of the divine presence dwelling in creation.[8] Christ brings a new, divinized humanity, and this is the basis for our own divinization. When Christ takes our nature, he not only cures mortality, heals the human condition, and addresses our guilt, but "by this marvelous sharing, our frailty is made eternal." To be eternal is a divine quality, a quality of the new man, Christ, who entered our human estate and shares his divine qualities with the people to whom he is united.[9]

## Baptism

Christ is the new man who makes a new people. This happens through the liturgy, which makes present Christ's newness. Leo the Great explains this by saying: "All that the Son of God did and taught for the reconciliation of the world, we have come to know not so much from an historical account of his actions in the past, but as we have experienced in the power of his works in the present. It is he who, brought forth from the Virgin Mother by the Holy Spir-

---

7. See 1 Cor 15 and Rom 5. For prayers about the newness of Christ, including the newly baptized person described as a "new man," see *GeV* 316, 353, 398, 527, 601; *Ve* 1331.

8. Lukken, *Original Sin in the Roman Liturgy*, 381. See, for example, Hilary of Poitiers, *On the Trinity* 9.40.9, and *Commentary on Matthew* 4.2.23.

9. See, for example, *GeV* 398 and 527. A prayer from the *Gelasian Sacramentary* (ca. 650) makes this same point: "It is, indeed, right that, lifting up our hearts, we adore the divine mystery [of the incarnation] by which the human condition, with the old and earthly law ceasing, is brought forth as a new and heavenly substance, marvelously restored" (*GeV* 14). From our old, fallen substance, Christ brings forth a new, divine one. Compare Leo the Great, *Sermon* 22.1.

it, makes fruitful his untainted Church with the same inspiration."[10] What Christ accomplished is not simply a matter of historical record, but something that is present in the sacraments. The same Spirit who wrought the union of God and man in the incarnation is the same one who works in the church to bring about our union with God.

This begins in the rite of baptism—something every Christian would have experienced—the first part of which is the exorcism. For the Latin church, exorcism is essential kenotic preparation if God is to dwell in us and deify us.[11] Everyone, by virtue of their lineage from the first Adam, is "held bound by the power of the devil" and unless one renounces the devil "he cannot obtain the grace given by the saving bath."[12] Originally, God "designed the human body and made it to be a dwelling for the divine Spirit" and therefore, in the first part of the baptismal rite, a bishop would pray for the catechumen's restoration: "All you armies of the devil, every power of the adversary, every violent clash of the enemy, every blind disordered phantasm, be rooted out and put to flight from this creature [*plasma*], that by the remission of all sins he may become a temple of the living God."[13] In exorcism, the catechumen (if we might borrow an apt phrase from the Eastern contemporary, Dionysius the Areopagite) "will do battle with every activity and with every being which stand in the way of his divinization."[14] For the Latins, exorcism is the self-emptying that participates in Christ's own kenotic death and prepares the way for sharing in his resurrection and therefore divinity. Leo says: "Even

10. Leo the Great, *Sermon* 63.6, author's translation: "Omnia igitur quae dei filius ad reconciliationem mundi et fecit et docuit, non in historia tantum praeteritarum actionum nouimus, sed etiam in praesentium operum uirtute sentimus. Ipse est qui de spiritu sancto ex matre editus uirgine incontaminatam ecclesiam suam eadem inspiratione fecundat" (CCL 138A). Compare Augustine's striking comment about the presence of Christ in the liturgy in *Sermon* 17.1.

11. Interestingly, the bulk of the baptismal rite is focused on exorcising the devil. This is true in both the Western and Eastern liturgies. For example, about forty percent of the words spoken in the eighth-century Byzantine liturgy are devoted to expelling Satan. See *Documents of the Baptismal Liturgy*, ed. E. C. Whitaker and Maxwell E. Johnson (Collegeville, Minn.: Pueblo Books, 2003), 109–23.

12. John the Deacon, *Letter to Senarius* 3, in *Worship in the Early Church: An Anthology of Historical Sources*, ed. Lawrence J. Johnson (Collegeville, Minn.: Liturgical Press, 2009), 4:39. This motif appears in the martyr literature as well: see Perpetua trampling the dragon at the foot of the ladder ascending to heaven in her first vision (*Passion* 4).

13. *Liber Ordinum: An Order of Baptism for Occasional Use* in *Documents of the Baptismal Liturgy*, 166. The manuscripts of the *Liber Ordinum* date from the eleventh century, though much of its content likely comes from the sixth and seventh centuries, hence its inclusion here.

14. Dionysus, *Ecclesiastical Hierarchy* 404A, in *Pseudo-Dionysus: The Complete Works*, trans. Colm Luibheid (New York: Paulist Press, 1987), 207.

while we renounce the devil and believe in God, while we pass into new things from old, while we put aside the 'image' of this 'earthly' human being and take on the form of that heavenly one, a kind of 'death' and a certain 'likeness of resurrection' happens."[15] And so, just as a new, divinized man emerged from the old in the incarnation, so too do we transition from oldness to newness as Christ's own divine life becomes manifest in us.

Not only is the catechumen exorcized, but so is the water used for baptism. Water was thought to be the abode of the ancient dragon (see Job 41:1) and so a dwelling place of demons. But Christ's own baptism sanctified the waters and made them usable for sanctifying. In a prayer for the Feast of the Birth of John the Baptist, we hear that John "washed the Author of Baptism Himself" so that "the nature of waters might conceive the effect of sacred purification for those to be sanctified in the flowing Jordan."[16] Maximus of Turin develops this theme in a deification key: "We are to be washed in the same spring in which Christ was washed so that we might become what Christ was."[17] Water is now the vehicle for sanctification, but it still needs to be purified. The prayer over the baptismal font from the *Liber Ordinum* reads: "Purge out from yourself the whole communion of demons ... so that having received the grace of sanctification you may restore in innocence to God, who is both yours and mine alike, those whom you receive in their sins."[18] Tertullian says "the Spirit comes from heaven," just as it did in the original creation, "and hovers over the waters [used for baptism] which it sanctifies with its presence. The waters, thus sanctified, are in turn granted the power to sanctify."[19]

It was a common idea that once purged of demons and subsequently blessed, the water became a dwelling place of God and therefore could bring believers to new birth. Isidore of Seville says, that in "the water ... *dwelleth all the fullness of the godhead bodily*."[20] Paulinus of Nola says that the Holy Spir-

---

15. Leo the Great, *Sermon* 63.6, in *St. Leo the Great: Sermons*, trans. Jane P. Freeland and Agnes J. Conway, Fathers of the Church (hereafter, FOTC) 93 (Washington, D.C.: The Catholic University of America Press, 1996), 276.

16. *Ve* 254.

17. Maximus of Turin, *Sermon* 13.2 in *The Sermons of St. Maximus of Turin*, trans. Boniface Ramsey, Ancient Christian Writers (hereafter, ACW) 50 (New York: Newman Press, 1989): "tingui debemus eodem fonte quo christus, ut possimus esse quod christus" (CCL 23).

18. *Documents of the Baptismal Liturgy*, 168. See Ambrose, *On the Sacraments* 1.18.

19. Tertullian, *On Baptism* 4. See *GeV* 445.

20. Isidore of Seville, *De Ecclesiasticis Officiis* 2.25.4, quoting Col 2:9, in *Documents of the Baptismal Liturgy*, 160.

it "marries the sacred water in the heavenly font" and because "water has received God into itself" it can bring forth "sacred progeny ... from an eternal seed."[21] Likening the water to Mary, Leo extends this reflection explicitly in the context of deification:

> Christ was made a man of our race, so that we might be able to become "partakers of the divine nature." He placed in the font of Baptism that very origin which he had assumed in the Virgin's womb. He gave to the water what he had given to his Mother. For, the same "power of the Most High" and "overshadowing" of the Holy Spirit that caused Mary to bear the Savior makes the water regenerate the believer.[22]

Like Mary, the baptismal font receives the power of the Holy Spirit, so that it can give us new life. Leo shows that this new life is divine life, a sharing in the divine nature. The same power that gives the world Christ in his divinized humanity is the same power that divinizes believers. The baptismal font, like Mary, is overshadowed with the Spirit and so has the power to bring new people to birth in the world.[23]

In Latin thought, baptism brings about a radical identification with Christ. "Taken up by Christ and taking on Christ," Leo says, "we are not the same after the purification of Baptism as we were before it. Instead, the bodies of those reborn turn into the flesh of the Crucified."[24] In many Latin baptisteries, the mosaic above the baptismal font depicted a naked Christ being baptized by John the Baptist in the Jordan River, which was clearly meant to mirror the bishop baptizing the naked believer in the font below. Even more striking are the mosaics that depict this scene with Christ in diminutive stature, as if he were a child.[25] Historically, of course, Christ was not a child when baptized, but Robin Jenson suggests that perhaps the image was meant to conflate Christ's baptism with the catechumen's. Christ identified himself with believers so they can become identified with him. The newly baptized—

---

21. Paulinus of Nola, *Epistle* 32.5, quoted in Robin Jensen, *Baptismal Imagery in Early Christianity: Ritual, Visual, and Theological Dimensions* (Grand Rapids, Mich.: Baker, 2012), 149.

22. Leo the Great, *Sermon* 25.5 (103).

23. An inscription over the Lateran baptistery (often attributed to Leo) combines this idea of the Spirit making the waters holy with the idea of bringing to birth a new people in Christ. It reads: "A people consecrated to the heavens is here born from a fruitful seed / established by waters made fertile by the Spirit. / Plunge in, O sinner, and be cleansed by the sacred flow. / Whom it receives old, the wave returns new." Quoted in Jensen, *Baptismal Imagery*, 53. Compare Faustus of Riez, *Sermon* 28.

24. Leo the Great, *Sermon* 63.6 (276).

25. See Jensen, *Baptismal Imagery*, 15–16.

also called neophytes, *infantes*, the reborn—had become *alteri Christi*, other Christs, just as he had become one of them.[26]

Baptism radically identifies us with Christ and makes us sharers in his divine nature. Everything else about the meaning and effects of baptism flows from this central insight. It is because baptism makes us partakers of the divine nature that Latin baptisteries were often designed in the shape of an octagon. For Latin Christians, the number eight signified the eschaton when God will be all in all. God created all things in six days, he hallowed the seventh day, when his rest was present to all creation, but the seventh day is a day without evening, it opens up into an eternal eighth day. The eighth day was also the day of resurrection, the day after the Sabbath when Christ rose from the dead, and so was a sign of eternal life.[27] In baptism, one was entering this eighth day, entering the final age of all things and becoming the new creation in which God was at rest.[28] A preface from the *Missale Gothicum* (ca. 700) for the Easter Vigil baptismal liturgy captures this powerfully:

> For this is the night which has knowledge of the saving sacraments, the night in which you offer pardon to sinners, make *new men* from old, from worn out old men restore full-grown infants, whom you bring from the sacred font renewed unto a *new creature*. On this night your people are *new* born and *brought forth unto eternal day*, the halls of the kingdom of heaven are thrown open, *by your blessed ordinance human conversation is changed to divine*.[29]

In baptism, we are united to Christ and participate in his resurrection, so we have entered into that day, the day we hope to enjoy fully in the end times. But already we have a foretaste because "on this night," we are born "unto eternal

---

26. In baptism, believers become identified with Christ in both his death and resurrection. This is based on the three key baptismal texts: Jn 3:5, Ti 3:5, and Rom 6. See Maxwell E. Johnson, *The Rites of Christian Initiation: Their Evolution and Interpretation* (Collegeville, Minn.: Liturgical Press, 2007), xiv, 112–13, 155. These meanings were written into the architecture and the rites. Baptismal fonts were often designed to evoke both the tomb and the womb. In the tomb, the old dies with Christ, and in the womb, a new birth occurs (see Jensen, *Baptismal Imagery*, 160–65). This parallels the double meaning of liturgical nudity in the baptismal rite as well: in taking off his clothes as he descended into the baptismal font, the catechumen was stripping off the old man and naked with the dying Christ; as he emerged on the other side, he was nude like a newborn infant, given new life in the risen Christ (ibid., 167).

27. See, e.g., Augustine, *City of God* 22.30, *Sermon* 259, and *Epistle* 55.9–13. See also the fine discussion by Jean Daniélou, *Bible and Liturgy* (Notre Dame, Ind.: University of Notre Dame Press, 2002), 261–86; see Jensen, *Baptismal Imagery*, 204–9.

28. See 1 Pt 3:20 for a biblical precedent.

29. Quoted in *Documents of the Baptismal Liturgy*, 262–63; emphasis added. Compare the epigraph in the Ambrosian Baptistry (quoted in Johnson, *Worship in the Early Church*, 3:87–88).

day," and "human conversation is changed to divine." It is no accident that Easter, the Feast of the Resurrection, was celebrated for eight days, the liturgical octave, another sign that the baptized had passed over into God's eternal day.

These octagonal baptisteries were often decorated with rich images of flora and fauna, an almost overwhelming fecundity meant to evoke the unspoiled Garden of Eden.[30] The baptistery, Jean Daniélou says, was "the Paradise from which Adam was driven out and to which baptism restores us."[31] This motif is seen not just in the decoration of church buildings, but also throughout the liturgical literature. In the *Liber Ordinum*, we hear the prayer of the blessing of the baptismal font, rich in paradisiacal imagery:

*Restore the innocence which Adam lost in paradise* which his wife let go, which the intemperance of gluttony devoured. Give a healthful draught to men who are upset by the bitterness of the apple; purge the disorders of mortals and with a divine antidote cure their age long distemper. Wash away the filth and squalor of the world: *Make a way through the wall of fire which protects the garden of paradise and open a flower-strewn path unto them that return*. May they receive the *likeness of God* which once was lost by the malice of the serpent.... May they *rise up unto rest*: may they be brought forward unto pardon: that being renewed in the mystic waters they may know themselves to be redeemed and reborn.[32]

These images and prayers are meant to convey the mystical reality that those who have union with Christ are no longer bound to their sins and now enjoy the grace that our original parents had. The likeness to God that they once had is restored because they now share God's life. In baptism, Tertullian says, "we are returned to God according to God's image, we who were once conformed to God's image."[33] We have become like him and likeness, for Tertullian, refers to God's eternal life.[34] For the Latins, the church is paradise because the church is Christ's body where we have communion with God and participate in his divine nature, thereby, enjoying the innocence and likeness to God that our first parents had.

---

30. See Jensen, *Baptismal Imagery*, 177–214. See also the funerary art on the cover of this book which depicts a young girl being baptized from a Spirit-infused heavenly font and surrounded by Edenic plants and animals.
31. Daniélou, *Bible and Liturgy*, 36. See Cyprian, *Letter* 73.11, where the church is called paradise in connection with 1 Pt 3:20. See also Augustine, *City of God* 13.21, and Zeno of Verona in *The Day Has Come*, 76.
32. *Documents of the Baptismal Liturgy*, 169; emphasis added. See also *Ve* 194.
33. Tertullian, *On Baptism* 5, in Johnson, *Worship in the Early Church*, 1:122.
34. Ibid.

Our restoration, though, is not just a return to original innocence, but a restoration to something better.[35] A famous Christmas prayer recorded in the *Verona Sacramentary* reads: "God, you who marvelously created the dignity of human substance and more marvelously reformed it: grant us, we ask, to be sharers in the divinity of your Son, Jesus Christ, who deemed it worthy to become a partaker of our humanity."[36] The reformation of our substance is "more marvelous" because it is superior to our original marvelous creation. This is because the incarnation grants us not just an Edenic harmony with God, but a sharing in God's own nature through the humanity of Christ. Another prayer in the *Verona* supports this idea: "not only do you make alive our earthly and mortal material which had died out"—that is, God not only restores the life which was lost in the Fall—"but you even make it divine."[37] We are restored to our first state, but then go beyond it because we are united to Christ's divinity. Leo fills out the thought of this prayer:

> Yet the merciful God wanted to help the creature "made in his own image" [Gn 1:27] through his only Son Jesus Christ—in such a way that the restoration of its nature should not be outside of that nature, and that the second creation should advance beyond the dignity of its original state.... It was a great thing to have received a form from Christ, but greater still to have its substance in Christ.[38]

Our re-creation in baptism is an advance upon our original creation because we now not only have form from Christ (our human nature), but share in his very own divine substance.

Emerging from the font, the newly baptized are clothed in white garments. These were understood as an outward sign of the inward change that had occurred in baptism. These garments were sometimes called "the chaste robes of innocence."[39] The baptized are now "dressed in heavenly vesture."[40] They are "clothed in blessed immortality."[41] Because of their baptism, they

---

35. See Ladner, *The Idea of Reform*, 133–316, for a wide-ranging discussion of this idea in the Latin Fathers.

36. *Ve* 1239. See *GeV* 27.

37. *Ve* 90: "terrenam mortalemque materiam non solum uiuificaris extinctam, sed efficeris et diuinam." Sometimes this advance on our original creation is spoken of in terms of "angelification." See *Ve* 1104; also Zeno of Verona, *The Day Has Come* 2.10.1 (85) and 2.11.7 (87).

38. Leo the Great, *Sermon* 72.2 (316).

39. Ambrose, *On the Mysteries* 7.34, in *Saint Ambrose: Theological and Dogmatic Works*, trans. Roy J. Deferrari, FOTC 44 (Washington, D.C.: The Catholic University of America Press, 1963), 17.

40. Zeno of Verona, *The Day Has Come* 1.23 (62).

41. *GeV* 516.

wear the wedding garment of Christ's flesh, which gives them access to the wedding feast of the eucharist.[42] Drawing on the Song of Songs, Ambrose talks about how the angels behold this baptismal transformation with awe. "The angels looked down and saw you coming. They saw the natural human state, until recently soiled with the gloom and squalor of sin, suddenly shine out brilliantly. This led them to say, 'Who is this that is coming up from the wilderness in white' [Song 8:5]? The angels, then, also stand and marvel."[43] John the Deacon says that the white garment signifies "the mystery of the risen Church" which has been transfigured just as Christ was on Mount Tabor.[44] In other words, the angels "stand and marvel" because the newly baptized are resplendent with God's own attributes.

## Anointing and the Imposition of Hands

Two rites follow: anointing and the imposition of hands. These rites are sometimes understood as one, sometimes as separate. Sometimes there are two anointings and one imposition of hands; sometimes both rites are lumped together under the name "confirmation."[45] Whatever the practice, though, the general meaning is the same: these rites configure the baptized to Christ as king and high priest in glory, they confirm that we are no longer slaves but have become adopted sons and daughters of God, and they bestow on us a full or fuller share of the Holy Spirit.

"All who have been regenerated in Christ," Leo says, "are made kings by the sign of the cross and consecrated priests by the anointing of the Holy Spirit."[46] John the Deacon highlights the Old Testament background of this anointing:

---

42. See Leo the Great, *Letter* 59.4. See also Chromatius of Aquileia, *Sermon* 14, and John the Deacon, *Letter to Senarius* 6, for white garment as wedding robe.

43. Ambrose, *On the Sacraments* 4:5, in Edward Yarnold, *The Awe-Inspiring Rites of Initiation* (Collegeville, Minn.: Liturgical Press, 1994), 129; see Song 3:6 and 8:5. See John Deacon, *Letter to Senarius* 6; Jerome, *Against the Pelagians* 3.15; Augustine, *Tractates on John* 65.3.

44. See John the Deacon, *Letter to Senarius* 6; Ambrose, *On the Mysteries* 7:34.

45. In the East, there seems to be no real tradition of handlaying; in the West, there seems to have always been one. For both East and West, the anointing rite is associated with the Holy Spirit, and this association becomes increasingly clear in the fourth century during the time of the pneumatological debates (Johnson, *The Rites of Christian Initiation*, 174).

46. Leo the Great, *Sermon* 4.1 (25).

Then, once the baptized have put on white garments, each person's head is anointed with holy chrism. In this way the baptized are able to understand that the kingdom and a priestly mystery have met in them. Priests and kings were once anointed with the oil of chrism so that, on the one hand, the priests might offer sacrifice, and on the other hand, so that the kings might govern the people.[47]

The anointed share in the priesthood of Christ; they are given the grace to offer their lives as an acceptable sacrifice: "We vow and return to him his gifts in us and the gift that is our very selves," Augustine says. "On the altar of the heart, we offer to him a sacrifice of humility and praise, inflamed with the fire of charity."[48] They also reign with Christ who sits at God's right hand. Filled with the Holy Spirit, they rule wisely over brute creation, over themselves, and others; they can judge all things according to the mind of God, but are judged by no one.[49] This is a dignity not just for those who have formal authority in the church, but for every Christian. "All Christians," Leo says, "who live spiritual lives according to reason recognize that they have a part in the royal race and the priestly office. What could be more royal than the soul in subjection to God ruling over its own body? What could be more priestly than dedicating a pure conscience to the Lord and offering spotless sacrifices of devotion from the altar of the heart?"[50] As new Adams who have entered paradise, the baptized and anointed are restored to the dignity of their original priesthood in the Garden and have dominion over creation.

By sharing in Christ's divine nature, the newly baptized also share in his sonship. Leo, again, puts it eloquently: "You can be made again a child rather than an outsider. With this power, you who were born of flesh that is subject to decay can be 'born again from the Spirit' of God and can obtain through grace what you do not have through nature. If you acknowledge yourself to be a 'child' of God through the 'spirit of adoption,' you may dare to claim God as your 'Father.'"[51] After baptism, we have something that we did not have be-

---

47. John the Deacon, *Letter to Senarius* 6, in Johnson, *Worship in the Early Church*, 4:41. See also Ambrose, *On the Mysteries* 6.30.

48. Augustine, *City of God* 10.3, author's translation: "ei dona eius in nobis nos que ipsos uouemus et reddimus ... ei sacrificamus hostiam humilitatis et laudis in ara cordis igne feruidam caritatis" (CCL 47).

49. See Augustine, *Confessions* 13.22.32–13.23.34 for an account of what dominion over creation means for the Spirit-filled person renewed by baptism and anointing (see 1 Cor 2:15). See also Peter Chrysologus, *Sermon* 148.

50. Leo the Great, *Sermon* 4.1 (25). See also Augustine, *Confessions* 13.22.32.

51. Leo the Great, *Sermon* 22.5 (85).

fore, so we are something we were not before. We have a share in the divine nature, and therefore we are, in truth, sons and daughters of God.

The laying on of hands signifies this as well. We see this in the two other interrelated meanings associated with these rites: manumission from slavery and adoption. John the Deacon fits these two meanings together well:

> One is instructed by the Church's ministry which imposes a blessing, namely, a laying on, of the hand so that one might know who he is or will be: from being condemned, a person is made holy; from being unjust, one becomes just; and finally a servant becomes a son or daughter. In this way whoever was lost in the first parent is restored by the gift of a second parent and possesses the paternal inheritance.[52]

By nature, that is, by our first birth, we belong to the devil. In the exorcism rite, we renounce our allegiance to the devil and profess our allegiance to our new family. Through the bishop, the newly baptized are manumitted from slavery and adopted into God's family.[53] Peter Chrysologus alludes to this same meaning when he tells his catechumens:

> What is more awesome ... that He Himself is born into your state of slavery, or that He makes you to be free children of His own? That He takes your poverty upon Himself, or that He makes you His heirs, yes, co-heirs of His unique Self? It is indeed more awesome that earth is transformed into a heaven, that man is changed by a deification [*deitate*], and that those whose lot is slavery get the rights of domination.[54]

The context of Roman adoption law brings out the deification dimension of these ideas in a rather suggestive way. According to Robin Jensen, adoptees "renounced their former family name and kinship relations. All their prior liabilities were voided and their previous (or birth) family lost any claim to support or loyalty. The adoptee not only started a new life but was rendered debt free."[55] This may very well be in the background of the triple renunciation of the devil that preceded the rite of baptism. Furthermore, "adoptees also took

---

52. John the Deacon, *Letter to Senarius* 3, in Johnson, *Worship in the Early Church*, 4:39.

53. See Alistair C. Stewart, "Manumission and Baptism in Tertullian's Africa: A Search for the Origin of Confirmation," *Studia Liturgica* 31 (2001): 129–49. In the back of Tertullian's thought seems to be not only manumission, but adoption as well. Tertullian claims that the handlaying rite comes from Jacob's final blessing over Joseph's sons when he adopted them by crossing his arms (foreshadowing our adoption in Christ) (*On Baptism* 8; see Gn 48:1–22).

54. Peter Chrysologus, Sermon 67, in *Saint Peter Chrysologus: Selected Sermons and Saint Valerian: Homilies*, trans. George E. Ganss, FOTC 17 (Washington, D.C.: The Catholic University of America Press, 1953), 92.

55. Jensen, *Baptismal Imagery*, 60.

the social rank of their new father, possessed all the rights of succession and inheritance due any child of the family."⁵⁶ If these Roman laws are in the background of the Latin theology of baptism and handlaying, then we can ponder what it means to "take the social rank of their new Father" and "possess all the rights of succession and inheritance."

For the Latins, the handlaying rite was also understood to confer the Holy Spirit. Tertullian says: "The flesh is shadowed with the imposition of hands, that the soul also may be illuminated by the Spirit."⁵⁷ Tertullian describes this outpouring as a marriage in which the Holy Spirit is wedded to the believer, both body and soul.⁵⁸ Cyprian says, "They who are baptized in the Church are brought to the prelates of the Church, and by our prayers and by the imposition of hands obtain the Holy Spirit, and are perfected with the Lord's seal."⁵⁹ For some Latins, the Holy Spirit was not believed to be given in baptism, but only in this post-baptismal rite.⁶⁰ For others, this rite was a new outpouring of the Spirit, a kind of Pentecost, which expanded the spiritual capacity of the baptized by bestowing on them the sevenfold gift of the Holy Spirit.⁶¹ Either way, the gift of the Spirit was another way by which the newly baptized partook of the divine nature.

In the *Gelasian Sacramentary* Chrism Mass (usually Holy Thursday, when the oils for anointing where consecrated), we hear that God will make the anointed "partakers of eternal life and sharers of heavenly glory."⁶² Ambrose has a similar understanding. After quoting 2 Peter 1:4, he speaks of the transformation the Spirit works in us in the "confirmation" rite: "For as we die in Christ, in order to be born again [in baptism], so, too, we are sealed with the Spirit, that we may possess His brightness and image and grace ... [and] that the Holy Spirit may portray in us the likeness of the heavenly image."⁶³ The outpouring of the Holy Spirit here makes us God-like by giving us a share in

---

56. Ibid.
57. Tertullian, *On the Resurrection* 8, in Ante-Nicene Fathers (ed. Roberts et al.) (hereafter, ANF), vol. 3.
58. See Tertullian, *On the Soul* 41.4, and *On the Resurrection* 63.
59. Cyprian, *Letter* 72.9, in ANF 5.
60. See, e.g., Tertullian, *On Baptism* 6–7.
61. "The spirit of wisdom and understanding, the spirit of counsel and strength, the spirit of knowledge and godliness, and the spirit of holy fear" (Is 11:2); see Ambrose, *On the Mysteries* 7.42.
62. *GeV* 388.
63. Ambrose, *On the Holy Spirit* 1.6.79, in Johnson, *Worship in the Early Church*, 3:20. Ambrose uses the Spirit's divinizing us as an argument for the divinity of the Holy Spirit (1.6.80).

*his* brightness, image, and grace. We are no longer earthly, but have the likeness of the heavenly image.

## Eucharist

For the Latins, baptism and confirmation are ordered toward the eucharist, and indeed these sacraments mutually illumine one another. There is not only a symbolic relationship but also a kind of mystical identity between the baptized and anointed congregation and the eucharist. Augustine likens the congregation to scattered grain that is gathered together, ground in exorcism, mixed with water in baptism, baked with the Holy Spirit in the anointing, and transformed into the eucharist.[64] But these symbolic elements point to a real relationship: just as the eucharist has become the body of Christ, so, too, the congregation. "So if you are the Body of Christ and its members," Augustine tells his congregation, "it is your mystery that has been placed on the Lord's table; you receive your own mystery."[65] Picking up on Augustine's thought, Fulgentius of Ruspe says that the baptized "not only ... are sharers in the very sacrifice, but ... they are the holy sacrifice itself."[66] For Augustine, though, the congregation both *is* the body of Christ and must also *become* the body of Christ. This is why he exhorts them, "Be what you see [on the altar], and receive what you are."[67] Being the body of Christ is both a grace and a task. Baptism makes us the body of Christ, but a mixed body. The body needs to be further conformed to its divine head. The eucharist, the unmixed body of Christ, is the primary means of advancing this transformation. It does so, as we will see later, with our cooperation, with our grace-filled moral efforts by which we are able to unite our Christ-configured lives to the eucharist.[68]

Partaking of the eucharist brings about a divine union that transforms be-

---

64. See, for example, Augustine, *Sermon* 229.1 and 272; see also *Didache* 9.
65. Augustine, *Sermon* 272; author's translation: "si ergo uos estis corpus christi et membra, mysterium uestrum in mensa dominica positum est: mysterium uestrum accipitis," in Patrologia Latina (ed. Migne) (hereafter, PL), 38:1247.
66. Fulgentius of Ruspe, *Letter* 12.24, in *Fulgentius: Selected Works*, trans. Robert B. Eno, FOTC 95 (Washington, D.C.: The Catholic University of America Press, 2010), 493.
67. Augustine, *Sermon* 272; author's translation: "estote quod uidetis, et accipite quod estis" (PL 38:1247–48).
68. See Augustine's complex discussion of the relationship between Christian lives as a sacrifice and the church's sacrifice in his discussion of true worship in *City of God* 10.1–6.

lievers in various ways. The *Verona Sacramentary* says that through the eucharist believers are made "sharers" (*consortes*) or "partakers" (*participes*) in "the divine nature,"[69] "the divine power,"[70] "heavenly things,"[71] and "heavenly joy."[72] This participation in God's life does many things for us: it abolishes sin and strengthens our frailty,[73] it takes up our weakness and gives us a share of divine power instead,[74] it purifies us,[75] it renews us and brings us back to life,[76] and, perhaps most beautifully, it adapts us to itself.[77] The most common effect of the eucharist, though, as seen in the pattern of prayers in the *Verona* (and *Gelasian*), is that we are "remade" (*reficere*).[78]

The union effected in the eucharist is often understood in nuptial terms. As noted above, the white garment received after baptism can signify the wedding garment that gains the baptized access to the eucharist, "the table of the heavenly bridegroom."[79] At the altar, Ambrose says, Christ calls to the newly baptized, "Let him kiss me with the kisses of his lips."[80] This union through the eucharist, Leo argues, communicates Christ's own life to us. "The participation in the body and blood of Christ does nothing else but that we pass over into what we receive, and we carry everywhere, in spirit and flesh, him in whom we have died, have been buried, and have risen."[81] As we eat the body and blood of Christ, we are more deeply united to Christ and our bodies and souls take on more and more the quality of what we consume in the eucharist.

---

69. *Ve* 525.
70. *Ve* 1269.
71. *Ve* 914. Compare *GeV* 448: "divine things."
72. *Ve* 876.
73. *Ve* 876.
74. *Ve* 1269.
75. See *Ve* 222 and 1041.
76. *Ve* 1078.
77. *Ve* 1256.
78. See *Ve* 230, 477, 548, 803, 903. See related words "renew" and "vivify": *Ve* 891, 908, 1078. See *GeV* 166 and 1175.
79. John the Deacon, *Letter to Senarius* 6, in Johnson, *Worship in the Early Church*, 4:41.
80. Ambrose, *On the Sacraments* 5.5, quoting Song 1:1, in Yarnold, *Awe-Inspiring Rites*, 142. A late antique marginalia on Jerome's *Commentary on Ezekiel* notes that "the sacred place where the body of Christ is kept, who is the true bridegroom of the Church and of our soul, is called *Thalamus* [in Latin] and *Pastophorion* [in Greek]," that is, "a bridal chamber" (author's translation). For another fascinating account of the union of martyrs and Christ in their relics in the altar, see Paulinus of Nola, *Letter* 32.7.
81. Leo the Great, *Sermon* 63.7 (author's translation): "Non enim aliud agit participatio corporis et sanguinis christi, quam ut in id quod sumimus transeamus, et in quo commortui et consepulti et conresuscitati sumus, ipsum per omnia et spiritu et carne gestemus" (CCL 138A).

It is important to note that even though we "carry Christ everywhere, in body and in spirit," we do not transform him into ourselves, but we are transformed into him. In a striking passage from the *Confessions* (interestingly, the central passage of the central book), God reveals to Augustine the transformative power of the eucharist. Augustine relates, "I heard Your voice from on high: 'I am the food of grown men; increase and you will eat Me. You will not change Me into you as food of your flesh, but you will be changed into Me.'"[82] Normally, when we eat something, we transform it into ourselves. We chew our food, digest it, break it down into its component parts, until it courses through our veins and becomes a part of our bodies. But the eucharist is not ordinary bread; for Augustine, it is "the body and blood of the Word."[83] When we "eat the Word," we do not incorporate him into us, but we are incorporated into him. When we "eat the Word," we do not change him, but he changes us.

The eucharist has the power to do this because the bread and wine undergo a real change during consecration.[84] For Augustine "when the word enters that bread and this wine it becomes the body and blood of the Word."[85] Pope Gelasius says: "Certainly the sacraments of the body and blood of Christ, which we receive, is a divine thing. On account of this and through the same 'we are made partakers of the divine nature' (2 Pet. 1:4)."[86] Because the sacrament is a "divine thing" (*diuina res*), it has the power to communicate divinity to us. For Ambrose, Christ's humanity is made present in the eucharist, but this is not separable from his divinity, so we partake of the divine nature through the eucharist. "The grace and efficacy of Christ's real human nature" is made available to us,[87] he says, and "because one and the same Jesus Christ our Lord possessed both divinity and a body, you too, by receiving his flesh, share in his divine substance by means of his food."[88]

---

82. Augustine, *Confessions* 7.10.16; author's translation.
83. Augustine, *Sermon* 229.1; author's translation.
84. See Ambrose, *On the Mysteries* 9.50 and *On the Sacraments* 6.3.
85. Augustine, *Sermon* 229.1; author's translation.
86. Pope Gelasius, *De duabus naturis in Christo aduersus Eutychem et Nestorium* 14, quoted in Edward J. Kilmartin, *The Eucharist in the West: History and Theology*, ed. Robert J. Daly (Collegeville, Minn.: Liturgical Press, 1998), 41.
87. Ambrose, *On the Sacraments* 6.3, in Yarnold, *Awe-Inspiring Rites*, 146.
88. Ibid., 6.4 (147). Our deification through the eucharist was so firmly fixed an idea in the Latin mind that Hilary of Poitiers could use it as the basis for one of his arguments for the substantial unity of the Father and the Son (see *On the Trinity* 8.13–17).

After receiving the eucharist for the first time, the newly baptized in many places would also drink from a chalice filled with milk and honey.[89] In partaking of the sacraments, the new Christian has arrived at the Promised Land. That land is not a geographic place, but our own glorification in Christ. The *Verona Sacramentary* records a beautiful prayer that explains that the milk and honey "signify the union of the heavenly and earthly substance in the Lord Jesus Christ."[90] John the Deacon comments on this part of the rite, saying:

And so the land of promise is the land of the Resurrection, a land leading to everlasting happiness; it is nothing other than the land of our body which in the resurrection of the dead attains glorious incorruption and peace. Therefore this form of the sacrament is offered to the baptized so that they may understand that only the baptized, not others, share in the Lord's Body and Blood, that they receive the land of promise, that beginning this journey they, like children, are nourished with milk and honey.[91]

The milk and honey is taken with the eucharist, and so it is joined together in meaning. The Promised Land is our resurrected body, glorious with incorruption and peace. The eucharist is already realizing this promise in us. Our very bodies are the destination, that is, when Christ's resurrection will be fully manifest in us. This is a journey of transformation or transfiguration which starts now in our participation in the sacraments.

## Life in Christ

The profound transformation that occurs in the rites of initiation calls for an equally profound change in our way of life: "Realize, O Christian, your dignity," Leo famously exhorts his congregation, reminding them of their baptism. "Once made a 'partaker of the divine nature,' do not return to your former baseness of life."[92] Cyprian takes up this theme as well by interpreting baptism in light of Paul's discussion of bearing the image of the heavenly man (1 Cor 15:47–49):

---

89. There is evidence of this practice in Rome and North Africa (as well as Ethiopia and Syria) from the second to the sixth century. See Johnson, *The Rites of Christian Initiation*, 69–71, 85, 100–101, 167–68, 188–89, 222, 302.
90. *Ve* 205.
91. John the Deacon, *Letter to Senarius* 12, in Johnson, *Worship in the Early Church*, 4:43.
92. Leo the Great, *Sermon* 21.3 (79).

But we cannot bear the heavenly image, unless in that condition wherein we have already begun to be, we show forth the likeness of Christ. For this is to change what you had been and to begin to be what you were not, that the divine birth might shine forth in you, that the deifying discipline [*deifica disciplina*] might respond to God, the Father, that in the honour and praise of living, God may be glorified in man.[93]

We partake in the divine nature by our baptism and this calls forth a certain way of life which makes that new divine life shine forth. That way of life is a "deifying discipline" which advances our participation in divinity. A prayer in the *Verona* captures this dynamic well. It says that "we fell away from the happiness of paradise by violating divine precepts," and so beseeches God that we "may return to access of eternal beatitude through the keeping of Your commands."[94]

For the Latins, we also advance in deification by meditating on scripture, both in the context of the liturgy and in private prayer. John Cassian says that by continuously meditating on the words of scripture, the word of God dwells in us until we are "formed in its likeness" and made into "a kind of ark of the covenant."[95] For Jerome, "the Gospel *is* the body of Christ"[96] and, just like the eucharistic body of Christ, we should feed on it to be spiritually nourished: "Since, the flesh of the Lord is true food and his blood is true drink, we only have this good in the present time ... if we feed on his flesh and drink his blood, not only in [the eucharistic] mystery, but also in the reading of the scriptures. For, true food and true drink—which is acquired from the word of God—is the knowledge of the scriptures."[97] Scripture, like the eucharist, has the power to transform us. Augustine understands the transformative power of scripture as the presence of the Holy Spirit from whose heat "no one can hide" (Ps 19:6). Hearing scripture, then, means encountering God and, in particular, the fire of his judgment. Scripture, for Augustine, has the power to destroy our old selves and give life to our new selves. "So," he says, "for the time being treat the scripture of God as the face of God. Melt in front of it."[98]

---

93. Cyprian, *On Jealousy and Envy* 14–15 (ANF 5); translation slightly modified.
94. *Ve* 194.
95. Cassian, *Conferences* 14.8.2, trans. Boniface Ramsey (Mahwah, N.J.: Paulist Press, 1997).
96. Jerome, *In Psalmum* 147; author's translation: "ego corpus iesu euangelium puto" (CCL 78).
97. Jerome, *Commentarius in Ecclesiasten* 3; author's translation: "porro, quia caro domini uerus est cibus, et sanguis eius uerus est potus ... hoc solum habemus in praesenti saeculo bonum, si uescamur carne eius et cruore potemur, non solum in mysterio, sed etiam in scripturarum lectione. uerus enim cibus et potus, qui ex uerbo dei sumitur, scientia scripturarum est" (PL 23:1039).
98. Augustine, *Sermon* 22.7, commenting on Ps 68; *Sermons*, trans. Edmund Hill, in *The Works of*

Augustine roots the transformative power of scripture in the *admirabile commercium*. In his commentary on the Psalms, he discusses how each Psalm is spoken by Christ in the first person. The "I" of the Psalms is always Christ, either Christ speaking in the head or Christ speaking in his body. When we pray the psalms, we are speaking in the voice of Christ or Christ is speaking through us.

> But in fact he who deigned to assume the form of a slave, and within that form to clothe us with himself, he who did not disdain to take us up into himself, did not disdain either to transfigure us into himself [*transfigurare nos in se*], and to speak in our words, so that we in our turn might speak in his. This is the wonderful exchange [*mira commutatio*], the divine business deal, the transaction effected in this world by the heavenly dealer.[99]

For Augustine, this is a consequence of the radical identity that is established in baptism where "we have become not only Christians, but Christ himself."[100] In Christ—or, as Christ—Christians see as Christ sees and read as Christ reads. Michael Cameron comments on this: "Their reading skills as Christians grow out of the 'astounding exchange' of redemption that gave rise to the *totus Christus*. Its members not only read the Bible's words as words about Christ the head: *they live as Christ inside these words and so speak them as their own words.*"[101]

This "synergy" or "co-operation" between Christ and believer can also be seen in the Latin understanding of prayer, fasting, and almsgiving. Our observance of them, Leo says, "brings us to the image and likeness of God" and inseparably joins us to the Holy Spirit.[102] This is because our observance is not so much our observance as it is God's work in us.[103] Maximus of Turin, for

---

*Saint Augustine: A Translation for the 21st Century*, ed. John E. Rotelle (Brooklyn, N.Y.: New City Press, 1990), 2:46. This is precisely what Augustine describes happened to him in the Milan garden when he first encountered the word of God in scripture. See Augustine, *Confessions* 8.12.29.

99. Augustine, *En. 2 Ps.* 30.1.3; *Expositions of the Psalms*, trans. Maria Boulding, in *Works of Saint Augustine*, 1:322–23.

100. Augustine, *Tractates on John* 21.8; author's translation: "ergo gratulemur et agamus gratias, non solum nos christianos factos esse, sed christum" (CCL 36).

101. Michael Cameron, *Christ Meets Me Everywhere: Augustine's Early Figurative Exegesis* (Oxford: Oxford University Press, 2012), 289.

102. Leo the Great, *Sermon* 12.4 (53): "ad imaginem et similitudinem dei peruenit et a sancto spiritu inseparabiles facit" (CCL 138A).

103. See Leo the Great, *Sermon* 63.7. See also Gregory the Great, *Dialogues II: Life and Miracles of Saint Benedict* 16 and 30.

example, says: "When we fast often, part of God's power dwells in us since it is God himself who fasts."[104] For Maximus this is a consequence of the incarnation and our participation in Christ through baptism. Christ poured his Spirit out and so "made every Christian to be what Christ is."[105] Christ was in the world like leaven in dough, he says, and Christians share in that, spreading grace throughout the whole world. "Whoever, therefore, sticks to the leaven of Christ becomes in turn leaven as useful to himself as he is helpful to everyone else and, certain of his own salvation, he is made sure of the redemption of others."[106] The baptized and anointed have the Holy Spirit who configures their lives to Christ, making them an acceptable sacrifice, indeed, a eucharistic sacrifice. Christians become *alteri Christi*, other Christs, who even share in Christ's own salvific activity in the world.

## Conclusion

The wide-ranging and diverse presence of deification in the Latin liturgical literature should hopefully put to rest the misconception that the Latins did not believe in deification. Deification is a pervasive theme that enriches and unites the other themes in the liturgy. From the many scattered liturgical references to deification a pattern emerges that amounts to a coherent theology of deification in the Latin church. Christ is the new man who comes to make us new by offering us a share in his newness. What is new about Christ is precisely the fact that in the incarnation he has united divinity and humanity in himself. Christ, then, is the start of a new humanity, one where divinity dwells in humanity, and he offers us the same. Through the sacraments, we are invited into this transfiguring union that gives us the power of the Holy Spirit who conforms us to Christ and unites our actions to God's. The pattern of deification ideas in the Latin liturgical literature confirms that the Latin church of the patristic period widely believed that, as Augustine claimed, God desires to "make his worshipers into gods."

---

104. Maximus of Turin, *Sermon* 35.4, in *The Sermons of St. Maximus of Turin*, trans. Boniface Ramsey, ACW 50 (New York: Newman Press, 1989).
105. Maximus of Turin, *Sermon* 33.3.
106. Ibid.

*Thomas Heffernan*

## 2. DYING TO BECOME GODS
*Deification in the* Passion of Perpetua and Felicity

While the belief in deification is present in the earliest Latin Christian *Acta Martyrum*, that genre does not employ the philosophical language of Justin or Irenaeus, nor is some rhetorical variation of the *admirabile commercium* formula employed. Rather the understanding of how a human can achieve such an exalted status is depicted in the historical martyrologies as an integral part of the narrative, expressed in richly metaphoric discourse, which shows the martyr participating by grace in one of the divine attributes. Such desire for an intimate union with God is present as early as the Ignatian letters (ca. 110–25) and exists in the earliest Greek *Acta Martyrum*, dating from the mid-second century, notably in the *Martyrdom of Polycarp*, the *Letter of the Churches of Lyons and Vienne*, and the *Acts of Justin*.[1] The two earliest Latin martyrologies, the subject of my investigation, date from the end of the second century and early third century respectively and are both from *Africa Proconsularis*, notably the *Scillitan Martyrs* (ca. 180) and the *Passion of Perpetua and Felicitas* (ca. 203; hereafter, *Passion*). Neither of these Latin texts employs philosophical discourse, or exhibits a Middle Platonist influence—an influence that is partly responsible for the language of such apologists as Justin, Tatian, and Irenaeus. As these narratives belong to a genre that does not employ technical philosophical language, I will illustrate how the *Passion of Perpetua*

---

1. On the Ignatian letters, see Paul Foster, "The Epistles of Ignatius of Antioch (Part I)," *The Expository Times* 117, no. 12 (2006): 487–95.

*and Felicity* particularly represents deification through its emphasis on transcendence, incorruptibility, the gift of healing, revivifying the dead, and an intimate union with God reserved for the martyr alone. Although the multiple voices in the *Passion* are never explicit about what intimacy with God entails, it appears, however, that they understood it as a type of divine possession. The martyr's experience of the indwelling presence of God was so intense that the somatic and psychic boundaries separating the human and divine blurred.

## The Matter of Genre

Martyrological texts, unlike the early Christian apologies, draw on a diverse generic tradition that had a rich literary tradition antedating the advent of Christianity. Already by the late first century the literature of martyrdom in both the Greco-Roman and Jewish traditions was a multifaceted and polyglot amalgam of diverse traditions including, but not limited to, the influence of the Peripatetic school of biography, Stoicism's concern for self-fashioning and the exercise of free will, the *exitus illustrium virorum*, Roman emperor worship, the *laudatio funebris*, book 6 of the *Aeneid*, Philo's *Life of Moses*, Plutarch's *Parallel Lives*, the figures of Enoch and Elijah and the various Jewish-Christian texts composed about their ascensions, the depiction of vicarious martyrdom in the Books of Maccabees, the passion narratives in the Gospels, and the account of Stephen's death in Acts 6:8–8:1. These multifarious traditions were part of the rich intellectual inheritance of the early Christian authors as they fashioned the stories of their own Christian heroes to substitute for the idealized heroic biographies of the Jews and pagans.

### Acta Martyrum

The genre of the Christian *Acta Martyrum* contains both *Acta* and *Passiones*. The *Acta*—of which the *Scillitan Martyrs* is the earliest example in Latin—are brief narratives that purport to present the actual judicial interrogations, and thus provide an "historical" record of cross-examinations between the prosecuting authority and the accused. They are rhetorically unadorned and focus on the civil authorities' representation of the illegality of the martyr's belief and its socially disruptive nature. The accused are given an opportunity to recant and be pardoned or to continue in their belief and die. The accuser is frequently depicted as an oppressing authority and the accused as innocent victim. Their deaths are treated with considerable economy and little drama. The *Scillitan Martyrs* and the *Act of Saint Cyprian* are representative of such narratives. The text of the *Scillitan Martyrs* is very brief, but there is one significant instance suggestive of deification: the belief in Carthaginian Christianity that the martyr's profound anticipation of union with God could actually result in their spiritual presence in heaven even before the precise moment of their death. The martyr Nartazalus says to the proconsul that because they will die for their faith (employing the present tense emphatically), "*today we are* martyrs in heaven" (*Hodie martyres in caelis sumus*).[2]

## Passiones Martyrum

The *Passiones*, on the other hand, are the principal heirs to the diverse literary traditions mentioned above. They illustrate these themes employing epideictic rhetoric, celebrating with the highest praise the great heroism of the martyr and the ignoble cowardice, cruelty, and lack of justice of the persecutors.[3] They depict the perennial struggle between good and evil, between God and Satan, and they are uncompromisingly binary in their representation of the opposing points of view. They employ encomium and panegyric, and occasionally remind one of motifs in the contemporary Hellenistic novels such as the *Martyrdom of Pionius* and the *Acts of Paul and Thecla*.[4] They are designed to arouse in their listeners the desire to imitate the martyrs. The martyr becomes the paradigmatic expression of Christian heroism. They focus on the *agōn* (test) and *hupomonē* (endurance) of the martyr. Their basic plot structure is the test, that is, they situate their hero or heroine in an unavoidable conflict with an oppressive civic authority where death or capitulation is the only outcome. The outcome, although almost always a vindication of the

---

2. "Acta Scillitanorum," in *Atti e passioni dei Martiri*, ed. A. A. R. Bastiaensen et al. (Milan: Lorenzo Valla, 1987), 15. See J. W. van Henten, "Martyrdom, Jesus' Passion and Barbarism," *Biblical Interpretation* 17, no. 1 (2009): 239–64.

3. Cicero believed that epideictic rhetoric was the appropriate format for historical writing; see his *Brutus, Orator*, trans. G. L. Hendrickson and H. M. Hubbell (Cambridge, Mass.: Harvard University Press, 1939), 20.66 (355): "History is nearly related to this style [i.e., epideictic]. It involves a narrative in an ornate style ... and speeches of exhortation [*et hortationes*]." See also T. Penner, *In Praise of Christian Origins: Stephen and the Hellenists in the Lukan Apologetic Historiography* (London: T and T Clark, 2004), and S. E. Parsons, *Ancient Apologetic Exegesis* (Eugene, Ore.: Wipf and Stock, 2015), 76.

4. "Martyrium Pionii," in *Atti e passioni dei Martiri*, 453–77. See also Herbert Musurillo, *The Acts of the Christian Martyrs* (Oxford: Clarendon Press, 1972), xxix. On the novel see J. W. Barrier, *The Acts of Paul and Thecla* (Tübingen: Mohr Siebeck, 2009), 30.

Christian truth, is never certain. The dramatic imperative of "the test" requires that failure is at least a possibility as a martyr may recant and apostatize.[5]

The representations of the events depicted in some of the *Acta Martyrum*, particularly in the *Passiones*, were composed using classical epideictic rhetoric as the principal rhetorical model and frequently use anecdotes from the non-Christian traditions as models shaping their narratives. Unlike the apologists, who seek to refute the arguments of their opponents through philosophical discourse, the martyrologies employ the existing traditions of heroic discourse and build their *aretologies* employing motifs from them. For example, the themes of Jewish martyrdom exemplified in such popular and well-loved texts as 2 and 4 Maccabees were well represented in the earliest Christian martyr narratives, and were influential in Paul's theology of martyrdom as an atoning sacrifice (Rom 3:25) and in the Gospel writer's understanding and depiction of Christ's passion.[6] Allusions to the righteous elder Eleazar also appear in the earliest Christian martyrdoms. In the *Martyrdom of Polycarp* (ca. 160), the hostile governor interrogates the aged Polycarp about his belief and says if he swears by the genius of the emperor, he will free him. The old bishop refuses to recant his Christianity, lest—like his Old Testament ancestor Eleazar—he betray his old age, his faith, and his flock. Polycarp's comment is an unmistakable echo of Eleazar's remarks to Antiochus (see *Mart. Poly.* 9.3 and 2 Mc 6:23–28). In the *Letter of the Churches of Lyons and Vienne*, the young man Ponticius endures his cruel torments "like a man" (1.54), an echo of the voice from heaven which voices urges Polycarp to "be strong and be a man" (9.1). Classical allusions are also present in the *Passiones*. For instance, the scene in which Perpetua covers her thigh (20.4) strongly suggests the redactor's familiarity with the story of Polyxena's death (Euripides, *Hec.* 569–70).

---

5. Musurillo, *Letter of the Churches Martyrs of Lyons and Vienne*, 1.11: "Yet others were shown to be still untrained, unprepared, and weak, unable to bear the strain of the great conflict. Of these about ten in all were stillborn ... blunting, indeed, the eagerness of those who had not yet been arrested."

6. J. W. van Henten, *The Maccabean Martyrs as Saviours of the Jewish People*, Supplements to the *Journal for the Study of Judaism* 57 (Leiden: Brill, 1997). See also Jarvis J. Williams, *Christ Died for Our Sins: Representation and Substitution in Romans and Their Jewish Martyrological Background* (Eugene, Ore.: Pickwick, 2015).

## The *Passion of Perpetua and Felicity*: Structure and Context

The *Passion of Perpetua and Felicity* is the oldest representative of the *passiones* in the Latin tradition and it is the principal subject of my discussion.[7] It was written sometime during the games honoring Geta Caesar, held in Carthage in March 203 and autumn 209. There is a Greek exemplar of the *Passion* extant, but it is, as I have argued elsewhere, mid-third century.[8] The *Passion* is a composite work in the hands of possibly four different authors: Redactor 1 (chaps. 1 and 22b), Vibia Perpetua (chaps. 3–10), Saturus (chaps. 11–14), and Redactor 2 (chaps. 2 and 14–21a), two of whom claim autobiographical status and one of whom is at once a convert, an imprisoned catechumen, and an educated elite female named Vibia Perpetua. My discussion of deification will necessarily have to consider the radically differing contexts for each of the principal authorial narratives and the extent to which we can make assumptions about their understanding of the Christian tradition. The four narratives are dominated by the following thematic categories: Redactor 1, polemic and ecclesial; Perpetua, sacrificial; Saturus, eschatological; and Redactor 2, historical narrative.[9]

The first-person narrative of Vibia Perpetua is the most singular voice in the *Passion*, the one that has received the most attention in the history of the text, and which provides the most historical information. Although she never gives her name, Redactor 2 provides both her *nomen* Vibia and a *cognomen* Perpetua, indicating by virtue of these two names that she is a member of the *honestiores* (individuals who according to Roman law had status and property; thus she was not a freed woman). The Vibii clan is well attested in *Africa Proconsularis* and Italy and they were a family of some distinction.[10] The Redac-

---

7. Thomas J. Heffernan, *The Passion of Perpetua and Felicity* (Oxford: Oxford University Press, 2013). All quotations in Latin, Greek, and translations are from this text.

8. Heffernan, *The Passion*, 79–99, and Petr Kitzler, *From Passio Perpetuae to Acta Perpetuae: Recontextualizing a Martyr Story in the Literature of the Early Church* (Berlin: De Gruyter, 2015), 24–29.

9. While Redactor 2 does not explicitly remark on the belief in deification in this persecuted community, it is clear that Redactor 1 believes that the Holy Spirit is present in his martyrs "may witness that one and the same Holy Spirit is always working among us [*et eundem semper Spiritum Sanctum usque adhuc operari testificentur*]" (21.11).

10. A. Pillet, *Histoire de Sainte Perpétue et de ses compagnons* (Lille: Librairie de J. Lefort, 1885), 66, and Naomi J. Norman, "Death and Burial of Roman Children: The Case of the Yasmina Cemetery at Carthage, Part II, The Archaeological Evidence," *Mortality* 8, no. 1 (2003): 40.

tor reports that she is a catechumen (*catechumena*), well-born (*honeste nata*), liberally educated (*liberaliter instituta*), honorably married (*matronaliter nupta*). The Greek version goes further and remarks that her marriage was a prominent ἐξόχως),[11] that she was twenty-two years of age (*annorum viginti duorum*), and that she had a small child at breast (*infantem ad ubera*). It is difficult to generalize about the education of female elite in the empire, and particularly outside of Italy, but her narrative suggests someone educated at home (well beyond the level provided by a *grammaticus*), likely until she was a teenager.[12] We learn that she spoke Latin, Greek, possibly Punic, and there is evidence in her narrative that she read Plato in a miscellany of favorite Greek authors.[13] We are on less firm ground when we ask how she understood the Christian idea of deification and to what extent that understanding was informed by her classical education. To answer this question we need to inquire into her knowledge and understanding of second-century African Latin Christianity.

## Perpetua Dreams of Intimacy with God

The narrator notes that she was a catechumen and thus a convert. We do not know how far along she was in the catechumenate. Hippolytus (of Rome, ca. 215) indicates that the typical length of time in preparation as a catechumen was three years.[14] It seems most unlikely that she was this advanced, as this would likely make her a catechumen before or at the very beginning of her marriage. She has one infant who is nursing, and there is no mention of other children. Given her father's antagonism toward her conversion to Christianity, it does not appear that he would have countenanced her marriage (nor would a suitable suitor be willing) and approved the *ius coniubii* if he knew

---

11. For a singular reading of Perpetua's class see Kate Cooper, "A Father, a Daughter and a Procurator: Authority and Resistance in the Prison Memoir of Perpetua of Carthage," *Gender and History* 23, no. 3 (2011): 685–702. But see my "Ius Conubii or Concubina: The Marital and Social Class of Perpetua in the *Passio Sanctarum Perpetuae et Felicitatis*," *Analecta Bollandiana* 136 (2018): 14–42.

12. Paul McKechnie, "St. Perpetua and Roman Education in AD 200," *L'antiqué classique* 63 (1994): 279–91, but see Walter Aemling, "Femina liberaliter instituta – Some Thoughts on a Martyr's Liberal Education," in *Perpetua's Passions: Multidisciplinary Approaches to the Passio Perpetuae et Felicitatis*, ed. J. Bremmer and M. Formisano (Oxford: Oxford University Press, 2012). Aemling's argument is not persuasive.

13. Jørgen Mejer, "Ancient Philosophy and the Doxographical Tradition," in *A Companion to Ancient Philosophy*, ed. M. L. Gill and P. Pellegrin (Oxford: Wiley-Blackwell, 2009), 20–34.

14. Hippolytus, *The Apostolic Tradition*, trans. B. S. Easton (Cambridge: Cambridge University Press, 1962), chap. 17 (43).

she was becoming a Christian. She was married *sine manu* and so remains under her father's *potestas*. Thus she was likely not married for more than two years before her arrest. I assume for this discussion that her conversion came after her marriage and that she was new to Christianity. Therefore, her understanding of her new faith provided in her narrative was not advanced, and her Christianity was in dialogue with her classical education. Moreover, Christianity had only been in Carthage for a generation before her narrative (ca. 175).

## The Martyr's *Mos Christianorum*

Perpetua's is the longest narrative in the *Passion* and it contains certain cruces that show a belief in a promise of deification to martyrs: her apocalyptic vision of heaven (chaps. 3 and 4), her healing of the dead Dinocrates (7 and 8), and her fight with the devil in the Amphitheatre (10). Her autobiographical reminiscences and her complex visionary dreams show her chief understanding of Christianity as an opportunity for profound personal transformation. Her dreams reveal that she and this small community of eschatological Carthaginian Christians saw Christianity as a way to remake the self through grace and thereby attain transcendence, incorruptibility, and an intimate union with God.[15] That journey of personal transformation, however arduous, required a radical reconfiguration of the self which allowed the martyr to embrace suffering and death in order to achieve intimacy and union with God in heaven. What results from this early deep introspection, which is made possible by grace, is a sweeping new evaluation of all existing relationships and social custom. Her dreams reveal an understanding of Christianity that is radically eschatological, but not preterist. It does, however, require severing non-Christian ties. Although in her dream narratives she provides positive glimpses of her spiritual journey toward union with God, it is clear from her narratives that she pays a great psychic price in loosening the ties that bind her to family. Her agony at these losses, although concealed in her account, are accessible in her denial of the importance of such loss, and they are present in what she appears to understand as resolved depictions of her new Christian relationships with her father and her son. Although she traverses the path to

---

15. See Michael Lattke, *Odes of Solomon*, trans. Marianne Ehrhardt (Minneapolis, Minn.: Fortress Press, 2009), Ode 15: "I have put on incorruption through His name: and have put off corruption by His grace."

martyrdom heroically and with supreme rhetorical panache, her journey is accomplished with a great and unresolved emotional cost.

She espouses a Christianity that insists that once she fully embraces her faith she will be reborn, and that once the shell-like chrysalis of the old person is discarded the Christian will emerge a newborn creation. This journey to God for this small group of converts also required an abandonment of social and domestic responsibilities, family ties, motherhood, being a dutiful daughter and wife, and even gender identity. All civic and personal responsibilities are peripheral and obstructions to the journey. These Carthaginian Christians understood Christ's rebuke to his disciples, "If anyone comes to me and does not hate father and mother, wife and children, brothers and sisters—yes, even their own life—such a person cannot be my disciple" (Lk 14:26), as a literal mandate to abandon one's kin and embrace a new family of spiritual brethren.[16] The community of martyrs replaces the revered Roman *mos maiorum*—crucial for full participation in the social order—with a *mos Christianorum*, a virtual antithesis of the older Roman verities.[17] Perpetua and her fellow Christians understood that to embrace God's invitation to greater intimacy in heaven, to become God's chosen vessels, they had to die to the world and to all domestic attachments, no matter how dear. In order for the union with God to progress, these radically eschatological Christians effaced their former social allegiances. Such rejection of social norms led to punishment. They believed that such persecution provided the annealing seal of martyrdom and was required for them to embrace Christianity in its fullest expression. Their journey to everlasting life begins with their recognition that grace is actively operating in them, drawing them ineluctably toward a more intimate and privileged union with God, which union must first embrace suffering and death. Perpetua and her fellow martyrs believed she had already received extraordi-

---

16. "Si quis uenit ad me et non odit patrem suum aut matrem aut uxorem aut filios aut fratres et sorores et animam suam, non potest meus discipulus esse." All quotations from the Latin Bible are from the *Vetus Latina: The Remains of the Old Latin Bible*, newly assembled following Petrus Sabatier and edited by the Archabbey of Beuron under the direction of Roger Gryson (Turnhout: Brepols, 2000). Judging from Speratus's reply to Proconsul Saturninus in the *Scillitan Martyrs*, the *Vetus* was available in Carthage ca. 180 or earlier.

17. See my "*Nomen Sacrum*: God's Name as Shield and Weapon in the *Acts of the Christian Martyrs*," in *Scripture and Pluralism: Reading the Bible in the Religiously Plural Worlds of the Middle Ages and Renaissance*, ed. Thomas J. Heffernan and Thomas E. Burman (Leiden: Brill, 2005), 19.

nary powers from God and that she was able to share God's power and Christ's redemptive work in history.

In the third chapter, after she has radically reidentified herself to her father in an expression of ontological personhood as a Christian (*Sic et ego aliud me dicere non possum nisi quod sum, Christiana*, 3.2), and thus rejecting all earlier identities as daughter, Carthaginian, and Roman matron, she remarks that she was baptized. Immediately after baptism, she says that the Spirit spoke to her (*et mihi Spiritus dictavit*, 3.5). The Greek text, always more specific and explicitly biblical and theological, identifies the third person of the Trinity as this confiding Holy Spirit (τὸ πνεῦμα τὸ ἅγιον). Perpetua then reveals gnomically that the spirit told her that all she should expect from the water (*ab aqua* / Τοῦ ὕδατος) is the ability to endure physically the torment of her impending martyrdom.[18] Her visionary dreams also serve as a type of consolation for her, and most importantly for her audience. Her dreams, by dramatically representing the prophecy of their fate and their triumph over death through martyrdom, enable the martyrs and their audience to construct a scenario where they—although apparent victims in the eyes of the state—emerge transformed by grace. Her spiritual *journey* requires a reversal of all the expectations of the traditional *mos maiorum* and social decorum required of an elite female. Prison becomes a palace (3.9), victim becomes victor (18.1), fathers and daughters change places (9.2), women become men and men women (10.7), and a humiliating death in the arena becomes a triumphal entry to a sanctified life (21.11).[19]

## Ascent to Heaven

Chapter 3 prepares the listener/reader for the next step in Perpetua's movement towards martyrdom and transcendence in chapter 4. Her spiritual itinerary begins with her house arrest in chapter 3 and her journey of faith will shortly bring her to a meeting with God in heaven at the end of chapter 4. In chapter 3, we learned that she could speak with the Lord and received great gifts from him; in 4, we are given the first evidence of her visionary ability in her dream of the ladder. Chapter 4 opens in the middle of a conversa-

---

18. The Greek appears to be indebted to Mt 3:11. See also Jas 5:11 and Justin, *Dial.* 14.86.138.
19. For a more complete discussion of these motifs of reversal see T. J. Heffernan and J. E. Shelton, "*Paradisus in Carcere*: The Vocabulary of Imprisonment and the Theology of Martyrdom in the *Passio Sanctarum Perpetuae et Felicitatis*," *Journal of Early Christian Studies* 14, no. 2 (2006): 217–23.

tion with her fellow martyr who notes her great reputation in the community—he calls her *Domina* (the Greek reads κυρία), which we shall hear again from the mouth of her sorrowful father (5.5)—and that all Christians know that she receives divine visions. She repeats what we have already learned in chapter 3, that she is able to speak with the Lord (*sciebam fabulari cum Domino*) whose great benefits (*beneficia tanta*) she has known. The listener/reader is thus introduced to Perpetua as an intimate of God and a prophetess, and is now ready to move to the next step where she will reveal the proof of her divine intimacy and privilege—the vision of her future death.

The dream narrative is not the immediate experience of the dream but her reconstruction of her now conscious understanding of that oneiric experience. Her narrative is the stuff of the remembered unconscious. The listener/reader is not present with her during the dream, but we are there with her fellow martyr at the following day's retelling. Her report of the dream to her fellow condemned Christian is her conscious reshaping of her dream's representation of her unconscious hopes and fears as she has reconstructed them on awakening in her prison cell.

The dream has its own unique internal logic. Perpetua's dream creates meaning through the employment of images, which appear superficially to lack coherence, but on deeper analysis they provide access to the psyche of the dreamer. She prefaces the vision with the remark that she asked for the vision and thus underscores its sanction by God. We learn much from the dream but lack some basic information concerning the context for the dream—Perpetua does not tell us where she had the dream, whether it was during the day or night, or what her emotional response was in the dream or on her waking. The dream elides any understanding of her emotional state. Events in the dream violate causal and temporal norms.

She says that she saw a great bronze ladder reaching to the heavens with iron instruments of torture attached to its sides. If one climbed carelessly or was not looking upwards—that is, toward heaven and God and paradoxically not at the weapons—they would be torn to pieces. This use of the ladder as a motif of spiritual ascent—of the movement from earth to unification with God—is its earliest expression in Christian Latin and is an important deification motif in the Greek Fathers.[20] A large threatening serpent lay at the lad-

---

20. See, e.g., Gregory of Nazianzus, *Oration* 43.71, and John Chrysostom, *Homilies on John* 83.5.

der's lowest rung blocking the way. The listener is presented with an impossible journey. Her *agon* and the listener's *vade mecum* have begun. She next relates that her teacher Saturus is the first to climb and on reaching the top calls for her to follow, warning her to be careful of the serpent. She steps onto the serpent's head as if it were the first step (see Gn 3:15). Before she steps on his head, however, she makes her only mention of Christ and says, "In the name of Jesus Christ, he will not hurt me" (4.6). The name of Christ was commonly used from the first century as a type of onomastic shield from evil (Mk 9:38–41), and this is why it occurs at this initial juncture.[21] She next reports that she saw an enormous garden (*locus amoenus*) where a large, white-haired man dressed in shepherd's clothes sat in the middle of the garden milking sheep. He raised his head, looked at her and welcomed her, calling her *tegnon* / τέκνον—a tender expression typically reserved in Classical Greek for use between parent and child. The shepherd welcomes her and in effect adopts her as part of his *familia*, a well-known theme of deification (Gal 4:5).[22] The image of the Good Shepherd is a syncretic figure both of the consoling divine father and a reminder to the reader of her alienation from her natural beloved parent.[23] She then says that the shepherd gave her "cheese that he had milked ... and I received it in my cupped hands and ate it" (*de caseo quod mulgebat ... et ego accepi iunctis manibus et manducavi*, 4.9).[24]

This scene has received an encyclopedic amount of commentary, and I will not rehearse it. The crucial matter for this discussion is not the issue of how one can get cheese instantly from fresh milk (an example of literary brachylogy) but the meaning of this nourishing gift from the hands of the shepherd.[25] As soon as she consumes his offering to her, the many thousands "dressed in white" cry out *Amen*. The cry is doxological and is reminiscent of that in Revelation 3:14, where Jesus is referred to as the "Amen, the witness,

---

21. Heffernan, "Nomen Sacrum," 10–28.

22. M. Kajava, *Roman Female Praenomina: Studies in the Nomenclature of Roman Women* (Rome: Institutum Romanum Finlandiae, 1994), 242.

23. Quodvultdeus identified Perpetua's father explicitly as the figure of the Good Shepherd. See his *De tempore barbarico*, ed. R. Brown, Corpus Christianorum: Series Latina 60 (Turnhout: Brepols, 1976), 431.

24. Jn 2:1–10. See Tertullian, *De corona* 3.9 for the newly baptized who on leaving the immersion immediately eat milk and honey.

25. Images of Christ (albeit unbearded and young) as the Good Shepherd date from the early third century and appear to have been known earlier; see Jn 10:1–21.

the faithful, the true, the beginning of creation of God" (ὁ ἀμὴν ὁ μάρτυς, ὁ πιστὸς, καὶ ἀληθινός, ἡ ἀρχὴ κτίσεως τοῦ θεοῦ). Justin notes that those present at the eucharist said "Amen" immediately after the celebrant has given thanks for the gift of bread and wine mixed with water as a prayer of thanksgiving for the Eucharist (*1 Apol.* 66). Polycarp ends his prayer of thanksgiving for his impending martyrdom by audibly intoning "Amen" immediately before the pyre is lighted (*Mart. Pol.* 14.3). He thus hallows his impending death as a type of liturgical sacrifice. The utterance here in the *Passion* has all of these overtones of a eucharistic thanksgiving, martyr as witness and sacrifice.

We learned in chapter 3 that Perpetua is an intimate with God and that she seeks greater union with him. Her recent baptism is a reminder of that growing intimacy. The eucharist is the apogee of such intimate union, as it allows her in eating the sacred meal to take God/Christ inside herself. She now has a physical share in his divinity. Her dream is a very physical depiction of consuming the eucharist. The elements of the dream—the lactating sheep, the nursing Good Shepherd, her reception of the gift in joined hands, the cry of *Amen* of those standing around and on awakening still eating (*conmanducans*) something sweet (4.10)—are deeply suggestive of what has happened to her thus far and what she hopes will happen in the future. She is being brought ever more deeply into her desired union both spiritually and physically with God. From a mélange of events, the dream creates a rationale for what is happening and what will happen.

In addition to a eucharistic reading, the Good Shepherd anecdote is also a symbolic figural representation seeking to restore the tragically severed relationship with her birth father. She has had a painful break with her father, who noted that he loved her more than her brothers. She is a nursing mother. Her infant son lives because she provides him milk. The child was removed from her. Her anxiety at his absence brought his return. The Good Shepherd's nurturing gift of milk reassures her that her child will survive her death and that for her sacrifice she will receive the gift of heaven. She says immediately on waking that "we ceased to have any hope in this world" (*coepimus nullam iam spem in saeculo habere*, 4.10). The reader is at once reminded of the earlier unhappy scene with her natural father. Yet, in her dream we have the depiction of a new father, a beneficent good father, depicted as a shepherd, who understands her, who supports her, nourishes her, and will save her and not abandon her. Those dressed in white who stand around the Good Shepherd are echoes of the martyrs in the Book of Revelation who live in heaven surrounding God's throne. They are her new civic community, her new heavenly family, replacing her former domestic circle. She will soon join their company as a fellow martyr and already has a foretaste in this vision of that blessed life when God will be fully present in her.

She concludes the dream by telling her fellow prisoner that "we knew we would suffer, and we ceased to have any hope in this world" (4.19). Her interpretation of the dream seems at first wildly eccentric because, after all, the dream presented a scene of consolation and hope. However, the dream is deeply eschatological and is to be contrasted with what we know of their situation from chapter 3—that they are in a fetid, hot, and violent Roman prison awaiting their uncertain fate at the hands of the authorities (a description not unlike the place in which she later finds her brother). The good that they have found is not in this world, in this reprehensible prison, but the true good awaits them in heaven. And lastly, if they persevere in their faith and die heroically as martyrs they will share—as those martyrs do who are already there—in the eternal beatific life of God. And her dream is prophetic: she has truly been given the gift of prophecy, as they do shortly die in the arena.

Perpetua's dream brings together a number of unresolved issues which will play an important role in her next dream vision. Immediately before her dream of the ladder to heaven and the meeting with the Good Shepherd she expressed worry about her infant son who was weak from hunger. Once she was able to suckle him he recovered. Her dream extends this motif of nurturing and being nourished. The Good Shepherd feeds her the mysterious soul enhancing curd-like milk, which he has milked from the sheep. Immediately before her next dreams of her brother Dinocrates, Perpetua and her fellows are called before Hilarianus, the procurator who finds them guilty of being Christians. He condemns them, yet she notes that rather than fearing she returned to her prison cell joyfully. She then remarks that her father has refused to return her child to her, but that God providentially has made the baby no longer want the breast and that she did not suffer from the mastitis inflammation (*neque mihi fevorem fecerunt*, 6.8) when she suddenly stopped nursing. However, the maternal and nursing instinct does not disappear, despite her remarks that she "might not be tormented by worry for my child or by the pain in my breasts" (6.8). Her ensuing two dreams of her brother Dinocrates depict a type of complex exorcism of her maternal anxieties for her child and a celebration of the presence of the curative power of almighty God working miraculously through her to restore the dead to life. She is given the special gift of being a mediator for the healing power of God.

## Saving Dinocrates: The Martyr as Mediator of God's Healing Power

Perpetua's first dream of her natural brother Dinocrates is prompted by her involuntary cry of the child's name, a cry which came to her unbidden, suddenly and mysteriously.[26] She thus represents herself as a vessel in which God's power is made manifest. Dinocrates's name cascades a history of their past associations, culminating in her revelation that he died at seven from a loathful cancer of the jaw. She interprets the unbidden name as a sign from God that she is being singled out to pray for him. She enters a prayer-like trance and immediately has a vision of the child Dinocrates suffering in a kind of Tartarus (see 2 Pt 2:4). He is filthy, hot, and thirsty, desperately trying to quench his thirst. On awakening from her vision, she concludes remarkably that despite the great gulf that separates them—he is after all dead and in some difficult to distinguish afterlife location—she is able to help him. She prays night and day so that "this gift might be given to me" (*ut mihi donaretur*, 6.10). The nature of the gift is unspoken, but we learn in chapter 8, the second dream of Dinocrates, that it is nothing less than the divine-like power of bringing life to the dead. Chapter 7 is also suffused with her unavoidable but here unmentioned loss of her own child who, like her brother Dinocrates, is taken from her, needs to drink/nurse, and from whom she will be separated by death. The dream coalesces the profound sadness and hope for her own infant with her passion to save Dinocrates. In saving her brother she unconsciously saves her child.

---

26. The Latin version uses the nominative *vox* as the subject of *profecta est*, underscoring the involuntary gift-like nature of the cry, whereas in the Greek Perpetua is the subject and initiates the cry ἀφῆκα φωνήν. The Latin emphasizes the power of God working in her. The Latin and Greek choice of words indicate differently the process of her recall of Dinocrates. The Latin uses *commemorata*, while the Greek uses the word ἀνάμνησιν with what feels like an effort to suggest that she makes Dinocrates present again (see Lk 22:19).

Her second vision of the child Dinocrates is brief, and it is deliberately set (in the Latin version) during the day. The setting of the dream in the day de-emphasizes the visionary and dreamlike quality of the night, when dreams normally occur. (The Greek, striving to be more literary, however, sets the scene in the night, underscoring God's presence at all times, day or night.) Perpetua's dream emphasizes the power of God operating through her even though she is depicted as physically constrained by the Roman chains. Immediately before providing the details of Dinocrates's changed situation, she remarks that she is locked in painful stocks, dirty and thirsty. She has a vision of the child in the same Hades-like place as she found him in the prior vision, but now he is clean, well-dressed, and refreshed; where there was a wounding, disfiguring cancer there is now only a scar. Much of this dream is concerned with Dinocrates being able to satisfy his thirst. She notes that the pool of quenching water, which was formerly out of reach, is now wondrously lowered to his navel. Perpetua is a concise author, and small details when given are significant. The height of the pool (*ad umbilicum pueri* / ἕως τοῦ ὀμφαλίου αὐτοῦ) evokes memories of maternity, of nurturing, of her life giving connection to her infant son now severed from her. Because of God's special gift of his power to her, her child will survive as did her brother Dinocrates. Although the chapter explicitly states that she saw Dinocrates in the same physical place where she first saw him, some ancient and medieval readers suggest he has been translated to some distinctly Christian place.[27] That reading owes more to medieval exegesis than the text allows, but the text explicitly states that a dead child, who died from a disfiguring and loathsome facial cancer, has been made whole and restored to some mysterious semblance of spiritual life through her efficacious prayer, a prayer made possible by God working through her.

Perpetua's dreams have moved dramatically from the initial gift of prophecy to a revivification of the dead. Her employment of powers of revitalization associated with God, although hitherto known only to her and a few of the condemned community, are growing ever greater as she moves toward martyrdom and the full realization of deification. As she grows in such authority, the presence of God in her should become increasingly manifest. And it does. In chapter 9 the pagan military adjutant Pudens in charge of the prison pub-

27. Manuscript Monte Casino 204, f. 172r, ca. last third of the eleventh century and the most complete text of the *Passion*, adds after the phrase *de poena* the words *ad requiem sanctam iustorum*.

licly recognized some "great power" (*magnum virtutem*) in the condemned and honors them with additional visitation privileges.[28] The three dreams we have examined show Perpetua maturing in her faith, progressing from a community leader to an intimate of God who can speak with him, share in his gift of prophecy, and act as a vehicle through which she can channel God's power to restore the dead to life. This growth in her understanding of her increasing intimacy with God is also contingent on her progressive separation from her role as daughter, mother, sister, and citizen. Chapter 9 also allows her an opportunity to grieve for her earthly father's terrible sadness to lose his beloved daughter. Her father's despondent cry at her feet as he is about to lose his only daughter in the amphitheater vividly contrasts with her apparently stoical resignation concerning her own child's loss in chapter 6. The difference between the representation of father and daughter centers on the father's belief that on Perpetua's death he will have lost his precious child forever, but Perpetua having cured and rescued her long dead brother Dinocrates now knows that there is no death for the Christian and that once dead to the world she will be more fully alive and that her child will be united with her. We are now ready for her last dream vision.

## The Invincibility of the Martyr

Her final vision has received more commentary than any other aspect of the narrative, and perhaps rightly so as it does present a novel depiction of a woman's sudden miraculous assumption of a man's body in order to engage in a cosmic struggle against Satan (see Mt 4:1–11), allegorically depicted as a *pankration* celebrating the birthday of the Caesar Geta.[29] This is her final struggle and greatest test. If we also read the dream visions as a progressive revelation of the immanence of God working in and manifesting that presence in his elect, these dreams serve as indicators of her increasing intimacy with God, her increasing participation in and active employment of the divine at-

---

28. The Greek, always seeking to draw a theological lesson goes much further than the Latin, making the explicit the root of the power in God (Καὶ δοξάζειν τὸν θεόν).

29. Augustine, *Sermo* 282, cited in "Sechs neue Augustinuspredigten. Teil 1 mit Edition dreier Sermones," ed. I. Schiller, D. Weber, and C. Weidmann, *Wiener Studien* 121 (2008): 227–84. Note the Greek text underscores the martyrs' distinctly male heroism ἀνδρειώτατοι (21.2) where the Latin is gender-neutral *fortissimi* (21.2).

tributes and her role, while still alive, as *miles Christi*.³⁰ In her initial dream she was given the gift of prophecy, which—like the *urceolus* she mentioned in that vision—transformed her identity (3.2). The second and third dreams show her gradually assuming more authority and redirecting divine power as she is able through God's grace to liberate her pagan dead brother through her prayers from his suffering.³¹ Her final dream presents her figuratively as a Christ figure, an *alter Christus* who is able to conquer the power of Satan, the prince of the world, who appears in the guise of an Egyptian wrestler.³² The text states that she is not able to kill Satan because he is a demon. Only God or someone privileged to participate in God's power can overcome him.³³ The Latin text clearly illustrates this power coming directly from God powerfully assisting her when it says, employing the passive form of the verb, that during their struggle she "was raised up into the air" (*Et sublata sum in aere*). The Greek text identifies this power using the active voice as coming solely from her: "And I arose in the air" (καὶ ἰδοὺ ἐπῆρα ἀπὸ ἀέρος, 10.11). The grammatical choices are significant. She does defeat the devil in the contest. The *lanista* congratulates her on her victory as a woman: "Daughter, peace be with you" (*Filia, pax tecum*). She has immediately resumed her gender and concludes her struggle with the conviction that victory will be hers.

This dream's narrative allows for multiple readings. Aside from the overtly Christian reading of the struggle against Satan, there is also the narrative of a young educated Carthaginian woman's yearning to be free of the rigid social proscriptions demanded by Roman Carthaginian customs—a freedom she sees in Christianity. Perpetua's closest associates in life are all males: her father, her brother, her son, her absent husband, Saturus, and the other five male martyrs—Pudens, Pomponius, Optatus, Aspasius, and Rusticius. She only mentions her mother once (3.8), and the Redactor never adds anything to Perpetua's mention of her. Perpetua lives in a male world. To be powerful in

---

30. 2 Tm 2:3: συγκακοπάθησον ὡς καλὸς στρατιώτης Χριστοῦ Ἰησοῦ (share in suffering as a good soldier of Christ Jesus). All New Testament Greek quotations come from *Novum Testamentum Graecae Nestle-Aland* (Münster: Hendrickson, 2012). Lactantius credits Donatus with the first use of the phrase in Latin.

31. See *Acts of Paul and Thecla* (ca. 160–90?), chap. 29, where Thecla prays for immortality for the dead pagan girl Falconilla.

32. See Jn 12:31: ὁ ἄρχων τοῦ κόσμου τούτου, and as an equal adversary to Christ in 1 Pt 5:8: ὁ ἀντίδικος διάβολος.

33. Tertullian, *Scorpiace* 6.

this world is to be male or to assume that persona. She found liberation from such paradigmatic Roman roles as daughter, wife, and mother in the Christian church. Her confession of martyrdom now confers leadership, authority, and respect.[34] Her psychic evolution has allowed her to jettison crucial socially constructed identity markers as daughter, wife, mother and replace them with Christian prophet, healer, warrior, and on her death God's spouse, joined in an intimate union with him. The narrator, apparently unwilling to push the identification with Christ as far as Perpetua does, refers to her in more acceptable gendered language, stating that after her triumph over Satan she walks in to the amphitheatre on her last day on earth as "a wife of Christ, and darling of God" (*ut matrona Christi, ut Dei delicata*, 18.2).

## The Eschatological Dream of Saturus

Saturus's vision begins immediately following Perpetua's request that anyone who wishes to write of their death is free to do so. Saturus's vision is radically different from that of Perpetua. His is more self-consciously literary, bookish, abstract, philosophically indebted to a mélange of contemporary ideas on the survival of the soul (from the Presocratics to the Stoics). He employs common Hellenistic metaphors of light to underscore spiritual illumination found in Plato's myth of the cave, in Cicero, and in current Christian eschatological teaching, and he is particularly indebted to the Book of Revelation.[35] Unlike Perpetua's dream, which is redolent with information of her actual lived experience, Saturus provides no details of his earthly existence. Of the fifteen times the personal pronoun (*ego*) is used in the almost 3,700 words of the complete narrative, it is never used by Saturus, who always using plural forms, whereas Perpetua uses it eleven times.[36]

---

34. "Optatum episcopum ad dexteram et Aspasium presbyterum doctorem ad sinstram .... Et miserunt se ad pedes nobis" (13.1).

35. In Cicero's *Tusculan Disputations*, ed. J. E. King (Cambridge, Mass.: Harvard University Press, 1927), 1.12.27 (32), Cicero has the figure of "M" argue that death is not the annihilation of the soul but rather that death represents a transition to "a kind of moving and changing of life" (*quandam quasi migrationem commutationemque vitae*). See his intention to divinize his daughter Tullia in *Att.* 12.36.1. See also S. Cole, *Cicero and the Rise of Deification at Rome* (Cambridge: Cambridge University Press, 2013), 30.

36. 4.2: [Perpetua] "Et ego quae me sciebam fabulari cum Domino," and 11.4: [Saturus] "et dixi Perpetuae."

Redactor 2 introduces this chapter underscoring that it is a genuine dream from Saturus himself (*Saturus ... suam edidit*). Saturus's dream describes his and Perpetua's posthumous ascent to God's heavenly throne (*"Passi" inquit "eramus, et exivimus de carne,"* 11.1), their theophany—when they enter heaven as blessed souls and have their audience with God—and finally their return to the world outside the gates of heaven, where dissonance abounds. The reward for their martyrdom is to be in the presence of God for eternity. Saturus opens his narrative by revealing that they have suffered (*passi eramus*) and died (*exivimus de carne*); they are now being carried towards heaven by four angels (*ferri a quattuor angelis*) to the throne of God somewhere in the east (*in orientem*). Although they are dead, their souls are alive; furthermore their souls have materiality and mass. The martyrs, unlike all other Christians at the time, are given the divine gift of immortality immediately on death. Polycarp is said to have been "crowned with the crown of immortality" on his martyrdom and Blandina by her suffering and death "won the crown of immortality."[37]

Saturus is at pains to emphasize the physicality of their spirits with somatic metaphors throughout the dream. He says that they traveled not on their backs (*non supini*), as we would expect the dead to be laid out, but upright, leaning forward as if climbing a hill (*clivum ascendentes*), and when they arrived at the garden (a *locus amoenus*) they crossed it on foot (*Et pedibus nostris transivimus*). Once there, they saw (*Ibi invenimus*) and not only recognized other martyrs who died in an earlier pogrom but called them by name and entered into conversation with them (*Et quaerebamus*), and when they met God he caressed their face (*traiecit nobis in faciem*) with his palm (*de manu*).[38] Saturus makes the significant remark, almost as an aside, that they "could not see his [God's] feet" (*cuius pedes non vidimus*, 13.3), underscoring the distinctive nonphysical nature of God in contrast to the two of them who arrived in the *locus amoenus, nostris pedibus*. The martyrs are the only Christians Saturus meets in heaven, thus underscoring that these Carthaginian Christians believed that the martyrs alone were unique sharers in God's eternal substance before Christ's Second Coming.

---

37. See *Martyrdom of Polycarp* 17.1 and the *Letter of the Churches of Lyons and Vienne* 1.42 (Blandina). See also Tertullian's understanding of the soul is both immortal and material and that even righteous Christian souls, in his *Anima* 22.2: "Definimus animam dei flatu natam, immortalem, corporalem, effigiatam, substantia simplicem, de suo sapientem."

38. The Greek suggests even greater intimacy with God, an embrace: τῇ χειρὶ περιέλαβεν.

The martyrs are brought to the ethereal residence of God whose walls appear *as if* made of light. Even light, that most immaterial substance accessible to human sensory experience, can only hint at the utter immateriality of the divine realm. God's *domus* in contrast to the emphasis on the martyrs' spiritual physicality, and their recent all too physical prison, is a likeness of a building; it is constructed entirely *as if* of light. Saturus depicts God sitting on his throne as an aged man with white hair (*quasi hominem canum*) but a youthful face, whose feet they could not see. The narrative represents a familiar biblical image of God but minimizes his corporeality. Unlike the two of them who, although dead, walk on their very physical feet, their vision of God explicitly excludes feet. God does not need human locomotion. The martyrs who are welcomed and caressed by God appear as sinless beings. After their audience with the Lord, they are commanded to play (*ludite*). This very deliberate choice of words suggests innocent children playing in a prelapsarian sinless state.

The early Latin church appears to have had a "rigorist" understanding of the spiritual status of the righteous Christian immediately on death. Tertullian, for example, notes that only the martyrs, enjoying God's special privilege and being sinless, go to heaven immediately on their death for union with God. All others, no matter how closely they adhered to the message of the Gospel, must await in Hades for the Second Coming. Tertullian intimates that even martyrs elect to live outside the world in a state of grace without sin and share unique spiritual gifts.[39] The command *ludite* also reminds the listener of Perpetua's brother Dinocrates (8.3), made whole through her intercessory prayers, and her infant son. The martyr is depicted as a direct witness of God and able to resolve the most grievous conflict and forgive sin. This latter point receives greater emphasis when her bishop Optatus and her priest Aspasius throw themselves at her feet begging that she resolve their differences. The clerics are subordinate to the martyr's paramount authority. The clerics are depicted not in heaven, but they await and meet the martyrs as they emerge from their meeting with God outside *in front of* the gates of heaven (*ante fores* / εἴδομεν πρὸ τῶν θυρῶν, 13.1). Unlike the martyrs, they are not worthy to enter heaven.

---

39. Tertullian, *Ad martyras* 1.1, writing to those imprisoned for their confession of faith addresses them as *benedicti martyres designati*.

## Felicity's Truth: God Dwells in My Soul

Redactor 2, who claims to have been an eyewitness to their imprisonment and persecution in the amphitheater, records a powerful instance of a deification theme in his description of the slave girl Felicity while in the throes of a difficult childbirth. Although all the martyrs have been condemned to die on the anniversary of Caesar Geta's birthday, Felicity, the slave girl who accompanied Perpetua, has been granted a stay of execution because she is in her eighth month of pregnancy. Roman law proscribed killing a pregnant woman, as the fetus was the property of her spouse or in this instance her owner. To kill the miscreant, in this instance Felicity, would be to deny the owner of his property. Hence, the fetus was protected as an asset.[40] The martyrs, however, on learning this, despair that she will not die with them, but be sacrificed later and thus her consecrated blood shed later with common criminals (*et ne inter alios postea sceleratos sanctum et innocentem sanguinem funderet*, 15.2).[41] The condemned Christians pray successfully for the immediate and quite miraculous delivery of her baby daughter. The redactor frames his presentation of God's immanence by narrating Felicity's painful delivery in her prison cell. There the prison guard taunts her, mocking her cries and berating her with such remarks, as "if you are suffering so much now, what will you do when you are thrown to the beasts" (15.5). Felicity replies, "Now I alone suffer what I am suffering, but then there will be another inside me, who will suffer for me, because I am going to suffer for him" (*Modo ego patior quod patior; illic autem alius erit in me qui patietur pro me, quia et ego pro illo passura sum*, 15.6).[42]

Felicity's reply is the most explicitly and self-consciously theological remark put in the mouth of the martyrs and shows not only the redactor's familiarity with Paul's remarks in Romans and 1 Peter 1:6, 2:19, and 4:12–17, where the importance of suffering for Christ as an ideal is insisted upon, but suggests knowledge of earlier martyr narratives and the uniquely Carthaginian emphasis on martyrdom as the highest expression of *imitatio Christi* as a way

---

40. The subject is complicated in Roman law but Ulpian is clear that the expectant mother cannot be executed until parturition; see *Digest* 2.3.48 and 19.3.

41. The Greek version does not contain an adjective corresponding to *sanctum* but only ἀθῷον corresponding to *innocentem*.

42. Did this radical immanence of God above influence Augustine in *Confessions* 3.6.11, "tu autem eras interior intimo meo" (you were more in me than I am in myself)?

to secure a sure union with God. Indeed, one might say that this identification and possession of Christ inside Felicity greatly exceeds an understanding of the trope of imitation. She possesses God, and God possesses her. Felicity believes that both her flesh and spirit are filled by God. While such possession is nowhere stated quite so explicitly as in the case of Felicity, we do find analogous sentiments about God's presence with the martyrs at their moment of greatest trial in Ignatius of Antioch's *Epistle to the Ephesians* (15.3), the *Martyrdom of Polycarp* (2), and in the figure of the martyr Blandina in the Letter of the Churches of Lyons and Vienne.[43] Felicity's remark not only acknowledges that she is suffering for her God (she does not use the name Christ) but that God—because he recognizes her ultimate sacrifice—will join her, enter into her, unite himself in some mystical union to her suffering, take her suffering upon himself, and shield her from pain.[44] The redactor's understanding of the unique reward of martyrdom allows him to construct a narrative in which Felicity's God is one who creates a demonstrable physical and spiritual union with her, dwelling inside her while she is yet alive. Felicity has becomes a living God-bearer, a Θεοφόρος, to adopt an Ignatian epithet.[45]

Although the *Passion* is not a learned work of Christian apology it nonetheless does represent a coherent belief that for the Christian martyr there is a unique call to share as a participant in the real presence of God to those who are open to his grace and die for him. Perpetua and her companions died true to their faith so that they could join and become one with the mystical body of God, to live in heaven and share in a mysterious union with God for eternity.

## *Illuxit dies victoriae:* New Life in the Amphitheatre

The God-bearing martyrs process to the amphitheater on the day of their execution joyfully, singing psalms, their faces radiant with light and visibly trembling, not from fear but with joy. This their last day on earth is the "the day when their victory dawned" (18.1). Those universal human verities such

---

43. Ignatius of Antioch, *Epistle to the Ephesians* 15.3: "and He may be in us as our God, which indeed He is"; *Martyrdom of Polycarp* 2, "the Lord was there present holding converse with them"; and *Letter of the Churches of the Martyrs of Lyons and Vienne*, "and because of her intimacy with Christ."
44. Felicity's patient acceptance of death uses the typically Roman and Stoic values of patient forbearance to subvert the established social and moral authority of the state.
45. In the dedicatory inscription to the *Epistle to the Romans* (Ἰγνάτιος ὁ καὶ θεοφόρος) and throughout many of the genuine letters.

as "death as end" and "life as beginning" are reversed: death now leads to life while continued life here is death. Ignatian sentiments redolent with a deep yearning for intimacy and union with God (Rom 4:1) infuse the final three chapters (19–21), which focus on the martyrs and their suffering in the arena. The martyrs' deaths in the amphitheater are not only a triumph of conscience over the barbarousness of the Roman state, but they also represent a cosmic victory over death itself (1 Cor 15:54) and over Satan. Their struggle is eschatological and cosmic. Their deaths are also the final and crucially necessary step in their movement toward union with God. The day of the martyrdom provides them with the chance to manifest, to witness, that they—this very afternoon in the Carthage amphitheatre—will offer themselves freely as an oblation to God. The text is quite clear that their martyrdom is sacrificial and one that is purely volitional. Perpetua emphasizes this act of free agency when she protests to the tribune: "We came here freely, so that our freedom might not be violated; therefore we handed over our lives" (*Ideo ad hoc sponte pervenimus, ne libertas nostra obduceretur; ideo animam nostram addiximus*, 19.5). The martyrs have discussed how they want to die, even down to the details predicting what beasts will kill them. The narrative moves back and forth between the jeering, frenzied bloodlust of the crowd in the stands and the deep calm and peace of the martyrs in the arena.

The Redactor interrupts the flow of his narrative of their processional walk to the amphitheater with a flashback to Perpetua's final dream and her defeat of the Egyptian whom she then identified as the devil. He notes Perpetua was "singing a hymn already trampling on the head of the Egyptian" (18.7). His allusion collapses time as the two events are juxtaposed simultaneously. The former event is predictive of the outcome of the present, the triumph of the martyrs and the obliteration of evil. Moments before her fight with the Egyptian, Pomponius—whom I have discussed elsewhere as a syncretic figure as a type of Christ—tells Perpetua, "Don't be afraid, I am here with you, and I will struggle with you" (10.4). These words are an echo of Jesus' words to his disciples (see Acts 18:10 and Mt 28:20). Christ is present in the arena and the Holy Spirit in Perpetua. Her remarks and those of the Redactor convey to the Christian audience that the offering of the self, which action they are about to witness, is a ritualized reenactment of the death of Christ at the hands of the Roman authorities. Such a sacrificial reenactment through mimesis transforms the representation of their suffering into identity: the model being depicted is consubstantial with the martyr. At this moment of their consuming sacrifice the distinction of personhood, albeit present, is blurred—Christ, God, the Holy Spirit are all present with and in the martyr but they act as one. The narrative reports that during her struggle and immediately after being gored by the mad cow, she "awakened, as if from a sleep" for "she was so deep in the spirit and in ecstasy" (*adeo in spiritu et in extasi fuerat*, 20.8). The martyrs die one after another heroically manifesting their faith and achieving their hoped-for union with God in heaven. The Redactor concludes as he began, by praising and testifying to the indwelling of the Holy Spirit in his faithful ones: "For these new deeds of courage too may witness that one and the same Holy Spirit is always working among us even now" (21.11).

*Mark A. Frisius*

## 3. SEQUESTERED IN CHRIST
*Deification in Tertullian*

Tertullian of Carthage is routinely seen as standing at the head of the Latin patristic tradition. His influence upon Western Christianity has been significant and wide-ranging. The imprint of his thought is found in the ongoing theological and ecclesiastical discussions of the third, fourth, and fifth centuries, particularly within the development of theological vocabulary.[1] Further, his surviving corpus of thirty-one works indicates that Tertullian was a significant figure for the emergence of a Western Latin tradition.[2]

In spite of his literary significance, little is known about Tertullian the man. There is no universally agreed-upon date of birth, his works appear like a whirlwind and then abruptly cease, and there is no agreed upon date of death.[3]

---

A version of this chapter was read at the seminar on "Deification in the Latin Patristic Tradition" at the XVII International Conference on Patristic Studies at Oxford in August 2015. The author wishes to thank the seminar participants for insightful comments given at that time.

1. Later Latin theologians often turned to Tertullian, who was among the first to use what would become key theological terms, including *sacramentum*, *trinitas*, *persona*, *substantia*, and *satisfactio*. See Geoffrey D. Dunn, *Tertullian* (New York: Routledge, 2004), 10. Andrew McGowan argues that part of Tertullian's lasting Trinitarian impact was related to his adherence to the "New Prophecy," which made him "ecclesially marginal" in the Carthaginian church that leaned toward Praxean modalism. See Andrew McGowan, "Tertullian and the 'Heretical' Origins of the 'Orthodox' Trinity," *Journal of Early Christian Studies* (hereafter, *JECS*) 14, no. 4 (2006): 456–57.

2. In addition to these surviving Latin texts, Tertullian is also assumed to have written a number of treatises in Greek which have not survived. See Dunn, *Tertullian*, 163.

3. Timothy Barnes suggests ca. 170 as a date of birth and speculates that Tertullian may have been

Although Tertullian gives few clues in terms of his autobiography,[4] there is much that can be said about the character of his writing and scholarship. In particular, his writing style and command of rhetoric imply that Tertullian was the recipient of a thorough Roman education.[5] Tertullian was most certainly a respected layman who made significant contributions to the church of Carthage and left a significant legacy for the development of theology.

In light of the significance of Tertullian for the emergence and development of Latin Christianity, this study will suggest that Tertullian has a distinctive understanding of deification, which is rooted in the incarnation and the eschaton. I will demonstrate that Tertullian viewed the *imitatio Christi* not just in legalistic and forensic terms, but also in transformative terms wherein the full human is conformed to the obedience of Christ. Further, it will be seen that Tertullian's distinctive view of Christ as the sequester between God and humans provides a paradigm in which flesh and spirit are perfected by God, beginning in the here and now and finding completion in the eschaton. Tertullian sees this process as bringing about the full restoration of the human, which includes the reception of the divine image and qualities. In order to demonstrate this, I will examine the role of *imitatio Christi*, the identity of Christ as the sequester between God and man, and Tertullian's understanding of angelification.

## Modern Challenges

The vast scope and impact of Tertullian's contributions not only make him worthy of discussion in this volume, but also present a number of challenges to the modern interpreter. In approaching Tertullian, the reader discovers a dizzying array of topics presented within an individualized polemical

---

martyred shortly after the completion of his final text in 212. See Timothy D. Barnes, *Tertullian: A Historical and Literary Study* (Oxford: Clarendon Press, 1985), 58–59.

4. Dunn provides an apt summary of what may be pieced together about the life of Tertullian (Dunn, *Tertullian*, 3–11). Jerome, *On Illustrious Men* 53 (Nicene and Post-Nicene Fathers [ed. Schaff], 3:373), provided a standard description of Tertullian's biography which was generally accepted until the work of Barnes provided a thorough challenge (Barnes, *Tertullian*, 3–29).

5. Tertullian's command of rhetoric is thoroughly examined in Robert D. Sider, *Ancient Rhetoric and the Art of Tertullian*, Oxford Theological Monographs (Oxford: Oxford University Press, 1971). Tertullian would have completed, at a minimum, the tertiary level of Roman education. See Geoffrey D. Dunn, *Tertullian's Adversus Iudaeos: A Rhetorical Analysis* (Washington, D.C.: The Catholic University of America Press, 2008), 29. For his knowledge of the Roman legal system, see below.

context. Writing over a span of approximately sixteen years, Tertullian developed and refined his theology within the prism of conflict and in response to emerging situations.[6] Given this situational approach, it is best to recognize that Tertullian was not always entirely consistent in his theology, and that no one idea or concept fully embodies his position.[7] Thus, Tertullian was a theologian with depth and layers to his thought, and there are many pieces to the puzzle of his theology. However, within this difficulty, there is also opportunity as areas of Tertullian's thought may have been overlooked by previous scholars.

In addition to his unique contributions, Tertullian also demonstrated dependency on the works of Irenaeus.[8] His dependency includes the description of the Valentinians, the succession of bishops, and the character of the apostles.[9] However, in spite of the multiple areas of dependency, there is near-universal agreement that Tertullian abandoned Irenaeus on the issue of deification.[10] Thus, it becomes necessary at the outset to summarize elements of the current state of thought on deification in Tertullian.

Gösta Hallonsten argues that Tertullian abandons Irenaeus because of anthropological considerations. He suggests that in his earliest writings, Tertullian considers the spiritual part of the human as partaking of the Holy Spirit, which was breathed in the body. This would have oriented the human toward full communion with God, that is, toward fulfilling the human likeness of

---

6. Barnes, *Tertullian*, 55. Barnes suggests that Tertullian was active between 196/97 and 212.

7. This is ably demonstrated in Dunn's contribution on Tertullian's soteriology. In this article, Dunn concludes that no one theory of the atonement is preferred by Tertullian; rather, he makes use of the theory which best fits his current argument. See Geoffrey D. Dunn, "A Survey of Tertullian's Soteriology," *Sacris Erudiri* 42 (2003): 61–86. Elsewhere, Dunn, while commenting on the importance of dating Tertullian's works, aptly notes, "Tertullian was selective and conscious of the occasion. One cannot refer simply to one passage in one text to demonstrate Tertullian's opinion on a matter. Instead, one needs to survey his output developmentally or comparatively, as well as rhetorically" (Dunn, *Tertullian*, 8–9).

8. Barnes, *Tertullian*, 220–21; S. L. Greenslade (ed.), *Early Latin Theology* (Louisville, Ky.: Westminster Press, 1956), 65–73. *Adversus Valentinianos*, beginning in chap. 6, demonstrates significant dependency upon *Against Heresies* 1.1–1.8, in Ante-Nicene Fathers (ed. Roberts et al.) (hereafter, ANF), 1:316–28. *Val.* 5.1 indicates that Tertullian is following the work of Irenaeus, and is the only instance where Tertullian names Irenaeus (ANF 3:506).

9. Irenaeus, *Against Heresies* 3.3–5 (ANF 1:415–18); Tertullian, *Prae.* 32 (ANF 3:258) on the succession of bishops; and *Prae.* 27 (ANF 1:256) on the character of the apostles.

10. On Irenaeus's view on deification, see Norman Russell, *The Doctrine of Deification in the Greek Patristic Tradition* (Oxford: Oxford University Press, 2006), 105–10. Below, I will suggest that there is a clear parallel between Irenaeus and Tertullian on the aspect of Christ's work as the mediator/sequester.

God.¹¹ However, in his later writings, Tertullian changed his language and described humans as receiving the *flatus* (breath) of God rather than the Spirit of God. Hallonsten suggests that this has a distinctive effect on his anthropology and essentially establishes humanity as a species distinct from God. This allowed Tertullian to avoid any suggestion of the Gnostic idea that humans have a divine spark,¹² and in Hallonsten's analysis marked a significant modification of Tertullian's idea of *imago Dei* and led to a rejection of deification.¹³

Gerald Bray suggests that the differences between Tertullian and Irenaeus can be found in the conception of sin which leads to a distinction in the understanding of union with God. For Irenaeus, sin is related to the fact that humans are inferior to God, at least in part, because humans are finite and thus bound to sin. In response, Christ divinizes human nature so that death can be conquered and natural shortcomings can be overcome. This allows for human participation in the life of God.¹⁴ Tertullian tends to view sin as an act of the will. The divine humanity of Christ is then described in terms of obedience that leads to the human goal of the imitation of Christ.¹⁵ Thus, Tertullian is depicted as concerned with rigoristic morality and having "no room in his theology for Irenaeus' latent concept of deification."¹⁶

However, others have noted that some deification terms and concepts are present in Tertullian. Jared Ortiz, in his brief summary of Tertullian's understanding of deification, notes several isolated phrases that present various concepts related to deification.¹⁷ However, these only touch the surface of deification issues and do not consider if deification is woven into Tertullian's larger

---

11. Hallonsten points to *Bapt.* 5.7 (ANF 3:671–72) wherein the language of image and likeness are brought together. See Gösta Hallonsten, "*Theosis* in Recent Research: A Renewal of Interest and a Need for Clarity," in *Partakers of the Divine Nature*, ed. Michael J. Christensen and Jeffrey A. Wittung (Grand Rapids, Mich.: Baker Academic Press, 2007), 285 and 291.

12. Ibid., 285–86. Although Hallonsten does not include it, this is a reference to *Marc.* 2.9.4–5 (ANF 3:304–05). However, here it is important to note that Tertullian is specifically focused on removing culpability for sin from the Spirit of God.

13. Hallonsten, "*Theosis* in Recent Research," 286.

14. Gerald Bray, *Holiness and the Will of God: Perspectives on the Theology of Tertullian* (London: Marshall, Morgan, and Scott, 1979), 88–89.

15. Ibid., 89–91.

16. Ibid., 90.

17. Jared Ortiz, "Deification in the Latin Fathers," in *Called to Be Children of God: Deification in the Catholic Tradition*, ed. Fr. David Meconi, SJ, and Carl E. Olson (San Francisco: Ignatius Press, 2016), 64–65.

theological constructs, or if deification was anything more than simply a minor topic.

Norman Russell notes that Tertullian was the first Latin author to use deification-related terms.[18] From his study it becomes apparent that Tertullian primarily uses deification language to speak about the character and nature of God, establishing three particular areas of theological usage. The first use established a defense of monotheism in the face of the proclamation of other gods. In *Apologeticum* 11.10, Tertullian examines the Euhemeristic views of his pagan opponents, insisting that they support a monotheistic position as a supreme God must exist to provide the power for deification.[19] In his further critique of the behavior of those whom the pagans have deified, Tertullian reveals a distinctive connection between deification and morality. In *Adversus Marcionem* 1.7.1, Tertullian considers Psalms 81–82 and argues that the presence of the assembly of gods, who share the name god, does not necessitate that the reality of divinity is shared.[20] In this way, the concept of deification does not impinge upon the supremacy of God, and monotheism is maintained.[21] The second theological usage is found in *Adversus Hermogonem* 5, wherein Tertullian declares that deification is an act of God's grace rather than the result of some inherent property within the human.[22] The third theological usage is designed as a comment on the divinity of Christ, and is located in *Adversus Praxean* 13.[23] In this instance, Tertullian comments on the deification of humans and its relationship to the identity of Christ. He suggests that if it is proper to apply the title of god to faithful men who have become sons of God, then it is even more proper to apply the name God to the true Son of God.[24] In each case, Tertullian does not argue against the concept of deification, but

---

18. Russell, citing Oroz Reta, notes that Tertullian uses three terms, *deificari*, *deificatio*, and *deificus*. See Russell, *Doctrine of Deification*, 326; José Oroz Reta, "De l'illumination à la deification de l'âme selon saint Augustin," ed. Elizabeth Livingstone, Studia Patristica 16 (Louvain: Peeters, 1993), 372. Each instance of these deification terms occurs in conjunction with Tertullian's use of Ps 82:1, wherein God judges amidst the other "gods," and 82:6, wherein the sons of the Most High are called "gods."

19. ANF 3:28. Russell, *Doctrine of Deification*, 326.

20. ANF 3:275.

21. Ibid.

22. *Herm.* 5 (ANF 3:479–80). Tertullian is clear that an element of the divine is present in the human. However, this element was given by God and rightly belongs to God. This counters the idea of Hermogenes who held that matter was eternal.

23. ANF 3:607–8.

24. Russell rightly identifies this as an example of Tertullian's use of an *a fortiori* argument. See Russell, *Doctrine of Deification*, 326.

also does not expound upon it; rather, his main focus is on the implications for understanding God rather than the human, although, in the final example, Tertullian implicitly accepts some form of human deification.

Russell's final example evidences a secondary concern of deification language which centers on the human possibility for deification. In *Adversus Marcionem* 2.25.4,[25] Tertullian suggests that although Adam's fall was a disaster there was still hope, which was grounded in the future taking of humanity into divinity.[26] This appears to be a clear deification statement and, Russell suggests, a possible allusion to 2 Peter 1:4.[27] Russell concludes by suggesting the possibility that Tertullian is describing the change into the substance of angels and the reception of an incorruptible nature.[28]

This essay seeks to challenge the majority view that there is no place for deification in the thought of Tertullian. I will situate deification within the prism of Tertullian's understanding of the incarnation and eschatology. In this, deification is more than a minor topic with a few scattered mentions in his corpus, but is integral to his soteriology.

## Holiness in This Life

It is no secret that Tertullian had a distinctively rigorist approach to the Christian life. For Tertullian, the Christian life in the here and now is typified by moral transformation that affects both the flesh and the soul. Typically, scholars characterize this transformation within a forensic or judicial model, but this unnecessarily limits the understanding of Tertullian's view on moral transformation.[29] I suggest that his understanding of moral transformation is rooted in the concept of *imitatio Christi*, wherein the Christian, through obedience, conforms to Christ's divine humanity.

---

25. ANF 3:317.
26. See below for a further explication of this passage.
27. Russell, *Doctrine of Deification*, 326. I disagree with Russell's suggestion that Tertullian is referencing 2 Pt 1:4 for two reasons. First, there is no verifiable evidence that Tertullian is familiar with 2 Pt or otherwise uses the text. See Mark A. Frisius, *Tertullian's Use of the Pastoral Epistles, Hebrews, James, 1 and 2 Peter, and Jude* (New York: Peter Lang, 2011), 13–15. Second, the concept of participation in the divine nature is an idea already present in Irenaeus and does not need to be traced back to 2 Pt.
28. Russell, *Doctrine of Deification*, 327. He will reference Tertullian's thought in *Marc.* 3.24 (ANF 3:341–42).
29. Justo L. González, *A History of Christian Thought*, vol. 1, *From the Beginning to the Council of Chalcedon* (Nashville, Tenn.: Abingdon Press, 1987), 173–74; Bray, *Holiness and the Will of God*, 34.

Part of Tertullian's understanding of moral transformation is certainly rooted in Christ as the teacher of righteous living. Within this conception, Christ provides instruction and examples for the Christian life.[30] As a result, Christ delivered the new law and strengthens the free will to live according to the commandments.[31] Thus, the basis of salvation becomes obedience to the teachings of Christ and rewards and punishments are based on a meritorious system.[32] Thus, at least part of the moral transformation is defined within a judicial environment and is based upon human merit.[33]

However, moral transformation for Tertullian is not encompassed by only living in accordance with Jesus' teachings, but has the ultimate goal of the *imitatio Christi*. This is rooted within Tertullian's theology of the incarnation, wherein the divine humanity of Christ fully obeyed and thus sets the pattern for humanity. The moral imperative is thus found in the character of Christ, and this makes possible the restoration of the likeness to God. The human will, which was defined as disobedient, is transformed into obedience and the entirety of the human together participates in the imitation of the obedience of Christ.[34] Thus, although obedience is the primary lens through which the *imitatio Christi* was understood, it encompassed more than rote legalism and rather involved the transformation and restoration of the human into the likeness of God.

Although Tertullian's view of rigoristic obedience was strengthened by his embrace of Montanism, this movement does not erase the idea of conformity to Christ.[35] During Tertullian's Montanist phase, the Paraclete was clear-

---

30. A. J. Wallace and R. D. Rusk, *Moral Transformation: The Original Christian Paradigm of Salvation* (New Zealand: Bridgehead, 2011), 263.

31. J. N. D. Kelly, *Early Christian Doctrines* (Peabody, Mass.: Hendrickson, 2004), 177; Bengt Hägglund, *History of Theology*, trans. Gene J. Lund (St. Louis, Mo.: Concordia, 2007), 56.

32. Hägglund, *History of Theology*, 56.

33. Here, it is significant to note that Tertullian is primarily responding to the Marcionite emphasis on divine, nonjudgmental love, which would have been severely damaged by a meritorious system that allowed for punishment (ibid.).

34. The incarnation demonstrated that both flesh and soul are part of God's redemptive plan (Bray, *Holiness and the Will of God*, 83). Tertullian reasons that if the soul, which was the primary culprit in the Fall, is saved, then the flesh too can be saved. Rigorism becomes necessary to reshape the flesh as it remains weak and could possibly mislead the soul (ibid., 91).

35. The generally accepted date for Tertullian's migration to Montanism is 207–8. See Christine Trevett, *Montanism: Gender, Authority and the New Prophecy* (Cambridge: Cambridge University Press, 1996), 71; William Tabbernee, "The World to Come: Tertullian's Christian Eschatology," in *Tertullian and Paul*, ed. Todd D. Still and David E. Wilhite (New York: Bloomsbury, 2013), 259. Tertullian certainly

ly understood as bringing stricter discipline to a church that has matured or come of age.[36] Although this may appear to be a movement away from *imitatio Christi*, it is best understood as the fulfillment of the concept. The Paraclete's teachings were the logical extension of the teachings of Christ and made clear their ethical implications.[37] In this model, the Paraclete teaches what is commanded by Christ and Christ continues to provide the model for the Christian life. Here, it is important to see that Tertullian is not only describing juridical ethics but sees ethics as also entailing participation with the Holy Spirit, who is pictured as wedded to human flesh.[38] Thus, the *imitatio Christi* is fully revealed through the Paraclete, and yet this modern progressive ethical revelation is consistent with Christ's teachings.[39] Thus, following the discipline of the Paraclete brings the Christian into conformity with the will of Christ and the Christian takes on the likeness of Christ.

Moral transformation and rigoristic discipline are completed and fulfilled by being brought into conformity with the teaching of Christ. Tertullian thus provides a rigoristic vision of the Christian life where the believer is formed by the *imitatio Christi* which is completely revealed through the Paraclete. Through discipline, the body and soul become obedient, which is how Tertullian describes Christ's divine humanity.[40] Thus, it becomes possible in the here and now for humans to become like Christ.[41] This is the initial framework for

---

held to rigorist tendencies prior to his movement to Montanism, which appears to have created a hardening in his vision of discipline. See Francine Cardman, "Tertullian on Doctrine and the Development of Discipline," ed. Elizabeth Livingstone, Studia Patristica (Berlin: Akademie Verlag, 1985), 141.

36. Trevett, *Montanism*, 119–20. Trevett notes the idea that this perfected discipline brings Christians up "to the mark." Tertullian was clear that the Paraclete does not introduce new doctrine; only stricter discipline. This often led to issues with the bishops on the identity of orthopraxis. See William Tabbernee, *Fake Prophecy and Polluted Sacraments: Ecclesiastical and Imperial Reactions to Montanism* (Leiden: Brill, 2007), 144–45.

37. Ibid.

38. *Res.* 63.3 (ANF 3:594)

39. Here, Tertullian references the ancient will of Christ, which is an allusion to Old Testament Christophanies. See Tabbernee, *Fake Prophecy*, 154. This is a key corollary as it prevents Tertullian's Trinitarian doctrine from being imperiled by the insertion of a false division within the economy of God.

40. Bray, *Holiness and the Will of God*, 90. In particular, the soul is being restored into the image of Christ's soul.

41. Anders Petersen suggests that the concept of the gods as role models, particularly within utopian religions, is inherently connected with the divinization of religious adherents. He notes that this is particularly present in Tertullian's depiction of the imitation of the suffering of Christ. See Anders Klostergaard Petersen, "Attaining Divine Perfection through Different Forms of Imitation," *Numen* 60 (2013): 9–15.

an understanding of deification, which will, in Tertullian's thought, become fully realized in the eschaton.

## From Mediator to Sequester

The incarnation and the eschaton are distinctly linked in the thought of Tertullian and connect with his theology of deification. In the incarnation, Tertullian understands that Christ takes up human nature and joins it to the divine. It is through this incarnational activity that humans may in the present conform to the image of Christ and may hope to take up the divine nature in the eschaton. This moves the soteriological discussion beyond the concept of redemption and ushers in an eschatological conclusion. Thus, the impact of the incarnation carries beyond the cross, resurrection, and ascension and extends to the Second Coming, wherein deification becomes a reality for the Christian.[42] The far-reaching extent of the incarnation is immediately visible in Tertullian's identification of Christ as mediator.[43]

The language of Christ as the mediator between God and humanity is present only in 1 Timothy 2:5,[44] which Tertullian references four times.[45] The first occurrence is found in *De carne Christi* 15.1, where Tertullian refutes what he sees as the erroneous Valentinian claim that Christ only had spiritual flesh, which was not human or born of a human.[46] In response, Tertullian quotes a series of passages that prove, in his mind, that the savior was a man. Included in this litany was 1 Timothy 2:5, with Tertullian's emphasis being on the "man"

---

42. On the significance of the incarnation for Tertullian, see Eric Osborn, *Tertullian: First Theologian of the West* (Cambridge: Cambridge University Press, 1999), 140–41.

43. The concept of a mediating figure between the divine and human was common in Ancient Near Eastern religions and Greek religions and was not uniquely Christian. See A. Oepke, "μεσίτες," in *Theological Dictionary of the New Testament*, ed. Gerhard Kittel, trans. Geoffrey Bromiley (Grand Rapids, Mich.: Eerdmans, 1967), 599–603.

44. The language of Christ as mediator of the New Covenant is found in Heb 8:6, 9:15, and 12:24, but these passages do not discuss him as mediator between God and man.

45. Frisius, *Tertullian's Use*, 130.

46. *Carn.* 15.1 (ANF 3:534–35). For the chronology of Tertullian's works, I follow Barnes, who located *De carne Christi* in 206 (Barnes, *Tertullian*, 55). Einar Thomassen suggests that this concept is prevalent in Eastern Valentinian doctrine, which adhered more directly to the teaching of Valentinus. The flesh of the savior is often rendered as the spiritual seed of Sophia which was put on when the savior descended. See Einar Thomassen, *The Spiritual Seed: The Church of the Valentinians* (Leiden: Brill, 2008), 41–42; see Birger Pearson, *Ancient Gnosticism: Traditions and Literature* (Philadelphia: Fortress Press, 2007), 148–49.

Christ Jesus. In his rendering of this verse, Tertullian translates μεσίτης as *mediator*.

The Roman judicial system allowed a presiding judge to summon a mediator to settle disputes, typically in areas regarding property or inheritance. The mediator was considered an expert in the area of dispute and was often empowered to insure an equitable distribution of the common property in question.[47] To accomplish this, it was necessary that the mediator be independent from all involved parties, thus insuring neutrality and trust.

Overall, the concept of the mediator would not have been distinctly helpful to Tertullian in his dispute with the Valentinians.[48] Although the mediator brought both sides together and, in a sense, belonged to each without distinction,[49] the concept would have been limited by the fact that the mediator was not connected with either party. This would not have provided a sufficient answer to the Valentinians as it could be construed as indicating a lack of true divinity and true human flesh. Thus the usefulness of 1 Timothy 2:5 in *De carne Christi* was found not in Christ as the mediator, but in the linkage of Christ with man. In subsequent works, Tertullian would return to this passage and, in every case, he changed his translation of μεσίτες from *mediator* to *sequester*. This change was intentional, unprecedented,[50] and signaled a shift in his use of this passage. In particular, the focus shifts from an emphasis on the manhood of Christ to the conjoining of divinity and humanity.

### Christ the Sequester in *De resurrectione carnis*

Although the sequester functioned within the realm of mediation and property law, the position was distinct from the mediator. The mediator was an independent go-between while the sequester was purposefully connected

---

47. In this activity, the roles of the mediator and the arbiter were closely related. See Adolf Berger, *Encyclopedic Dictionary of Roman Law* (Philadelphia: The Lawbook Exchange, 1953), 365–66.

48. Whether Tertullian had a professional relationship with the Roman legal system may be left to one side. What is clear, given his Roman education, is that Tertullian had a working knowledge of legal concepts. See David I. Rankin, "Was Tertullian a Jurist?," ed. Elizabeth Livingstone, Studia Patristica 31 (Leuven: Peeters, 1997), 338–39 and 342; Dunn, *Tertullian*, 3–4; Barnes, *Tertullian*, 22–29.

49. Oepke, "μεσίτες," 619.

50. In the *Vetus Latina*, which contains multiple translations of 1 Tm, there are no other examples of μεσίτες in 1 Tm 2:5 being translated with *sequester*. See Hermann Frede (ed.), *Epistulae ad Thessalonicenses, Timotheum, Titum, Philemonem, Hebraeos*, in *Vetus Latina* (Freiburg: Herder, 1975–82), 25.1:448.

with the disputing parties. The position of sequester became necessary owing to abuse of laws covering *usucapio*.[51] It had become possible for one party to acquire ownership of disputed property by prolonging legal proceedings until the statute of limitations expired. In this, the original court proceedings regarding ownership were circumvented and the party with physical possession became the legal owner. To counteract this abuse, the sequester became the legal owner of the disputed object until a proper legal decision could be rendered. Thus, the sequester received a deposit from the disputing parties and guaranteed the viable return of the object in question.[52]

This rendering of 1 Timothy 2:5 occurs twice in *De resurrectione carnis*, a later text also directed against the Valentinians.[53] The first occurrence is found in chapter 51, which is, in Robert Sider's rhetorical analysis, the crowning point for his argument against the Valentinians.[54] They claimed, on the basis of 1 Corinthians 15:50–56,[55] that flesh and blood are excluded from the kingdom of God. Tertullian disputes this claim, and contends that the passage describes the exclusion of sinful flesh from heaven. However, he maintains that it is possible for human flesh to be transformed so that it is proper for the kingdom of God on the basis that Jesus is currently in heaven and has flesh.

The first element of Tertullian's response is to provide a description of the flesh of Christ. He will identify Christ as both the Word and the last Adam. In this sense, the flesh of Christ is purer than fallen human flesh and is a restoration of the original creation. This ideal human flesh is maintained by Christ in heaven and will return at his Second Coming.[56] Tertullian is clear that this

---

51. On the Roman process of *usucapio*, see David Johnston, *Roman Law in Context* (Cambridge: Cambridge University Press, 1999), 57–58. *Usucapio* was a legal principle whereby ownership could be established based upon length of physical possession of property.

52. Reinhard Zimmerman, *The Law of Obligations* (Oxford: Oxford University Press, 1996), 219–20.

53. *De resurrectione carnis* is a follow up to *De carne Christi*, which was written in late 206 or 207 (Barnes, *Tertullian*, 55). The text is alternately referred to as *de resurrectione mortuorum*.

54. Robert Sider, "Structure and Design in the '*De Resurrectione Mortuorum*' of Tertullian," *Vigiliae Christianae* (hereafter, *VC*) 23, no. 3 (1969): 191.

55. The key verse is 1 Cor 15:50, which reads: "I declare to you, brothers and sisters, that flesh and blood cannot inherit the kingdom of God, nor does the perishable inherit the imperishable" (NIV). See Outi Lehtipuu, "'Flesh and Blood Cannot Inherit the Kingdom of God': The Transformation of the Flesh in the Early Christian Debates Concerning Resurrection," in *Metamorphoses: Resurrection, Body and Transformative Practices in Early Christianity*, ed. Turid Karlsen Seim and Jorunn Økland (Berlin: Walter de Gruyter, 2009), 157–58.

56. Tertullian typically describes the first advent as occurring in humility, while the second advent

is not metaphorical flesh or vague fleshliness, but is the historical flesh of Christ which retains its substance and form and is physically recognizable.[57] The point is that Christ was fully human while on earth and retains this full humanity while in heaven.[58]

In *De resurrectione carnis* 51.2, Tertullian describes how Christ preserves the flesh in heaven; however, the identity of the flesh of Christ is expanded to become paradigmatic of all human flesh.[59] Tertullian highlights this preservation through the use of sequester. In his description, Christ becomes the legal possessor of the flesh, which has been given by God, who as the creator had a legitimate claim to the flesh, and man, who currently inhabits the flesh and thus can also make a claim to it. Although Tertullian's primary focus was to indicate that Christ has taken flesh to heaven, he does discuss the restoration of the flesh. In his role as sequester, Christ was duty bound to restore flesh to humanity; however, Tertullian is clear that the flesh which is returned is perfect flesh (*summae totius*) which is completely and entirely restored to a prelapsarian condition.[60] Thus, one of the ultimate impacts of the incarnation is the eschatological perfection and return of human flesh, a key concept in deification and a result of the flesh being taken up by Christ and joined with his being.

The presence of Christ as the sequester not only had an effect upon the flesh, but also upon the soul. Tertullian describes a mutual exchange between Christ and humanity, wherein Christ received the deposit of the flesh but also gave the deposit of the Spirit. This deposit, referred to as the earnest money, guaranteed the return of the flesh.[61] The implication is that, until the eschaton, the Spirit belongs to humanity and joins the human to the divine. This significantly impacts the status of the human soul, as the sequester provided

---

is one of victory. See Geoffrey D. Dunn, "Two Goats, Two Advents and Tertullian's *Adversus Iudaeos*," *Augustinianum* 39 (1999): 259–60.

57. Tertullian suggests that Christ retains the *substantia et forma*. The *forma* is the outer expression of the substance, which Christ retains in spite of the wounds he received. The *substantia* referred to the constitutive material of a thing and is used by Tertullian within a Trinitarian context in *Adversus Praxean* (Osborn, *Tertullian*, 131). For a discussion of different perspectives of Tertullian's use of *substantia*, see Osborn, *Tertullian*, 133–36.

58. In contrast with Marcion, Tertullian highlights that real flesh is necessary for suffering, death, and resurrection which were the core of the Christian message (ibid., 107).

59. ANF 3:584–85.

60. *Res.* 51.2 (ANF 3:584–85).

61. In Roman law, the earnest money belonged jointly to both parties and was the guarantee that a disputed item would be fully returned (Berger, *Encyclopedic Dictionary*, 367). The presence of the *arrabonem* insured that each party had the right to back out of a deal, but only at the cost of the earnest.

a path for the reception of the Spirit by humanity. Thus, even though in Tertullian's later thought Adam is described as receiving only the inferior breath of God at creation, as opposed to the Spirit, it is not as anthropologically devastating as Hallonsten suggests because the work of the sequester allowed for unity between God and the human soul.[62] This works side by side with *imitatio Christi* and indicates that the soul has been elevated to a superior status and, with the reception of the Spirit, participates in God here and now.

The concept of the sequester challenges the traditional understanding of Tertullian as primarily interested in present, rigoristic moralism, which is seen as disciplining the weaker flesh and preventing it from leading the soul back into disobedience.[63] The sequester broadens our understanding and suggests that the flesh is not only disciplined to prevent another fall of the soul, but is being joined with the divine so that the flesh is prepared for eschatological conformity with Christ. At the eschaton, the divinized flesh becomes a reality for humans and is rejoined with the soul which has imitated Christ through the Spirit and been transformed by him. This provision of the sequester is, at least in part, appropriated by the believer through baptism. In baptism, there is a distinctive sense that the human nature is restored to an original, prelapsarian condition through the cleansing and renewing effects of the water.[64] This enables the beginnings of deification in the present. Baptism is thus a necessary element in human salvation and provides the human with the means for receiving transformation back into the image of God. All of this is possible for the baptized believer, as baptism restores the body and soul to the prelapsarian condition and enables the beginnings of deification in the present.[65]

This concept is further demonstrated in the remainder of chapter 51, which focuses on the implications of Christ returning the deposit of the flesh.

---

62. Compare the earlier *Bapt.* 5.7 (ANF 3:672) with *Marc.* 2.9.4–5 (ANF 3:304–5). These texts are respectively dated to 198–203 and 208 (Barnes, *Tertullian*, 55). See Hallonsten, "*Theosis* in recent research," 285–86; Bray, *Holiness and the Will of God*, 69. Tertullian held to a traducianist position for the ongoing production of souls.

63. Bray, *Holiness and the Will of God*, 93.

64. See *Bapt.* 5.6–7 (ANF 3:672), where Tertullian indicates that humans will be restored to the likeness of God by receiving once more the Spirit of God which had been lost as a result of sin. See Dunn, "A Survey of Tertullian's Soteriology," 67 and 71–73. The presence of the sequester suggests that the flesh is not as fragile after baptism as Bray suggests. See Bray, *Holiness and the Will of God*, 93.

65. In *Bapt.* 9.2 (ANF 3:673), Tertullian sees Christ as restoring human nature to its original sense. This is done through identifying Moses's action of turning the water at Marah from bitter to sweet as a prefiguring of Christ's work in baptism. See Dunn, "A Survey of Tertullian's Soteriology," 72.

Perhaps the most significant element is that it becomes possible for human flesh to be subject (*patiantur*) to incorruption and immortality,[66] as long as two distinctive elements have occurred. First, death must be overcome as its presence has led to the corruption of the flesh. This corruption is not natural to the flesh,[67] which means that ultimately death must be destroyed, as nothing that is subjected to death can take on incorruption. Death is therefore defeated in the return of Christ, which enables the second element: the transformation (*demutabimur*) of the human flesh. That which was formerly subject to corruptibility and mortality is changed because the sequester has preserved the flesh. Thus, human flesh, as a result of being joined to the divine sequester, takes on the properties of the divine.

Tertullian returns to the image of Christ as sequester in *De resurrectione carnis* 63, which is the concluding chapter. Tertullian reiterates that the flesh will indeed rise again with absolute integrity. He is able to make this forceful statement on the grounds that Christ is the sequester between God and man who personally safeguards his own flesh, the flesh of each individual person, and the concept of human flesh, in the presence of God.[68] In a clear parallel with Irenaeus, Tertullian describes the role of the sequester as restoring (*reddet*) God to man and man to God.[69] In this sense, Tertullian suggests that humanity and divinity are being brought back together into the original prelapsarian relationship.[70]

Later, in chapter 63.4, Tertullian envisions the restoration of the flesh as it is witnessed by the soul. Regardless of the circumstances of death and the disbursement of the body, the flesh is safeguarded in God's presence and is restored at the Second Coming. He describes the flesh of the individual as being

---

66. Tertullian is clear that this applies to actual human flesh rather than metaphorical flesh. This is done through a reference to 1 Cor 15:53, where Tertullian suggests that Paul is touching his own body while saying "this [*istud*] mortal" and "this [*istud*] corruptible." This makes the passage a personalized statement from Paul and allows Tertullian to suggest that *istud* requires a palpable expression. See *Res.* 51.9 (ANF 3:584–85).

67. Corruptibility and mortality cannot be natural to human flesh, otherwise the incarnate Christ would have been subjected to them. See *Carn.* 3 (ANF 3:522–23) and *An.* 52 (ANF 3:229).

68. *Res.* 63.1 (ANF 3:593–94).

69. Irenaeus, *Against Heresies* 3.18.7 (ANF 1:448). In this section, which is clearly on deification, Irenaeus suggests that the mediator joins man to God so that humans become partakers of incorruptibility. In this, the mediator presents man to God and reveals God to man.

70. Andrew Louth, "The Place of *Theosis* in Orthodox Theology," in *Partakers of the Divine Nature*, ed. Michael J. Christensen and Jeffrey A. Wittung (Grand Rapids, Mich.: Baker Academic Press, 2008), 35–39, suggests that the return to a prelapsarian state is a key element of deification.

summoned to the final judgment where, evoking Genesis 3:22, it is told, "'Behold, the man is become as one of us!'—thoroughly 'knowing' by that time 'the evil' which she had escaped [*evasit*] 'and the good' which she has acquired [*invasit*]."[71] It is in the eschaton that the flesh has fully escaped evil and taken possession of good. This indicates that Tertullian's eschatological vision identifies the soul being reunited with the deified flesh, with the result being the deification of the whole human. The individual believer and God are thus fully reconciled through the work of the sequester.[72]

This is consistent with Tertullian's other main use of Genesis 3:22, which is located in *Adversus Marcionem* 2.25, and is directly applicable to his thought on deification.[73] Here, Tertullian counters the Marcionite suggestion that the Old Testament God is capricious in his differing treatment of Adam and Cain.[74] Tertullian maintains that the distinction lies with Adam freely acknowledging his sin, which made him a candidate for restoration. Thus, although Adam was given up to death, hope is found in the declaration that Adam is becoming as one with God. Tertullian views this as a future consequence of the human being taken into the divinity, stating: "Now, although Adam was by reason of his condition under law subject to death, yet was hope preserved to him by the Lord's saying, 'Behold, Adam is become as one of us'; that is, in consequence of the future taking of the man into the divine nature."[75]

---

71. *Res.* 63.4 (ANF 3:594). This section includes a quotation from Gn 3:22: "And the LORD God said, 'The man has now become like one of us, knowing good and evil'" (NIV).

72. Tertullian is clear that the flesh shares guilt with the soul and thus the whole person must be present at the final judgment. See Eliezer Gonzalez, "Anthropologies of Continuity: The Body and Soul in Tertullian, Perpetua, and Early Christianity," *JECS* 21, no. 4 (2013): 488–89.

73. Gn 3:22 is also present in *Prax.* 12 (ANF 3:611–12) where the first person plural serves as evidence for distinction within God, as the Father is speaking to the Son. This places an identification of Christ at the heart of the passage.

74. Although both were guilty of sin, Adam's punishment was seen as less severe than Cain's. The Marcionites also suggested that the Old Testament God was ignorant as he was unaware of Adam's sin and of Adam and Eve's location; see *Marc.* 2.25 (ANF 3:316–17).

75. *Marc.* 2.25.4 (ANF 3:317). In the final clause, "divine nature" is more properly rendered as "divinity," with the Latin stating: "Ecce Adam factus est tanquam unus ex nobis, de futura scilicet adlectione hominis in divinitatem." Throughout *Adversus Marcionem* book 2, Tertullian uses *divinitas, divinitatis* in conjunction with the concept of the divine attributes, particularly justice and goodness (*Marc.* 2.1.2; 2.2.4; 2.9.4; 2.10.1; 2.13.5; 2.24.2; 2.29.1, 3). Thus, Tertullian is suggesting that humans take up characteristics that are properly applied to the divinity.

Here, Tertullian notes that both Adam and Eve are examples of confession. Tertullian suggests that Adam is guilty of the Fall and bears responsibility for the consequences; however, Eve is mentioned as a full participant in the restoration. On Tertullian's view of Eve and her participation in the Fall, see

Two important elements for Tertullian's understanding of deification emerge from Genesis 3:22. The first is that Tertullian has a sense that deification is the restoration of the human. Humans become what they were created to be, which is paralleled with being taken up into the divine nature. Further, Tertullian appears to treat deification as a foregone conclusion for the future of the believer; becoming one with God is the consequence of being taken into the divine nature. The second significant element is the Christological nature of his understanding of Genesis 3:22. Tertullian joins together the concept of Adam becoming as one with God with the work of Christ in joining the humanity to the divinity. Thus, deification becomes a key corollary of Tertullian's Christology and involves the full restoration of the whole human, which is the ultimate goal of the sequester.

## Christ the Sequester in *Adversus Praxean*

The final occurrence of Christ as sequester is *Adversus Praxean* 27, wherein Tertullian disputes a corollary of Praxeas's modalism.[76] Having already established that Praxeas denies the distinction between Father and Son, Tertullian is at pains to explain a distinction within the Praxean construction of the divine monarchy. According to Tertullian, Praxeas claimed that the Father is the Spirit and Christ, while the Son is flesh and Jesus.[77] This position allowed Praxeas to maintain distinction within an overall position of unity that did not require him to sacrifice the ontological identity of Spirit to identify the Son of God as flesh.

Tertullian disputes this distinction through the use of logic, noting that like breeds like. In this case, Mary conceived by the Spirit; therefore, what was brought forth must also be Spirit and the angelic pronunciation of Luke 1:35

---

F. Forrester Church, "Sex and Salvation in Tertullian," *Harvard Theological Review* 68, no. 2 (1975): 83–101, and Dyan Elliott, "Tertullian, the Angelic Life, and the Bride of Christ," in *Gender and Christianity in Medieval Europe: New Perspectives*, ed. Lisa M. Bitel and Felice Lifshitz (Philadelphia: University of Pennsylvania Press, 2010), 16–33.

76. ANF 3:624. *Adversus Praxean* was written in 210/11 (Barnes, *Tertullian*, 55). On Praxean modalism, see Kelly, *Early Christian Doctrines*, 120–21; Kevin B. McCruden, "Monarchy and Economy in Tertullian's *Adversus Praxeam*," *Scottish Journal of Theology* 55, no. 3 (2002): 326–34.

77. Tertullian suggests that they may have derived this separation of Jesus and Christ from the Valentinians. See *Prax.* 27 (ANF 3:624). Some elements in Valentinian thought appear to suggest that Christ was a production of the divine mother (Sophia) while she was outside of the Pleroma. Christ then returned to the Pleroma and later sent Jesus as savior (Pearson, *Ancient Gnosticism*, 149).

applies to the Spirit, not the flesh.[78] Thus, the Son cannot be solely relegated to the flesh, and the logical outcome is that the Word, who is a divine person, must have been incarnate. For Tertullian, this is the only reasonable conclusion and the Praxean separation of flesh and Spirit in the Word is defeated.

However, Tertullian realizes that his conclusion that the Word is incarnate needs additional explanation to avoid other Christological heresies. He offers two possible ways to comprehend the coming together of flesh and Spirit in Christ. The first possibility is through transfiguration; however, this position must be discarded as it suggests change in God,[79] and would imply the creation of a third compound that was neither divine nor human.[80] Tertullian will maintain a clear distinction between the flesh and Spirit, highlighting that each nature maintains its unique characteristics. In this, Tertullian limits the *communicatio idiomatum* as the distinctive properties of each nature are not communicated to the other. However, Tertullian allows for the communication of the status of each nature and thus maintains overall unity within the person of Christ.[81]

---

78. In this passage, Gabriel pronounces, "So the holy one to be born will be called the Son of God" (NIV). Praxeas applied this pronunciation to the flesh which provided evidence that the Son was flesh.

79. As its name suggests, transfiguration involved the destruction of the former and becoming just the latter. This would suggest that Christ was ceasing to be divine and was in the process of becoming just the flesh. Tertullian is clear; God cannot cease to be Spirit and cannot become anything else. These would violate God's immutability and Spirit nature, which are the bedrock elements of Tertullian's understanding of God (Osborn, *Tertullian*, 140–41). Here, it is important to note that Tertullian is only referencing transfiguration as an understanding of the incarnation, and is in no way referencing Jesus' transfiguration on the mountain (see Mt 17:1–13 and parallel passages).

80. Tertullian refers to *electrum*, which he identifies as a substance composed of gold and silver. The gold and silver change each other, with the result being neither gold nor silver. Later, Tertullian returns to this illustration to claim that if transfiguration were true, then neither the human nor the divine would be readily apparent in the work of Jesus. However, as they are readily apparent, transfiguration cannot be correct. See *Prax.* 27.8–9 (ANF 3:624). Electrum was an early alloy used in coins in Lydia and Persia. Some scholars believe that electrum was abandoned because the amount of gold and silver present could not be verified, although others have called this into question. See Christopher Howgego, *Ancient History from Coins* (London: Routledge, 1995), 1–4.

81. Here, I disagree with Rankin's assertion that Tertullian is not denying *communicatio idiomatum*. Rankin argues, through comparison with Leo the Great and Cyril of Alexandria, that Tertullian is solely providing a distinction of the properties and not a limitation of *communicatio idiomatum*. See David I. Rankin, "Tertullian and the Crucified God," *Pacifica* 10 (1997): 306–8. My approach is more nuanced and consistent with his concept of compenetration. Elsewhere, Tertullian has language that appears to support elements of the *communicatio idiomatum*, particularly noting that God was born, suffered, and died. See *Carn.* 5.2 (ANF 3:525); Kelly, *Early Christian Doctrines*, 151–52. Tertullian notes, and is comfortable with, this paradox. Although the concept of *communicatio idiomatum* would later become popular, there is no clear evidence that it was in widespread use prior to Tertullian (Rankin, "Tertullian and the Crucified God," 301).

Tertullian is therefore left with the difficulty of identifying how the Word has two natures, each of which is wholly preserved and identifiable. Tertullian's answer to this apparent contradiction is the concept of compenetration. In this theory each nature retains its unique identity while being combined together, so that the person of Christ contains the divine and human nature.[82] As Tertullian concludes this key Christological passage, he identifies Christ as the sequester, which he understands as an affirmation of the divine and human nature coexisting in the one person. Thus, for Tertullian, the sequester represents the full joining of humanity to divinity in the person of Christ.

In his description of Christ as the sequester, Tertullian clearly articulates significant elements of deification. He describes a mutual exchange whereby Christ fully owns and perfects human flesh and gives the Spirit for the perfection of the soul. This restorative process is a present reality which is completed in the eschaton when Christ the sequester restores the flesh to the soul and the human takes possession of good and is taken into the divine nature.

## *Adversus Marcionem* 2.27

The concept of the present and future restoration of humanity is also present in *Adversus Marcionem* 2.27, which is a key chapter for Tertullian's thought on deification. In this chapter, Tertullian disputes that the incarnation is a degradation of the divinity. He proclaims the necessity of the incarnation as otherwise God could not engage (*congressus inire*) with humanity.[83] Humans are too weak and fragile unless God tempers his strength with human emotions. Although the Marcionites viewed the incarnation as disgraceful, Tertullian asserts that Christ, in himself, joins together humanity and divinity for the purpose of bestowing upon humanity what he has taken from God.[84] Thus, Tertullian creates a picture of God accommodating himself to

---

82. Edward Yarnold, SJ, "'*Videmus duplicem statum*': The visibility of the two natures of Christ in Tertullian's *Adversus Praxean*," ed. Elizabeth Livingstone, *Studia Patristica* 19 (Leuven: Peeters, 1989), 289–90; Brian E. Daley, "'One Thing and another': The Persons in God and the Person of Christ in Patristic Theology," *Pro Ecclesia* 15, no. 1 (2006): 29; Lawrence B. Porter, "On Keeping 'Persons' in the Trinity: A Linguistic Approach to Trinitarian Thought," *Theological Studies* 41, no. 3 (1980): 545–47.

83. *Marc.* 2.27.1 (ANF 3:318); Charlotte Radler, "The Dirty Physician: Necessary Dishonor and Fleshly Solidarity in Tertullian's Writings," *VC* 63 (2009): 360.

84. *Marc.* 2.27.6 (ANF 3:318–19). In describing the Son, Tertullian states, "uniting in Himself man

human weakness for the purpose of not only redemption, but also the reception of the divine life.

With this underlying understanding of the incarnation in place, Tertullian presents a series of statements detailing a threefold sense of the ramifications of the relationship between God and humanity, stating, "God held converse with man, that man might learn to act as God. God dealt on equal terms with man, that man might be able to deal on equal terms with God. God was found little, that man might become great."[85] There is a progression that can be seen in this joining together. The first element is that God accommodates himself to humanity. Tertullian describes God as consorting with humanity so that humans learn to act like God. In this, humans are rigorously disciplined and the focus is on actions. The emphasis is therefore on present conformity to God. In the second element, humanity mirrors God; God deals equally with humans so that humans might deal equally with God. Here, Tertullian moves forward with the elevation of humanity wherein the human has been brought into a level place with God. This is directly related to his understanding of the sequester as the human and divine are completely brought together. In the third element, God is found small so that humanity might become great (*ut homo maximus fieret*). In this instance, Tertullian develops the concept of an exchange. Here, the sense of *communicatio idiomatum* is one that involves both status and properties as God takes on what it is to be human and humans take on what it is to be God. In this text, the present reality and the eschatological possibility of deification are integrated by Tertullian. As a result of the incarnation, humans are trained for holiness in the here and now through conformity to God.[86] However, the impact of the incarnation stretches further as humans are elevated to God and take on the qualities of God.

---

and God, God in mighty deeds, in weak ones man, in order that He may give to man as much as He takes from God."

85. *Marc.* 2.27.7 (ANF 3:319).

86. Rankin notes that this is a strong deification statement: "Here God condescends to come to man so that man might be lifted up to God. Here is 'accommodation' of the highest order; here is the '*theopoiesis*' (deification) of the Greeks; here is the 'admirabile commercium' (wonderful exchange) of Irenaeus, Athanasius and the Cappadocians." Rankin, "Tertullian and the Crucified God," 304.

## Angelification

The perfected human flesh, which is provided by the sequester, must be brought into harmony with this reception of the qualities of God. Tertullian provides for this harmony through an understanding of the angelification of the human, wherein humans receive an incorruptible nature. Tertullian often depicts the eschatological nature of the human in relation to humans receiving the angelic substance or nature, though he is not entirely consistent in terms of the exact identity of the angelic nature *vis-à-vis* human nature.[87] At points, Tertullian talks about Christ being made lower than the angels and angels having to be lowered to come to humanity in human form.[88] However, elsewhere Tertullian describes the human soul as superior owing to its creation in the divine image.[89] It is necessary for Tertullian to hold these points in tension owing to his understanding of the reality of the incarnation and the full humanity of Christ. As a result, Tertullian's position may be characterized as the following: the human material form is inferior to the angelic form, which is identified as *spiritu materiali*; by nature, the human soul is superior, but, owing to the Fall, it is currently inferior.[90] Thus, the transformation of the human into the angelic state is best understood as humanity taking on the incorruption of the flesh.[91] In *Ad Uxorem* 1.1.4 Tertullian asserts that in the eschaton humans receive the character and purity (*qualitatem et sanctitatem*) of the angels, but is clear that humans do not become angels.[92] Thus, when Tertullian describes humans as receiving the angelic substance, he is indicating a trans-

---

87. *Marc.* 3.24.6 (ANF 3:343, mistakenly labeled as chap. 25) is a standard location for this identification. This thought is based, at least in part, on Lk 20:36, "and they can no longer die; for they are like the angels" (NIV). See also Russell, *Doctrine of Deification*, 326–27. Here, it is important to note that Tertullian is describing the angelic nature of the good angels as he considered demons as angelic beings.

88. *Prax.* 16.4–5 (ANF 3:612) and *Marc.* 3.9 (ANF 3:328–29).

89. *Marc.* 2.8.2 (ANF 3:303–4).

90. Ibid.

91. *Marc.* 3.24.6 (ANF 3:343). In this passage, Tertullian puts together the change into the angelic substance with the investiture of an incorruptible nature.

92. ANF 4:39. Willemien Otten confirms the eschatological nature of this assertion and places it within the context of humans overcoming marriage. See Willemien Otten, "Tertullian's Rhetoric of Redemption: Flesh and Embodiment in *De carne Christi* and *De resurrectione mortuorum*," ed. Markus Vinzent, Studia Patristica 65 (Leuven: Peeters, 2013), 340. Kari Kloos notes that Tertullian is asserting that upward progression is logically subsequent to the downward movement of angels in a theophany. See Kari Kloos, *Christ, Creation and the Vision of God: Augustine's Transformation of Early Christian Theophany Interpretation* (Leiden: Brill, 2011), 59–60.

formation into an incorruptible nature which is the equal of the vague, undefined corporeality of the angels.[93] The concept of angelification allows Tertullian to tie together the eschatological dimension of his deification thought. The perfected human flesh receives the angelic nature, which can then receive incorruptibility, which is a key quality of God.

## Conclusion

Tertullian's understanding of deification is rooted in his incarnational and eschatological thought. Deification is only possible as a result of the incarnation as Christ joins man to God and God to man by taking up and perfecting human nature. Deification is an incarnational reality owing to the work of the sequester, which is potentially available for all humans. In baptism, the individual actualizes the possibility of deification and begins the process of being transformed and conformed to the image of Christ. In the present, the individual human, through moral discipline, lives out the *imitatio Christi* and is moved from disobedience to obedience. The work of deification does not only include the flesh, but the soul receives the Spirit which enables the soul to progress toward perfection as well. These initial elements of deification are fully realized in the eschaton when Christ the sequester returns the now-perfected human flesh, which has become like the angels, to the soul and the individual human is fully restored and receives the divine image and qualities. Humans thus take possession of the incorruptible nature and the connection between human and divine becomes a completed reality. With this understanding, it is clear that deification is a key element within the soteriological paradigm of Tertullian.

---

93. *Res.* 26.7 (ANF 3:564) and 36.6 (ANF 3:571) describe the transformation as a remaking of the flesh which takes on the clothing of incorruption. Elliott notes that in his later writings, Tertullian sees the angelic life as a substitute for eternity and bodily transformation into the incorruptible (Elliott, "Tertullian, the Angelic Life," 29).

*Benjamin Safranski*

## 4. AFTER THE FASHION OF GOD
*Deification in Cyprian*

While the literature about his fellow North Africans, Tertullian and Augustine, continues to grow, Cyprian's thought on deification has been little discussed by scholars.[1] This essay aims to fill this lacuna by locating Cyprian's thought on deification within a deeper examination of his ecclesiology, Christology, anthropology, and soteriology. To that end, it will proceed in three main parts. After introductory remarks, I will examine the ecclesial and sacramental foundation of deification as expressed in Cyprian's epistles and select treatises. Next, I will discuss how deification comes about through the conformation of the Christian to the image and likeness of God. Finally, I will explore the concept of deification by imitation of God's mercy, one of the most noteworthy aspects of Cyprian's account of deification.

---

1. Gustave Bardy, "Divinisation," in *Dictionnaire de Spiritualité*, ed. M. Viller et al., and continued by C. Baumgartner et al. (Paris: Beauchesne, 1957), 1390–98, mentions Cyprian twice. The first time, he mentions that Cyprian uses the word *deificus* in several places, but says that Cyprian is simply substituting this for *diuinus* in order to avoid repetition or rhyme (1390). The second time, when discussing the development of the doctrine, Bardy says that one can skip over Cyprian completely. Norman Russell, in *The Doctrine of Deification in the Greek Patristic Tradition* (Oxford: Oxford University Press, 2004), provides a helpful appendix on the Latin Fathers, but also jumps from Tertullian to Hilary. Jared Ortiz, "Deification in the Latin Fathers," in *Called to Be the Children of God: The Catholic Theology of Human Deification*, ed. Carl E. Olson and Fr. David Meconi, SJ (San Francisco: Ignatius Press, 2016), 65–66, counters this trend by discussing the third-century bishop of Carthage in continuity with those others. Ortiz portrays Cyprian's thought on deification as expressed primarily in his sacramental thought and as lacking the sense of dynamic movement towards the likeness of Christ that one finds in Tertullian et al.

It must be admitted that Cyprian does not use the technical vocabulary of deification in the same way that some of his contemporaries and successors do. Nowhere in his corpus do we find any quotations of, or allusions to, the standard biblical passages for deification, Psalm 82:6 and 2 Peter 1:4.[2] Nowhere does he directly describe men as "God" or "gods," and his few uses of specific deification vocabulary are ambiguous.[3] This is not surprising for a bishop whose short episcopacy (ca. 249–58) was largely defined by a battle against idolatry. Though Cyprian is better known for his exchange with Pope St. Stephen I regarding the baptism of schismatics, the shadow of the controversy over those who had lapsed during the Decian persecution hung heavy over the bishop of Carthage for his entire reign. With so many of his flock having fallen away by sacrificing to idols (or publicly claiming to have done so),[4] it is perhaps understandable that Cyprian would have shied away from language describing men as God or gods.

Cyprian does, however, describe the realities of deification in many ways and in many places. This essay will show that Cyprian's thought on salvation in both its present and future aspects is consistent with the more explicit descriptions of deification in some of the other Church Fathers. Working from the memory of the "old man" that died in his own baptism, Cyprian knows firsthand what it means to be reborn as a new man while still in one's earthly body. In that rebirth, the Christian begins to be divine through assimilation into Christ's body, adoption as a coheir with Christ, and sanctification as a temple of the Holy Spirit. It is by continuously living up to that rebirth that one merits the eternal reward; by imitating Christ that one merits the grace that ultimately results in the fullness of deification.

---

2. Michael Fahey, SJ, *Cyprian and the Bible: A Study in Third-Century Exegesis* (Tübingen: J. C. B. Mohr, 1971), 675–95, provides an exhaustive index of scriptural quotations and allusions in the Cyprianic corpus.

3. Cyprian's writings contain five uses of forms of the word *deificus*. One is in the treatise *Envy and Jealousy*, while four are in the epistles. The instance from *Envy and Jealousy* will be quoted below. Translators have tended to use "divine," "of God," or similar terms in their translations, avoiding the loaded term "deifying." In each of these instances, even if Cyprian intended to communicate a sense of deification, none of the contexts lend themselves to strong discussions of deification.

4. The former were the *sacrificati*, those who had actually offered the sacrifices demanded by imperial agents in Carthage. The latter belonged to a category known as the *libellatici*, those who had paid to obtain fraudulent documents (*libelli*) certifying that they had sacrificed, so that they could avoid the consequences of refusal. The two groups together constituted the *lapsi*.

## The Ecclesial and Sacramental Foundation for Deification

Cyprian's understanding of deification is rooted in his understanding of the church and the sacraments. It is well established that communion with the Catholic church through the sacraments, most notably baptism and the eucharist, is for Cyprian the way to gain access to the forgiveness of sins and the salvation won by Christ.[5] It has gone relatively unnoticed that it is in these same sacraments where deification begins. I will proceed to outline the deifying effects of the sacraments, paying special attention to the epistles and the treatises *To Donatus* and *On the Unity of the Catholic Church*.

### Baptism

Deification for Cyprian is begun by baptism and preserved and advanced by contemplation of divine things and right action. He ultimately describes it as the baptized being the dwelling place of God. The pneumatological rooting of baptism is prominent in Cyprian and is key for understanding his thought on deification. For Cyprian, baptism can be bestowed by the Catholic church alone because that is where the Holy Spirit dwells, and the Spirit is absolutely essential for sanctification.[6] Where the Spirit dwells, he dwells in fullness and is given in fullness. In baptism, the Spirit "is poured out completely upon the believer"[7] and "takes up His dwelling"[8] in him. If the baptized cooperates

---

5. *To Donatus* 3–5, in *Saint Cyprian: Treatises*, trans. Roy J. Deferrari, Fathers of the Church (hereafter, FOTC) 36 (Washington, D.C.: The Catholic University of America Press, 1958), 7–21; *On the Unity of the Catholic Church* 6, in *St. Cyprian: The Lapsed, The Unity of the Catholic Church*, trans. Maurice Bévenot, Ancient Christian Writers (hereafter, ACW) 25 (New York: Newman Press, 1956), 43–68; *Epistles* 69–75, in *The Letters of St. Cyprian*, trans. G. W. Clarke, ACW 43–44 and 46–47 (New York: Newman Press, 1984–89); as well as numerous other places in Cyprian's writings. See Abraham van de Beek, "Cyprian on Baptism," in *Cyprian of Carthage: Studies in His Life, Language, and Thought*, ed. Henk Bakker, Paul van Geest, and Hans van Loon (Leuven: Peeters, 2010), 143–64.

6. *Ep.* 69.11 (40–41) and 70.3.1 (47). For all parenthetical page numbers after citations, the source is the respective English translation listed alongside the first long-form citation.

7. *Ep.* 69.14.1 (43). A passage on 14.2 contains one of the best sources for arguing that Cyprian did have a "dynamic" view of growth into the likeness of Christ through deification. It reads: "Surely that spiritual grace, received equally by all believers in baptism, may be diminished or increased by our subsequent conduct in our own lives" (43; translation adjusted). This will be supported below, when it is shown that in the treatises deification is tied very intimately with God-like action for Cyprian. See Clarke, notes on letter 69 in ACW 47:186n39 and 188n47.

8. *Ep.* 69.15.2 (44).

with the Spirit by his way of life, he is given power by God to live in a way that he could not live otherwise.⁹ For Cyprian, it is this new way of life that is the manifestation of God's effective dwelling in us.

The deifying effects of baptism are especially highlighted in the treatise *To Donatus*, an attempt by the newly baptized Cyprian to extol the benefits of life in Christ to an interlocutor who is not entirely convinced or is struggling with complete commitment. Cyprian reflects on the changes he experienced in baptism. He finds it hard to believe that God could be so merciful "so that anyone might be born again and animated into new life by the bath of saving water, he might abandon what he had been before, and, although the structure of the body remained that of a human [*corporis licet manente conpage hominem*], he might change in soul and mind."¹⁰ The use of the word *hominem* creates a contrast between what the body is (human) and what the changed mind and soul are. This passage raises the question, of course, of what the soul and mind of the baptized change into so that they are no longer considered simply human.¹¹

Cyprian goes on to describe his own baptism in such a way that sums up very neatly his thought on conversion, salvation, and deification. When his sins had been washed away by baptism, he writes, "a light from above poured itself upon my expiated and pure breast."¹² That light was "a heavenly Spirit" which through baptism "restored me into a new man."¹³ This allowed Cyprian to understand that the sinful part of him was the old man, the earthly man, and that "what the Holy Spirit already was animating had begun to be of God [*Dei esse coepisse*]."¹⁴ The Holy Spirit is infused into the baptized and begins to change him into something more than he was; something "of God," something divine.

Chapters 14 and 15 close out *To Donatus* with additional testimony to this change. When the baptized has been graced with salvation and is "close to God in his mind," he begins more and more to raise his eyes to heavenly

---

9. *To Donatus* 5 (10–11). See Van de beek, "Cyprian on Baptism," 144–46.

10. *To Donatus* 3 (8–9, translation adjusted).

11. This is echoed in chap. 8 of *On Mortality* (199–221). Cyprian explains that, due to the conditions of our "original" or earthly birth, our bodies share the weaknesses of those who have undergone that birth (i.e., all of humanity). Our spirits, however, which have been reborn in baptism, are different: "As long as we are here in the world we are united with the human race in equality of the flesh, we are separated in spirit" (205).

12. *To Donatus* 4 (9, translation adjusted).

13. Ibid. (9–10, translation adjusted).

14. Ibid. (10, translation adjusted).

things.[15] This happens by the free gift of God pouring his Spirit into the believer. As this happens, "the soul gazing upon heaven recognizes its Author, higher than the sun and more sublime than all this earthly power, [and] it begins to be that which it believes itself to be."[16] What does the soul "believe itself to be"? While Cyprian does not say explicitly, it makes sense to connect this change back to chapter 3, where the soul and mind are said to change into something not simply human. It seems, then, that Cyprian had in mind a change in the soul in the direction of God,[17] whom it was contemplating. This change ultimately results in God taking up his dwelling with the baptized. If the person keeps his gaze fixed on the heavenly things, understanding what he is called to be, God will adorn him spiritually more than the most glorious of earthly buildings, for in him "the Lord has moved into a temple, in which the Holy Spirit begins to live."[18]

The description of the change within the Christian is echoed and strengthened in chapter 11 of the treatise *That Idols Are Not Gods*. The last six chapters of this treatise comprise Cyprian's most extensive discussion of Christology and soteriology.[19] They are based to an extent on chapter 21 of Tertullian's *Apology*, but the passages that are relevant to deification are very much original. Cyprian explains the uniting of God and man in Christ as follows: "This is our God; this is our Christ who, as mediator of the two, puts on man, whom he leads to the Father. What man is, Christ wished to be, so that man also might be able to be what Christ is."[20] What is the "what" that Christ is and that we might be? Cyprian's answer is clear and telling: "This one is the power of God, the *ratio*, His wisdom and glory ... the Holy Spirit clothed in flesh."[21] We can become God's *ratio*; God's wisdom; God's glory—and are we

---

15. *To Donatus* 14 (19, translation adjusted): "Deo suo mente ... proximus." It should be noted that *proximus* can also carry the meaning of being very alike to someone or something.

16. Ibid., 20.

17. Because of Cyprian's silence, I hesitate to say directly that the soul is becoming divine or God-like, but that can be inferred.

18. *To Donatus* 15 (20).

19. The debate over the authorship of this treatise has a long history and should not be considered completely settled. In 2010, an excellent study by Hans van Loon ("Cyprian's Christology and the Authenticity of *Quod idola dii non sint*," in *Cyprian of Carthage*, ed. Bakker et al., 127–42) summarized the history of this question and offered fresh arguments for Cyprianic authorship. Though there are still lingering questions (in my opinion primarily stylistic ones), van Loon convincingly debunks the thematic and grammatical arguments made by scholars in the past such as Harnack and Diller.

20. *That Idols Are Not Gods* 11 (FOTC 36:349–60, at 358, translation adjusted).

21. Ibid. (357, translation adjusted).

not therefore deified? Whereas in *To Donatus* Cyprian had hinted at the deifying change that comes upon the Christian, in *That Idols Are Not Gods*, he describes it outright.

## Eucharist

Cyprian's thought on the eucharist and how it brings God to dwell in us effectively is expressed in several places. Two examples are especially helpful. Epistle 57 is a letter sent by Cyprian and the Carthaginian synod of Easter 253, wherein the African bishops tell Pope Cornelius in Rome that they have decided immediately to readmit to communion any of the lapsed who had been doing continuous penance since their fall. This was in view of another pending persecution, in the hopes that the reconciled would thus have the strength to face the trial the second time around. Cyprian portrays the giving of eucharist as arming the soldiers of Christ for the battle: "A man cannot be fit for martyrdom if he is not armed for battle by the Church; his heart fails if it is not fired and fortified by receiving the Eucharist."[22] As I mentioned in the preceding paragraph (with reference to *Ad Donatum*), it is the Spirit dwelling in us that gives us the power to act uprightly, as Cyprian hopes those facing persecution will do. Thus, the same Spirit of uprightness that manifests in Christian action after baptism is also strengthened by the eucharist.

In addition to providing arms for battle, the eucharist symbolizes and effects the union of Christians in Christ. In Epistle 63, Cyprian's most notable discussion of the eucharist, he explains why the eucharistic cup must contain both water and wine. He writes:

For Christ bore the burden of us all, having borne the burden of our sins. And so we can see that by water is meant God's people, whereas Scripture reveals that by wine is signified the blood of Christ. When, therefore, water is mixed with wine in the cup, the people are made one with Christ and the multitude of believers are bonded and united with Him in whom they have come to believe. And this bonding and union between water and wine in the Lord's cup is achieved in such a way that nothing can thereafter separate their intermingling. Thus there is nothing that can separate the union between Christ and the Church.[23]

---

22. *Ep.* 57.4.2 (58).
23. *Ep.* 63.13.1–2 (105). See 63.13.3 (105) and 69.5.2 (36).

The sensory imagery of the mingling of water and wine is important here. When water and wine are mingled in the eucharistic cup, not only do they become inextricably joined, but the characteristics of each become indistinguishable from those of the other—the water, for example, takes on the taste, smell, and appearance of the wine. The mixing of water and wine symbolizes our transformative union with Christ and also brings it about.[24]

## On the Unity of the Catholic Church

The union of Christ and Christians, effected through the sacraments in the church, is a major focal point for deification in *On the Unity of the Catholic Church*, Cyprian's exhortation to ecclesial unity. This is particularly true when Cyprian describes the relationships among God, the church, and the people who are its members. Cyprian's primary concern in this treatise (possibly originally a homily) is the unity of the visible church.[25] This unity requires one bishop in each place and unanimity of heart and mind, and gives expression to the invisible realities that underlie the church, her origins, and her mission.

*On the Unity of the Catholic Church* was occasioned by one of the great schisms of Cyprian's day (either that of Novatian in Rome or Felicissimus in Carthage). The entire work is essentially an argument that any presumptive bishop or congregation, cut off from the unity of the church founded on the episcopal college, is neither the church nor a member of it. His first argument for this fact is that, while Christ gave all of the apostles equal authority, he founded the church on one man (Peter), in order to show the unified nature of its source.[26] This unicity-in-multiplicity, expressed by the twelve apostles owing their unity to one of their number, is at the heart of the mystery of the church.

To make this clearer, Cyprian compares the unity of the church in its many manifestations throughout the world to that of the sun and its rays, a

---

24. One can see here the conceptual ancestry of later prayers spoken by the priest at the mingling that make the connection with deification more explicit. At least since the Middle Ages, the priest has prayed this prayer over the cup: "Per huius aquae et vini mysterium / eius efficiamur divinitatis consortes / qui humanitatis nostrae fieri dignatus est particeps."

25. I have surveyed the debates over several textual issues and the original context of *De unitate* in Benjamin B. Safranski, *St. Cyprian of Carthage and the College of Bishops* (Lanham, Md.: Lexington Books/Fortress Academic, 2018), 12–17.

26. *Unity*, chaps. 4 and 5 (ACW 25:46–48).

tree and its branches, and a river and the many streams to which it gives birth. What happens when you sever a member from its source, as the schismatics attempt to do? Cyprian writes:

> Cut off a ray from the body of the sun—the unity does not permit a division of the light; break off a branch from the tree, the broken piece cannot bud; dam off a stream from the source, the severed section dries up. Thus also the Church, imbued with the light of the Lord, stretches out her rays through the whole world, but it is one light which is diffused everywhere without the unity of the body being divided.[27]

This profound unity may be analogous to a sun or a river, but for Cyprian it is actually based on the unity of the Trinity.[28] After describing the church as our mother,[29] the spouse of Christ,[30] and Noah's ark,[31] Cyprian writes:

> The Lord says: "I and the Father are One," and again of the Father, Son, and Holy Spirit it is written: And the three are One. And does anyone believe that this unity, coming from divine stability, held together in the celestial mysteries [*sacramentis caelestibus cohaerentem*], can be torn in the Church and divided by the separation of conflicting wills? He who does not hold this unity does not hold the law of God, does not hold the faith of the Father and Son, does not hold life and salvation.[32]

It is telling that after Cyprian has quoted John 10:30 and given an interpretation of 1 John 5:8,[33] he refers to "this unity" without explaining that he means the unity of the church. Cyprian makes it clear that he is in fact writing about the unity of the church, a unity that cannot be torn by schism. This unity comes "from divine stability" and is "held together in the celestial mysteries." This latter phrase, *sacramentis caelestibus cohaerentem*, truly resists translation. What Cyprian seems to be saying is that ecclesial unity is a visible sign of the invisible truth of heaven—the truth of the relationships in the Trinity. So crucial is this ecclesial unity, and so closely tied to the unity of the Father and Son, that not holding the first precludes holding faith in the second.

---

27. *Unity* 5 (48, translation adjusted).
28. See *The Lord's Prayer* 23 (FOTC 36:127–59, at 147–48); Juan Antonio Gil-Tamayo, "«De unitate Patris et Filii et Spiritus sancti plebs adunata» (*De oratione dominica*, 23). La unidad trinitaria como fundamento de la unidad eclesial en Tertuliano y Cipriano de Cartago," *Scripta Theologica* 43 (2011): 9–29.
29. *Unity* 5 (48).
30. Ibid., 6 (48).
31. Ibid. (49).
32. Ibid. (translation adjusted).
33. See Maurice Bévenot, Notes on *Unity* (ACW 25:109n53).

After comparing the unity of the church to Christ's seamless garment, woven from the top down, "that is, from His Father in heaven,"[34] Cyprian asks the central question again: "Who therefore is so wicked and perfidious ... as either to believe it possible that the unity of God, the garment of the Lord, the Church of Christ could be divided, or to dare to divide it?"[35] Without belaboring the point, one should notice that Cyprian is strongly identifying the very unity of God with the church of Christ. One can no more be divided than the other.

This grounding of ecclesial unity in divine unity is essential for Cyprian's thought on deification because it goes beyond mere analogy and approaches identity. Because the unities are so closely allied, one can say that, for Cyprian, we participate in the life of the Trinity by our integration into the church through baptism and eucharist. As Abraham van de Beek has aptly written: "There is a unity of life in the Church that is embedded in the unity of God."[36] This embedding in the unity of God, which can readily be described as deification, is salvation for Cyprian, and it cannot be attained without integration in the church. In schism, one dis-integrates oneself from ecclesial unity and thereby loses the integration in the divine unity, the deification, that constitutes salvation.

### *The Lord's Prayer*

Cyprian also emphasizes our unity in Christ in chapters 8 through 11 of *The Lord's Prayer*, one of his most well-known treatises and one of the first extent treatises on prayer. In chapter 8, Cyprian expounds on the unity of the faithful indicated by the fact that we always pray "Our Father" and not "My Father," even when praying alone. Cyprian writes: "God, the teacher of prayer and concord, who taught unity, thus wished one to pray for all, just as He

---

34. *Unity* 7 (49).
35. *Unity* 8 (50, translation adjusted). The concluding pronoun "it" is not present in the original: "Quis ergo sic sceleratus et perfidus ... ut aut credat scindi posse aut audeat scindere unitatem Dei, uestem Domini, ecclesiam Christi?" I have translated the passage in the way I found least awkward in English, though this could create a subtly different sense of the identification of the terms *unitatem ... uestem ... ecclesiam*. If a singular pronoun were the object of *scindere*, then unity, garment, and church would be strongly shown to be one thing. As it is, Cyprian simply piles the phrases together without so much as an *et*, creating the balance between identity and diversity that, perhaps, he intended, and, regardless, is appropriate.
36. Van de Beek, "Cyprian on Baptism," 145.

Himself bore all in one [*quomodo in uno omnes ipse portauit*]."[37] Here, the unity of the church's members is grounded in Christ's taking on our common nature. God is always "our" Father because our sonship is inextricably linked with our common incorporation into Christ through the sacraments.

Insofar as we are sons of God through sacramental incorporation into Christ, we are also coheirs with him.[38] In chapters 9 to 11, Cyprian analyzes the opening words of the Lord's Prayer, "Our Father who art in heaven." Through this analysis runs a very strong theme of our sonship in Christ and the confidence with which we call God "Father" on account of this. "A new man, reborn and restored to his God by His grace says in the first place 'Father', because he has already begun to be a son."[39] The sonship of the baptized is such that he should begin to transfer the reverence due his earthly father to his heavenly Father alone. The theme of sonship comes to a peak in chapter 11. Cyprian asks: "How great is the indulgence of the Lord ... that He had so wished us to celebrate prayer in the sight of God, that we might call God 'Father' and, as Christ is the son of God for us also thus to be pronounced sons of God!"[40] In addition, Cyprian insists that those who are called sons should behave like sons: "We must act as sons of God.... Let us abide as temples of God, so that it might be apparent that God dwells in us."[41] This dwelling is of the Spirit and begins at baptism, demanding again a certain rightness of action on our part: "Let our action not be unworthy of the Spirit, so that we who have begun to be spiritual and heavenly people may ponder and do nothing except spiritual and heavenly things."[42] This is the call of the baptized Christian to be changed in what he is and what he does.

## Image and Likeness

Deification, for Cyprian, requires integration into the life of God through integration into the sacramental life of the church. It is expressed and deep-

---

37. *The Lord's Prayer* 8 (132).
38. Being coheirs with Christ essentially means inheriting those things promised in the formula of exchange: glory, wholeness, immortality, freedom. These attributes or possessions of Christ become ours through the incarnation. See below, 85–88, 89–93.
39. *The Lord's Prayer* 9 (133).
40. Ibid., 11 (135, translation adjusted).
41. Ibid. (136, translation adjusted).
42. Ibid. (translation adjusted).

ened, however, in several ways. One of these ways is through transformation into the image of God which, having begun in baptism, continues by our striving to live out our baptism in our actions. It is through our Christ-like acting in the world that the likeness of God in us is both expressed and increased. As it is increased, we become more and more what we began to be in baptism—spiritual creatures and children of God. Cyprian expresses this most directly in two treatises: *Jealousy and Envy* and *The Dress of Virgins*.

### Jealousy and Envy

For Cyprian, deification is closely connected to the behavior of the baptized Christian; conformation to God's image and likeness is described primarily as conformation in action. This is shown clearly in *Jealousy and Envy*, which is, as one might expect, an exhortation against those two vices and so deals with changes in thought and behavior that Cyprian sees as absolutely essential to the Christian life. Cyprian states that he is writing the treatise for those who are "jealous of the good that you see" and "envious of those who are better than you."[43] His intended audience, then, are those who have already made some progress in goodness. Much of the treatise consists of warnings against this jealousy that may appear good, on account of its good object, but is part of the "blind snares of a deceitful enemy, when brother by jealousy turns to hatred of brother."[44] Scriptural examples of the evils of jealousy and envy are mustered; the grievous effects on one's body and soul are described.

There is a turn in chapter 12. From here until the end of the treatise in chapter 18, Cyprian describes the attitudes and feelings that must dwell in the Christian heart in place of those pernicious ones. "Christian innocence ... simplicity of mind ... the same love with which [Christ] Himself loved the disciples."[45] These are the things that risk being destroyed by jealousy and envy. It is particularly in chapters 13–18 that, drawing on St. Paul, Cyprian explains the difference between the half-hearted, jealous Christian and the one who is living worthily in terms that are similar to discourse on deification. Cyprian specifically draws on 1 Corinthians 3 and Romans 8 to draw a contrast between the old, carnal man and the new, spiritual man. The new man, the

---

43. *Jealousy and Envy* 1 (FOTC 36:293–308, at 293).
44. Ibid., 3 (295).
45. Ibid., 12 (302–3).

one who is not jealous, is the "man already made full of the Holy Spirit and a son of God by heavenly birth."⁴⁶ Cyprian directly ties this new birth in the Spirit to the Christian's renewed way of acting:

If we are the sons of God, if we already begin to be His temples, if, having received the Holy Spirit, we live holily and spiritually, if we have lifted our eyes from the earth toward heaven, if we have raised our heart full of God and Christ to the supernal and divine things, let us not do anything unless it is worthy of God and Christ, as the apostle arouses and exhorts us.⁴⁷

Cyprian proceeds to quote Colossians 3:1–4: "For you have died and your life is hidden with Christ in God. When Christ, your life, shall appear, then you too shall appear with Him in glory."⁴⁸ This new life, as Cyprian explains, is the new life begun in baptism, where the old carnal man has died with his sins and the new spiritual man has risen with Christ.⁴⁹ The renunciation of sins such as jealousy and envy, therefore, should be a result of the Christian's being integrated into God's life through the sacraments.

At the end of chapter 14 and in chapter 15, Cyprian quotes 1 Corinthians 15, a classic text for showing the formula of exchange. Cyprian, though, does something unique with it. The end of Cyprian's quotation reads: "Just as we have borne the image of him who is of the earth, so let us bear the image of him who is of heaven."⁵⁰ In Paul's context, this is an argument for the resurrection of the body. Cyprian uses it to argue that we must act like Christ in order to become heavenly. He writes: "We cannot, however, bear the heavenly image [*imaginem*], unless, in that condition in which we have now begun to be, we show the likeness [*similitudinem*] of Christ."⁵¹ In chapter 15, Cyprian explains that imitation is the essence of likeness. He writes: "For this [to show the likeness of Christ] is to have changed what you had been, and to begin to be what you were not, so that the divine birth may shine in you, so that the deifying discipline [*deifica disciplina*] may respond to God the Father, so that, by the honor and praise of living, God may be illuminated in man [*Deus*

---

46. Ibid., 13 (303, translation adjusted).
47. Ibid., 14 (304, translation adjusted).
48. Ibid. (304–5).
49. See *The Lord's Prayer* 17 (141–42).
50. *Jealousy and Envy* 14 (305, translation adjusted).
51. Ibid.

*in homine clarescat*]."⁵² How does one bear the image of Christ, the heavenly man? He does this by living in the likeness of Christ, which means being changed into something he was not before. This change takes place when one undergoes the divine birth of baptism and the subsequent living out of baptism through Christ-like action. It is the *disciplina*, the training or education in the ways of God, that is deifying, that makes one like God.⁵³ When one acts like God, then *Deus in homine clarescat*, God may be made bright, clear, or evident in man.

This remarkable passage is only the beginning of chapter 15. Cyprian continues to explain that, when God is made bright in man, man himself is glorified. Cyprian writes that when Jesus delivered the Sermon on the Mount, he was "forming and preparing us for this glorification" and "instilling the likeness of God the Father" in us.⁵⁴ In other words, when we act like God (as the Sermon on the Mount exhorts us to do), we bear the image of the heavenly man and are glorified with the glory of the Father. To finish this dense chapter, Cyprian compares the human begetting of children by natural birth to God's begetting of children by spiritual rebirth: "If it is joyful and glorious for men to have children like themselves, and it delights even more to have begotten, if the remaining offspring resembles the father with similar features, how much greater is the joy in God the Father, when one is thus born spiritually, that in his acts and praises the divine generosity is proclaimed."⁵⁵ Through the grace of baptism and the maintenance of its character, we are made children like to the Father and coheirs with his only son. We are made so like the Father that his joy in us is greater than the joy of a human parent at a child born of his own flesh. God rejoices precisely because we show forth his features, inherited in baptism and displayed through God-like actions.

Cyprian finishes *Jealousy and Envy* in chapter 18 with a final reminder of what we must do in order to live forever with God. "Consider that only those can be called sons of God who are peacemakers, who, united by divine

---

52. Ibid., 15 (305, translation adjusted)
53. *Pace* Bardy (see above, note 1), it is only tangentially relevant why Cyprian chose *deifica* here, given that the denotations and connotations are different from those of *divina*. In addition, the close proximity of the description of change in the Christian, as well as the divine birth, makes it most appropriate to translate *deifica* as "deifying."
54. *Jealousy and Envy* 15 (305).
55. Ibid. (306, translation adjusted).

birth and law, correspond to the likeness of God the Father and Christ."[56] In this passage, the connections between baptism, right action, and adoption are highlighted once more. Those who are united by the divine birth of baptism and act rightly according to God's precepts are peacemakers. These peacemakers are neither jealous nor envious and therefore conform to the *similitudo* of God. Reborn as his sons, they resemble God because they act like God.

### *The Dress of Virgins*

This treatise on the value of celibacy and the ascetical life is one of Cyprian's most beautiful and has been extensively studied as one of the first treatises on these subjects. Before he begins his exhortations to the virtues particularly required in this state of life, Cyprian uses lofty language to describe the female religious whom he is addressing: "They are the flower of the ecclesiastical shoot, the beauty and ornament of spiritual grace, the image of God corresponding to the sanctity of the Lord, the more illustrious part of Christ's flock."[57] Cyprian's use of *imago* here is very telling. In *On Jealousy and Envy*, Cyprian said that to bear the *imago* of the heavenly man in 1 Corinthians 15 was held up as a sort of consequence of bearing the *similitudo* of Christ in our actions. In *The Dress of Virgins* 3, Cyprian calls the virgins the *imago Dei* and so is holding them up already as humans who imitate Christ quite closely.

Aside from a few scattered references to the inheritance of immortality or reigning with Christ,[58] the other significant passage regarding deification is in chapter 23 (the penultimate chapter). In this chapter, Cyprian summarizes the parallel between the old man and the new man, telling those who have

---

56. *Jealousy and Envy* 18 (308, translation adjusted).

57. *The Dress of Virgins* 3, trans. Sister Angela Elizabeth Keenan (FOTC 36:31–52, at 33, translation adjusted). Cyprian chooses a form of the verb *respondere* here as he does many times when describing the relationship a godly human has to the divine attributes. See above, the quotations from *Jealousy and Envy* 15 and 18.

58. Something should be said here about another use Cyprian makes of *imago* and *similitudo* in *The Dress of Virgins* 15. This chapter is in the midst of Cyprian's excoriation of makeup and jewelry as tools of the devil. He writes: "All women ... should be admonished that the work of God and his creature and matter [*plastica*] must in no way be adulterated ... God says: 'Let us make man to our image and likeness.' And someone dares to change and convert what God has made!" (44, translation adjusted). According to Fahey, *Cyprian and the Bible*, 676, this is Cyprian's only direct use of Gn 1:26, and it clearly refers the image and likeness of God in humanity to physical appearance. As has been shown, however, *imago* and *similitudo* are extremely important for salvation as deification to Cyprian. This shows the possibility of polyvalence for those (sometimes fraught) terms.

chosen celibacy that they are attaining to a greater reward and "the greater sanctity and truth of the renewed birth."[59] Those who live the celibate life well have turned to heavenly things in a greater degree than others. He once again quotes 1 Corinthians 15:47–49 and writes regarding the *imago* of the heavenly man: "Virginity bears this image, integrity bears it, sanctity and truth bear it, those who are mindful of the discipline of God bear it, upholding justice with reverence, steadfast in faith, humble in fear, strong in all endurance, mild in sustaining injury, quick in showing mercy, unanimous and harmonious in fraternal peace."[60] While maintaining that all can bear the image of God who are good, faithful, and just, Cyprian puts virginity in the first place. Read together with *Jealousy and Envy*, *The Dress of Virgins* strengthens the connection between upright action, conformation to the *imago Dei*, and salvation.

## Imitation of God

The treatise *Works and Almsgiving* could be considered the most polished and dense presentation of Cyprian's thought on deification. Building on the themes of baptism and *imago et similitudo*, *Works and Almsgiving* demonstrates that, for Cyprian, deification ultimately means imitating God's most incredible work: his immense mercy towards us, displayed primarily through the salvation offered in Christ. The treatise is an extended exhortation from scripture and reason to the giving of alms and care for the poor. Cyprian's overall argument is based on two points. First, God has been merciful to us and so shown us that we should act mercifully towards others. Second, God has revealed to us very clearly in both the Old and New Testaments that giving to the poor is one of the chief means of wiping away the sins that we commit after the cleansing of baptism. Almsgiving is, in fact, an expression of baptism's continuing efficacy in us.

Cyprian frames *Works and Almsgiving* with an *inclusio* that describes salvation in terms of Christ's incarnation and our glorification through it. Chapter 1 begins with the formula of exchange, articulated to highlight God's mercy:

Many and great, most beloved brothers, are the divine benefits by which the abundant and copious clemency of God the Father and of Christ has both worked and is

---

59. *The Dress of Virgins* 23 (51, translation adjusted).
60. Ibid. (translation adjusted).

always working for our salvation, because the Father has sent the son for our preservation and vivification so that He might be able to restore us, and because the son, having been sent, wished also to be a son of man in order to make us sons of God: He humbled Himself in order to raise up the people who before were lying prostrate, He was wounded in order to cure our wounds, He was a slave in order to drag slaves out to liberty. He tolerated dying in order to present immortality to mortals. These are the many and great gifts of divine mercy."[61]

Cyprian explains that God sent the Son to take on the attributes of fallen humanity (prostration, wounds, slavery, mortality) so that humanity might take on the attributes of divinity (sonship, exaltation, freedom, immortality).

In the central part of *Works and Almsgiving*, Cyprian ties the exchange into the theme of the treatise by explaining that the way in which we appropriate the divine attributes to ourselves is by acting as God acts, that is, with mercy towards the poor, and by doing what he has told us to do in scripture. In chapter 2, this is uniquely connected with baptism. Cyprian quotes Sirach 3:33 as follows: "As water extinguishes fire, so almsgiving extinguishes sin."[62] In baptism, all previous sins are washed away, and after that, the character of baptism makes the Christian and his actions like God: "And because the remission of sins is once given in baptism, the constant and continuous working of baptism performed after the fashion of God [*instar imitata Dei*] bestows pardon once again."[63] Forgiveness of sins is always in the forefront of Cyprian's thought on baptism. This forgiveness continues to be merited after baptism by the God-like working of baptism within us, expressed through almsgiving.

Why does Cyprian connect almsgiving so closely to baptism, and what relevance does this have for deification? Quite simply, as the gateway to the church and therefore the *sine qua non* of salvation, baptism in a way encompasses God's entire saving action and our appropriation of the same. As God has bestowed this gift on us, lifting us from our abject poverty of spirit, we are called likewise to lift our fellow humans from their poverty of body. God gives us the greatest thing he has to offer—his Son—through baptism. When we give what we have to those who desperately need it, we act similarly. The

---

61. *Works and Almsgiving* 2 (FOTC 36:227–53, at 227, translation adjusted).

62. Ibid. (228, translation adjusted): "Sicut aqua extinguit ignem, sic eleemosyna extinguit peccatum."

63. Ibid. (translation adjusted): "Et quia semel in baptismo remissa peccatorum datur, adsidua et iugis operatio baptismi instar imitata Dei rursus indulgentiam largiatur."

mercy that we bestow in charity bears a close resemblance to the mercy God shows us in baptism, and for good reason, as baptism working in us is *instar imitata Dei*, "after the fashion of God." We receive from God forgiveness for our sins when we bestow this mercy.

Cyprian draws on the quotation from Sirach 3 and many others from both Testaments to show that almsgiving wins forgiveness of sins.[64] These quotations, along with arguments against practical concerns one might have about giving away too much of one's patrimony, occupy the majority of *Works and Almsgiving*. The themes of inheritance and patrimony are used with great effect by Cyprian to show what heavenly things the Christian will receive in exchange for sharing earthly possessions: "Divide your returns with your God; share your profits with Christ; make Christ a partner with you in earthly possessions, that He might also make you a co-heir with Him of the heavenly kingdom."[65] This exchange strengthens what has been written above regarding how almsgiving leads to deification. When we share our material possessions with Christ present in the poor, he will share with us his spiritual possessions, which make us like God.

In chapter 25, Cyprian reaches the ultimate example of earthly charity done with heavenly motivation: the life lived by the first Christians in community with the apostles. All sold what they had and gave to the apostles to distribute as needed, "so great was the surplus in good works then as was the harmony in love."[66] Cyprian equates this degree of charity with the adoption won for us by the *admirabile commercium*: "This is truly to become a son of God by spiritual birth; this is to imitate the equity of God the Father by the heavenly law."[67] The fact that rebirth as children of God is equated with imitation of God's charity demonstrates Cyprian's focus on deification by imitation.[68] For Cyprian, our transformation into sons of God can never be di-

---

64. E.g., Prv 16:6, Is 58:1–9, Tb 12:8–9, Lk 12:33.
65. *Works and Almsgiving* 13 (239, translation adjusted).
66. Ibid., 25 (251, translation adjusted).
67. Ibid.
68. The formula of exchange is connected with godly behavior also in *To Fortunatus* 5: "We, redeemed and vivified by the blood of Christ, must place nothing before Christ, because neither did He place anything before us and He on account of us preferred evil things to good things, poverty to riches, servitude to domination, death to immortality, while we on the contrary in our sufferings prefer the riches and joys of paradise to the poverty of the world [*paupertati saeculari*], eternal dominion and reign to temporary servitude, immortality to death, God and Christ to the devil and antichrist" (313–44, at 317, translation adjusted). Because Christ made the ultimate sacrifice for us in his humbling, we must choose him above all else.

vorced from our God-like behavior; each leads back to the other in a perpetual cycle. God always acts justly, and so do his children. As God sends the rain and sun on everyone, "the possessor on the earth who shares his returns and profits with brotherly feeling, provided that he is fair and just with his gratuitous bounties, is an imitator of God the Father."[69]

Chapter 26 provides the closing of the *inclusio* begun in chapter 1 with a reflection on the exchange of earthly things for heavenly and our return to the Father by Christ:

> What, dearest brothers, will be that glory of the worker [*gloria operantium*]; how grand and consummate the joy, when the Lord begins to number His people, and, distributing the rewards for our merits and works, to grant heavenly things for the earthly, everlasting for the temporal, great for small, to offer us to the Father to whom he restored us by His sanctification, to bestow eternal immortality on us, for which He has prepared us by the quickening of His blood.[70]

The theme of exchange nicely closes out the line of thought begun in the first chapter. God has graciously and freely sent his son to us, and they both willed that he might take on what is ours. If we imitate God, freely giving for the good of others what we possess (our temporal and earthly goods), then we merit the bestowal of heavenly, spiritual goods that belong to God by nature (glory, immortality). The one who does this work of charity "accounts God a debtor."[71] Who could account God a debtor, one might ask, if not by virtue of something higher than fallen human nature? Echoing *Jealousy and Envy* 15, Cyprian writes that Christians are those "who already have begun to be greater than the age and the world."[72] The one who is greater in this way is the one who has risen above his fallen nature through imitation of the Father.

Imitation resulting in deification is described in another treatise as well. In *That Idols Are Not Gods*, Cyprian ties our deification to the heart of Christian living—suffering with Christ in order to follow him to glory: "What Christ is, we Christians will be, if we follow Christ."[73] This quotation closes the work, which is the closest thing that Cyprian wrote to a Christological

---

69. *Works and Almsgiving* 25 (252, translation adjusted).
70. Ibid., 26 (252, translation adjusted).
71. Ibid. (translation adjusted).
72. Ibid. (253, translation adjusted).
73. *That Idols Are Not Gods* 15 (360).

treatise. It is telling that Cyprian summarizes the work of Christ and the rewards of seeking and believing in him in this way.

## Conclusion

Though Cyprian did not write a treatise on salvation *per se*, it is the point toward which all of the lines of his teaching converge. The first step in salvation, baptism, occupied much of his time and energy for writing, as it comes down to us, and he was very concerned with the forgiveness that baptism brings to the sinner. This is not hard to understand, as he was an adult convert who, as he himself wrote, was a great sinner before his conversion. His gratitude for the forgiveness he received as well as the power to live a new life pervades all of his writings on baptism, conversion, and salvation. He had a sense, derived from personal experience and study of scripture, that baptism caused the sinner to begin being changed into something new, something heavenly, through his incorporation into the church, Christ's bride and body. When the baptized cooperates with the beginnings of this grace in the indwelling of the Spirit, when he acts in the likeness of his baptism, it is increased, and new power is given him to act like Christ. When he acts like Christ, he becomes the *imago Dei*. When he dies then, Christ bears him to the Father. At this point, the once wretched sinner is truly a child of God and coheir to the kingdom with Christ.

*James L. Papandrea*

## 5. LOANING AND BORROWING
### *Deification in Novatian*

As someone who generally gravitates toward the Latin West, I confess I have not spent a lot of time teaching on the doctrine of deification, or as it is commonly called, *theosis*. When I have taught on the subject in the past, I tended to default to what appears to be the standard practice of giving a brief nod to Irenaeus before jumping right to Athanasius, and then taking it from there. However, in my ongoing study of Novatian I have noticed that there are several stops one could make on a path, or a trajectory, that leads from Irenaeus to Athanasius. This essay will make a stop in Rome to see where Roman theology, and especially Novatian of Rome, fits into that trajectory. As I will demonstrate, the arc that will lead us to Novatian has as its focal point the concept of the *communicatio idiomatum*, which may have its roots as early as Callistus of Rome, but which finds its first real extant expression in Novatian himself.

In fact, we could make a brief stop in Rome even before Irenaeus, to see how the possibility of deification was already somewhat assumed. In Justin Martyr's *First Apology*, he acknowledges pagan Roman belief in the deification of emperors and then says, "we have learned that those only are deified who have lived near to God in holiness and virtue."[1] Although we cannot speculate from this passing comment what Justin's understanding of deifica-

---

1. Justin Martyr, *I Apology* 21, in Ante-Nicene Fathers (ed. Roberts et al.) (hereafter, ANF), 1:170.

tion might have been, at least we can see that he did not hesitate to use the language of deification when referring to the Christian vision of the afterlife.

Irenaeus's comment in the preface to book 5 of *Against Heresies* is well known: "the Word of God, our Lord Jesus Christ, who did, through his transcendent love, become what we are, that he might bring us to be even what he is himself."[2] He became like us so we could become like him. The exchange formula is presumably based on Paul's comments in 1 Corinthians 15:21–22 ("for just as in Adam all die, so too in Christ all shall be brought to life"), 2 Corinthians 8:9 ("for your sake he became poor ... so that ... you might become rich"), and Galatians 3:13–14 ("becoming a curse for us ... that the blessing of Abraham might be extended to the Gentiles").[3]

But in book 4, Irenaeus—who had been to Rome—goes even further, and says that finite humanity had received the immortal Son of God so that humans could become gods, that is, so that they could become immortal.[4] This was based on Psalm 82:6–7 and possibly 2 Peter 1:4 ("you may come to share in the divine nature"). Of course, Irenaeus points out that we will not become God because we cannot become uncreated, and therefore we cannot become immutably perfect, as logically it is too late for us to be perfect from the start.[5] This is, for Irenaeus, what prevents deification from becoming idolatrous. The point here is that Irenaeus's definition of deification—sharing in the divine nature—does not mean to become divine *per se*, but rather it means to become immortal. Deification, for Irenaeus, means that those who put their faith in God through Christ "shall receive a faculty of the Uncreated, through the gratuitous bestowal of eternal existence upon them by God."[6] The result of this is immortality, and this, as we will see, is picked up by Novatian.

We need to look at just one more thought from Irenaeus before we move on. In book 3, the bishop of Lyons is interpreting the passage in Psalm 82 that refers to humans as "sons of the Most High, and gods."[7] In that context, Ire-

---

2. Irenaeus of Lyons, *Against Heresies* 5, Preface (ANF 1:526).
3. Note that Novatian does not directly refer to any of these three "exchange" passages in Paul. However, as I will explain below, I believe that he does have 2 Pt 1:4 in mind at *De Trinitate* 15.7.
4. Irenaeus of Lyons, *Against Heresies* 4.38.1–4.39.2.
5. Ibid., 4.38.1–3.
6. Ibid., 4.38.3 (ANF 1:521).
7. Ps 82:6.

naeus refers to the deification of human nature as "promotion into God."[8] But what does that mean? He connects deification to our adoption as heirs of God and says that this adoption is the very reason for the incarnation. In other words, the Son of God became the Son of Man so that the sons and daughters of men might become sons and daughters of God. The result of this is that humans are able to receive, not just immortality, but immortality and incorruptibility.[9] This is possible because the Word of God became what we are (implying that he became corruptible and mortal) so that we could become what he is: specifically, incorruptible and immortal sons and daughters of God. Irenaeus uses union language here—we are united, or joined to, incorruptibility and immortality, because the Word of God was united with corruptible and mortal humanity—and in that union, the corruptible and the mortal were "swallowed up" by the incorruptible and the immortal.[10]

Although we have not yet arrived at a technical terminology such as "*hypostatic* union," there is a real ontological union assumed here between the divine and the human in the person of Christ. The Word of God, the divine *Logos*, united with humanity in order to raise humanity up to the level of divinity, at least with regard to incorruptibility and immortality. If Irenaeus had had 2 Peter in mind (and this is not at all certain), this is what it would mean to have a share in the divine nature. So the union with the divine Word affects the humanity that the Word takes up. But that is where Irenaeus stops. He does not say that the union also affects the divine nature in any way, and on this point he is consistent with his predecessors and his contemporaries. He would not have been ready to accept the concept of *communicatio idiomatum*, and as we will see, neither was Hippolytus. Nevertheless, this is where the trajectory is taking us: to Rome, and to the conflict between Hippolytus and Callistus.

---

8. Irenaeus of Lyons, *Against Heresies* 3.19.1 (ANF 1:448).

9. See Mark D. Nispel, "Christian Deification and the Early *Testimonia*," *Vigiliae Christianae* 53 (1999): 298–99 and 301.

10. Irenaeus of Lyons, *Against Heresies* 3.19.1 (ANF 1:449).

## Callistus

In other places, I have argued that Novatian of Rome was one of the pioneers of the doctrine of *communicatio idiomatum*.[11] I say "one of" because there is some evidence that it was already in the Roman air during the episcopacy of Callistus, who was bishop of Rome (r. 217–22). The evidence for this can be found in the writings of Hippolytus, in which he criticized Callistus for what he saw as a variety of moral and doctrinal failures.

To be fair, Hippolytus was primarily concerned with refuting the modalism of Sabellius and Noetus, and so his theological agenda focused on protecting the distinction between the three persons of the Trinity. In that context, he also seems concerned to protect the immutability of the divine by preserving a similar distinction between the two natures of Christ. However, in his enthusiasm for the "economy" of the Trinity, and in his zeal to remove the modalist heresy from the church, Hippolytus tended to lean to the opposite extremes: toward a kind of proto-Nestorianism, and toward adoptionism.[12] In fact, he admitted that Callistus accused him of being a "ditheist," which I take to mean that Callistus thought he made too much of a separation between the Father and the Son.[13]

Therefore, when Hippolytus saw what appear to be early forms of *perichoresis* and *communicatio idiomatum* in the teachings of Callistus, he accused the bishop of Rome of being a modalist.[14] However, we know that Callistus was not a modalist, because he excommunicated Sabellius.[15] In fact, Hippolytus himself inadvertently admitted that theologically, Callistus navigated a

---

11. My 1998 dissertation and 2011 monograph on Novatian are cited below.

12. See James L. Papandrea, *Novatian of Rome and the Culmination of Pre-Nicene Orthodoxy*, Princeton Theological Monograph Series 175 (Eugene, Ore.: Pickwick, 2011), 41.

13. Hippolytus, *Refutation of All Heresies* 9.6–7.

14. Hippolytus, *Against Noetus* 15. See also *Against Beron and Helix* 1, though the authorship of this document is in doubt. Note that Tertullian would also not accept the concept of *communicatio idiomatum*; see Tertullian, *Against Praxeas* 27.

15. Hippolytus claimed that Callistus only excommunicated Sabellius because of the pressure and accusations from Hippolytus himself, however it is clear that Hippolytus has admitted Callistus's orthodoxy in his comment about Callistus being the middle way between Sabellius and Theodotus. Accusations of modalism in Hippolytus's description of Callistus's teaching can be explained by Hippolytus's discomfort with Callistus's teaching on consubstantiality, and on the lack of consensus over the proper Greek term for "person." If *Against Beron and Helix* is by Hippolytus, there the word *hypostasis* is used of the substance of divinity, the oneness of the Trinity, rather than the three persons.

middle way between Sabellius (modalism) on the one hand, and Theodotus (adoptionism) on the other.[16] In reality, what Hippolytus saw in Callistus's teaching was a strong belief in the consubstantiality of the Son with the Father, along with early hints at *perichoresis*, and what is perhaps the earliest extant reference to a communication of idiomatic properties—and in fact the latter two are related, as the *communicatio idiomatum* is in a way a *perichoresis* of the two natures. In his *Refutation of All Heresies*, Hippolytus described Callistus's teaching as follows:

> For he [Callistus] says, "I will not profess belief in two Gods, Father and Son, but in one. For the Father, who subsisted in the Son himself, after he had taken unto himself our flesh, raised it to the nature of deity, by bringing it into union with himself, and made it one, so that the Father and Son must be styled one God" … and in this way he [Callistus] contends that the Father suffered along with the Son – for he does not wish to assert that the Father suffered.[17]

So if we read between the lines a bit, we can see what Callistus was teaching in Rome. He began with what we saw in Irenaeus, that the divine Son of God united with humanity so that humanity could be "raised to the nature of deity." This is a deification of Christ's human nature. But then he went further, by describing how *our* deification takes place: it happens because of the union of divinity with humanity in the incarnation, which affects not only the human nature of Christ, but all of humanity, due to the assumed consubstantiality of Christ's human nature with all of humanity. Furthermore, not only could the Son of God suffer as a human, but because of the consubstantiality of the Father and the Son, and the fact that the Father subsists in the Son (*perichoresis*), the Father could also suffer along with the Son—yet without saying that the Father suffered in any way that would compromise divine impassibility. What is at least implied here is that the union of divine with human in the person of Christ allowed that the divine could experience something of the suffering of humanity. As far as we can tell, for the first time, there is the possibility that the incarnation has some "effect" on God—that is, a communication of properties that runs in both directions.[18] And yet, as Hippolytus ad-

---

16. Hippolytus, *Refutation of All Heresies* 9.7. See Novatian, *De Trinitate* 30.6, where Novatian says that Christ was being crucified again between the two "thieves" of modalism and adoptionism.

17. Hippolytus, *Refutation of All Heresies* 9.7 (ANF 5:130–31).

18. Even Hippolytus admitted this to a certain extent, when he said "the impassible Word of God came under suffering." See Hippolytus, *Against Noetus* 15.

mits, Callistus "does not wish to assert that the Father suffered." So whatever he might say about the incarnation having an effect on the divine through the *communicatio idiomatum*, he was careful not to slip into a modalist patripassionism, or to compromise divine immutability.

## Novatian

Twenty years and four popes later, Novatian was active in Rome in the mid-third century. He was born around the turn of the third century, and ordained a priest by Fabian of Rome, probably in the late 230s. He must have written his magnum opus, *De Trinitate*, as a priest in the 240s. This document was well received at the time, and proved influential for later theologians.[19] The Roman emperor Decius ascended to the throne in the year 249, and by the end of that year he had instituted an empire-wide mandate to make sacrifices to the traditional gods in his honor, for the benefit of the empire. Among other things, his motivation was to force Christians to show their patriotism by participating in pagan worship. Many refused. When Pope Fabian was martyred in January 250, Novatian was chosen to be what some (including myself) have called the "acting bishop" of Rome, speaking for the Roman Christians, and writing letters on behalf of Rome to other metropolitans, including Cyprian of Carthage.[20]

After the death of Decius, when the persecution of Christians subsided for a while, the church found itself with an internal controversy over what to do with the "lapsed"—those who had complied with the emperor's edict and made the required sacrifice to save life and livelihood. All agreed that by their apostasy and idolatry they had effectively excommunicated themselves, but not all agreed that they could be reconciled to the table of the eucharist. Novatian became the leader of the rigorist party, which claimed that only God could forgive the unforgiveable sin (as they believed apostasy was), and which argued that reconciling the lapsed would be a slap in the face to the martyrs who gave their lives rather than deny the faith.

The church at Rome was finally able to hold an election for bishop in

---

19. See James L. Papandrea, *Reading the Early Church Fathers: From the Didache to Nicaea* (Mahwah, N.J.: Paulist Press, 2012), 144–47, and *Novatian of Rome*, 106–32.

20. A few of these letters are extant. See Papandrea, *Novatian: On the Trinity, Letters to Cyprian of Carthage, Ethical Treatises*, Corpus Christianorum in Translation 22 (Brussels: Brepols, 2015).

spring 251, and after over fourteen months of being the "acting bishop," Novatian lost the election to Cornelius, who advocated reconciliation for the lapsed. Some time after this, Novatian was apparently consecrated as a rival bishop of Rome, and accepted the position as leader of a rigorist schism, earning him the title "anti-pope." A synod at Rome excommunicated Novatian and any who would follow him, and this formalized the schism, which continued to grow throughout the empire. When the persecution heated up again under the emperor Valerian, it appears that Novatian was arrested and exiled, probably in the year 253. From his exile, he wrote "episcopal" letters to his flock, a few of which are extant.[21] In the year 258, Valerian recalled exiled Christian leaders and had them executed. Novatian died a martyr, probably still in a state of excommunication.[22] However, there are a few sources that relate a story that he was reconciled to the church just before his death, and there is a tradition of a feast day for Novatian on June 29.

Although Novatian was never a legitimately elected bishop, the document that is important for my purposes was written while he was still within the church, is considered completely orthodox, and was probably the reason

21. See ibid.
22. I have had the opportunity to visit the tomb of Novatian on two occasions, in the summers of 2014 and 2015. It is in a network of catacombs closed to the public, mostly under the church of San Lorenzo Fuori le Mura and the Via Tiburtina. Much of the catacomb is blocked off by the supports that hold up the streets, but the section with Novatian's tomb can be entered from an opening in a garden along the Via della Regina Elena. There has been some debate over whether this is in fact the tomb of our Novatian, however after seeing the tomb firsthand, I am convinced that it is. The inscription is original to the catacomb, the relevant section of which dates to within about a decade of the time of Novatian's death in the mid-third century. It says, "NOVATIANO BEATISSIMO MARTURI—GAUDENTIUS DEAC. FEC," which means, "Novatian the Most Blessed Martyr, (placed here) by the Deacon Gaudentius." For photos of the inscription and the entrance to the catacomb, see Papandrea, *Novatian of Rome*, 71–72. Furthermore, there are later embellishments to the tomb that strongly suggest the martyr's relics were being venerated in the fourth century. At one time it was asserted that the tomb was too small for an adult male, and it was speculated that perhaps the martyr's remains were brought to this catacomb much later. See Allan Fitzgerald, *Conversion through Penance in the Italian Church of the Fourth and Fifth Centuries: New Approaches to the Experience of Conversion from Sin* (Lewiston, N.Y.: Edwin Mellen Press, 1988), 27–28. However, I have measured the tomb myself (the tomb has been opened from the top and the relics are long gone), and it is large enough for a man five feet six inches tall, which is the average height for a third-century male. Therefore, I conclude that it is the theologian and "anti-pope" Novatian, who was placed in the tomb soon after his martyrdom, probably in the year 258. It is not clear why he would not be called a bishop in the inscription, though there are rumors that he was reconciled to the church before his death. In any case, his relics were venerated by his later followers, and in the fourth century the tomb was embellished with plaster decorations and paint. See Papandrea, *Novatian of Rome*, 68, and *Novatian: On the Trinity*, 15.

he was chosen to be the spokesman for the church of Rome.²³ Therefore, we can take the content of Novatian's *De Trinitate* as consistent with Roman orthodoxy in the mid-third century. As I have argued elsewhere, Novatian's understanding of the union of the two natures in the person of Christ anticipated the Chalcedonian definition in some very significant ways.²⁴ For Novatian, the two natures are distinct, but not separate; united, but not confused.²⁵ In fact, Novatian used Latin terms that might be associated with marriage to talk about the union of the two natures.²⁶ He wrote that the Word of God was like a groom, coming down out of his chambers to take up flesh like a bride, and then once united with his bride—human nature—he took it back with him, raising it up to his level.²⁷ So, for Novatian, the two natures are like a husband and wife, maintaining their individual integrity, and yet united in a way that they cannot be separated. (Remember that Novatian was a rigorist, so divorce is not an option.)

For Novatian, the incarnation *is* the union of natures.²⁸ And this union is not simply a union of wills, but is also a mutual reception and assumption. Each nature receives and assumes the other nature. By the mutual connection (*connexionem mutuam*) the flesh bears the Word of God (the Son of God), and the Word of God (the Son of God) accepts the frailty of the flesh.²⁹ And in accepting the frailty of the flesh, the divine Logos *experiences* (*experitur*) that frailty. So, for Novatian, the union of the two natures is one in which each

---

23. Canon 8 of the Council of Nicaea recognized the orthodoxy of the Novatians. A Novatianist bishop was at the council, and was not counted among the heretics.

24. James Papandrea, *The Trinitarian Theology of Novatian of Rome: A Study in Third-Century Orthodoxy* (Lewiston, N.Y.: Edwin Mellen Press, 2008), 318–19, and *Novatian of Rome*, 110–20. Novatian's understanding of the union of natures and the *communicatio idiomatum* presents the church with a precedent for Chalcedon's middle way between Nestorianism and Monophysitism. Novatian's own concern for the middle way can be seen in his statement that Christ was being crucified again between the two "thieves" of modalism and adoptionism, and also when he commented, "Therefore, one is not to lean toward one part and avoid the other part, since whoever ignores some portion of the truth could never possess the whole truth" (Novatian, *De Trinitate* 11.5 and 30.6).

25. Novatian is clear that the two natures are not confused or mixed to the point of diminishing either one, even though his language is imprecise and inconsistent. For example, he did use the word *permixtio* to speak of the union, but he also used the same word to describe the kind of union that the two natures do not have, that is, one in which they are "mixed-up." See *De Trinitate* 11.1; 24.8–10; 25.3, 5; see 24.9.

26. Ibid., 15.4, 26.2–3, 31.5. See Papandrea, *Novatian of Rome*, 115–18.

27. Novatian, *De Trinitate* 13.4–5.

28. Ibid., 23.7.

29. Ibid., 13.5.

nature is affected by the other. Novatian does not mean to imply that Christ's human nature ever existed apart from the divine nature in a "pre-affected" state "before the union." But he does assume that the *communicatio idiomatum* runs in both directions.

Novatian described the incarnation as a descent, a *kenosis*, to use the Greek term, relying heavily on Philippians 2:6–11.[30] He always maintained that this *kenosis* is not a form of change that would compromise divine immutability or impassibility.[31] Nevertheless, the *kenosis* resulted in a union of the two natures that Novatian described as a mutual sharing.[32] This mutual sharing, or receiving, is active on the part of the divine nature, but passive on the part of the human nature.[33] But it is still a union in which both natures receive something from the other. And this brings us to Novatian's understanding of the *communicatio idiomatum*.

## Loaning and Borrowing

Novatian is the first author to explain something that we might call the *communicatio idiomatum*.[34] Of course, he does not use that term. In *De Trinitate*, he says:

Because the Son of God descended when he took the Son of Man to himself, he has thereby made him the Son of God, because he associated and joined him to himself, the Son of God, so that when the Son of Man clings to the Son of God in the nativi-

---

30. Papandrea, *Novatian of Rome*, 74–96. Novatian's Latin term for *kenosis* is *exinaniuit* (*exanio*). For a detailed treatment of Novatian's exegesis of this passage, see Papandrea, *The Trinitarian Theology of Novatian of Rome*, 268–74. On the concept of *kenosis* in the context of the controversy between Cyril and Nestorius, see Paul Gavrilyuk, *The Suffering of the Impassible God: The Dialectics of Patristic Thought* (Oxford: Oxford University Press, 2004), 151–75.

31. Novatian, *De Trinitate* 13.5; 18.5; 22.6, 9; 24.7–11. Although Weinandy argues that any self-limitation must necessarily be a form of ontological change, Novatian would not agree, and he is careful to be clear that the *kenosis* does not include an ontological change for the Logos. See Thomas G. Weinandy, *Does God Change?* (Still River, Mass.: St. Bede's Publications, 1985), 114–18. The union that results from the *kenosis* is also not one that requires a separate previous existence for the human nature, despite the claims of Weinandy to the contrary (see ibid., 118–19).

32. Novatian, *De Trinitate* 13.5.

33. Ibid., 23.7. See Papandrea, *Novatian of Rome*, 114.

34. Papandrea, *The Trinitarian Theology of Novatian of Rome*, 313–18, and *Novatian of Rome*, 110–20. On the possibility that Origen held some notion of a *communicatio idiomatum*, see Papandrea, *Novatian of Rome*, 111n154.

ty, he might hold, loaned [*feneratum*] and borrowed [*mutuatum*] by the union itself, what he could not possess from his own nature.³⁵

Here Novatian is referring to the divine nature as the Son of God, and the human nature as the Son of Man, as we are already used to seeing in his predecessors.³⁶ But notice that in the incarnation, the divine nature (the Son of God) descends to join with the human nature (the Son of Man), which results in the divine nature loaning to the human nature the ability to become the Son of God. In other words, the human nature has borrowed divinity from the divine nature (which, as we will see, Novatian understands in terms of immortality)—and this is something that the human nature does not "naturally" possess.

But this loaning and borrowing does not happen only in one direction.³⁷ Unlike his predecessors, Novatian believed that the *communicatio* must work both ways, or deification would not be possible. Novatian says that in the

---

35. Novatian, *De Trinitate* 24.10. All English translations of Novatian are from Papandrea, *Novatian: On the Trinity*. The translations are based on the Latin text of *De Trinitate* in *Novatiani Opera*, ed. G. F. Diercks, Corpus Christianorum: Series Latina 4 (Turnholti: Typographyi Brepols Editores Pontificii, 1972). The entire passage reads as follows in Latin: "Nunc autem particulatim exponens tam magni sacramenti ordinem atque rationem euidenter expressit, ut diceret: Et quod ex te nascetur sanctum uocabitur Filius Dei, probans quoniam Filius Dei descendit, qui dum filium hominis in se suscepit, consequenter illum Filium Dei fecit, quoniam illum Filius sibi Dei sociauit et iunxit, ut dum filius hominis adhaeret in natiuitatem Filio Dei, ipsa permixtione feneratum et mutuatum teneret, quod ex natura propria possidere non posset."

36. See Irenaeus of Lyons, *Against Heresies* 3.19.1.

37. See Gavrilyuk, *The Suffering of the Impassible God*, 143–50. See also Papandrea, *Novatian of Rome*, 111n154. The *communicatio idiomatum* in Novatian is what has been called *communicatio idiomatum in abstracto* (communication of idiomatic properties between the natures). This has been called an "Alexandrian" version of *communicatio idiomatum*, however Cyril of Alexandria does not seem to fall into this camp. This is also the version that Weinandy attributes to Martin Luther (see Weinandy, *Does God*, 70, 98, 106). In any case, there is no hint in Novatian of what has been called *communicatio idiomatum in concreto* (communication of idiomatic properties from each nature to the "whole" person). This has been called an "Antiochene" version of *communicatio idiomatum*, and presumably it is motivated by a desire to protect the human nature from any Apollinarian or Monophysite diminishing of the humanity or the human will, and to protect the divine nature from any semblance of change that would imply passibility. See George Kalantzis, "Is There Room for Two? Cyril's Single Subjectivity and the Prosopic Union," *St. Vladimir's Theological Quarterly* 52, no. 1 (2008): 95–110, esp. 101–2. According to Kalantzis, Cyril of Alexandria is in the "Antiochene" camp. It seems to me that the *communicatio idiomatum in concreto* version would actually fall into the trap of creating a *tertium quid*, a person distinct from the natures. For Novatian, the person is not distinct from the natures (though the natures retain their distinct integrities), and the human nature has no existence before or apart from the divine. Furthermore, the *communicatio idiomatum* could not be by appellation only, as that would not allow for deification, and would ultimately lead to a Nestorian rejection of the Theotokos.

*kenosis* of the incarnation, the divine Logos *experiences* unspeakable, disgraceful things.[38] The divine nature of Christ can *experience* suffering because of the *kenosis*, yet without *actually* suffering in a way that would compromise divine impassibility.[39] The suffering of the divine nature is, in a sense, loaned by and borrowed from the human nature.

Humanity is not the Son of God by nature, and divinity is not the Son of Man by nature, yet each loans its natural property to the other. So, in the incarnation, the Son of Man "becomes" the Son of God. But this is not adoptionism, rather it is a deification of the human nature.[40] At the same time, the Son of God becomes the Son of Man—using that same *becoming* language from John 1:14, and that we saw in Irenaeus, yet all the time affirming that this becoming does not imply an ontological change in the divine nature.[41] The language of loaning and borrowing, and also of experiencing, allows Novatian to say that the divine nature "becomes" flesh without actually changing, and even more than that, it allows Novatian to say that the divine nature experiences suffering without actually suffering in a way that would compromise divine impassibility. This is because any suffering in which the divine nature participates is entirely voluntary.[42] But on the other hand, Novatian intuitively knew that some participation in the human condition was necessary for the incarnation to be more than a kind of proto-Apollinarian "putting on flesh."[43] Thus each nature loans something of its own to the other nature.

So what does the human nature borrow from the divine nature? As we

---

38. Novatian, *De Trinitate* 22.9. As noted above, the Latin word I have translated "experiences" is *experitur*, which de Simone had translated as "suffers."

39. Papandrea, *The Trinitarian Theology of Novatian of Rome*, 317.

40. Novatian, *De Trinitate* 24.5, 7. The difference is that the preexistent divine nature descends to raise the human nature up. Adoptionism, on the other hand, would imply that the glorification of the human nature occurred as a result of human merit, and that there was no descent of the preexistent Logos. In other words, adoptionism proposes that the flesh became the Word, not the other way around. We know that Novatian does not mean to imply a kind of adoptionism here, as he spends several chapters of the same document refuting all the various forms of adoptionism that he knew of. See Irenaeus of Lyons, *Against Heresies* 3.19.1. Novatian does not mean to imply by this that the human nature existed separately prior to the incarnation.

41. Novatian does seem to assume that the deification of the human nature is an ontological change, but he does not explain why or how the union affects the human nature ontologically, and the divine nature only temporarily—except perhaps that he assumes it is simply because the divine nature *cannot* be changed ontologically, and the human nature can.

42. Gavrilyuk, *The Suffering of the Impassible God*, 162–63.

43. Weinandy, *Does God*, 20.

have seen, only the Word of God is the Son of God by nature, but the Son of Man becomes the Son of God by virtue of the union.[44] Therefore, the union results in an exalted, glorified, status for the human nature. Novatian wrote:

Thus the heretics are urged to understand that Christ the human, the Son of Man, is also the Son of God, and that the Son of God is a human. That is, they must accept that the Word of God, who is God just as it is written, is also therefore the Lord Jesus Christ, joined from both, so that I could say united and compounded from both, into one harmony of both substances, humanity and God reciprocally associated with a bond of mutual unity.[45]

Notice the language of "hypostatic union"—"one harmony of both substances." It could be argued that here Novatian is an influence on the language found later in Leo's Tome. In any case, what is most important to note is that for Novatian, the union results in the loaning and borrowing of idiomatic properties, in which the human nature of Jesus Christ borrows divinity from the divine nature. More concretely, Novatian tells us that the divine nature loans to the human nature immortality (*immortalitas*).[46] Here is what Novatian wrote:

In this way, the frailty and limitation of the human condition is strengthened, improved, and raised up by him, so that by becoming used to perceiving the Son, at some time we also may be able to see the Father himself. Otherwise, one might be struck and carried away by the sudden and unbearable brightness of his majesty, so that one could not see the Father, who is the object of humanity's eternal desire.[47]

---

44. Papandrea, *The Trinitarian Theology of Novatian of Rome*, 316.

45. Novatian, *De Trinitate* 24.11. The Latin text of this passage is: "Ac sic facta est angeli uoce, quod nolunt haeretici, inter Filium Dei hominisque cum sua tamen sociatione distinctio, urgendo illos uti Christum, hominis filium hominem, intellegant quoque Dei Filium et hominem Dei Filium, id est Dei uerbum, sicut scriptum est, Deum accipiant atque ideo Christum Iesum Dominum ex utroque connexum, ut ita dixerim, ex utroque contextum atque concretum et in eadem utriusque substantiae concordia mutui ad inuicem foederis confibulatione sociatum hominem et Deum scripturae hoc ipsum dicentis ueritate cognoscant."

46. Novatian believed that Adam (humanity) would have been immortal had the Fall not occurred. Therefore, immortality is a restoration to humanity's originally intended God-like state. In *De Trinitate* 1.11, Novatian wrote, "As it happened, the first man brought cursed mortality upon himself, though he might have escaped it by obedience. Instead, in a self-destructive decision, he could not wait to make himself God." The irony is that by trying to be like God, humanity lost the very thing that would make us like God: immortality.

47. Novatian, *De Trinitate* 18.5. The Latin text of this passage reads: "Sic ergo et Christus, id est imago Dei et Filius Dei, ab hominibus inspicitur, qua poterat uideri. Et ideo fragilitas et mediocritas sortis humanae per ipsum alitur, producitur, educatur, ut aliquando Deum quoque ipsum Patrem, assueta

The union of the incarnation results in a deification of the human nature of Christ and, as we will see, that will make our deification possible.

Furthermore, unlike his predecessors and contemporaries, Novatian also believed that Christ's divine nature had received, or "borrowed," something from his human nature.[48] Novatian wrote that for the person of Jesus Christ to be truly human, he could not be invisible or omnipresent, or exhibit any number of other things he called "powers."[49] We might call some of these powers divine attributes, but Novatian saw them as properties of the divine persons rather than attributes of the substance of divinity itself. This explains why the Son can be visible, but the Father cannot. His point is that, to truly experience the human condition, Christ had to be circumscribed—localized in time and space, not to mention visible and tangible—and he must be able to suffer.[50] Therefore, Christ's divine nature received, not just flesh, but the limitations of the flesh, which Novatian called the weakness, or the *frailty* of the flesh. Novatian wrote: "The Word had descended, then truly through the mutual connection the flesh carries the Word of God and the Son of God accepts the frailty [*fragilitas*] of the flesh."[51] The result is that the person of Jesus Christ could "empty himself" of omnipresence, omnipotence, and even omniscience, so that he could truly experience the human condition. If he could not, then his humanity would be nothing more than an illusion.

Novatian clearly saw Philippians 2 as all-important for understanding the

---

Filium conspicere, possit ut est uidere, ne maiestatis ipsius repentino et intolerabili fulgore percussa intercipi possit, ut Deum Patrem, quem semper optauit, uidere non possit."

48. Human nature, as such, does have its own dignity. Novatian appears to be the first Christian writer ever to condemn slavery on the basis of humanity being created in the image of God. In *De Trinitate* 1.10, he wrote, "humanity must be free, since slavery is inconsistent with the dignity of the image of God."

49. For Novatian, the terms powers (*viribus*) and authority (*auctoritas*) are synonymous. See Papandrea, *Novatian of Rome*, 79–81.

50. Novatian, *De Trinitate* 24.10. The logic here is that if one person of the Trinity can assume a human nature without compromising divine immutability, and can suffer in the flesh, without compromising divine impassibility, then that person of the Trinity can also be circumscribed in the incarnation without compromising divine omnipresence.

51. Ibid., 13.5. The Latin text of this verse in context is: "Ac si de caelo descendit uerbum hoc tamquam sponsus ad carnem, ut per carnis assumptionem Filius hominis illuc posset ascendere, unde Dei Filius uerbum descenderat, merito dum per connexionem mutuam et caro uerbum Dei gerit et Filius Dei fragilitatem carnis assumit, cum sponsa carne conscendens illuc, unde sine carne descenderat, recipit iam claritatem illam, quam dum ante mundi institutionem habuisse ostenditur, Deus manifestissime comprobatur. Et nihilominus dum mundus ipse post illum institutus refertur, per ipsum creatus esse reperitur, quo ipso diuinitatis in ipso per quem factus est mundus et claritas et auctoritas comprobetur."

incarnation. Therefore he described the incarnation as a humiliation of the divine Word. He wrote:

> He became human, and by being born he took up the substance of flesh and body, the slavery which comes from the ancestors as a consequence of the sins of humanity. At that time he also emptied himself, since he did not refuse to take up the frailty of the human condition ... He empties himself when he descends to injuries and insults, when he hears unspeakable things, experiences disgraceful things, yet with such humility comes extraordinary fruit.[52]

To summarize, Novatian described the *communicatio idiomatum* as a loaning and borrowing, in which each of Christ's two natures receives something from the other nature, something that is idiomatic to the other nature. Specifically, the human nature receives *immortalitas* and the divine nature receives *fragilitas*. This reception of *fragilitas* does not imply an ontological change or actual suffering in the divine nature, but it does allow the divine nature to experience the human condition and the suffering that comes along with it—especially the passion of Jesus.[53]

## Novatian on Deification

Now we come to Novatian's understanding of deification. For Novatian, deification depends on the *communicatio idiomatum*, because it is in the union of the two natures that the human nature of Christ is deified. And that human nature he describes as *in nostra substantia* (in our substance).[54] So by virtue of the fact that Christ's human nature is consubstantial with humanity as

---

52. Ibid., 22.6, 9. See also 24.3–4. The Latin text for these verses (including some of the omitted text for context) is: "Ex quo probatur numquam arbitratum illum esse rapinam quandam diuinitatem, ut aequaret se Patri Deo, quin immo contra omni ipsius imperio et uoluntati oboediens atque subiectus, etiam ut formam serui susciperet contentus fuit, hoc est hominem illum fieri, et substantiam carnis et corporis, quam ex paternorum et secundum hominem delictorum seruitute uenientem nascendo suscepit, quo tempore se etiam exinaniuit, dum humanam condicionis fragilitatem suscipere non recusauit.... Exinanit se, dum ad iniurias contumeliasque descendit, dum audit infanda, experitur indigna, cuius tamen humilitatis adest statim egregius fructus."

53. The difference between *kenosis* and deification is that *kenosis* is not an ontological change in any sense that would compromise divine immutability. To say that the Word "became" flesh is to say that the Word assumed and united with flesh, but did not "change into" flesh (nor did the Word simply "put on" flesh). Deification, however, is an ontological change, not to the extent that human nature ceases to be human, but in the sense that it is glorified and granted the gifts of immortality and incorruptibility.

54. Novatian, *De Trinitate* 10.6.

a whole, the deification of his human nature makes our deification possible. This is how Novatian would interpret 2 Peter 1:4, the promise that we can share in the divine nature. In fact, Novatian does not seem to be working with the Pauline exchange passages at all, nor with Psalm 82. I am convinced that he is working from 2 Peter as well as probably Irenaeus, and is thus building on a Roman tradition that I believe we can already see in Callistus.

The Word of God (or Son of God) descended so that the Son of Man could ascend.[55] And because the Logos assumed our human nature, which Novatian described as "the substance of flesh," or "the substance of a body," what happened to his humanity can happen to ours as well.[56] That is, it can be deified, leading to our salvation.[57] In fact Novatian anticipates the maxim, "What is not assumed is not saved," when he says that "we could not realize our salvation in him if we could not recognize our solid body in him."[58] We could not hope for salvation if the Word of God had not assumed our humanity.

What we call deification, Novatian considered a process that includes our sanctification,[59] but ultimately results in our salvation—which for Novatian meant the granting of immortality. And this is the heart of the matter. Immortality is what it means to be like God. Sanctification, growing in holiness, is, of course, part of the process, but for Novatian the heart of salvation has to do with becoming immortal. Here is what Novatian says, in his argument against adoptionists who claimed Jesus Christ was a mere human:

> Now immortality is the partner of divinity, because divinity is immortal and immortality is the fruit of divinity. But certainly every human is mortal, and immortality cannot exist from what is mortal. Therefore, immortality cannot originate from Christ as a mortal human. But he says, "whoever will observe my word will never see death." Therefore the word of Christ confers immortality, and through immortality,

---

55. Ibid., 13.4–5.
56. Ibid., 21.13–16.
57. Ibid., 10.5–6, 8–9; 21.10; 22.2, 6; 24.1–2, 5; 25.6.
58. Novatian, *De Trinitate* 10.6. The Latin text for this passage in context is: "Neque igitur eum haereticorum agnoscimus Christum, qui in imagine, ut dicitur, fuit et non in ueritate, <ne> nihil uerum eorum quae gessit fecerit, si ipse phantasma et non ueritas fuit, neque eum qui nihil in se nostri corporis gessit, dum ex Maria nihil accepit, ne non nobis uenerit, dum non in nostra substantia uisus apparuit, neque illum qui aetheream siue sideream, ut alii uoluerunt haeretici, induit carnem, ne nullam in illo nostram intellegamus salutem, si non etiam nostri corporis cognoscamus soliditatem, nec ullum omnino alterum, qui quoduis aliud ex figmento haereticorum gesserit corpus fabularum."
59. Ibid., 18.3, 5; 29.16–17.

confers divinity. Since a human is mortal himself, he cannot make another immortal. But this word of Christ both offers and confers immortality, and certainly one who confers immortality is not human only, for if he were human only, he could not confer immortality. But by conferring divinity through immortality, he proves that he is God granting divinity, for if he were not God, he could not confer it.[60]

At this point, Novatian is demonstrating the divinity of Jesus Christ by arguing that Christ could not grant immortality if he were not divine. But notice how he connects immortality to divinity, almost equating the two concepts. Salvation is the granting of immortality, which can only be done by divinity, as "immortality is the partner of divinity" and "the fruit of divinity." This granting of immortality by divinity is deification. "*The word of Christ confers immortality, and through immortality, confers divinity*." Here, I believe Novatian is alluding to 2 Peter 1:4 and the sharing of the divine nature.[61] The end result for the individual who receives divinity is resurrection—what he calls in another passage, "the resurrection of immortality."[62]

---

60. Ibid., 15.7 (Jn 8:51, 2 Pt 1:4). The Latin text for this passage is: "Si homo tantummodo Christus, quomodo ait: Si quis uerbum meum seruauerit, mortem non uidebit in aeternum? Mortem in aeternum non uidere, quid aliud quam immortalitas est? Immortalitas autem diuinitati socia est, quia et diuinitas immortalis est et immortalitas diuinitatis fructus est. Sed enim omnis homo mortalis est, immortalitas autem ex mortali non potest esse. Ergo ex Christo homine mortali immortalitas non potest nasci. Sed qui uerbum custodierit, inquit, meum, mortem non uidebit in aeternum. Ergo uerbum Christi praestat immortalitatem et per immortalitatem praestat diuinitatem. Quodsi non potest exhibere ut immortalem alterum faciat ipse mortalis, hoc autem Christi uerbum exhibet pariter et praestat immortalitatem, non utique homo tantum est qui praestat immortalitatem, quam, si tantummodo homo esset, praestare non posset; praestando autem diuinitatem per immortalitatem Deum se probat diuinitatem porrigendo, quam, nisi Deus esset, praestare non posset."

61. I cannot say why Novatian did not simply quote 2 Pt 1:4. Irenaeus did not quote it. In fact, it seems no one quoted anything from 2 Pt before Origen, and although I have argued elsewhere that there is no evidence that Novatian had read Origen, they were contemporaries. There are possible allusions to 2 Pt 2:5 in Clement of Rome, *I Clement* 7.16, and Clement of Alexandria, *Stromata* 1.21. There are also possible allusions to 2 Pt 3:8 in Justin Martyr, *Dialogue with Trypho* 81, the *Epistle of Barnabas* 15, and Irenaeus of Lyons, *Against Heresies* 5.23, 28. Eusebius knew that there was some doubt regarding the authorship of 2 Pt (*Ecclesiastical History* 6.25.8), so it could be that early authors knew the document, but refrained from quoting it because of the authorship question. However, I believe that there are enough possible allusions to 2 Pt in the second and third centuries, including Cyprian of Carthage, with whom Novatian corresponded, that it is likely Novatian had the 2 Pt passage in mind when writing the text above. See Cyprian of Carthage, *Epistle* 7.1 and *Exhortation to Martyrdom* 10.

62. Novatian, *De Trinitate* 29.16–17. Paul also connected sanctification to resurrection in Phil 3:11–12.

## Conclusion

Novatian's definition of deification, if he were to give one, would begin with what would later be called the *hypostatic* union and the *communicatio idiomatum*: through the loaning and borrowing of idiomatic properties, the divine nature of Christ grants incorruptibility and immortality to human nature, which in turn makes it possible for our humanity to receive sanctification and immortality, culminating in resurrection and eternal life.[63]

There is a logical progression here, which might be described as links in a chain. The progression goes like this: the Trinity is connected to the Word/Son of God (consubstantiality); the Word/Son of God is connected to the Son of Man (*hypostatic* union); the Son of Man is connected to the human race (consubstantiality with human nature); and this is how humanity in general is connected to God. In other words, we are all united to the humanity of Christ through our common human nature;[64] and the humanity of Christ is united to the divine nature—the Word of God—through the hypostatic union and *communicatio idiomatum*; and the divine Word is connected to the Trinity (in fact, is the same divinity as the Trinity) through consubstantiality. Because of this chain of connection, two things are possible: God has firsthand experience of the human condition, and humans have the possibility to become deified. Of course, we can never become God, because we cannot go back in time and become uncreated, but we can become immortal through the descent of Christ in the incarnation, which leads to our eventual ascent in the resurrection.[65] Therefore the logical progression is: *kenosis > communicatio idiomatum > deification*. What Paul Gavrilyuk said with regard to Cyril of Alexandria was already true of Novatian and the Romans by the third century: Christ's *kenosis* makes possible our *theosis*.[66]

---

63. If it seems to the reader that deification is a mere afterthought in Novatian, that would only demonstrate that he did not feel the need to argue for it, and therefore, it was an assumption in the West by Novatian's time.
64. Novatian, *De Trinitate* 10.6. Note that Novatian described the human nature of Christ as being *in nostra substantia*.
65. Nispel, "Christian Deification and the Early *Testimonia*," 299.
66. Gavrilyuk, *The Suffering of the Impassible God*, 171.

*Janet Sidaway*

# 6. MAKING MAN MANIFEST
## *Deification in Hilary of Poitiers*

Hilary of Poitiers (ca. 315–ca. 367) is often considered as a stepping stone to Ambrose, Augustine, and Leo rather than a theologian in his own right, and until the late twentieth century received scant attention from English-language scholars. Although recent scholarship is redressing this imbalance,[1] Hilary's ideas of individual, rather than collective, transformation at the eschaton have received little attention, yet I would argue are more original and hence relevant to any study of deification in the West. Hilary's ideas were linked to a concept I describe as *anthropophany*, a word I have adopted from the early twentieth-century theologian Frank Weston. He suggested that the incarnation was not only a theophany, but at the same time, "an anthropophany: the perfect exhibition before God of the beauty and excellencies of manhood when framed without sin, developed without flaw, and continuously maintained in personal union with the eternal Son of God."[2]

Hilary similarly suggested that humans can aspire to the glory of this perfect man, revealed in Christ. Thus "anthropophany" neatly summarises Hilary's idea that man is "made manifest" in a dual sense.[3] Christ manifests the glory of

---

I would like to thank Jared Ortiz for his constructive suggestions in improving this essay.

1. By Paul Burns, Daniel Williams, Mark Weedman, Carl Beckwith, and Ellen Scully. Their major works on Hilary are listed at the end of this volume.

2. Frank Weston, *The One Christ: An Enquiry into the Manner of the Incarnation* (London: Longmans Green, 1914), 150. I am indebted to Lionel Wickham for pointing out the comparison.

3. "Man" is used as Hilary used the Latin *homo*, to refer to humankind in general.

perfect man, and we too can manifest that glory at the eschaton through our *profectus*, Hilary's favourite term to convey the onward momentum of man's progressive transformation. Christ, as God, enables us to progress to the perfection he personified as man, both through his life, death, resurrection, and ascension, and through his ongoing relationship with us through the eucharist. Hilary did not use the term *deification* to describe this progression, preferring periphrastic expressions such as "being made sharers in the glory of the body of God."[4] The term *glorification,* for which Hilary used *glorificare,* or its synonyms *clarificare* or *honorificare,* represents his emphasis on the process more accurately.[5]

In addition to the significance of individual transformation, Hilary also argued that there was a collective transformation, so that all of humanity was in some way incorporated into the body of Christ. Adolf von Harnack noticed that, in this respect, Hilary's thought was similar to that of Gregory of Nyssa, although von Harnack mistakenly reversed the chronological difference to suggest that Gregory influenced Hilary.[6] Hilary (ca. 315–ca. 367) preceded Gregory (ca. 330–ca. 395), but there is no evidence that Gregory knew Hilary's work. Nonetheless, the perceived similarity with Greek thought was such that Émile Mersch discussed Hilary amongst the Greek Fathers.[7] My purpose in focusing on the individual rather than the collective relationship with God is to draw attention to Hilary's original but neglected idea of anthropophany, to complement the studies that have been made of Hilary's ideas on the assumption of all humanity.[8] Indeed, both concepts are present in all three of Hilary's major theological works.

At times, some of the phrases Hilary uses could refer to individual or to collective humanity, and might be deliberately ambiguous.[9] His rhetorical

---

4. Hilary, *De trin.* 11.4.11: "conformes efficiendi gloriae corporis Dei." Translations from book 11 are mine; translations of the other books are drawn from Nicene and Post-Nicene Fathers (ed. Schaff) (hereafter, NPNF), vol. 9.

5. According to the Brepolis search engine, Hilary uses the root *glorific-* sixty-three times, *clarific-* fifty times, and *honorific-* thirty-nine times in the *De Trinitate.*

6. "The thought that Christ assumed the general concept of humanity occurs, though mingled with distinctive ideas, in Hilary, who was dependent on Gregory." Adolf von Harnack, *History of Dogma,* trans. James Millar (London: Williams and Norgate, 1897), 3:301.

7. In part 2, "The Doctrine of the Mystical Body in the Greek Fathers," under the chapter heading "Divinization by Incorporation in the Incarnate Word." Émile Mersch, *The Whole Christ,* trans. John R. Kelly (Milwaukee, Wis.: Bruce, 1938), 288–306.

8. Most recently by Ellen Scully, *Physicalist Soteriology in Hilary of Poitiers* (Leiden: Brill, 2015).

9. An example of such (possibly deliberate) ambiguity is discussed in note 48.

style and attempts to render Greek theological concepts into Latin also present a challenge to understanding his exact meaning, as Jerome noted.[10] Nevertheless, there are differences in emphasis in each work because of chronology, purpose, and genre, and these, as well as the specific context of his argument, should always be borne in mind when attempting to interpret his thought.[11]

Hilary wrote his first known work, the *Commentarius in Matthaeum*, probably before 353, and probably for fellow bishops. It is a detailed, almost verse-by-verse exegesis of the Gospel of Matthew. The theology is in the Latin tradition.[12] His last work, the *Tractatus super Psalmos*, written between 363 and 367, is also a work of exegesis, probably composed as a series of homilies for a specific local congregation before it was written down.[13] It examines fifty-eight psalms in detail. The exegetical genre, line-by-line commentary, and length make it challenging to discern particular themes, as Paul Burns commented ruefully in his study of the work.[14] Burns has, however, traced what he thinks is the most significant theme, flagged up by Hilary himself, that of "the model of the Christian life."

This theme also provides the backdrop to Hilary's most significant work, the twelve books of his *De Trinitate*, written mainly during his exile in the East between 356 and 360. *De Trinitate* has a good claim to be the first work of systematic theology in the West. Hilary blended pastoral, rhetorical, and polemical genres together to guide the reader on the progressively more difficult steps of the Christian journey towards perfection, a process he continually reinforced through his repetition of *profectus* and its cognates.[15] Hilary projected himself as "Everyman" by introducing the work with a brief rhetorical "autobiography" of his own spiritual development, and often reminded the reader that he too was on the journey of faith to "share in the glory of the body

---

10. Jerome commented that "adorned as [Hilary] is with the flowers of Greek rhetoric, he sometimes entangles himself in long periods and offers by no means easy reading to the less learned brethren" (*Ep.* 58.10.12; NPNF 6:122).

11. Hilary often reminded his readers of the importance of context when interpreting a text, and criticized the "heretics" for failing to do so. See *De trin.* 1.30.4, 2.31.3, 5.31.1.

12. *St. Hilary of Poitiers: Commentary on Matthew*, trans. D. H. Williams, Fathers of the Church 125 (Washington, D.C.: The Catholic University of America Press, 2012), 27–30.

13. Burns argues that Hilary wrote it for a circle of educated Christians in Gaul. Paul C. Burns, *A Model for the Christian Life* (Washington, D.C.: The Catholic University of America Press, 2012), 223.

14. Burns, *A Model for the Christian Life*, 20.

15. Analysed in detail in Janet Sidaway, *The Human Factor: Deification in Hilary of Poitiers' De trinitate*, Studia Patristica Supplement 6 (Leuven: Peeters, 2016).

of God," the ultimate goal of glorification.[16] It is therefore in *De Trinitate* that we find the clearest argument on anthropophany.

For Hilary, anthropophany was related to the *admirabile commercium*, often known as the exchange formula, which for him meant that we become the image of the ascended Christ. He summarised these ideas at the end of book 11 of *De Trinitate*: "Thus man is perfected as the image of God. For, having been made a sharer of the glory of the body of God, he advances into the image of the creator according to the planned formation of the first man. And man having been made new in the knowledge of God after sin and the old man, reaches the perfection of his condition."[17] By advancing into the image of the incarnate creator, who is manifest as the perfect man, we are made manifest as the people we were planned to be.

The steps of the argument begin with the fatherhood of God and the substantial co-equality of the Son. Hilary insisted that our salvation and glorification could only be effected if God the Son was equal in divinity to God the Father because he shared the Father's substance. Linked to this was the insistence that Christ should remain fully God after the incarnation, yet must also be fully human so that he shared our humanity as a brother. In Hilary's anthropocentric concept of deification, Christ's brotherhood with us was as important as the fatherhood of God. This was based on his novel interpretation of the transfiguration, which, he argued, demonstrated that Christ retained his humanity, albeit transformed and glorified, after the ascension. Because Christ was our brother, we too could share this glory. This interpretation of our glorification led Hilary to interpret 1 Corinthians 15:24–28 to mean that God would become "all in all" because through sharing the glory of the body of Christ, we would become the kingdom of God which is returned to God. These interlinked ideas will be discussed after an analysis of Hilary's theological development in the context of his own *profectus*.

---

16. See Hilary, *De trin.* 1.1–14.

17. Hilary, *De trin.* 11.49.22: "Consummatur itaque homo imago Dei. Namque conformis effectus gloriae corporis Dei, in imaginem creatoris excedit secundum dispositam primi hominis figurationem. Et post peccatum ueteremque hominem in agnitionem Dei nouus homo factus, constitutionis suae obtinet perfectionem, agnoscens Deum suum et per id imago eius, et per religionem proficiens ad aeternitatem, et per aeternitatem creatoris sui imago mansurus."

## Hilary's Background

Hilary was born around 315 into a Gaul just recovering from civil war. His family was likely to have been non-Christian. He was converted as an adult, and became the first bishop of Poitiers, probably before 353.[18] Christianity was not well established in Gaul; and there were probably only fifty bishops in the whole territory in 350.[19] Although his works attest that he had clearly received a good classical education in rhetoric, we know as little about his intellectual background as of his family circumstances.

His career as bishop was inseparably linked with the political, military, and ecclesiastical situation in the Roman Empire.[20] In 353, Constantius II (316–61), son of Constantine (ca. 272–337), and already ruler of the East, had finally become sole emperor following the suicide of the Western usurper Magnentius.[21] Like his father, he tried to unify the Christian church through getting agreement to one core statement of belief. Constantine had tried to achieve this in 325 at the council of Nicaea, where a creed was formulated that became the touchstone of later Nicene orthodoxy. Its main objective was to refute the teaching of Arius (ca. 280–336), a priest in Alexandria who preached that God the Son was subordinate to God the Father, who alone was God. This creed was unacceptable to Constantius and his advisors, who believed in a theology closer to "Arian" subordinationism.[22] Constantius had attempted to quell dissent in the East by getting agreement at the Council of Sirmium in 351 to a synodical letter that included a revised creed, and seems also to have

---

18. For more details see Williams, *St. Hilary of Poitiers: Commentary on Matthew*, 4–10. The main sources are Hilary's own scattered comments, and the chronicles of Sulpicius Severus. See *Sulpice Sévère, Chroniques, Texte critique,* ed. and trans. Ghislaine de Senneville-Grave, Sources Chrétiennes (hereafter, SC) 441 (Paris: Éditions du Cerf, 1999).

19. Jean-Remy Palanque, "Le Gaule chrétienne au temps de Saint Hilaire," in *Hilaire et son temps*, Actes du Colloque du Poitiers (Paris: Études Augustiniennes, 1969), 11–17, at 13.

20. For details of Constantine's actions and the policies which led to the Council of Nicaea, see T. D. Barnes, *Constantine: Dynasty, Religion and Power in the Later Roman Empire* (Oxford: Wiley-Blackwell, 2011), 107–11 and 120–22.

21. T. D. Barnes, *Constantius and Athanasius: Theology and Politics in the Constantinian Empire* (Cambridge, Mass.: Harvard University Press, 1981), 106.

22. "Arianism" tends to be used as a portmanteau term encompassing the divergent paths developed from the ideas attributed to Arius on the relationship God the Father and God the Son. Underlying the differences was the common position, *contra* the creed of Nicaea, that the Son was not equal to the Father, so they all rejected the key Nicene phrase that he was "of the same substance" (*homoousios*). See J. N. D. Kelly, *Early Christian Doctrines*, 5th ed. (London: Black, 1977), 247–51.

condemned Athanasius, Marcellus, and Photinus. It is likely that it was this document that Constantius wanted the Western bishops to sign, first at Arles in 353 and then at Milan in 355.[23] It is possible that Hilary was at the Council of Arles in 353, but almost certain that he was at the Council of Milan in 355, where the bishops Dionysius of Milan, Lucifer of Cagliari, and Eusebius of Vercelli refused to sign and were exiled. Hilary was not exiled until 356. The exact cause is not known but was perhaps linked to renewed rebellion on the Rhine border, and to his challenge to the authority of the bishop of Arles, Saturninus, who supported Constantius and "Arianism." Gaul was under the control of Constantius's nephew, Julian, who had been appointed caesar in 355, but it was Constantius who took the decision to exile Hilary to the East.

Hilary was able to move around comparatively freely in the Roman province of Asiana (modern Turkey), and was recognised as bishop by imperial troops as he was taken to Seleucia (modern Silifke) in 359 to a church council organised by Constantius for another attempt to reach a creed acceptable to all sides (the so-called dated creed of Sirmium). A parallel council had been organised in the West at Ariminum (modern Rimini). Despite heavy imperial pressure, there was still no overall agreement. Hilary then accompanied some of the bishops to Constantinople where Constantius finally got agreement to the document, albeit a slightly altered version.[24] In 360 or 361, Hilary left Constantinople, probably during the confusion caused by the uprising against Constantius by Julian in 360. After his return, he worked with Eusebius of Vercelli to reintroduce pro-Nicene theology into Gaul and Italy. Hilary died around 367.

## Anthropophany and the Exchange Formula

The historical summary shows what a huge impact the theological controversies of the 350s had on Hilary's personal life. They also contributed to his ideas of deification, at the heart of which was his interpretation of the exchange formula. The shorthand used for this is "God became man so man

---

23. The evidence and inferences to support this are set out in Barnes, *Constantius and Athanasius*, 110 and 273n9.

24. The complex evolution of the document is charted by J. N. D. Kelly, *Early Christian Creeds*, 3rd ed. (London: Longman, 1972).

could become God," a phrase attributed to Athanasius,[25] although the first known formulation of the idea in the early church was by Irenaeus.[26] Hilary's first understanding of it most likely came from his biblical exegesis, as the exchange formula was ultimately derived from various biblical texts.[27] Hilary's interpretation of the exchange formula in *De Trinitate* differed from other patristic interpretations, however, because it emphasized the exchange in terms of the individual's relationship with the ascended Christ rather than the collective glorification of incorporation into the mystical body of Christ.

The controversies contributed to Hilary's theological development by focusing his attention on the soteriological significance of the relationship between God the Son and God the Father. As noted above, Arius taught that the Son was subordinate. The "Arians" themselves rejected two other interpretations of the relationship, associated with Marcellus of Ancyra (ca. 285–374) and his deacon, Photinus of Sirmium (active mid-fourth century). Marcellus had been deposed in 336 because he was associated by his opponents with an earlier "heretic" Sabellius, hence views attributed to him were often labeled Sabellianism. He was accused of asserting that Father and Son were a monad; that the Son was preexistent, and that the incarnate Christ existed only to fulfill a specific, finite soteriological purpose, and for a finite time.[28] Photinus developed Marcellus's emphasis on the undivided monad, to teach that the Son of God had no separate existence and that Christ was a son of God by adoption not by nature.

In his pre-exile *In Matthaeum*, Hilary showed awareness of the dangers of subordinationism, Sabellianism, and adoptionism.[29] In *De Trinitate*, with

25. Athanasius, *De incarn.* 54: "For he became man that we might become divine." Translation from R. W. Thomson, *Athanasius: Contra Gentes and De Incarnatione* (Oxford: Oxford University Press, 1971), 269.

26. Irenaeus, *Against Heresies* V, *Praef.* 36, SC 153 (Paris: Éditions du Cerf, 1969), 14: "Jesum Christum Dominum nostrum, qui propter immensam suam dilectionem factus est quod sumus nos, uti nos perficeret esse quod est ipse" (our Lord Jesus Christ, who did, through his transcendent love, become what we are, that he might bring us to be even what he is himself). All translations of Irenaeus are drawn from Ante-Nicene Fathers (ed. Roberts et al.) (hereafter, ANF), vol. 1.

27. Notably 2 Cor 8:9; Gal 4:4–6; Rom 8:14–17, 8:29; 1 Jn 3:1–2. See Daniel Keating, *Deification and Grace* (Naples, Fla.: Sapientia Press, 2007), 16–21.

28. See Joseph Lienhard, *Contra Marcellum: Marcellus of Ancyra and Fourth Century Theology* (Washington, D.C.: The Catholic University of America Press, 1999), 31–62.

29. D. H. Williams, "Monarchianism and Photinus of Sirmium as the Persistent Heretical Face of the Fourth Century," *Harvard Theological Review* 99 (2006): 187–206.

greater knowledge of the issues from his exile in the East, he tackled them directly. He refers to their "heresies" separately and collectively throughout the work, and combines them in his culminating eschatological argument of book 11. The common thread to his objection to them all was that none of their views of Christ's relationship to God the Father allowed the exchange formula to take effect. "Arian" subordination, by denying the equality of the Son with the Father, denies "the mystery of our salvation." If the Son, and hence the incarnate Christ, did not share the Father's divinity, how could he save us? "For the apostle leaves it in no doubt that it must be confessed by all, that the mystery of our salvation is not an impairment of divinity but a *sacrament of great godliness*."[30] If, as the so-called Marcellans argued, the incarnate Christ was restricted to his life on earth, and his power was finite, how could he provide continuity for our humanity after death? "Either he is not God as a result of his condition of subjection, or in surrendering the kingdom he is not in the kingdom, or in there being an end, his disappearance follows upon the end."[31] If, as the so-called Photinians argued, Christ was a "mere man," he did not have God's power on earth nor could he act as a physical mediator for humanity after death: "Photinus maintains his [Christ's] manhood, though in maintaining it he forgets that Christ was born as God before the worlds."[32]

Hilary did not attack these views simply because their adherents were attempting to replace the creed of Nicaea with alternative confessions of faith; he attacked them because he thought they contradicted what the baptismal creed taught and what the eucharist embodied. When in exile, in response to a request from bishops back in Gaul requesting information on all the recent creeds and councils, he told them they did not need a written creed as they had the "perfect and apostolic faith" (*perfectam atque apostolicam fidem*) which they learned at baptism: "For you do not desire the duty of the hand to write what you have believed in your hearts and confessed with your mouth for salvation. For as bishops you do not have to read what you believed as reborn neophytes."[33] He defended the creed of Nicaea because it encapsulated what he had learned as a

---

30. *De trin.* 11.9.19: "Non enim apostolus ambigit, quin hoc ab uniuersis fatendum sit, mysterium salutis nostrae non esse contumeliam diuinitatis, sed magnae pietatis sacramentum."

31. *De trin.* 11.21.3: "aut dum regnum tradit, non sit in regno, aut dum finis est, finem eius defectio consequatur."

32. *De trin.* 7.7.20: "Hominem autem Fotinus usurpat, sed in usurpato sibi homine natiuitatem Dei ante saecula ignorat."

33. Hilary, *Syn.* 63, in *Patrologia Latina* (ed. Migne), 10:523B: "Neque officium manus ad scriben-

catechumen, and from his subsequent biblical exegesis, and it was on these that he based his arguments of how we "become God" through our own *profectus*.

## The Fatherhood of God

Hilary used the concept of fatherhood to assert the indivisibility of the substance of God the Father and God the Son.[34] He accused the "heretics" of ignoring the scriptural teaching that God is Father. He urged them to "remember that the revelation is not of the Father manifested as God, but of God manifested as Father."[35] The name "God the Father" itself signified the relationship: "The very fact that He bears the name of *Father* reveals Him as the cause of His Son's existence."[36] In book 7, Hilary emphasized the link between birth and nature. *Natura* derived from *nativitas*, birth, because *nativitas* meant sharing of substance: "For everything that is born can only exist in that nature by which it is born."[37] In book 9, he emphasizes this again, combining *nativitas*, *natura*, and *substantia*: "The fact of birth [*natiuitas*] did not make Him God with a different nature [*natura*] nor did the generation, which produced His substance [*substantia*], change the nature [*substantiae natura*] in kind."[38]

He had possibly learned of the concept of shared substance of God the Father and God the Son from Tertullian[39] and Novatian,[40] as Hilary refers to

---

dum desiderastis, qui quod corde a vobis credebatur, ore ad salutem profitebamini. Nec necessarium habuistis episcopi legere, quod regenerati neophyti tenebatis." *De synodis* was written in 358/59.

34. Peter Widdicombe has shown the importance of this concept in the patristic writers of the East, but there has been no equivalent study of the West. Peter Widdicombe, *The Fatherhood of God from Origen to Athanasius* (Oxford: Oxford University Press, 2000).

35. *De trin.* 3.22.33: "Memento non tibi Patrem manfestatum esse quod Deus est, sed Deum manifestatum esse quod Pater est."

36. *De trin.* 4.9.8: "In ipso enim quod Pater dicitur, eius quem genuit auctor ostenditur." Hilary's use of divine names is discussed by Tarmo Toom, "Hilary of Poitiers' *De Trinitate* and the Name(s) of God," *Vigiliae Christianae* 65 (2010): 456–79.

37. *De trin.* 7.21.41: "quia uniuersa nativitas non potest non in ea esse natura unde nascatur."

38. *De trin.* 9.37.15: "dum subsistens natiuitas non alterius naturae Deum perficit, neque generatio, quae substantiam prouehebat, substantiae naturam demutauit in genere."

39. Tertullian, *Adversus Praxean* 19.8: "rationem reddimus qua dei non duo dicantur nec domini sed qua pater et filius duo, et hoc non ex separatione substantiae sed ex dispositione" (We are rendering an account how the expressions "two gods" or "two lords" are not used, but how the Father and the Son are two, and this [is] not as a result of separation of substance, but as a result of ordinance). Translation from Ernest Evans, *Tertullian's Treatise against Praxeas* (London: SPCK, 1948).

40. Novatian, *De trin.* 31.20.89: "haec uis diuinitatis emissa ... rursum per substantiae communionem ad Patrem reuoluitur." Novatian, *Opera quae supersunt*, ed. G. F. Dierks, Corpus Christianorum: Series Latina 4 (Turnhout: Brepols, 1972).

the "commonality of the paternal substance" three times in *In Matthaeum*[41] in a phrase similar to one used by Novatian. But at this point he seemed ignorant of the concept of eternal generation of the Son.[42] Hilary's developing ideas of the fatherhood of God was probably the impetus for his later insight on eternal generation which was the main focus of the final book 12 of *De Trinitate*.[43]

### Christ as Son of God and Son of Man

By establishing through the fatherhood of God that the consubstantial Son was equal in divinity, Hilary was able to assert the reality of the incarnate Christ's humanity without prejudice to his divinity. The basis of Hilary's insistence on the dual natures of the incarnate Christ was Philippians 2:6–8. The text is often associated in modern theological minds with *kenosis*, the "self-emptying" of God.[44] What Hilary meant may not be what some modern theologians would recognize. For Hilary, the incarnation did not mean that the Son was any the less divine. Divinity was immutable but could be self-limiting: "The emptying of the form is not the abolition of the nature: because he who empties himself is not lacking in himself."[45] From this, Hilary argued that Christ's miracles showed his divine power worked in tandem with his human faculties: "In all the varied acts of power and healing which He wrought, the fact is conspicuous that He was man by virtue of the flesh He had taken, God by evidence of the works He did."[46]

Such statements led to accusations by scholars such as Richard Hanson that Hilary had a docetic Christology.[47] When read in context, however, Hil-

---

41. *In Matt.* 8.8.12: "sed soli hoc Christo erat debitum, soli de communione paternae substantiae haec agere erat familiare"; 12.18.8: "et communione paternae substantiae Domino detrahentes"; and 31.3.3: "de infinitate paternae substantiae exstitisse."

42. See Williams, *Commentary on Matthew*, 29.

43. Argued by Joseph Moingt, "La Théologie Trinitaire de St Hilaire," in *Hilaire et son temps*, Actes du Colloque du Poitiers (Paris: Études Augustiniennes, 1969), 163.

44. See S. W. Sykes, "The Strange Persistence of Kenotic Christology," in *Being and Truth: Essays in Honour of John Macquarrie*, ed. A. Kee and E. T. Long (London: SCM Press, 1986), 349–75. He summarizes the changing interpretations since the patristic era.

45. *De trin.* 9.14.15: "Ergo euacuatio formae non est abolitio naturae: quia qui se euacuat, non caret sese; et qui accepit, manet" (author's translation).

46. *De trin.* 2.28.3: "Tantum illud in uniuersis virtutum et curationum generibus contendum est, in carnis adsumptione hominem, Deum uero in gestis rebus existere."

47. R. P. C. Hanson, *The Search for the Christian Doctrine of God* (Edinburgh: T and T Clark, 1988), 501.

ary is emphatically not docetic, as his soteriology depends on Christ's humanity. *In Matthaeum* demonstrates that Hilary was already unequivocal on the human as well as the divine nature of Christ. He emphasized that the Son became truly human in order to save us: "There was in Jesus Christ the whole man [*homo totus*] ... he fulfilled in himself the sacrament of our salvation."[48] He argued that, because sin came through the flesh, it could only be defeated in the flesh,[49] hence Christ assumed the fragility of the human body in order to buy it back.[50] But Hilary also argued that the incarnate Son's divine power was not restricted to the strength of the human body: "And the assumption of the body does not imprison the nature of his power."[51]

The exegetical genre of *In Matthaeum* means that there is no extended analysis of such statements. In *De Trinitate*, Hilary's greater awareness of the theological developments and the new type of systematic work he was writing prompted extensive analysis on the link between Christ's humanity and our salvation. In book 1, he reminded his readers: "[Christ] suffered as man to the utmost that he might put powers [i.e., of sin] to shame."[52] In book 9, refuting the claim that the Son was subordinate to the Father, he reminded them of Philippians 2:6–8: "can you be ignorant that the dispensation for your salvation was an emptying of the form of God?"[53]

The dual natures of Christ on earth were reflected by his two different relationships to God the Father, both as God the Son and as man: "Where the glory of Christ is, there God is his Father, but where Christ Jesus is, there the Father is his God, having him as his God by dispensation when he is a slave, and as Father in glory when he is God."[54] Our salvation depended on both

---

48. *In Matt.* 2.5.2: "Erat in Iesu Christo homo totus ... in se sacramentum nostrae salutis expleuit." This is a good example of Hilary's ambiguity. Does *homo totus* refer to Christ as the perfect man, or to Christ who encompasses all of humanity? The former is preferred by Paul Burns in *The Christology in Hilary of Poitiers' Commentary on Matthew* (Rome: Institutum Patristicum Augustinianum, 1981), 100. Philip Wild prefers the latter in *The Divinization of Man according to Hilary of Poitiers* (Mundelein, Ill.: St. Mary of the Lake Seminary, 1950), 60. Charlier credits him with deliberate ambiguity. See A. Charlier, "L'Église corps du Christ chez saint Hilaire de Poitiers," *Ephemerides Theologicae Lovanienses* 41 (1965): 456.

49. *In Matt.* 3.2.6: "non enim erat a Deo diabolus, sed a carne uincendus."

50. *In Matt.* 9.7.10: "ad redemptionem suam fragilitatem corporis uirtus adsumpsit."

51. *In Matt.* 9.7.9: "Et adsumptio corporis non naturam uirtutis inclusit."

52. *De trin.* 1.13.40: "ad ultimum in hominem passus, ut potestates dehonestaret."

53. *De trin.* 9.51.15: "ignorandum existimas, hanc dispensationem salutis tuae exinationem formae Dei esse?"

54. *De trin.* 11.17.22: "ut Christi ubi claritas est, ibi Deus Pater eius sit, ubi uero Christus Iesus est,

natures. Hilary was not interested in the mechanics of salvation beyond this one essential element of the two natures of Christ: "For He took upon Him the flesh in which we have sinned that by wearing our flesh He might forgive sins."[55]

But the duality did not make Christ's physical body less human. He "had been born of a virgin, from cradle and childhood he had grown to man's estate, through sleep and hunger and thirst and weariness he had lived man's life.... And why? These things were ordained for our assurance that in Christ is complete [*solum*] man."[56] It was because Hilary believed in the full and perfect humanity of the incarnate Christ that he developed his ideas on Christ's brotherhood with us, through which we could share the glory of the ascended body of Christ at the eschaton, that is, achieve our own anthropophany. We find the fullest exposition of this concept in *De Trinitate* book 11.[57] Hilary carefully structured the work to lead the reader by progressive stages along his journey of faith. By book 11 Hilary had reached the point when he needed to educate the reader about why and how we are glorified. The brotherhood of Christ was pivotal.

## Our Brotherhood with Christ

According to Gilles Pelland, Hilary was the first Latin writer to use *frater* and *fraternitas* in this context.[58] Hilary's key text for this was John 20:17b: "[Jesus said] But go to my brothers and say to them, 'I am ascending to my Father and your Father, to my God and your God.'" As our brother, the incarnate Christ is "our man Christ," *homo noster Christus*.[59] He "contains in himself the

---

ibi Pater Deus suus sit, habens Deum suum in dispensatione cum seruus est, et Patrem in claritate cum Deus sit."

55. *De trin.* 1.13.34: "Carnem enim peccati recepit, ut in adsumptione carnis nostrae delicta donaret, dum eius fit particeps adsumptione non crimine."

56. *De trin.* 3.10.21: "Namque natus ex uirgine a cunis et infantia usque ad consummatum uirum uenerat; per somnum sitim lassitudinem lacrimas hominem egerat, etiamnum conspuendus flagellandus crucifigendus. Quid ergo? Nobis solum hominem in Christo haec erant contestatura."

57. I am very grateful to Lionel Wickham for drawing my attention to the significance of book 11 at a conference on Hilary in Poitiers in 2002. His paper was published as "Le livre 11 et l'apothéose de l'homme-Dieu," in *Dieu Trinité d'hier à demain avec Hilaire de Poitiers*, ed. Dominique Bertrand (Paris: Éditions du Cerf, 2010), 241–51.

58. *La Trinité III, Livres 9–12*, trans. G. M. de Durand, Ch. Morel, and G. Pelland, SC 462 (Paris: Éditions du Cerf, 2001), 322n3.

59. *De trin.* 11.19.34.

whole of our nature as a result of the assumption of flesh."[60] Hilary's emphasis on the brotherhood of Christ was as important to his anthropology as his emphasis on the fatherhood of God was to his Christology. It was the key to his argument of how we "become God." Christ is our brother because the humanity that God the Son assumed was a humanity that, in Hilary's view, had been planned to become perfect. In book 11, in the context of the eschaton, he speaks of "the planned formation of the first man."[61] The ideas and phrasing are similar to Irenaeus. Irenaeus argued that "God recapitulated in Himself the ancient formation of man, that He might kill sin, deprive death of its power, and vivify man."[62] Irenaeus also used the same term to emphasize the physical reality of the human Christ.[63] Whether or not there was a direct influence, the similarity suggests that Hilary agreed with the Irenaean concept that man was formed in the image and likeness of the incarnate God, who guided us to the perfection planned for us but lost by sin.[64]

When Hilary refers to the "planned formation of the first man," he therefore explains that, through sharing the glorified body of Christ, humans can achieve the glory that had been planned for them, because, through the incarnation, individual humans could become the image of God through sharing the Son's humanity. This concept was summarised in the passage already quoted: "Thus man is perfected as the image of God. For, having been made a sharer of the glory of the body of God, he advances into the image of the creator according to the planned formation of the first man."[65] Through the *profectus* of *noster homo*, Christ, and our own *profectus*, we too can attain the perfection planned for Adam, the first man: "And man having been made new in the knowledge of God after sin and the old man, reaches the perfection of his condition."

60. *De trin.* 11.16.1: "Ipse autem uniuersitatis nostrae in se continens ex carnis adsumptione naturam."

61. *De trin.* 11.49.24: "dispositam primi hominis figurationem."

62. Irenaeus, *Against Heresies*, SC 211 (Paris: Éditions du Cerf, 1974), 3.18.7: "Deus hominis antiquam plasmationem in se recapitulans, ut occideret quidem peccatum, euacuaret autem mortem et uiuicaret hominem."

63. Ibid., 3.16.6: "In omnibus autem est et homo plasmatio Dei et hominem ergo in semetipso recapituletus est" (But in every respect, too, He is man, the formation of God; and thus He took up man into Himself).

64. See Denis Minns, *Irenaeus: An Introduction* (London: T and T Clark, 2010), 74.

65. *De trin.* 11.49.22: "Consummatur itaque homo imago Dei. Namque conformis effectus gloriae corporis Dei, in imaginem creatoris excedit secundum dispositam primi hominis figurationem."

An important part of this argument was that Christ did not lose his physical humanity after the ascension. Hilary followed the lead of Tertullian in affirming that there was physical continuity for human bodies after death,[66] but, more audaciously, Hilary also claimed continuity of Christ's human body. The transfiguration narrative was central to his argument.

## The Transfiguration

Hilary's interpretation of the transfiguration combined both strands of his concept of how man is made manifest through anthropophany: the glory of Christ revealed as perfect man, and the possibility that we can share it. In *In Matthaeum*, Hilary discussed the transfiguration (Mt 17:1–7) as part of his exegesis of the whole Gospel. It is the earliest surviving Western work to discuss it,[67] although presumably earlier Matthew commentaries had also done so. Hilary's interpretation might well have been original, however, as he links the passage to his emphasis on Christ as the perfect man, *homo totus*. Moses became visible to teach that "the glory of the resurrection is ordained for human bodies."[68] The cloud and the voice from heaven (Mt 17:5) signified that "after the loss of the world, after the willing acceptance of the cross, after the death of the body, [Christ] had confirmed by his exemplary action the glory of the heavenly kingdom through the resurrection of the dead."[69] Christ's body is transfigured and glorified, as ours will be in the kingdom of heaven. This link between the transfiguration, the resurrection of the dead, and the kingdom of heaven provides evidence that before his exile Hilary already interpreted the transfiguration as prefiguring our own corporeal resurrection as perfected human beings.

---

66. In the *Apologeticum* 48.4.35, Tertullian emphasized that what is being judged is the action of the flesh, so the flesh must be there: "Ideoque repraesentabuntur et corpora, quia neque pati quicquam potest anima sola sine materia stabili, id est carne, et quod omnino de iudicio dei pati debent animae, non sine carne meruerunt intra quam omnia egerunt" (it is not right that souls should have all the wrath of God to bear: they did not sin without the flesh, within which all was done by them).

67. According to Driscoll, this is the only Western interpretation unaffected by the East. His assertion depends on the problematic assumption that the West was untouched by the Eastern exegetical tradition in ca. 350. Jeremy Driscoll, "The Transfiguration in Hilary of Poitiers' '*Commentarius in Matthaeum*,'" *Augustinianum* 24 (1984): 396.

68. *In Matt.* 17.2.14: "humanis corporibus decreta esse resurrectionis gloria doceretur."

69. Ibid., 17.3.5: "qui post saeculi damnum, post crucis uoluntatem, post obitum corporum regni caelestis gloriam ex mortuorum resurrectione facti confirmasset exemplo."

In book 11 of *De Trinitate*, Hilary used the same text to argue that the ascended body, both of Christ and our own, is still in some sense recognizably corporeal and individual. He interpreted the transfiguration not as a revelation of Christ as God but of Christ as glorified, perfect man, that is, an anthropophany, not a theophany: "Therefore the glory of the body coming into the kingdom was revealed to the apostles. For the Lord stood in the condition of his glorious transformation with the glory of his reigning body revealed."[70] It was a body (*corpus*) which was transformed and revealed, and on our behalf the apostles were then promised the same glory.[71] Hilary reinforced the point when he linked the transfiguration to Matthew 13:40–43: "At the end of the age ... the righteous shall shine like the sun in the kingdom of their Father" (NRSV). He then combined it with Philippians 3:21: "He will transform the body of our humiliation so that it may be conformed to the body of his glory, by the power that enables him to make all things subject to himself" (NRSV). This reinforced his point that we share in Christ's glorious body: "Again, we have [*habemus*] ourselves as sharers in the form of the glory of his body shining in the Kingdom of the Father as if in the sun's glory, in which having been transformed on the mountain he showed the appearance of his Kingdom to the apostles."[72] By using the first-person plural, as he often did, Hilary reminded his readers that he was also on the journey of individual transformation.[73] Hilary has now prepared his readers to understand 1 Corinthians 15:24–28, Philippians 3.21, and the all-important Philippians 2:6–8 through the lens of the transfiguration.

## 1 Corinthians 15:24–28: We Become the Kingdom of God

The text had become one of the most contentious battlegrounds of the so-called heretics. It contributed to Hilary's ideas of anthropophany because he interpreted it as confirmation of the equality of God the Father and God

---

70. *De trin.* 11.37.9: "Gloria itaque uenientis in regnum corporis apostolis demonstrata est. Nam in habitu Dominus gloriosae transformationis suae constitit, regnantis corporis sui claritate patefacta."

71. *De trin.* 11.38.1: "Et huius quidem gloriae consortium apostolis pollicens."

72. *De trin.* 11.38.13: "Habemus rursum conformes nos gloriae corporis sui in regno Patris tamquam in solis claritate fulgentes, in qua habitum regni sui apostolis in monte transformatus ostendit."

73. For another example, see *De trin.* 10.70.27: "Non per difficiles nos Deus ad beatam uitam quaestiones uocat, nec multiplici eloquentis facundiae genere sollicititat" (For God does not call us to the blessed life through arduous investigations; he does not tempt us with the varied arts of rhetoric).

the Son, and of the Son's continuity with us through which we are glorified. It is through this glorification, he argued, that God becomes all in all: that is, humanity has achieved the perfection originally planned for it.

Hilary introduced the text by explaining how he will refute both "Arian" subordinationism and the view attributed to Marcellus that Christ's kingdom will end: "Three things therefore are summoned for examination according to the order of the words, first the end [*finis*], next surrender [*traditio*], then subjection [*subiectio*]: so that through these either Christ might cease to exist at the end, or he might not retain the kingdom by surrendering it, or he might exist in subjection to God outside the nature of God."[74] Hilary then provides an extensive analysis of the three key words. In contrast to the "Arians," Hilary interprets the subjection (*subiectio*) of Christ as a demonstration of filial obedience, not proof that the Son is subordinate. In contrast to the "Marcellans," *traditio* is handing over the kingdom but not losing it; *finis* is fulfillment, not annihilation, at the eschaton.

Hilary had already rejected any suggestion that, in the context of God, "to give" meant to lose. Citing Matthew 11:27 ("all things have been handed over by the Father to me") and Matthew 28:18 ("all power is given to me in heaven and earth"), Hilary pointed out that "if therefore to have given is to have lost possession, the Father too did not possess what he had given."[75] Now Hilary makes the original and startling claim that we, as humans, become the kingdom of God which the Son will return to God: "Therefore he will hand over the kingdom to God the Father, not by handing it over in such a way that he yields in power, but because we will become the kingdom of God having been made sharers in the form of the glory of his body."[76] In the next sentence, he reiterated that Christ has made us the kingdom by glorification: "For he did not say, 'He will hand over *his* Kingdom' but 'he will hand over *the* kingdom,' handing us to God when we have been made the kingdom through the glorification of his body."[77] By repeating the phrase *conformes gloriae corporis*

---

74. *De trin.* 11.25.1: "Tria igitur secundum dictorum ordinem in quaestionem uocantur, primum finis, deinde traditio, deinde subiectio: ut per haec aut desinat Christus in fine, aut regnum tradendo non teneat, aut extra Dei naturam Deo subiectus existat."

75. *De trin.* 11.29.12: "Si igitur dedisse caruisse est, pater quoque his quae dedit caruit."

76. *De trin.* 11.39.1: "Tradet ergo regnum Deo Patri, non ita tamquam tradens potestate concedat, sed quod nos conformes gloriae corporis sui facti regnum Dei erimus."

77. *De trin.* 11.39.3: "Non enim ait 'Tradet suum regnum,' sed 'Tradet regnum,' effectos nos per glorificationem corporis sui regnum Deo traditurus."

from Philippians 3:21, and connecting it to 1 Corinthians 15:24–28, Hilary developed his argument eschatologically to show that handing over the kingdom did not mean a loss for Christ, but that God would be "gaining mankind for himself as God rather than losing God through mankind."[78] He has "gained man" because man has become the perfected human exemplified and glorified by Christ so that God will become all in all: "we believe that he [the Son] is both glorified in the body since he reigns in it, and afterwards will be made subject so that *God might be all in all.*"[79]

The same understanding of *traditio* as gain rather than loss informed Hilary's argument for corporeal continuity, and linked to his statements that transformation (often using the word *demutatio*) did not mean destruction. Hilary had cited the transfiguration as evidence that the ascended Christ retains our nature, and he now argued that at the ascension Christ's human body was not discarded (*abiectio*) but "transformed as a result of the subjection, not because the body has been destroyed through ceasing to exist, but because it has been changed through glorification."[80] Hilary linked this transformation with our own. Because we have been made sharers of Christ's glory, our own bodies will also be transformed, so that "these our originally earthly bodies pass into the condition of a superior nature and become sharers in the glory of the Lord's body."[81]

The argument that, because of this, "we will become the kingdom of God" related to Hilary's understanding of our individual relationship to Christ at the eschaton, the last stage of our *profectus*. In other contexts, Hilary interpreted the kingdom differently. In *In Matthaeum*, Christ was the "kingdom of Heaven," as the prophets foretold and John the Baptist had preached (5.6.12). But in his commentary on Matthew 5:14, Hilary argued that Christ was suggesting an analogy between himself and the city constructed on a mountain. By our union with his flesh (*consortium carnis*) we become inhabitants of that

---

78. *De trin.* 11.40.17: "adquirens sibi Deo potius hominem, quam Deum per hominem amittens."

79. *De trin.* 11.41.7: "quia et clarificatum in corpore dum in eo regnat et postea subiciendum ut Deus omnia in omnibus sit credimus."

80. *De trin.* 11.40.15: "non abiecto corpore, sed ex subiectione translato, neque per defectionem abolito, sed ex clarificatione mutate." Hilary makes the same point in the *Tractatus super Psalmos*, referring to 1 Cor 15:42 (*Tr. Ps.* 2.41.21).

81. *De trin.* 11.43.16: "Cum igitur haec nostra terrenorum corporum origo in habitum naturae potioris excedat et conformis gloriae dominici corporis fiat."

city, a theme developed in the *Tractatus super Psalmos*.[82] Later in *In Matthaeum* Hilary interpreted the text of Matthew 22:2–3, which compares the kingdom of heaven to a wedding feast, to illustrate the mystery of eternal life and the eternal glory of the resurrection.[83] Even in *De Trinitate* book 11 Hilary referred to the kingdom prepared for us from the foundation of the world (11.24 and 11.39, citing Mt 25:34), and recalled that Jesus told his disciples that his kingdom was not of this world (11.32, citing Jn 18:36). The variety of Hilary's interpretations reflects his response to the richness of the biblical allusions: the kingdom is internal, it is external, it always was, always is, and always will be, yet is not yet. None of these precludes his particular interpretation of 1 Corinthians 15:24–28.

In the final chapter of book 11, Hilary associates 1 Corinthians 15:24–28 with Philippians 2:6–8. He reminds us that "he who, when he was in the form of God, was found in the form of a slave must again be confessed *in the glory of God the Father*."[84] But in what could be called a "reverse kenosis," it was Christ's human nature which was now glorified through his *profectus* as "perfect man," and it is this glory which we share: "For that subjection of the body, through which what is corporeal to him is consumed into the nature of the Spirit, establishes him who besides God is also man, to be God *all in all*, but that our Man becomes it through progress. But we shall advance into the glory of the Man whose form we share."[85] Because Christ is our brother we not only share his body in this life, we will share it at the eschaton.[86]

---

82. The "heavenly city" becomes an important metaphor for Hilary in the *Tractatus super Psalmos*, and Burns shows how Hilary adapts it at specific stages of the work as he develops his theme of the three stages of human transformation. See Burns, *The Model of the Christian Life*, 179.

83. *In Matt.* 22.3.8: "Uerum hic nuptiae uitae caelestis et in resurrectione suscipiendae aeternae gloriae sacramentum est."

84. *De trin.* 11.49.2: "Qui enim, cum esset in Dei forma, repertus est in forma serui, rursum confitendus est *in gloria Dei Patris*."

85. *De trin.* 11.49.14: "Subiectio enim illa corporis, per quam quod carnale ei est in naturam Spiritus deuoratur, esse Deum omnia in omnibus eum qui praeter Deum et homo est constituit, noster autem ille homo in id proficit."

86. In the *Tractatus* Hilary's interpretation of 1 Cor 15:24–28 confusingly suggests we are the kingdom and yet are about to be handed over into the kingdom: "sed nos, qui regnum eius sumus, Dei Patri traditurus in regnum" (*Tr. Ps.* 148.8.24). Scully discusses the passage in the context of her argument that Christ assumed the whole of humanity at the moment of his incarnation (*Physicalist Soteriology*, 176–79).

## Deification through the Sacraments

There is another dimension to Hilary's concept of deification: the sacraments of baptism and the eucharist. Throughout his writings, Hilary emphasizes the sacrament of baptism as the first step in our *profectus*, but where appropriate to his theme shows how the eucharist anticipated and reenacted our glorification at the eschaton.

It was his interpretation of the creed of Nicaea as an affirmation of the baptismal confession and liturgy of the church that motivated his defence of it. Hilary cited what sounds like part of a baptismal creed in *In Matthaeum*: "Those who come to baptism first confess that they believe in God the Son and in his passion and resurrection, and by the mystery of this confession the faith is given."[87] He also emphasized the role of worship as a route to knowledge of God, explaining its importance to his own *profectus*, "understanding God by worship alone as I do."[88]

Hilary refers to the eucharist less frequently. It is mentioned obliquely in *In Mattheum* and the *Tractatus super Psalmos*. In the former, discussing Matthew 9:14, Hilary interprets Jesus' statement that there is no need to fast when the bridegroom comes to mean that that no one will lack the "sacrament of the holy food" (*sacramentum sancti cibi*) in Christ's presence, "for the heavenly food is received by faith in the resurrection."[89] References to the eucharist in the *Tractatus super Psalmos* are scattered, and relate to its eschatological role.[90] His only sustained discussion of the eucharist is in *De Trinitate* 8.13–17, where he emphasizes the theological link between the shared nature of God the Father and God the Son with our sharing in the body of Christ through the eucharist, and hence our sharing of his glory.

The context was Hilary's refutation of the "heretics" (in this case the "Arians"), who alleged that the text "I and the Father are one" (Jn 10:30) referred to a union of will, not of nature (8.5–12).[91] Hilary pointed out the incongruity between this interpretation of the text set alongside other texts, particularly

---

87. *In Matt.* 15.8.2: "Venturi enim ad baptismum, prius confitentur credere se in Dei filio et in passione ac resurrectione ejus et huic professionis sacramento fides redditur."

88. *De trin.* 11.44.1: "Deum sola veneratione intelligenti."

89. *In Matt.* 9.316: "In fide enim resurrectionis sacramentum panis caelistis accipitur."

90. See Scully, *Physicalist*, 190n3.

91. In his brief overview of the eucharist in Hilary's works, Boris Bobrinskoy wondered why the use of the eucharist to prove the unity between Father and Son was so rare in the anti-Arian arguments. See

"I am in the Father, and you in me and I in you" (Jn 14:19–20) and "That they may all be one, as Thou Father art in me and I in thee, that they also may be in us" (Jn 17:21). His logic was that denial that the Father and the Son were one by nature also meant the denial of Christ's promise that "he that eats my flesh and drinks my blood abides in me, and I in him" (Jn 6:55–56). Hilary argued that we could not be one with God if there were only a union of will between God the Father and God the Son: "How can a union of will be maintained, seeing that the special property of nature received through the sacrament is the sacrament of a perfect unity?"[92] Hilary then elaborated on the reality of the sacrament, and emphasized its link to the reality of Christ's consubstantiality with the Father: "For now, both from the declaration of the Lord himself, and our own faith, it is verily flesh and verily blood. And these, when eaten and drunk, bring it to pass that both we are in Christ and Christ is in us."[93]

Hilary argued that, by sharing Christ's flesh, we too in some mysterious way become a part of God. We live in him though his flesh, while Christ, through his birth as Son of God, retains his divine nature.[94] Hilary concluded his argument on the eucharist by referring back to Christ's statement that "the glory which you [God the Father] have given me, I have given to them" (Jn 17:22). Hilary's interpretation was that "since both through the glory of the Son of God bestowed upon us and through the Son abiding in us according to the flesh, and with us united in him corporeally and inseparably, the mystery of the true and natural unity should be preached."[95] Hilary thus linked the eucharist with the fatherhood of God, through which Father and Son share the same nature, and the brotherhood of Christ, through which we can share his humanity and hence his glory.

---

"Eucharistie et mystère du salut chez Hilaire," in *Hilaire et son temps*, Actes du Colloque du Poitiers (Paris: Études Augustiniennes, 1969), 235–41, at 239.

92. *De trin.* 8.13.22: "quomodo uoluntatis unitas adseritur, cum naturalis per sacramentum proprietas perfectae sacramentum sit unitatis?"

93. *De trin.* 8.14.12: "Nunc enim et ipsius Domini professione et fide nostra uere caro est et uere sanguis est. Et haec accepta adque hausta id efficiunt, ut et nos in Christo et Christus in nobis sit."

94. *De trin.* 8.16.15: "nos naturaliter secundum carnem per eum uiuimus ... dum in se per natiuitatem habet Patrem in uirtutute natura."

95. *De trin.* 8.17.7: "um et per honorem nobis datum Dei Fili, et per manentem in nobis carnaliter Filium, et in eo nobis corporaliter et inseparabiliter unitis, mysterium uerae ac naturalis unitatis sit praedicandum" (author's translation).

## Conclusion

Hilary had an unusual but rich theology of deification. In *De Trinitate* he focuses on the way we can "become God" in the sense of sharing in the perfect, glorified humanity of the incarnate Son. This was based primarily on his interpretation of the transfiguration as anthropophany rather than theophany, and his exegesis that 1 Corinthians 15:24–28 meant God becomes all in all when we are transformed into glory. For Hilary, the exchange formula was therefore anthropocentric. Only because Christ is our brother, can we "become God" through sharing his glorified body, after a *profectus* initiated in baptism and maintained through the eucharist. We will then be made manifest as the people we were planned to be, because Christ as perfect man made himself manifest to us.

*Fr. Brian Dunkle, SJ*

## 7. BEYOND CARNAL COGITATIONS
*Deification in Ambrose of Milan*

In the concluding essay of a recent collection on deification, Gösta Hallonsten criticizes a trend in scholarship that fails to distinguish adequately between Eastern and Western approaches to the topic.[1] Reprising Yves Congar's "Deification in the Spiritual Tradition of the East," Hallonsten claims that basic differences in anthropology underlie distinct soteriologies: in the East we find a "dynamic" account of humanity created in the image and likeness of God, while in the West "we see the tendency to distinguish nature and grace in a way that is foreign to Eastern tradition."[2] According to Hallonsten, most studies that identify a doctrine of deification in Latin authors impose an Eastern theological anthropology on a "static" Western account.

Although the critique is directed primarily against scholars of the medieval and Reformation period, a cursory review of deification in the work of the fourth-century theologian Ambrose of Milan might suggest that the

---

1. Gösta Hallonsten, "*Theosis* in Recent Research: A Renewal of Interest and a Need for Clarity," in *Partakers of the Divine Nature: The History and Development of Deification in the Christian Traditions*, ed. Michael J. Christensen and Jeffery A. Wittung (Madison, N.J.: Fairleigh Dickinson University Press, 2007), 286; for further reflection on the motives and approaches of recent studies, see Paul Gavrilyuk, "The Retrieval of Deification: How a Once-Despised Archaism Became an Ecumenical Desideratum," *Modern Theology* 25 (2009): 647–59.

2. Hallonsten, "*Theosis* in Recent Research," 286; see Yves Congar, "La déification dans la traditions de l'Orient," *La vie spirituel, Supplément* 44 (1935): 91–107. For a recent response, see Luke Davis Townsend, "Deification in Aquinas: A *Supplementum* to *The Ground of Union*," *Journal of Theological Studies* 66 (2015): 204–34.

bishop fits neatly into Hallonsten's taxonomy.[3] While Ambrose is so dependent on Greek sources that he has been called a "plagiarist" by both ancient and modern readers, he never renders the Greek term *theosis* and related deification language into Latin.[4] Furthermore, Ambrose employs the nature/grace distinction much more often than any previous theologian.[5] Perhaps, then, Ambrose is a prime case of a major Latin doctor favoring a static Western anthropology that anticipates the two-tier nature/supernature distinction of Neo-Scholasticism over the dynamic Greek vision captured by the term *theosis*.[6]

An alternative view appears in the ninth-century theologian John Scotus Eriugena, a famous mediator between Greek and Latin: he takes Ambrose as a singular representative of the pervasive presence of deification in the Latin tradition.[7] In his *Periphyseon* Eriugena writes: "But the use of this term—I mean, 'deification'—is most uncommon in Latin books, although we find its idea [*intellectus*] among many of them, and above all in Ambrose."[8] In

---

3. Ambrose is often cited in overviews of deification—see, e.g., Daniel Keating, *Deification and Grace* (Naples, Fla.: Sapientia, 2007), 18, and Édouard des Places, "Divinisation," in *Dictionnaire de spiritualité ascétique et mystique*, ed. Charles Baumgartner et al. (Paris: Beauchesne, 1957), 3:1394–95—but rarely treated in his own right. I have found only one (inadequate) study: Augustyn Eckmann, "Deification of Man in St. Ambrose's Writings," in *Being or Good? Metamorphoses of Neoplatonism*, ed. Agnieszka Kijewska (Lublin: Wydawnictwo KUL, 2004), 199–210. J. Warren Smith, *Christian Grace and Pagan Virtue: The Theological Foundation of Ambrose's Ethics* (Oxford: Oxford University Press, 2010), 178, aligns Ambrose's approach to deification with the Alexandrian tradition; see also Ernst Dassmann, *Die Frömmigkeit des Kirchenvaters Ambrosius von Mailand: Quellen und Entfaltung* (Münster: Aschendorff, 1965), 127–29.

4. On Ambrose the "plagiarist," see Harald Hagendahl, *Latin Fathers and the Classics* (Göteberg: Göteberg Elanders, 1958), 372; Jerome, prologue to translation of Didymus, *On the Holy Spirit*. See also Hugo Rahner, "Die Gottesgeburt: Die Lehre der Kirchenväter von der Geburt Christi im Herzen des Gläubigen," *Zeitschrift für Katholische Theologie* 59 (1935): 383n1. For a succinct response to the claims of plagiarism, see Luigi Pizzolato, *La dottrina esegetica di sant'Ambrogio* (Milan: Vita e Pensiero, 1978), 5–7.

5. See Smith, *Christian Grace*, 159–78; on the law and grace in Ambrose, see Viktor Hahn, *Das Wahre Gesetz: Eine Untersuchung der Auffassung des Ambrosius von Mailand vom Verhältnis der beiden Testamente* (Münster: Aschendorff, 1968), 349–52.

6. As in, e.g., John McGuckin, *The Westminster Handbook to Patristic Theology* (Louisville, Ky.: Westminster John Knox, 2004), 149.

7. On Eriugena and Latin sources, see Willemien Otten, "The Texture of Tradition: The Role of the Church Fathers in Carolingian Theology," in *The Reception of the Church Fathers in the West*, ed. Irena Backus (Leiden: Brill, 1997), 1:31–44, and Goulven Madec, "Jean Scot et les Pères latins: Hilaire, Ambroise, Jérôme et Grégoire le Grand," in his *Jean Scot et ses auteurs: Annotations érigéniennes* (Paris: Études augustiniennes, 1988), 54–62.

8. Eriugena, *Periphyseon* 5 (Corpus Christianorum. Continuatio Mediaevalis 165:1217): "Sed huius nominis (deificationis dico) in latinis codicibus rarissimus est usus, intellectum uero eius apud multos et maxime apud Ambrosium inuenimus. Sed quare hoc euenit, non satis nobis patet. An forte sensus ipsius

this chapter, I follow Eriugena to argue for Ambrose's commitment to a robust vision of deification. After discussing possible reasons for the absence of the term *deificatio* in Ambrose, I present Ambrose's treatment of deification in three parts. First I examine the *intellectus* of the term by treating the motifs of deification that speak directly of God's union with humanity through Christ as found in Ambrose's use of formulas of divine/human exchange and 2 Peter 1:4; these texts tend to appear in doctrinal and ascetical works aimed at the "advanced," although Ambrose does employ 2 Peter 1:4 more widely to link deification to the sacraments. I then treat themes of divine adoption and "image and likeness," which imply indirectly the union between God and the baptized; these motifs appear often in Ambrose's exhortations to all Christians to be conformed to the divine life. In the words of Eriugena, I suggest that Ambrose took the *intellectus* of deification to be "incomprehensible and unbelievable to those who cannot manage to move beyond carnal cogitations," and hence he speaks differently to "professional Christians" (*inter sapientes*) than he does to neophytes.[9]

In the third part of this chapter, I reconsider Hallonsten's critique in light of Ambrose's understanding of the themes of deification. Hallonsten maintains that Western theological anthropology draws heavily on the distinction between nature and grace in contrast to the Eastern emphasis on image and likeness. I will suggest that Ambrose often deploys the *natura/gratia* pair to articulate an account of deification that would be accessible to a diverse congregation. In part, perhaps, because of his sense that the technicalities of deification are proper only to advanced audiences, Ambrose uses the language of nature and grace for mixed congregations when he explains God's divinizing humanity—itself created "to the image and likeness" of the Son, the true image—beyond created limits.

---

nominis (quod est ΘΕΩΣΙΣ, quo maxime graeci utuntur), significantes sanctorum transitum in deum, non solum anima sed etiam et corpore, ut unum in ipso et cum ipso sint, quando in eis nil animale, nil corporeum remanebit, altus nimium uisus est ultraque carnales cogitationes ascendere non ualentibus incomprehensibilis et incredibilis, ac per hoc non publice praedicandus; sed de eo inter sapientes tractandum." Unless otherwise noted, all translations are my own.

9. For Origen expressing similar reservations, see *Contra Celsum* 3.37; Russell, *The Doctrine of Deification*, 162.

## Ambrose the Theologian

"Snatched from the tribunals," as he reports, while still a catechumen and elected bishop of Milan in 374, Ambrose had much to learn when he began to compose his theological treatises and sermons in the late 370s.[10] As the pastor of the capital of the western Roman Empire, he played a special role in mediating the Christian faith to the court of the emperors Gratian, Valentinian II, and Theodosius. Indeed, Ambrose's proximity to civil power has prompted many scholars to treat him primarily as a *Kirchenpolitiker*, an ecclesiastical operator working to extend and secure the Milanese church's influence in secular affairs.[11]

While historians focus on Ambrose's church politics, theologians tend to emphasize his dependence on earlier thinkers. Ambrose is often portrayed as a mouthpiece for his sources and *Quellenforschung* dominates in studies of his writings.[12] To be sure, Ambrose read widely in Greek theology and mastered the thought of Philo, Origen, Basil of Caesarea, Didymus the Blind, and Athanasius; he also borrowed heavily from the Latin writings of Hilary of Poitiers and Cyprian of Carthage.[13] Yet treatment of Ambrose the "transmitter" generally presumes that he adds little to the theological tradition that he inherits.

Recent work, however, has engaged Ambrose's thought on its own terms, as a rich and sophisticated contribution to the pro-Nicene consensus of the late fourth century.[14] Ambrose rarely channeled unaltered what he found in his sources.[15] Scholars have examined Ambrose's distinctive language and vi-

---

10. For a recent and accessible account of Ambrose's life and work, see Cesare Pasini, *Ambrogio di Milano: Azione e pensiero di un vescovo* (Milan: Edizioni San Paolo, 1996); translated by Robert Grant as *Ambrose of Milan: Deeds and Thought of a Bishop* (Staten Island, N.Y.: St. Paul, 2013).

11. Hans von Campenhausen, *Ambrosius von Mailand als Kirchenpolitiker* (Berlin: de Gruyter, 1929). For a more recent representative, see Neil McLynn, *Ambrose of Milan: Church and Court in a Christian Capital* (Berkeley: University of California Press, 1994).

12. On the predominance of such "source research" in Ambrose studies, see Marcia Colish, *Ambrose's Patriarchs: Ethics for the Common Man* (Notre Dame, Ind.: University of Notre Dame Press, 2005), 9–12.

13. For studies on Ambrose's sources, see entries for individual ancient authors in Giuseppe Visonà, *Cronologia Ambrosiana/Bibliografia Ambrosiana (1900–2000)* (Milan: Biblioteca Ambrosiana, 2004).

14. The classic treatment of Ambrose's spirituality remains Ernst Dassmann, *Die Frömmigkeit des Kirchenvaters Ambrosius* (Münster: Aschendorff, 1965), who traces Ambrose's development chronologically. On Ambrose's theology more broadly, see Christoph Markschies, *Ambrosius von Mailand und die Trinitätstheologie: kirchen- und theologiegeschichtliche Studien zu Antiarianismus und Neunizänismus bei Ambrosius und im lateinischen Westen (364–381 n. Chr.)* (Tübingen: Mohr, 1995).

15. See, in particular, Thomas Graumann, *Christus interpres: Die Einheit von Auslegung und*

sion of Christology and Trinitarian theology, especially as found in his early treatises *On the Faith* and *On the Holy Spirit*, when he writes against "Arians" in northern Italy. In these works, Ambrose develops Eastern thought in Latin terms to express the Son as true God, coeternal and one in substance with the Father.[16] His pneumatology underscores the Spirit's cooperation with the Father and the Son in the work of creation and sanctification.

This theological synthesis influences all of Ambrose's writings.[17] Often inserting resonant phrases with antiheretical intent, Ambrose maintains core commitments to Nicene dogma throughout his career. Although the chronology of Ambrose's works remains disputed, there is little evidence that he changed his thoughts on major issues.[18] Thus, even one of his earliest sermons, *On Paradise*, presumes the Son's consubstantiality and coeternity with the Father.[19] His letters to the emperors Gratian, Valentinian II, and Theodosius often emphasize the role of conciliar orthodoxy in grounding civic order.[20] Likewise, the Nicene features of his hymns, though often implicit, suggest their role in communicating doctrine to his Milanese congregation.[21]

Although common themes and biblical motifs appear throughout Ambrose's corpus, his doctrinal and ascetical works often exhibit a greater theological sophistication than his catechetical sermons, which in turn communicate broad ethical concerns.[22] Ambrose's catechetical preaching on the patriarchs presents the moral teachings of Christian scripture pertinent to the swelling ranks of "ordinary" believers who were entering the church in

---

*Verkündigung in der Lukaserklärung des Ambrosius von Mailand* (Berlin: Walter de Gruyter, 1994), on Ambrose's use of Origen, and Hervé Savon, *Saint Ambroise devant l'exegese de Philon le Juif* (Paris: Études augustiniennes, 1977), for Ambrose and Philo.

16. See especially Daniel Williams, *Ambrose of Milan and the End of the Nicene-Arian Conflicts* (New York: Clarendon, 1995).

17. The best complete edition of Ambrose's works is now *Sancti Ambrosii Episcopi Mediolanensis Opera* (Milan: Città Nuova, 1977–2004). Not all of his works have been translated into English, but for a guide to available versions see Visonà, *Bibliografia Ambrosiana*.

18. For dating, I rely on Visonà, *Bibliografia Ambrosiana*, 58–138.

19. *Par.* 3.13.

20. See, e.g., *Ep.* 72, to Valentinian on the Altar of Victory.

21. Brian Dunkle, SJ, *Enchantment and Creed in the Hymns of Ambrose of Milan* (Oxford: Oxford University Press, 2016).

22. See Colish, *Ambrose's Patriarchs*, 3; note, however, the cautions of Ivor Davidson, who in his review underscores the difficulty of contextualizing many of Ambrose's works. "Book Review of Marcia Colish, *Ambrose's Patriarchs: Ethics for the Common Man*," *Scottish Journal of Theology* 63 (2010): 235–37.

the late fourth century.²³ While much of this preaching was edited and therefore "polished" before publication, we still find evidence of especially practical counsel throughout.

In all of these writings, Ambrose returns often to the dynamics of salvation and, in particular, human elevation to the divine achieved through the incarnation.²⁴ The metaphors Ambrose employs to articulate human salvation range widely, from the "ransom theory" involving the trope of the "hook" of Christ's human nature ensnaring the Devil, to the economic vision of Christ repaying the debt accrued by humanity on account of sin, to the depiction of Christ as the paragon of virtue sent to teach holiness to the people.²⁵ Despite the range of models, Ambrose often expounds these soteriological motifs consistently, according to an *intellectus* of deification that draws especially from Greek sources.

## Ambrose's Sources on Deification

Ambrose develops his thoughts on deification in dialogue with, among others, Philo, Origen, Athanasius, Basil, and Didymus.²⁶ Yet even as Ambrose recruits the tropes and biblical motifs of deification, he adopts them for his particular theological concerns.

On the one hand, Ambrose seems deliberately to avoid his sources' technical language for deification, choosing to speak of the dynamic in alternative terms. Ambrose's treatise *On the Holy Spirit*, for instance, draws heavily from Basil's treatise of the same name, which contains the Cappadocian's most famous treatment of deification, including the reference to the effects of the Spirit as "becoming a god."²⁷ While Ambrose's treatise does follow Basil in

---

23. In addition to Colish, *Ambrose's Patriarchs*, and Smith, *Christian Grace and Pagan Virtue*, see the seminal study by Graumann, Christus interpres.

24. For a still-valuable brief synopsis of Ambrose's teaching on human restoration, with relevant citations, see F. Homes Dudden, *The Life and Times of St. Ambrose* (Oxford: Clarendon Press, 1934), 624–26.

25. See the summary given by Homes Dudden, *Life and Time of St. Ambrose*, 605–12. See also Angelo Madeo, *La dottrina soteriologica di S. Ambrogio* (Bergamo: Cattaneo, 1943).

26. See the overview in Marcia Colish, *Ambrose's Patriarchs*, 1. Otto Faller's editions (Corpus Scriptorium Ecclesiasticorum Latinorum [hereafter, CSEL] 78 and 79) include essential apparatuses for his sources.

27. Translation modified from Jackson in Russell, *The Doctrine of Deification*, 209.

affirming the life in the Spirit effected through baptism,[28] the text nowhere claims that the Spirit makes us gods.[29] Basil's strong phrase has been elided in this particular borrowing.

*On the Holy Spirit* also seems to avoid the term "deification" when it appears another of its sources, Athanasius's *Letter to Serapion*. Arguing against those who subordinate the Spirit within the Godhead, Athanasius writes:

> But if "we become sharers of the divine nature" [2 Pt 1:4] by participation in the Spirit, someone would be insane to say that the Spirit is of a created nature and not of the nature of God. For it is because of this that those in whom the Spirit comes to be are deified [θεοποιοῦνται]. And if he deifies [θεοποιεῖ], there is no doubt that his nature is of God.[30]

Athanasius takes the fact of deification as a premise to support an argument about the status of the Spirit: the Spirit's power to deify, which everyone admits, implies the Spirit's full divinity. We find in Ambrose a nearly identical claim: "Who, then, can dare to say that the Holy Spirit is separated from the Father and the Son, since through Him we are worthy to be in the image and likeness of God, and through Him it happens, as the Apostle Peter says, that 'we are partakers of the divine nature' [2 Pt 1:4]?"[31] To be sure, similar claims appear in Basil and Didymus,[32] yet neither employs 2 Peter in the corresponding passages; hence, Athanasius is probably Ambrose's source. Moreover, the parallel in Ambrose's statement between the language of "image and likeness" and the Petrine citation indicate that Ambrose, too, shares a "dynamic" notion of the individual teleologically ordered to the divine nature; that is, like Athanasius, Ambrose maintains that through God's action we approach the divine image to which we have been previously conformed. Ambrose adopts not only the language and the scriptural support from Athanasius but also the basic logic, the *intellectus*, of his source. Nevertheless, he offers no equivalent for θεοποιοῦνται. While Ambrose professed the idea of deification, he does not use the language.

---

28. *Spir.* 1.6.79, see Basil, *De Spiritu Sancto* 26.64.

29. See *Spir.* 1.8.93. To be sure, there may be different emphases in the two authors; see Russell, *The Doctrine of Deification*, 209, for discussion of Basil as "more eschatological" in this passage than Athanasius had been; perhaps Ambrose has returned to Athanasius's original.

30. *Ad Serapionem* 1.24.4.

31. *Spir.* 1.6.80 (CSEL 79:48).

32. Basil, *De Spiritu Sancto* 24.56; Didymus, *De Spiritu Sancto* 1.17–19.

All attempts to explain this absence must remain speculative, yet in Ambrose's case we have two particular concerns that distinguish him among his Latin-speaking contemporaries. The first reason is style: Ambrose is a cautious Latinist who avoids neologisms, often quoting Greek words and phrases directly rather than attempting to translate them.[33] To be sure, forms of *deificus* appear in earlier Latin authors, notably Cyprian of Carthage.[34] But none of these are classical writers—Ambrose prefers Cicero to Cyprian—and many such references are suspect even for Augustine, who does occasionally speak of *deificatio*.[35] This hesitation, of course, accounts only for the absence of the *deus-facere* root, and not the identification of men as gods, as we saw, for instance, in Ambrose's use of Basil. Still, a certain traditionalism characterizes Ambrose's Latin style.

Second, Ambrose's cultural formation may have informed his linguistic choices. As a former Roman administrator and, in the words of Christopher Dawson, "the most Roman of the Fathers," Ambrose would have been especially sensitive to the pagan resonances of the language of deification.[36] We find some evidence in the most "Roman" of his writings, his letters to Valentinian II composed during the controversy over the Altar of Victory.[37] While Symmachus, the prefect of Rome, adopts traditional Roman usage in labeling an emperor as *diuus* or "divinized," Ambrose leaves the term conspicuously absent from his address to the emperor, identifying Valentinian as *Christianissime*: a superlative, but orthodox, term.[38] Perhaps Ambrose's imperial formation, unique among the Fathers, made him particularly averse to addressing mere mortals with Roman terms that implied elites could be objects of idolatry.[39]

---

33. See, e.g., *Exa.* 1.3.8.

34. See, e.g., *De zelo et liuore* 15.

35. See David Vincent Meconi, *The One Christ: St. Augustine's Theology of Deification* (Washington, D.C.: The Catholic University of America Press, 2013), 86–87, on Augustine's reticence.

36. Christopher Dawson, *Religion and the Rise of the Western Culture* (New York: Sheed and Ward, 1950), 38.

37. For the text of the exchange and some commentary, see J. H. W. G. Liebeschuetz, *Ambrose of Milan: Political Letters and Speeches* (Liverpool: Liverpool University Press, 2005), 61–94.

38. On Ambrose's *Romanitas* in these debates, see Glen Bowersock, "From Emperor to Bishop: The Self-Conscious Transformation of Political Power in the Fourth Century A.D.," *Classical Philology* 81 (1986): 304, and James Sheridan, "The Altar of Victory: Paganism's Last Battle," *L'antiquité classique* 35 (1966): 197.

39. This might be especially true if, as Colish argues, the audience for Ambrose's catechetical

## Formula(s) of Exchange

Despite the terminological gap, Ambrose's sophisticated *intellectus* of deification appears especially in his use of the standard motifs of divinization. He often employs variants of the "formula of exchange" in his early ascetical and dogmatic works. As many have noted, the formula seems most dependent on Paul's reference in 2 Corinthians 8:9 to the benefits to humanity achieved through the incarnation: "Thus, although he was rich, the Lord Jesus became poor, that we might become rich by his poverty."[40] This account of the incarnation enabling the exchange between the richness of God and the poverty of humanity appears throughout Ambrose's corpus.[41] Often Ambrose cites Paul's words to encourage his audience to embrace poverty in imitation of Christ rather than to emphasize God's action making us rich, that is, he uses 2 Corinthians 8:9 in a "non-deifying" sense.[42] Yet in a lengthy description from his early treatise *On Noah*, Ambrose engages the soteriological implications of this exchange:

> God, however, since he is everlasting, transfers the inheritance of his divine substance to just men and he himself, while being in need of nothing, gives what is his without any cost [to himself] of giving. The partakers of his goods do not weigh him down, and he enjoys his goods more by as much as we use them. Accordingly, the Lord Jesus became poor, although he was rich, so that we might be enriched by the poverty [2 Cor 8:9] of him who fulfilled each covenant with his own blood, so that he might make us co-heirs of his life and heirs of his death, by whom we have both fellowship [*consortium*] in life and the advantage of his death.[43]

Ambrose explains divine benevolence as a bestowal of God's wealth to poor humanity, a theme he borrows directly from Philo, his main source for the treatise.[44] Yet Ambrose's insertion of the Pauline text linked to deification

---

orations comprised primarily "persons with domestic and public responsibilities ... familiar as well with Roman law and ethics" (*Ambrose's Patriarchs*, 17).

40. In Ambrose's version: "denique dominus Iesus pauper factus est, cum diues esset, ut illius inopia nos ditaremur" (*Noe* 10.35; CSEL 32.1:435). For a study on Ambrose's use of the passage, see Michel Poirier, "'Christus pauper factus est' chez saint'Ambroise," *Rivista di storia e letteratura religiosa* 15 (1979): 250–57, which focuses on the trope in Ambrose's preaching on wealth and poverty.

41. In doctrinal works, see *Fid.* 3.7.52 and 5.12.146; letters, e.g., *Ep.* 17.11; preaching, *Luc.* 2.41 and 4.6.

42. E.g., *Ex. uirg.* 5.30.

43. *Noe* 10.35 (CSEL 31.1:435).

44. See Savon, *Saint Ambroise devant l'exegese de Philon*, 1.86. Philo's original appears at *Questions and Answers on Genesis* 2.10.

changes the tenor of the interpretation. In Philo God grants his "riches"—divine blessings—on the just man; Ambrose interprets the "riches" as Christ's divine inheritance offered through his "impoverishing" incarnation. By further identifying the main fruit of this inheritance as *"consortium* in life" Ambrose implies that the characteristic divine attribute offered to humanity is immortality. Hence, even in one of the most "plagiarized" of Ambrose's treatises, we find that the *intellectus* of deification is a central concern.

In his compositions addressed to "elite" Christian audiences, Ambrose explores further implications of the Pauline language in the terms of divine/human exchange established by Athanasius.[45] The incarnation enables not only the divine gift of immortality but also virtues beyond human capacities. Indeed, Ambrose's earliest and most explicit use of the classical exchange formula occurs in *On Virgins* (378), where he attributes to the practice of virginity a divine origin that enables virgins to become divine: "Let no one, then, be surprised if they are compared to the angels who are joined to the Lord of angels. For who would deny that this mode of life, which we don't easily find on earth, except since God descended into the members of an earthly body, has its source in heaven? Then a Virgin conceived, and the Word became flesh that flesh might become God."[46] The incarnation allows for the divinization of the human body because the incarnation both exemplified and enabled the heavenly practice of virginity; virgins dwell beyond even angels because their flesh is divinized. Although Ambrose hardly examines the mechanics of this "exchange," he offers a clear account of the implications of Christ's divinity for human holiness. Moreover, it should be noted that the exchange formula, speaking directly of the elevation of human capacities in the divine and even the deification language of "becoming God," appears in an ascetical treatise, in a work, that is, dedicated to a group of Christian "professionals."[47]

Elsewhere Ambrose develops his account of the human benefit of the exchange to extend beyond immortality and the gift of "godlike" virginity, to en-

---

45. For a brief treatment, see Russell, *The Doctrine of Deification*, 166–87.
46. *Virg.* 1.3.11 (*Sancti Ambrosii Episcopi Mediolanensis Opera* [hereafter, *SAEMO*] 14/1.113).
47. See Susanna Elm, "Gregory of Nazianzus: Mediation between Individual and Community," in *Group Identity and Religious Individuality in Late Antiquity*, ed. Jörg Rüpke and Éric Rebillard (Washington, D.C.: The Catholic University of America Press, 2015), 89–107, for the claim that Gregory's use of *theôsis* is part of an elite discourse.

tail a limited human participation in heaven itself. In perhaps his most famous treatise, *On the Faith*, Ambrose writes:

So that while he grants himself as a partaker of our weakness in the flesh, he makes us partakers of the divine nature in his power. But in neither one nor the other have we any natural fellowship with the celestial generation of Christ, nor is there any subjection of divinity in Christ. But as the Apostle has said that in him through that flesh which is the pledge of our salvation, we sit in the heavens [Eph 2:6] even though we don't really sit there, so also he is said to be subject in us through the assumption of our nature.[48]

Here combining the language of exchange with a reference to 2 Peter 1:4 (which I treat below), Ambrose explains the possibility of fellowship (*consortium*) with God in relation to Christ's assumption of humanity and his concomitant humiliation. Ambrose also includes the distinction between Christ's natural divinity and humanity's adopted sonship, along with the preservation of the co-equality of the Father and the Son in the incarnation, convictions that by his day were standard for Nicene theologians.[49]

Thus, exchange formulas are not merely decorative insertions drawn from the tradition, but rather they inform the development of Ambrose's Christology. In the anti-Apollinarian treatise *On the Sacrament of the Lord's Incarnation*, Ambrose states the exchange in plain terms: "I did not have what was his; he did not have what is mine. He assumed what is mine so that he might share what is his. He assumed it not to confuse, but to complete it."[50] Here Ambrose deploys the trope against his Apollinarian opponents: genuine salvation requires a complete exchange between what is human and what is divine in Christ. Unless Christ's humanity is the same as ours, and not some confusion of a divine soul and a human body, we have no hope of sharing in his true divinity.[51] In works aimed at theologians, both Nicene and Apollinarian, the rhetoric of the formula of exchange is appropriate to the learned audience.

---

48. *Fid.* 5.14.179 (CSEL 78:282–83).
49. See, e.g., Athanasius, *CA* 1.39.
50. *Incarn.* 4.23 (CSEL 79:235).
51. With parallels in Gregory of Nazianzus, *Ep.* 101.5: "What is not assumed is not saved."

## 2 Peter 1:4

The reference in 2 Peter to God's power to make Christians "partakers of the divine nature" plays an equally prominent role in Ambrose's doctrinal work.[52] As Daniel Keating argues, direct quotation of this text is generally quite rare in the early church; hence, Ambrose's penchant for the passage is striking.[53] To be sure, some of the references are unrelated to the human experience of deification, properly speaking. In *On the Faith*, 2 Peter 1:4 gives scriptural warrant for the Nicene use of the terms *substantia* and *natura* to express God's being;[54] in *On the Sacrament of the Lord's Incarnation*, the citation establishes the Son's divine nature as necessary for his role in sharing divinity;[55] finally, in *Hexameron*, Ambrose includes a reference to 2 Peter 1:4 to make clear that creation in itself is not "a partaker of the divine substance."[56] Ambrose refers to partaking in the divine nature most often when reflecting on the creator rather than on the creature.

In certain writings about the sacraments, however, Ambrose cites 2 Peter 1:4 to emphasize the human participation in the creator. In the passage from *On the Holy Spirit* cited above, he relates the Holy Spirit to the deifying effects of baptism and unction. Because baptism occurs in water and the Spirit, the Spirit must be equal to the Father and the Son in effecting human elevation to the divine: "Through him we are worthy to be in the image and likeness of God, and through him it occurs, as the Apostle Peter says, that 'we are partakers of the divine nature?'"[57] Baptism in water and the Spirit confers participation in God's life, in a dynamic intimately linked to humanity's creation in God's image.

Likewise, when preaching to initiates in his mystagogy *On the Sacraments*, Ambrose uses the bold Petrine language to awe his congregation and to reinforce the incomprehensibility of what they have experienced: "Because our Lord Jesus Christ himself is partaker both of divinity and of the body, you

---

52. On the biblical text, see James M. Starar, *Sharers in Divine Nature: 2 Peter 1:4 in its Hellenistic Context* (Stockholm: Almqvist and Wiksell International, 2000).
53. Keating, *Deification and Grace*, 36–37.
54. *Fid.* 1.19.129.
55. *Incarn.* 8.85.
56. See the edition of Gabriele Banterle, *Opere esegetiche I. I sei giorni della creazione*, SAEMO 1 (Milan: Biblioteca Ambrosiana, 1979), for the apparatus and notes on parallels.
57. *Spir.* 1.6.80 (CSEL 79:48).

too, who receive his flesh, participate through that very food in his divine substance."[58] Reference to 2 Peter 1:4, generally reserved to doctrinal reflection on the divine nature, is especially appropriate in mystagogical preaching precisely because Ambrose *wants* to speak of a mystery beyond the neophytes' imagining.[59] Thus, Ambrose's most remarkable reference to 2 Peter supports my main argument that the tropes of deification appear in Ambrose's works aimed at educated Christians, *except when* Ambrose wants to emphasize the singular wonder of the sacraments.

Ambrose's use of 2 Peter 1:4 in sacramental contexts may represent a certain development in his *intellectus* of deification.[60] According to Ernst Dassmann, the sacraments do not seem to play a "deifying" role in Ambrose's early, dogmatic works, which rather tend to emphasize ascetic perfection.[61] Perhaps Ambrose determined that Peter's account of human participation in the divine nature should be linked less to ascetical practices that were potentially confused for self-mastery and more to the reception of Christ's sacramental self-offering.[62] Ambrose came to see that participation in the divine nature is not a goal achieved by the Christian elite but rather a gift received when the church is washed in water and the Spirit and consumes Christ's humble body.

---

58. *Sacr.* 6.1.4 (CSEL 73:73); see Cyril of Jerusalem, *Mystagogical Catechesis*, 4.3 (Sources Chrétiennes 126 and 134), who introduces 2 Pt 1:4 precisely here as well. While the talk of Christ as a "partaker of divinity" may appear "inadequate" according to Chalcedonian standards, Ambrose seems to have in mind a Christology of the "giant of twin substance" apparent in his hymn "Intende Qui Regis Israel"; see *Fid.* 5.22 and Brian E. Daley, "The Giant's Twin Substances: Ambrose and the Christology of Augustine's *Contra sermonem Arianorum*," in *Augustine: Presbyter Factus Sum*, ed. Joseph T. Lienhard, Earl C. Muller, and Roland J. Teske (New York: Peter Lang, 1993), 477–95.

59. The language is probably an accurate reflection of Ambrose's preaching: Christine Mohrmann, "Le style oral du 'De Sacramentis' de Saint Ambroise," *Vigiliae Christianae* (hereafter, *VC*) 6 (1952): 168–77; see also *Fid.* 4.8.86 and *Spir.* 2.6.61.

60. Ambrose also seems to cite 2 Pt 1:4 in a sacramental context in a letter to his friend Irenaeus (*Ep.* 11), although the reference is ambivalent.

61. Dassmann, *Die Frömmigkeit*, 129.

62. For a parallel sacramental emphasis in Augustine's later reflections on deification, see Meconi, *The One Christ*, 175, citing Karl Adam. On themes of participation in Ambrose's final work, the *Exposition on Ps 118*, see Gerald Boersma, "Participation in Christ: Psalm 118 in Ambrose and Augustine," *Augustinianum* 54 (2014): 173–97.

## Divine Adoption

While the exchange formulas and the language of 2 Peter 1:4 are employed for distinctive theological and catechetical ends, the broader dynamic of deification appears everywhere in Ambrose's writings. Like many of his contemporaries, Ambrose invokes certain features of deification by employing the language of divine adoption: God communicates his divinity to humans by making them sons of God through grace. The primarily Johannine motif is examined at length in his doctrinal treatise *On the Faith*. In books 4 and 5, Ambrose explains that the incarnation of the Son of God makes possible the identification of Christians as *filii dei*. Generally, he refers to divine adoption to speak of the Son's role in performing a divine work. Thus he explains in book 5, "Indeed, every creature serves, but the Son of God, who makes from servants sons of God, does not serve."[63] Ambrose uses the motif of divine adoption much like the formulas of exchange and 2 Peter, primarily to establish Christological orthodoxy: Christ can make sons of God because he is God.

At the same time, Ambrose also treats the effect of divine adoption on Christians, especially by linking adoption and sanctification. The holy are identified as sons of God. In *Hexameron* we find: "The soul that is conformed to the Lord Jesus is in the image of God, and those who are conformed to the Son of God are saints."[64] Preaching in the *Hexameron* to a congregation of initiates, Ambrose employs the language of divine elevation in broad terms. He also links adoption to creation in the image and likeness, the final theme of deification that influences Ambrose's theology.

## Image and Likeness

The reference to Genesis 1:26 in the passage above reflects the pervasive role of humanity as made unto the *imago dei* in Ambrose's anthropology. Because humanity is created in the image and likeness of God, participation in the divine relates to the perfection of a primordial relationship.[65]

---

63. *Fid.* 5.11; see *Spir.* 2.7.64 and 2.8.82, where the language again establishes a doctrinal point, namely the full divinity of the Spirit.

64. *Exa.* 6.8.46 (CSEL 32,1:237).

65. In general, Ambrose does not distinguish between "image" and "likeness"; Dudden, *Life and Times of St. Ambrose*, 612n3. For a recent treatment, see Gerald Boersma, *Augustine's Early Theology of Image: A Study in the Development of Pro-Nicene Theology* (Oxford: Oxford University Press, 2016), 87–134.

Ambrose's most extensive treatment appears in his commentary on Genesis 1 in the *Hexameron*, and his discussion of the sixth day in particular. In chapter 8 of the section on that day, he explores at length the relevance of the *ad imaginem dei* for deification. Following Basil, he first clarifies that the divine image subsists in the soul rather than in the body. Developing Basil's thought further, however, Ambrose claims that the image of God is manifest especially in the soul's capacity to imagine the extent of the world:[66]

Thus the soul that is unto the image of God [*ad imaginem dei*] acts not just by corporeal means, but by an acuity of heart that sees what is absent, in its gaze traveling across the sea, in its vision racing all over, investigating what is hidden, applying its senses here and there in a single instant to the ends of the whole earth and the secrets of the world; this is the soul that is joined to God, adheres to Christ, descends to Hell, and, set free, dwells in heaven.[67]

Ambrose first argues for the soul's capacity for a certain omnipresence: like God, who is not circumscribed by spatial boundaries, the soul can be many places at once. His description suggests certain innate "divine" features of the soul, a psychology that would be especially fit for a robust account of the soul's elevation to God through deification. But then Ambrose develops the features of this innate omnipresence in a Christological key: through its adherence to Christ, the soul can travel also to the underworld (*infernum*) and to heaven (*in caelo*). Ambrose develops Basil's thought to argue that the soul in the process of divinization is conformed to Christ in his passion, descent, and ascension.

The Christological contours of this image are emphasized throughout Ambrose's corpus. Thus, commenting on Psalm 38, he writes: "In what image then does the human being walk? He walks in fact in the one to whose likeness he was made, that is, to the image of God; but the image of God is Christ, who is the splendor of God's glory and the image of his substance."[68] We see a progressive ordering of the soul created "to the image" elevated to unity in

---

66. Jan den Boeft, "Delight and Imagination: Ambrose's Hymns," *VC* 62 (2008): 425–40, argues that this is an Ambrosian invention.

67. *Exa.* 6.8.45 (CSEL 32.1:236); see *Psal. 118*, 5.32 and 8.23.

68. *Psal.* 38.24.1 (CSEL 64:202). Ambrose likewise consistently distinguishes our formation *to the image* (or *likeness*) from Christ as the image in *Psal. 118* 10.16 (CSEL 62:212): "Si intellegas imaginem, uidebis ad imaginem; homo enim non est imago dei, sed ad similitudinem factus est."

"the image" of God, that is Christ himself.[69] Thus, "the image" conforms humanity "to the image."

Elsewhere Ambrose indicates particular features of this likeness: conformity to the image of God involves flight from sin;[70] the image is interior rather than exterior.[71] Likewise, reason (or *intellectus*) is linked to the image of God, as he notes in commenting on Psalm 48: "Because the person did not understand that he was in honor—it is honor, of course, because whoever was made capable of reason was made unto the image of God—he was likened to the beasts that have no sense; but the one who understood [*intellexit*] is likened to angels."[72] In various terms, then, Ambrose presents the divine likeness as elevating humanity above terrestrial limits.

Unlike the language of divine exchange and participation, which tend to be limited to doctrinal and ascetical works, the language of *ad imaginem dei* appears throughout Ambrose's corpus. Given the scriptural source and its prominence in all early Christian literature, this should be expected. Still, it shows that Ambrose frequently used familiar or "non-scandalous" language to remind his congregation that their human nature was dynamically ordered to the divine life. Eriugena's claim that deification is "most of all" present in Ambrose among Latin authors may find special warrant in the bishop's emphatic focus on human beings created in the divine image.

## Nature and Grace

Moreover, the broad outlines of Ambrose's strategy support Eriugena's suggestion that Latin theologians may have thought the language of *deificatio* was "incomprehensible" to those who could not transcend "carnal cogitations." At the same time, I maintain that Ambrose often rendered the doctrine of deification in terms of the distinction between nature and grace.[73] As Am-

---

69. The distinction is important for understanding the proper ordering of human nature to perfection in Christ. Thus, in *On the Faith* he writes, "Quod igitur tibi usurpas, filio dei derogas, cum utique nisi per imaginem dei ad imaginem dei esse non possis" (*Fid.* 1.7; CSEL 78:21). Augustine may have entertained (and abandoned) this position early in his career; see Roland Teske, "The Image and Likeness of God in St. Augustine's *De Genesi ad litteram liber imperfectus*," *Augustinianum* 10 (1990): 445.

70. E.g., *Psal.* 36.73.1.

71. *Inst.* 3.30 and 3.40; *Ep.* 9.69.19; on the inner man, see Smith, *Christian Grace and Pagan Virtue*, 22–23.

72. *Psal.* 48.20.1 (CSEL 64:373).

73. For Ambrose on grace, see Antonio Bonato, "Incidenze della Grazia in Sant'Ambrogio," in

brose's preaching turned to address catechumens, that is, beginners, he often used the language of nature and grace to communicate the process of deification in a pastoral context. This development helps explain not only the absence of *deus-facere* language but also the reduced role that the other tropes of deification play in these texts.

There is little evidence of nature and grace deployed in tandem in early Christian writings. A few references develop the Pauline distinction between divine law and grace to apply it to nature and grace.[74] Tertullian makes some reference to the pair in *De Anima*: "This will be the force of the divine grace, stronger indeed than nature, which possesses in us the free power of the will underlying it, which Greeks call *autexousia*," one of the earliest suggestions that divine grace somehow supervenes on nature, indicating that grace renders possible the movement of the natural will to God.[75] A few Greek sources make a similar suggestion, but nowhere in the surviving literature do we find a programmatic juxtaposition of nature and grace.[76]

When we come to Ambrose, however, the pair acquires a fixed and somewhat technical sense. Ambrose employs nature and grace both independently and as a pair throughout his career.[77] *Gratia*, for Ambrose, has meanings ranging from any "gift" at all to God's action in created existence; *natura* has a broad valence that comprises both the cosmos and theological terms (that is, the "divine nature"). Yet Ambrose distinguishes grace from nature to identify God's work beyond the regular order of the cosmos. For instance, he notes in the late work *On the Mysteries* that the *natura* of rock in Exodus 17:6 would never have produced water were it not for divine *gratia* accomplishing the miracle.[78] Grace, then, becomes an equivalent for God's operation beyond the order he has established.

At the same time, the distinction applies to the moral order, where Am-

---

*Dizionario di spiritualità biblicopatristica: i grandi temi della S. scrittura per la "lectio divina,"* ed. Salvatore Alberto Panimolle and Franco Bolgiani (Rome: Borla, 1992), 270–321, and Eduardo Toraño López, *La teología de la Gracia en Ambrosio de Milán* (Madrid: Facultad de Teología "San Dámaso," 2006).

74. The Pauline background is Eph 2:3–7.

75. *De anima* 21.6 (Corpus Christianorum: Series Latina 2.814): "Haec erit uis diuinae gratiae, potentior utique natura, habens in nobis subiacentem sibi liberam arbitrii potestatem quod αὐτεξούσιον dicitur, quae cum sit et ipsa naturalis atque mutabilis, quoquo uertitur, natura conuertitur."

76. See, e.g., Origen, *Fragmenta in Lucam* 174; on Origen and grace and nature, see Benjamin Drewery, *Origen and the Doctrine of Grace* (London: Epworth Press, 1960), 64.

77. See Baziel Maes, *La loi naturelle selon Ambroise de Milan* (Rome: Gregorianum, 1967), 60–64.

78. *Myst.* 9.51.

brose identifies certain acts as good by nature and other acts as graced, transcending natural demands. In the early *On Widows*, he links the Pauline precept/counsel pair to nature and grace: "A precept calls one back to nature, while the counsel encourages one to grace."[79] Building on Ambrose's account of the Stoic notion of the natural law, the distinction between grace and nature shows the place of transcendent ends for human agents.

Ambrose's catechetical works clarify that both nature and grace are gratuitous participations in the divine. In preaching on Joseph, Ambrose interprets the silver cup that Joseph both places and discovers in Benjamin's sack (Gn 44:1–17) as a type for Christ's role in bestowing creation and salvation: Christ finds valuable in us what belongs to him, the same wealth that he has placed in humanity: "We possess the silver of nature, we also possess the silver of grace. Nature is the work of the Creator, grace the gift of the Redeemer."[80] There is no sense that nature is simply inert material to be transformed by grace; rather, human nature contains a divine gift that is integral to its graced redemption. The *argentum* of nature and grace is the same stuff.

Moreover, Ambrose explicitly links grace and human deification in viewing the primordial loss of status as "gods" to a loss of grace. In his early homily *On Paradise*, Ambrose links one of the standard biblical references to deification to the terms of grace. Like many of his predecessors, Ambrose identifies the serpent's promise to Eve that eating the fruit of the forbidden tree would make her and Adam "like gods" (Gn 3:5) as a treacherous inversion of the theme of deification. Ambrose argues that when they in fact ate the fruit they lost their path to divinity by losing their "grace": "And he tricked them with the 'humans are as gods.' For not only did humans cease to be as gods, but even those who were quasi-gods, that is, those to whom it was said, 'I said to you, you are gods' [Ps 82:6], lost their own grace."[81] Here Ambrose links divine status to the presence of grace. In this early popular work, Ambrose presents the first sin as a loss both of grace and of divinity.

Indeed, Ambrose presents God's graced operation directly to deification, clarifying what the incarnation brings to the created image of God. One passage from *On the Sacrament of the Lord's Incarnation* suggests precisely this

79. *Vid.* 12.72 (*SAEMO* 14/1.304).
80. *Ios.* 11.63 (CSEL 32.2:112).
81. *Par.* 13.61; there is no corresponding grace/divinity connection in Philo's treatment of the text in *Questions and Answers on Genesis*, Ambrose's source for much of the work.

overlap between the work of grace and the dynamic of deification and may mark the shift I am identifying, where deification talk dovetails with the diction of nature and grace. Speaking of exchange, Ambrose explains that the incarnation was necessary to elevate humanity to the divine life. He writes:

> Therefore he received from us what he offered as his own for us, so that he might redeem us from what was our own; and what was not our own he granted to us from his own divine bounty. Thus he offered himself according to our nature that he might accomplish a work beyond our nature.... and many things will you find in him both according to nature and beyond nature.[82]

For Ambrose the work of the incarnation is not only a process of atonement for sin, a redemption from a fallen state, but rather a conferral of what is beyond the human condition. This rescue to the divine, that is, deification, is expressed in terms of the work that is done "beyond nature."[83]

Nature, grace, and deification are further linked in Ambrose's catechetical treatise on *Elijah and Fasting*. Here Ambrose explores the theme of "drunkenness" (*ebrietas*) as distinguished between one of guilt and one of grace: "There is therefore a drunkenness of guilt and one of grace; and perhaps this latter one, of grace, is also of nature, because we who are made according to the image and likeness of God should be filled with the Holy Spirit."[84] Here interweaving the theme of image and likeness, which, according to Ambrose, are naturally inherent in humanity, and the fullness of the Spirit, which is divine, Ambrose relies on the language of nature and grace to express what is standard in the "dynamic" tradition of deification.[85]

Ambrose's use of nature and grace, then, is not a mere "transactional" and commoditized account of deification.[86] Rather, by employing the pair Ambrose extends the purview of God's action in the cosmos beyond human elevation to comprise all that is "natural." At times, as in his treatment of the Book of Exodus, he speaks of the "nature" of a mineral and the "grace" of the miraculous; at other times, though, the action of grace is limited to the virtuous ac-

---

82. *Incarn.* 6.54 (CSEL 79:250).
83. See also *Hel.* 21.20.
84. *Hel.* 16.61 (CSEL 32.2:448).
85. See *Psal. 118* 1.9, on the "observation of the commandments of God increasing the grace of its own nature."
86. McGuckin, *The Westminster Handbook*, 149: "The pre-Augustinian Latin ideas on grace were more discrete and 'transactional.'"

tions of the individual. Especially in the catechetical works, grace is precisely what incorporates the Christian into the divine life.

## Why the Language of Nature and Grace?

Why, then, does Ambrose favor the trope of nature and grace in these works? If "deification" talk is incomprehensible, Ambrose's preference for the language of nature and grace may render the same dynamic in a pastoral register. Indeed, I have focused on citations of the pair in texts that speak to the neophytes' experience of God's action through their incorporation into the community of the baptized. While I do not have the space to explore the connection here, it is worth noting that Ambrose's contemporary "pastoral" theologian, John Chrysostom, who was preaching in the East in the same period, also employs the language of nature and grace in relation to human elevation.[87] In the popular preaching of both pastors, the preference for the nature/grace pair seems to parallel a general avoidance of the chief motifs and terms of deification.[88]

Thus, Ambrose uses nature and grace to articulate the difference between ordinary, fallen life and the life in the Trinity. The role of grace in elevating human perception and virtue communicates deification to a congregation intent on the concrete difference that their initiation brings; these are not monks, but they want to know how baptism changes them. He can cite grace's elevation of nature in celebration of the eucharist and in scriptural miracles. Speaking of the consecration, he states: "Thus how many examples must we use to show that the bread is not what nature has formed but what the blessing has consecrated, and that the force of the blessing is greater than the force of nature, because nature itself is transformed by the blessing."[89] Likewise, grace is key for enacting the soul's participation in the life of God.[90] For Ambrose the pastor, the nature/grace pair, more than the language of exchange and partic-

---

87. See John Chrysostom, e.g., *Contra Anomoeos* 10.35 and *In Heb* 7.6. Gérard Philips, "La grâce chez les Orientaux," *Ephemerides Theologicae Lovanienses* 48 (1972): 37–50, focuses on Palamas and contemporary Orthodox theology. Palamas has ἡ θεοποιὸς χάρις, i.e., "deifying grace" (e.g., *Epistula* 5 *ad Acindynum et Barlaam* 5.15–16).
88. Russell, *The Doctrine of Deification*, 233.
89. *Myst.* 9.50 (CSEL 73:110); see *Sacr.* 4.4.18.
90. *Psal. 118* 20.30.459.

ipation in divine substance, offers a ready tool for explaining the distinction between the divine and human roles in the process of deification.

## Conclusion

While Ambrose employs deifying motifs throughout his career, a general pattern suggests that the clear divine/human exchange formulas and direct citations of 2 Peter are more characteristic of his ascetical and dogmatic writings, where they are employed mostly to establish what the Father, Son, and Holy Spirit can perform in humanity and what humanity can experience through the incarnation. This essay, then, has attempted to track this development in a synthesis. With Eriugena as an authority, I have highlighted the range of concerns in Ambrose that attest to an ample, if flexible, vision of human elevation into divine grace. Although Ambrose's patriarch treatises and catechetical works might focus more on the practice of human virtues through the language of grace, this preaching nonetheless presupposes a theological anthropology that affirms the dynamic interaction of God and human beings rendered possible by the incarnation of the Word, a concern common to all theologians of the fourth century. In Ambrose's day, at least, talk of deification, nature, and grace should be seen not in competition but as complementary.

*Vít Hušek*

# 8. REBIRTH INTO A NEW MAN
*Deification in Jerome*

Jerome (ca. 347–420) is known as the foremost biblical scholar of the ancient Latin church and a fervent promoter of ascetic ideals. He was well versed in Latin, Greek, and Hebrew as well as in classical and ecclesiastical literature. From about 373, he spent much of his life in the East, mostly in Antioch and Bethlehem, except for the period he spent as the secretary of Pope Damasus in Rome between 382 and 385. He is the father of the Latin Bible, the Vulgate, but also an author of biblical commentaries and a translator of Origen's and Didymus's commentaries.

All this may lead one to suppose that on deification Jerome would have had much in common with the Greek Fathers, yet an examination of Jerome's work gives us the opposite impression at first. Despite his vast knowledge of Greek literature, his fondness for analyzing Hebrew and Greek words, and his affection for comparing Greek and Latin translations, Jerome never uses any of the Greek expressions for deification.[1] Neither does he use the Latin words *deificare*, *deificatio*, or their derived forms.[2] Unlike some other

---

This study is a result of research funded by the Czech Science Foundation under the project GA ČR P401/12/G168, "History and Interpretation of the Bible."

1. See Norman Russell, "The Greek Vocabulary of Deification," appendix 2 in *The Doctrine of Deification in the Greek Patristic Tradition* (Oxford: Oxford University Press, 2004), 333–44. We may guess whether the reason is that none of the terms is used in the Septuagint or the New Testament.

2. The Patrologia Latina Database and CETEDOC/The Library of Latin Texts were consulted.

Latin authors, he does not describe divinization using the terms *commercium* or *commutatio*. When using the language of *glorification*, Jerome describes the glory of God[3] or glorification of the human body after the resurrection (with a focus on discordances in the biblical text).[4] On that account, it is not surprising that Gustav Bardy, in his survey of Latin patristic thought on deification, does not even mention Jerome's name.[5]

The purpose of this essay is to argue that the doctrine of deification holds a place in Jerome's thought, even if this is not apparent at first glance. It will be shown that Jerome emphasizes the Christological, sacramental, moral, and ascetical dimensions of deification. His understanding of deification is based on adoptive sonship, which enables us to become sons of God and to participate in divine life. Our adoption and participation in God calls every Christian to pursue moral excellence, though it finds its eminent form in the "angelic life" of virgins and hermits. Finally, this essay illustrates Jerome's concern to save the adequate value of our free decisions as we grow in sonship and participate more in God.

## Adoptive Sonship

Jerome explicitly links the Latin word *adoptio* with the Greek New Testament term υἱοθεσία[6] and repeatedly emphasizes the difference between Christ's divine sonship and human adoptive sonship. Christ is the eternal Son of God by his nature, but we become sons of God through adoption. Commenting on the verse in Ephesians 1:5, "He destined us in love to be his sons through Jesus Christ," Jerome follows Origen's interpretation and explains this difference both theologically and terminologically. Christ "always was and never experienced a beginning of his existence," in contrast to those "who previously did

---

3. E.g., *Epistle* 106.12 (Corpus Scriptorium Ecclesiasticorum Latinorum [hereafter, CSEL] 55:255): "*Universum semen Iacob, magnificate eum,* pro quo in Graeco scriptum sit, δοξάσατε αὐτὸν, id est 'glorificate eum.' Sed sciendum, quod, ubicumque in Graeco 'glorificate' scriptum est, Latinus interpres 'magnificate' transtulerit."

4. *Ep.* 119 (CSEL 55:446–69) dealing with "the most difficult question of the apostle Paul," i.e., the interpretation of 1 Cor 15:51 (with regard to the contradictory reading of various Greek manuscripts) and 1 Thes 4:17.

5. Gustave Bardy, "Divinisation: Chez les Pères Latins," in *Dictionnaire de spiritualité*, ed. Marcel Viller et al. (Paris: Beauchesne, 1957), 3:1389–98.

6. *Ep.* 121.9 (CSEL 56.1:40): "*Quorum est,* inquit, *adoptio,* quae significantius Graece dicitur υἱοθεσία." The word υἱοθεσία occurs five times in the New Testament: Rom 8:15, 8:23, 9:4; Gal 4:5; Eph 1:5.

not exist."⁷ Accordingly, Jerome says, the word ὁρισθέντος ("declared," Rom 1:4) is used for Christ, while the words προορίσας ("destined," Eph 1:5) and προορισθέντες ("having been destined," Eph 1:11) are used for us.⁸ To become adoptive sons of God, we have first to "receive faith in and knowledge of his Son Jesus Christ.... Before we existed we were predestined and then we received the spirit of adoption when we believed in the Son of God."⁹

Inspired by Psalm 81:6, "I say, 'You are gods, children of the Most High, all of you,'" Jerome modifies his vocabulary; not only are we called "sons of God" but also "gods."¹⁰ A contrast between Christ and us is emphasized again. While Eunomius and Arius stress the similarity between Christ's and our sonship, Jerome states that we "are gods" not by our nature but by grace (*quod dii sumus, non sumus natura, sed gratia*).¹¹ The reason that God created peo-

---

7. *In epistolam ad Ephesios* 1.1.5, in Patrologia Latina (ed. Migne) (hereafter, PL), 26:448C; trans. Ronald Heine, *The Commentaries of Origen and Jerome on St. Paul's Epistle to the Ephesians* (Oxford: Oxford University Press, 2002), 87.

8. *In Eph.* 1.1.5 (PL 26:448C–D): "Differentiam vero Graeci sermonis προορίσας et ὁρισθέντος Latinus sermo non explicat. Superior quippe sermo ad eos refertur, qui antea non fuerunt, et priusquam fierent, de his cogitatum est, et postea substiterunt. Inferior vero de eo quem nulla cogitatio, voluntas nulla praecessit, sed semper fuit, et numquam ut esset, accepit exordium. Unde recte nunc de his qui cum ante non essent, postea substiterunt, dicitur προορισθέντες. De Filio vero, hoc est, de Domino nostro Iesu Christo, in alio loco scriptum est ὁρισθέντος, quia semper cum Patre fuit, et numquam eum ut esset, voluntas paterna praecessit. Ex quo colligitur semper Patrem, semper fuisse Filium, et in quibus aeternitas coaequalis est, eamdem esse naturam" (*Commentaries*, trans. Heine, 87). See Origen, *In epistolam ad Ephesios* 1.5, in J. A. F. Gregg, "The Commentary of Origen upon the Epistle to the Ephesians," *Journal of Theological Studies* 3 (1902): 235.

9. *In Eph.* 1.1.5 (PL 26:448D–449A): "Nec non etiam hoc inferendum, quod cum praedestinet nos, sive praefiniat Deus, in adoptionem filiorum per Iesum Christum; tamen non ante filii esse possumus, nisi Filii eius Iesu Christi fidem et intelligentiam recipiamus. Et ille quidem natura Filius est; nos vero adoptione. Ille numquam Filius non fuit: nos antequam essemus, praedestinati sumus, et tunc spiritum adoptionis accepimus, quando credidimus in Filium Dei" (*Commentaries*, trans. Heine, 88, translation modified). See *In Eph.* 1.1.9 and 2.3.14 (PL 26:453B–D and 489D–490A); *Adversus Iovinianum* 2.29 (PL 23:326A–C); *In Ecclesiasten* 4.7–8 (Corpus Christianorum: Series Latina [hereafter, CCL] 72:286); *Tractatus in Psalmos* 109.3 (CCL 78:224); *Tract. Ps. alt.* 88.4 and 88.7 (CCL 78:408 and 410).

10. *Tract. Ps.* 81.6 (CCL 78:86); *In Matthaeum* 4.23.8–10 (CCL 77:212–13).

11. *Tract. Ps.* 81.6 (CCL 78:86): "Audiat Eunomius, audiat Arrius, qui dicunt Filium Dei similiter esse filium, ut nos sumus. Quod dii sumus, non sumus natura, sed gratia." For Jerome's authorship of *Tract. Ps.* and Origen's influence, see Lorenzo Perrone, "Riscoprire Origene oggi: prime impressioni sulla raccolta di omelie sui Salmi nel *Codex Monacensis Graecus 314*," *Adamantius* 18 (2012): 41–58, at 55–56; Alessandro Capone, "Folia uero in uerbis sunt: parola divina e lingua umana nei *Tractatus in Psalmos* attribuiti a Gerolamo," *Adamantius* 19 (2013): 437–56; Lorenzo Perrone, "*Codex Monacensis Graecus 314*: 29 Psalmenhomilien des Origenes," in Origenes, *Die neuen Psalmenhomilien: Eine kritische Edition des Codex Monacensis Monacensis Graecus 314*, Die griechische christliche Schriftsteller der ersten Jahrhunderte (hereafter, GCS) NF 19 (Berlin: de Gruyter, 2015), 1–72, at 8–9.

ple is "so that they may become gods" (*ut de hominibus dii fiant*).[12] Not only are kings and princes invited to "become gods" and adoptive sons; this invitation is extended to all (Ps 81:6, *omnes*).[13] The adoptive children of God may be called "gods" or also "holy" (see 1 Pt 1:16), with the same differentiation: Christians are called gods "according to grace" (*secundum gratiam*), not "by nature" (*natura*).[14] Metaphorically, Jerome also uses the language of "gods" for those who abandon human vices and adopt a divine way of thinking (e.g., the remnant of Israel),[15] for the patriarchs and prophets (who also "have received the spirit of adoption"),[16] and for the apostles (e.g., when Peter, on all of their behalf, confesses that Jesus is the son of God).[17] In comparison with Origen, whose distinction between the proper (*principaliter*) and inexact (*abusive*) use of the term "god" seems to be echoed here,[18] Jerome is much less willing to call the saints and the perfect Christians "gods," as if they ceased to be men,[19] and repeatedly emphasizes that God and men do not share the same nature.

What, then, is the positive content of adoptive sonship and our "being gods"? Jerome explains it using an image of Christian growth and maturation. "Be as I am, for I was as you are," says St. Paul (Gal 4:12a). The Apostle becomes weak on account of those who are weak (see 1 Cor 9:22), that is, those who cannot be addressed "as spiritually minded people."[20] As they are not yet

---

12. *Tract. Ps.* 81.6 (CCL 78:86): "*Quotquot enim eum receperunt, dedit eis potestatem filios Dei fieri.* Propterea feci hominem, ut de hominibus dii fiant. *Ego dixi: dii estis, et filii Excelsi omnes.* Videte quanta sit dignitas: et dii vocamur, et filii." See *In Matth.* 4.23.8–10 (CCL 77:212–13): "Et ne infinita replicem, quomodo unus per naturam Deus et unus Filius, non praeiudicat caeteris ne per adoptionem dii vocentur, et filii."

13. *Tract. Ps.* 81.6 (CCL 78:86): "Non dixit: *Ego dixi: dii estis,* reges et principes, sed *omnes*: quibus aequaliter corpus dedi et animam et spiritum, aequaliter donavi et deitatem et adoptionem."

14. *Tract. Ps.* 76.14 (CCL 78:58–59): "Si uolumus ut Xpistus habitet in nobis, simus sancti: Dei enim uia in sancto est. *Quis Deus magnus sicut Deus noster?* Sicut enim *sunt dii multi, et domini multi* (hoc loquitur apostolus. *Deus stetit in synagoga deorum. Ego dixi: dii estis, et filii Excelsi omnes.* Et ad Moysen *dedi te deum Faraonis*): sancti dii dicuntur. Illi secundum gratiam dii, tu enim natura Deus es."

15. *In Michaeam* 1.2.11–13 (CCL 76:454–55).

16. *In Eph.* 2.3.5–7 (PL 23:479C–D) (*Commentaries*, trans. Heine, 145). See Origen, *Commentarius in Iohannem* 20.27 and 20.29 (GCS 10:363 and 367).

17. *In Matth.* 3.16.15–16 (CCL 77:140); see *In Gal.* 1.1.11–12 (CCL 77A:25).

18. Origen, *Commentarius in Canticum canticorum*, prol. 2.34 (GCS 33:71); see Russell, *Doctrine of Deification*, 145–46.

19. See Russell, *Doctrine of Deification*, 146 and nn 47–52.

20. *In epistolam ad Galatas* 2.4.12a (CCL 77A:120): "Quod dicit tale est: quomodo *ego* vobis infirmis sum factus infirmus et non potui loqui ut spiritualibus sed quasi carnalibus et parvulis in Christo." Translated by Andrew Cain, *St. Jerome, Commentary on Galatians* (Washington, D.C.: The Catholic University of America Press, 2010), 168.

ready for solid food, he feeds them with the milk of the Gospel (see 1 Cor 3:1–2). The Apostle does not wish for them "to remain infants forever" but to guide them "gradually to adolescence and then adulthood," urging them to develop "a taste for greater things."[21] For Jerome, the Christian's growth is the imitation of Christ who "emptied himself and took on the form of a servant and was found in appearance as a man [see Phil 2:6–8], so that we 'become gods from humans' [*ut nos dii fieremus ex hominibus*, see Ps 81:6] and no longer die but be raised with Christ [see 1 Cor 3:1] and be called his friends [see Jn 15:15] and brothers [see Jn 20:17]."[22]

For Jerome, adoptive sonship and our "becoming gods" consist in the Son of God assuming our human condition in order to communicate to us his life and a new relationship with God. A similar expression of the great exchange is based on Galatians 3:13, "Christ redeemed us from the curse of the law by becoming a curse for us." Jerome adds:

> An insult to the Lord is therefore a reason for us to boast. He died so that we might live. He descended into Hades so that we might rise to heaven. He became foolish so that we might become wise. He emptied himself of the fullness and form of God and assumed the form of a servant so that the fullness of divinity might dwell in us and so that we might go from being servants to masters.[23]

Our adoption as children of God is closely related to baptism. Although Christ is free from sin, he receives the baptism of repentance to inculcate in others the need to be cleansed through baptism and "be born as sons by a new spiritual adoption" (*in filios nova spiritus adoptione generari*).[24] After the resurrection, the apostles receive the grace of the Holy Spirit to forgive sins, to

---

21. Ibid.: "Quia necdum poteratis solido cibo vesci, Evangelico vos tantum lacte potavi nolens in aetate vos semper infantiae permanere, sed paulatim ad adolescentiam et iuventutem usque perducere, ut solidum cibum possetis accipere; ita et vos debetis esse *sicut et ego* sum, perfectiora videlicet sapere, dimisso lacte, ad fortiores cibos et ad pabula transire maiora."

22. Ibid. (120–21, translation modified): "qui non rapinam arbitratus est se esse aequalem Deo, sed semetipsum exinanivit formam servi accipiens et habitu inventus est ut homo, ut nos dii fieremus ex hominibus et non ultra moreremur, sed consurgentes Christo amici eius diceremur et fratres ut esset discipulus sicut magister et servus sicut Dominus."

23. *In Gal.* 2.3.13b–14 (CCL 77A:93; trans. Cain, 144): "Iniuria itaque Domini nostra gloria est, ille mortuus est ut nos uiueremus, ille descendit ad inferos ut nos ascenderemus ad caelum, ille factus est stultitia ut nos sapientia fieremus." See Alexey Fokin, "The Doctrine of Deification in Western Fathers of the Church: A Reconsideration," in *Für uns und für unser Heil. Soteriologie in Ost und West*, ed. Theresia Hainthaler et al. (Innsbruck: Tyrolia Verlag, 2014), 207–20, at 210.

24. *In Gal.* 2.4.4–5 (CCL 77A:108; trans. Cain, 157).

baptize, to make people sons of god, and to "bestow upon the faithful the spirit of adoption."²⁵

Baptism, the water of rebirth, transforms our human life into a "new creation" (2 Cor 5:17). We are buried with Christ in baptism before being raised with Him (see Col 2:12) or—as Jerome puts it—"reborn into a new man" (*in novum renati hominem*). Therefore, "we should believe that we are now already what we will become."²⁶ This is "a new creation [see Gal 6:15], into which our lowly body is being transformed into the glorious body of Christ [see Phil 3:21]."²⁷ Our future body can be neither circumcised nor kept uncircumcised (see Gal 5:6). It is "not to say that its substance changes; it is just different in glory."²⁸

## Participation in Divine Life

Jerome links adoptive sonship with participation in divine life. In a passage from the *Tractates on the Psalms*, Jerome uses "adoption" and "participation" as parallel terms. "There is only one true God and many are called 'gods' by participation in Him, just as there is the only Son of God and many are called 'sons' by adoption."²⁹

Similarly, Jerome links participation in God and likeness with God. Those who have been united with Christ in a death such as his will be united with him upon the resurrection, according to the Apostle (see Rom 6:5). Jerome here moves from the vocabulary of "likeness" (ὁμοίωμα, *similitudo*) to

---

25. *Ep.* 120.9 (CSEL 55:494): "Primo igitur die resurrectionis eius acceperunt [*sc.* apostoli] spiritus sancti gratiam, qua peccata dimitterent et baptizarent et filios dei facerent et spiritum adoptionis credentibus largirentur."

26. *In Gal.* 3.6.15 (CCL 77A:224; trans. Cain, 265): "Nos qui iam nunc in baptismate Christo consurreximus, in novum renati hominem, nec *circumcisioni*, nec *praeputio* serviamus, sed quod futuri sumus iam nunc nos esse credamus."

27. *In Gal.* 3.6.15 (CCL 77A:223; trans. Cain, 264): "Cum enim sancto mundus fuerit crucifixus, nequaquam est ei *circumcisio* et *praeputium*, non Iudaeus neque gentilis, *sed nova creatura* in quam transfiguratur corpus humilitatis nostrae conforme corporis gloriae Christi."

28. *In Gal.* 3.6.15 (CCL 77A, 223–24; trans. Cain, 265): "Cum de corpore humilitatis transformati fuerimus in corpus gloriae Domini Iesu Christi, illud habebimus corpus quod nec Iudaeus possit incidere nec cum *praeputio* custodire gentilis, non quo aliud iuxta substantiam sit, sed quo iuxta gloriam sit diversum."

29. *Tractatus in Psalmos series altera* 10.8 (CCL 78:363–64): "Sicut enim unus est verus Deus, et si multi sunt dii qui participatione illius appellantur, et unus est filius Dei unigenitus, alii autem adoptione vocantur."

"participation" (*participatio*), and more specifically, from "likeness of resurrection" (ὁμοίωμα τῆς ἀναστάσεως, *similitudo resurrectionis*) to "participation in life" (*vitae participes*): "Those who were made partakers of his death will also be made partakers of [his] life."³⁰

Jerome draws explicitly on the participation language of 2 Peter 1:4 three times, in *Adversus Iovinianum* in each instance.³¹ He follows closely the biblical text and uses the vocabulary of *consortium* (not *participatio*) without mercantile or ontological connotations. His focus is on the incarnation and its moral and ascetical implications. Our participation in God's substance is made possible by the incarnation and is explained by means of the exchange formula. The purpose behind the Word becoming flesh (see Jn 1:14) is "that we might pass from the flesh into the Word." The Word does not cease to be divine; our human nature is not changed but "the glory is increased."³²

While we live in this earthly life, our participation in God consists in pursuing moral excellence. If we fail to reach perfection, then the whole process of that growth is worthless. Jerome, again, gives us the image of the grape and its maturation "through many stages between the vine and the winepress." Similarly, the Christian goes through stages of "infancy, childhood, adolescence, and young adulthood, until he becomes a mature man." If the work is not brought to an end, which indicates perfection and moral excellence, and "if the work lacks that final touch," the whole effort is in vain.³³ However, we

---

30. *In Abacuc* 2.3.10–13 (CCL 76A:641): "Qui facti fuerant participes mortis huius, vitae quoque participes fierent." See Rom 6:5, Εἰ γὰρ σύμφυτοι γεγόναμεν τῷ ὁμοιώματι τοῦ θανάτου αὐτοῦ, ἀλλὰ καὶ τῆς ἀναστάσεως ἐσόμεθα.

31. *Adv. Iov.* 1.39, 2.19, 2.29 (PL 23:267A, 314C, 326A–B). The reference to 2 Pt 1:4 in *Adv. Iov.* 2.19 (PL 23:314C) is rather marginal: "Et quomodo nos sumus Pater et Filius et Spiritus sanctus unus Deus, sic et unus populus in ipsis sit, hoc est, quasi filii charissimi, *divinae consortes naturae*."

32. *Adv. Iov.* 2.29 (PL 23:326B–C): "Verbum caro factum est, ut nos de carne transiremus in Verbum. Nec Verbum desiit esse quod fuerat: nec homo perdidit esse, quod natus est. Gloria aucta est, non mutata natura," in Nicene and Post-Nicene Fathers, Series 2 (ed. Schaff) (hereafter, NPNF), 6:410.

33. *In Gal.* 2.4.15–16 (CCL 77A:125; trans. Cain, 172–73): "Beatus est qui ambulat in virtutum via, sed si ad virtutes usque perveneris; nec prodest a vitiis recessisse nisi optima comprehendas, quia non tam initia sunt in bonis studiis laudanda quam finis. Sicut enim in vinea multi usque ad prelum uvae gradus sunt, et primum necesse est ut vitis gemmet in pampinis, spem promittat in floribus, dehinc ut flore decusso futuri botri species deformetur paulatimque turgescens uva parturiat ut pressa torcularibus dulcia musta desudet, ita et in doctrina singuli beatitudinum sunt provectus: ut audiat quis verbum Dei, ut concipiat, ut in utero animae eius adolescat et ad partum usque perveniat, ut cum pepererit, lactet, enutriat et per infantiam, pueritiam, adolescentiam, iuventutem ad perfectum virum usque perducat. Cum ergo singuli, ut diximus, gradus iuxta provectus suos habeant beatitudinem, si finis et, ut ita loquar, extrema manus operi defuerit, totus labor irritus fiet." See *In Gal.* 2.4.19 (CCL 77A:131–32).

must never claim that we have already reached our goal or achieved perfection; rather, we should forget the things which are behind us and focus on the things which are ahead (see Phil 3:12–15), admit our own imperfection, and keep in mind that we "rather seek than have found" (*magis quaerere quam invenisse*).[34]

In other words, we reap what we sow (see Gal 6:7). The person who sows in the Spirit—in Jerome's words, "a spiritual hearer"—will reap eternal life from the Spirit. At the time of harvest, our humanity will also be transformed. Although Jerome consistently denies any change of human nature, this time he uses an overstatement by saying that we sow in the Spirit as men, "but when we begin to reap eternal life, we will perhaps cease to be men" (*homo fortasse esse desistit*).[35] The present is a time for sowing, for enacting works of the Spirit, or of the flesh. The harvest is "the future judgment of all works."[36] Unlike some other Latin authors, Jerome does not develop the Platonic concept of participation and its ontological implications in this context. Rather, he declares again that our participation in God is not a change of human nature. In his own words: "You see, then, we are privileged to partake of His substance [*in consortium substantiae eius assumimur*], not in the realm of nature, but of grace."[37]

Finally, Jerome uses the language of participation in connection with virginity. In *Adversus Iovinianum* 1.39, he quotes, rephrases, and comments on extensive passages from Peter's letters.[38] He draws a connection between virginity and eschatological promises. An inheritance that is "imperishable, undefiled, and unfading, kept in heaven" for us, "ready to be revealed in the last time" (see 1 Pt 1:4–5); hope in eternal life, where people "neither marry nor are given in marriage" (Mt 20:30; see 1 Cor 7:38); all describe, according to

---

34. *In Ezechielem* 13.44.1–3 (CCL 75:644). See *Adv. pelag.* 1.15 (CCL 80:18–19).

35. *In Gal.* 3.6.8 (CCL 77A:214; trans. Cain, 256): "Qui legem carnaliter intellegit repromissiones quoque carnales et quae in praesenti saeculo corrumpuntur exspectat; qui autem spiritalis auditor est *seminat in spiritu* et *de spiritu metet vitam* sempiternam. Simul notandus ordo sermonis et cum superioribus copulandus, quod *homo* vocatur *in spiritu seminans* qui, quando coeperit *vitam metere* sempiternam, *homo* fortasse esse desistet."

36. *In Gal.* 3.6.9 (CCL 77A:215; trans. Cain, 257).

37. *Adv. Iov.* 2.29 (PL 23:326B): "Vides ergo quod in consortium substantiae eius assumimur, non naturae esse, sed gratiae" (NPNF-II 6:410, translation modified). The contrast between nature and grace also holds for the unity of the church in Christ, see *Adv. Iov.* 2.29 (PL 23:326A–B): "We are not one in the Father and the Son according to nature, but according to grace" (NPNF-II 6:410).

38. 1 Pt 1:3–5, 13–16, 18–19, 22–23; 2:5, 9; and 2 Pt 1:4, 2:9–10 and 12–14.

Jerome, "the privileges of virginity."[39] In a subsequent passage, Jerome paraphrases 2 Peter 1:4 by linking virginity with participation in divine nature: "Great and precious are the promises attaching to virginity which He has given us, that through it we may become partakers of the divine nature."[40]

## Angelic Life

Virginity leads us to a link between deification and the "angelic lives" of hermits and virgins. The references to angelic life are found mostly (but not exclusively) in Jerome's letters.[41] Writing to Eustochium (in his famous *Libellus de virginitate servanda*), Jerome states that he will not flatter her by expounding the "beatitude of virginity" (i.e., the blessedness of the virgin's state of life), setting her "among the angels" and putting the world beneath her feet.[42] Nevertheless, he frequently uses the image of angelic life.[43] Several paragraphs later, reflecting his own experience of a spiritual battle against temptation, Jerome describes that sometimes, after many tears and straining his eyes to heaven, he felt himself "in the presence of the angelic hosts."[44]

Jerome is quite clear that virgins and hermits do not become angels. Rather, what he describes is a *likeness* with angelic life (*comparatio, similitudo*), where human nature (*natura et substantia*) is not changed and physical corporeity is not taken away. Fifteen years later, Jerome is even more explicit on this in his letter to Theodora:

---

39. *Adv. Iov.* 1.39 (PL 23:266C): "Ubi incorrupta praedicatur haereditas, et immaculata, et immarcescibilis, et praeparata in coelis, et in tempus novissimum reservata, et spes vitae aeternae, quando non nubent, neque nubentur, ibi aliis verbis virginitatis privilegia describuntur" (NPNF-II 6:377).

40. *Adv. Iov.* 1.39 (PL 23:267A): "Grandia nobis et pretiosa virginitatis promissa donavit, *ut per hanc efficiamur divinae consortes naturae, fugientes eam quae in mundo est concupiscentiam corruptionis*" (NPNF-II 6:377).

41. Andrew Cain, *The Letters of Jerome: Asceticism, Biblical Exegesis, and the Construction of Christian Authority in Late Antiquity* (Oxford: Oxford University Press, 2009), 6 and 202.

42. *Ep.* 22.2 (CSEL 54:146): "Nulla in hoc libello adulatio – adulator quippe blandus inimicus est –, nulla erit rhetorici pompa sermonis, quae te iam inter angelos statuat et beatitudine virginitatis exposita mundum subiciat pedibus tuis." In *Jerome: Selected Letters*, trans. Frederick Adam Wright, Loeb Classical Library 262 (Cambridge, Mass.: Harvard University Press, 1933), 57.

43. See Neil Adkin, *Jerome on Virginity: A Commentary on the Libellus de virginitate servanda (Letter 22)* (Cambridge: Francis Cairns, 2003), 30–32.

44. *Ep.* 22.7 (CSEL 54:154): "Et, ut mihi ipse testis est dominus, post multas lacrimas, post caelo oculos inhaerentes nonnumquam videbar mihi interesse agminibus angelorum" (trans. Wright, 69). See *Ep.* 49.14 (CSEL 54:372).

Now when it is said that they neither marry nor are given in marriage but are as the angels in heaven [see Mt 22:30], there is no taking away of a natural and real body but only an indication of the greatness of the glory to come. For the words are not *they shall be angels* but *they shall be as the angels*: thus while likeness to the angels is promised, identity with them is refused. *They shall be*, Christ tells us, *as the angels*, that is like the angels; therefore they will not cease to be human. Glorious indeed they shall be, and graced with angelic splendour, but they will still be human.[45]

As we see, "angelification" is not a change in human nature or a taking away of the physical body.[46] What, again, is the positive content of angelic life? In another letter to Eustochium, Jerome describes asceticism as the anticipated fulfillment of eschatological promises, even in this world: a likeness with the angelic way of life and an increase in glory:

What the Lord promises to us is not the nature of angels but their mode of life and their bliss. And therefore John the Baptist is called an angel even before he is beheaded, and all God's holy men and virgins manifest in themselves even in this world the life of angels. When it is said *ye shall be like the angels*, likeness only is promised and not a change of nature.[47]

The designation of John the Baptist as an angel is significant. Jerome alludes to Matthew 11:10 (also in Lk 7:27; quoting Mal 3:1): "This is the one about whom it is written, 'See, I am sending my messenger [*angelum meum*] ahead of you.'"[48] His aim is to emphasize that the likeness with the life of angels has already begun in our earthly life. The same stress is found in a letter to Demetrias. Here, Jerome explains that divine grace together with strict fasting enable the virgin "even in its earthly tenement to live the angelic life."[49] Later in the same letter, he reminds us that the virgin should take care of God's

---

45. *Ep.* 75.2 (CSEL 55:31–32): "Quando dicitur: *non nubent neque nubentur, sed erunt sicut angeli in caelis*, non natura et substantia corporum tollitur, sed gloriae magnitudo monstratur. Neque enim scriptum est, *erunt angeli*, sed: *sicut angeli*, ubi similitudo promittitur, veritas denegatur. *Erunt*, inquit, *sicut angeli*, id est similes angelorum: ergo homines esse non desinunt, incliti quidem et angelico splendore decorati, sed tamen homines."

46. See also *In Isaiam* 16.58 (CCL 73A:677–78): "Et haec dicimus, non quo substantiam glorificati corporis denegemus, sed quo opera pristina in his qui angelorum sunt similes, penitus auferamus."

47. *Ep.* 108.23 (CSEL 55:341): "Non substantiam nobis angelorum, sed conversationem et beatitudinem repromittit, quomodo et Iohannes Baptista, antequam decollaretur, angelus appellatus est et omnes sancti ac virgines dei etiam in isto saeculo vitam in se exprimunt angelorum. Quando enim dicitur: *eritis similes angelorum*, similitudo promittitur, non natura mutatur" (NPNF-II 6:208).

48. See also *Ep.* 38.3 (CSEL 54:291).

49. *Ep.* 130.10 (CSEL 56.1:191): "et humano corpori angelorum impetratur conversatio" (NPNF-II 6:267).

servants who serve the Lord day and night, "who while they are on earth live the angelic life."⁵⁰ Another image Jerome uses to describe the earthly dimension of angelic life is "a new household," formed by the Son of God on earth from those who have decided to become virgins or hermits, so "that as He was adored by angels in heaven He might have angels also on earth."⁵¹

The angelic life, then, has nothing to do with removing human nature and becoming someone else. Unlike adoptive sonship of all the baptized, angelic life, for Jerome, concerns a limited group of virgins and hermits who decide to follow Christ in a radical way, and who may experience an anticipated fulfillment of eschatological promises. On the other hand, their way of life is not detached from the church, as they serve as a reminder to other Christians of what we have been promised and what we may experience, even in this earthly life.

## The Spirit of Slavery and the Value of Voluntary Human Decisions

Jerome is aware that adoptive sonship and virginity do not exclude our free decision. Rather, as we grow in adoption and participation in God, we are less and less led by the fear of slaves and more and more enjoy the freedom of sons and every step of our spiritual progress is not a result of necessity but of our free choice.

The spirit of adoption is closely connected with the value of free human choice, which is the opposite of the spirit of slavery. Jerome's spiritual or "deeper" interpretation of Galatians 4:22–23 identifies two groups: those who are imbued with the spirit of slavery with the children of Hagar, the slave woman, and those who have received the spirit of adoption with the children of Sarah, the free woman.⁵² The spirit of slavery and the spirit of adoption may also be understood as the literal and spiritual interpretation of scripture. The Jewish

---

50. *Ep.* 130.14 (CSEL 56.1:195): "servorum dei et pauperum spiritu habere curam, qui diebus et noctibus serviunt domino tuo, qui in terra positi imitantur angelorum conversationem" (NPNF-II 6:269).

51. *Ep.* 22.21 (CSEL 54:178): "Statim ut filius dei ingressus est super terram, novam sibi familiam instituit, ut, qui ab angelis adorabatur in caelo, haberet angelos et in terris" (trans. Wright, 99–101).

52. *In Gal.* 2.4.22–23 (CCL 77A:138): "Verum illos qui habeant spiritum servitutis iterum in timore ex *ancilla* generari Aegyptia; eos autem qui spiritum adoptionis acceperint ex Sara *libera*." See *In epistolam ad Titum* 1.1a (CCL 77C:5–6).

emphasis on the latter is typical of the state of fear, while Christians aim at a deeper understanding.[53] Besides this interpretation, Jerome provides a more nuanced view. Instead of opposing the Old and New Testaments, he considers two kinds of interpretation, literal and spiritual, and two respective "hermeneutical orientations" of its readers. A literal interpretation corresponds to the state of slavery and the spirit of fear, while true "sons of Sarah," free children of God, "aspire to loftier meanings and desire to construe Scripture allegorically."[54] Thus, the duality of literal and spiritual interpretation may be applicable within the church, "whereby some are deemed to be slaves and others free on the basis of their varying degrees of understanding." Moreover, Jerome considers the varying degrees of our spiritual progress. Those who follow the literal meaning (*historiam*) are sons of the slave woman. True sons of Sarah recognize Jesus when "their hearts catch fire"; similarly, the eyes of the disciples of Emmaus are opened upon recognizing Him at the breaking of the bread (see Lk 24).[55] In this context, again, we see that to become a slave, or a free son, is not a matter of necessity but of choice. God desires everyone to be his son and to do what is right voluntarily. However, those who receive the spirit of slavery may be led by their fear of punishment and, on that account, cease to commit evil. "The fear of the Lord is the beginning of wisdom" (Prv 9:10), but God wishes for us to replace the fear of slaves with the glory of sons.[56]

---

53. *In die dominica Paschae* 2 (CCL 78:549): "Vos habetis scripturas, et nos intellegentiam scripturarum: vos legitis libros, et nos in eum, qui in libris scriptus est, credimus: vos tenetis paginas, nos sensum paginarum: vos conplicatis membranas animalium mortuorum, nos possidemus spiritum vivificantem."

54. *In Gal.* 2.4.24b–26 (CCL 77A:141–42; trans. Cain, 188): "Sunt qui *duo Testamenta* et aliter intellegant ut Scripturam divinam, tam veterem quam novam, iuxta diversitatem sensus eorumque sententiam qui legunt aut ancillam interpretentur aut liberam et eos qui adhuc litterae serviant et spiritum timoris habeant in servitutem de Agar Aegyptia velint esse generatos, eos autem qui ad superiora conscendant et allegorice velint sentire quae scripta sunt filios esse Sarae."

55. *In Gal.* 2.4.24b–26 (CCL 77A:142; trans. Cain, 189): "Unde melius esse ut non solum de his qui in ecclesia sunt pro diversitate (ut supra diximus) intellectuum alios servos, alios liberos arbitremur, sed etiam de uno eodemque homine, quamdiu sequitur historiam, ancillae eum esse filium, cum autem aperiente Iesu Scripturas incensum fuerit cor eius et in fractione panis inspexerit eum quem antea non videbat, tunc et ipsum Sarae filium nominari."

56. *In Malachiam* 1.6–7 (CCL 76A:907): "Simulque consideremus, quod filius ac servus in scripturis sanctis voluntate fiat, non necessitate naturae. Qui enim spiritum adoptionis acceperit, in filium Dei vertitur; qui autem spiritum servitutis in timorem, Dei servus efficitur. Vult itaque primum Deus, ut filii eius simus, et bonum voluntate faciamus; si hoc consequi volumus, ut saltem servos nos habeat et a malis per suppliciorum formidinem recedamus.... Deus omnipotens sciens differentiam filii et servi, et a filio gloriam, a servo timorem expetit: *Principium enim sapientiae timor Domini*, ut de timore servorum, ad filiorum gloriam transeamus."

Similarly, virginity is not a command because "what is freely offered is worth more than what is extorted by force."[57] The accent on a voluntary decision seems to have been very important for Jerome, as he repeats several times that the Apostle "does not lay a snare upon us, nor does he compel us to be what we do not wish to be."[58] Moreover, it seems hard to command virginity and "to force men against their nature and to extort from them the life that angels enjoy."[59] The statement that virginity is against nature (*adversum naturam*) is moderated by an explanation that virginity goes beyond human powers.[60] This is why it is not a command but a counsel, and also why virgins deserve higher rewards and are compared to angels.[61]

However, Jerome is not an uncritical promoter of human freedom. Rather, he tries to keep a triple balance.[62] First, Jerome advocates the balance between the sovereignty of God's decisions and the effort of voluntary human decisions. On the one hand, God "works all things according to the counsel of his will" (Eph 1:11), wishing "all men to be saved" (1 Tm 2:4); but on the other hand, a human being can be an image of God only when behaving well as a result of freedom, not out of necessity.[63]

Second, he looks for a balance between God's mercy and justice. The for-

---

57. *Ep.* 22.20 (CSEL 54:171): "Quia maioris est mercedis, quod non cogitur et offertur" (trans. Wright, 97).

58. *Adv. Iov.* 1.13 (PL 23:242): "Non imponit nobis Apostolus laqueum, nec cogit esse quod nolumus" (NPNF-II 6:357). See also *Adversus Helvidium* 21 (*PL* 23:215): "Neque tamen alicui necessitate imponit aut laqueum," and *In Ezech.* 14.46.12–15 (CCL 75:698): "Unde et uirginitas maior est nuptiis, quia non exigitur nec redditur sed offertur." See Adkin, *Jerome on Virginity*, 176.

59. *Ep.* 22.20 (CSEL 54:171): "Durissimum erat contra naturam cogere angelorumque vitam ab hominibus extorquere et id quodam modo damnare, quod conditum est" (trans. Wright, 97).

60. The point that virginity is optional had already been made by Fathers before Jerome, as well as the idea that virginity runs counter to nature and makes virgins similar to angels. The combination of all these motifs in one passage is found in Athanasius, *Letter to Virgins*. For the Coptic text, and the French translation (by L.-Th. Lefort), see S. Athanase, *Lettres festales et pastorales en copte*, ed. L.-Th. Lefort, Corpus Scriptorum Christianorum Orientalium (hereafter, CSCO) 150 (Louvain: Durbecq, 1955), 81–82, and CSCO 151 (Louvain: Durbecq, 1955), 62–63. For the English translation (by David Brakke), see *Athanasius and the Politics of Asceticism* (Oxford: Clarendon Press, 1995), 279–80. This passage appears to be Jerome's source in *Ep.* 22.20; see Adkin, *Jerome on Virginity*, 176–78.

61. *Adv. Helv.* 21 (PL 23:215): "Et quamquam de virginitate praeceptum Domini non habeat: quia ultra homines est; et quodammodo impudentis erat, adversum naturam cogere, alioque modo dicere. Volo vos esse, quod angeli sunt: unde et virgo majoris est mercedis."

62. See my paper "'Perfection Appropriate to the Fragile Human Condition': Jerome and Pelagius on the Perfection of Christian Life," *Studia Patristica* 67 (2013), 385–92.

63. See *In Eph.* 1.1.11 (PL 26:454C–455B); *In epistolam ad Philemonem* 14 (CCL 77C:96–97); similarly *Adv. Iov.* 2.3 (PL 23:284D–288B).

mer does not consist in the final restoration of all things regardless of our virtues or vices. God looks at human deeds and often withholds promised benefits from those who turn to evil, or contrarily, refrains from imposing promised punishments when people turn to repentance.[64]

Third, a balance is to be kept between the effort of will and the final outcome. Jerome is well aware that individual people are given unequal gifts. Marriage and virginity are both gifts from Christ but "in the Church there is diversity in the gifts of Christ."[65] Jerome does not see any injustice in this diversity, affirming that different gifts correspond to different rewards.[66] Neither celibacy nor marriage prevail "without works, since even faith, which is specially characteristic of Christians, if it has not works, is said to be dead."[67] On the other hand, the effort of the will deserves reward even when the act itself, which a person decides to carry out, is not realized for another reason. God takes into account the faith of that person and "fills in" the void of the act.[68] This is exactly the case with salvation, which not only depends upon God, but upon human cooperation. The culmination of salvation is, beyond doubt, an act of God, while it is man's task to try and strive,[69] aided at every step by the grace of God.[70]

## Conclusion

In summary, Jerome appears cautious and conservative on the topic of deification. He does not use words related to *deificare*. Rather, he draws on the complementary terms: adoptive sonship and spiritual adoption; "becoming gods" and participation in divine life; and "rebirth into a new man" and angelic life.

Jerome's understanding of deification stems from St. Paul's adoptive son-

---

64. *In Ionam* 3.10 (CCL 76:410).
65. *Adv. Iov.* 1.8 (PL 23:222A): "Diversa sunt dona Christi" (NPNF-II 6:352).
66. *Adv. Iov.* 1.8 (PL 23:221D–222A).
67. However, Jerome does not resist the temptation to add that it is better to be a servant of Christ, not of a woman, and "to serve not the flesh, but the spirit." *Adv. Iov.* 1.11 (PL 23:225C): "Nihil enim prodest absque operibus coelibatus, et nuptiae, cum etiam fides, quae proprie Christianorum est, si opera non habuerit, mortua esse dicatur.... Quanta felicitas, non uxoris servum esse, sed Christi; non carni servire, sed spiritui!" (NPNF-II 6:354).
68. See *In Matth.* 2.11.30 and 4.25.29 (CCL 77:87 and 242–43).
69. *In Ezech.* 1.3.2 (CCL 75:31); *In Ieremiam* 1.9.2; 3.15.2; 6.17.4; 6.20.4 (CCL 74:10, 129, 304, 309–10).
70. See *Ep.* 133.5–6 (CSEL 56.1:248–51); *Adv. pelag.* 1.1–2, 1.5, 1.28, 3.11 (CCL 80:6–8, 9, 35, 111).

ship. The effect of "spiritual adoption" is that we become "sons of God"; and even more, we are called "gods." We are all created by God with the only aim "that we may become gods."[71] Those who are buried with Christ in baptism and have been raised with him are "reborn into a new man."[72] Therefore, the process of our transformation has already begun and "new creation" becomes present in our lives.[73]

The spirit of adoption is linked with freedom on three levels: a dichotomy between the spirit of freedom and the spirit of slavery finds its first parallel in the Jewish stress on the latter, in contrast to the Christian effort at a deeper understanding; the second parallel is indicated by two kinds of hermeneutical orientation of the readers within the church (literal or spiritual); and the third parallel corresponds to the progressive degrees of our spiritual growth.

Adoptive sonship is participation in divine life. Our transformation is a counterpart to incarnation: the Word becomes flesh so that "we might pass from the flesh into the Word"[74] and Christ "emptied himself and took on the form of a servant" so that we might "go from being servants to masters" and "become gods from humans."[75] When the process of Christian growth is brought to an end, our humanity is transformed and we "perhaps will cease to be men."[76]

The realization of this potential divinity calls for a moral and ascetic practice. Nothing less than moral excellence is satisfactory. Christian perfection is not required immediately after baptism. The process of moral growth and maturation starts with an acknowledgment of one's own imperfection and goes through many stages towards an ever-deepening perfection. Yet, if it is not brought to moral excellence, the whole effort is in vain.

A prototype, model, or an eminent mode of human kinship with God is virginity, a way of life that anticipates eschatological promises and future glory. The ascetic life is also compared to the life of angels. The angelic life of virgins and hermits has nothing to do with the shedding of human corporeity;

---

71. *Tract. Ps.* 81.6 (CCL 78:86).
72. *In Gal.* 3.6.15 (CCL 77A:224).
73. Ibid. (223).
74. *Adv. Iov.* 2.29 (PL 23:326B–C).
75. *In Gal.* 2.4.12a (CCL 77A:120–21).
76. Ibid., 3.6.8 (CCL 77A:214).

rather, it is a manifestation of the mode of the life of angels and an anticipation of future promises, even in this world.

Jerome consistently states that our adoptive sonship, participation in divine life, and angelic life is not a change of human nature. This may be the reason of his frequent remarks on the contrast between nature and grace. Against the Arians, who assert that Christ is distinct from and subordinate to God the Father, Jerome emphasizes the difference between Christ's eternal sonship according to nature and our adoptive sonship according to grace. In contrast to the Manichees, who assert that the human soul is of the same nature as God, Jerome stresses that there is only one true God, and that we are called "gods" through our participation in him. What lies behind this anti-Arian and anti-Manichean rhetoric is an echo of the Origenist controversies that led Jerome—previously a great admirer of Origen's work but later an avowed critic—to deny any ontological change, to avoid the direct language of divinization, and to reject the Platonic metaphor of the soul's ascent.

To conclude, Jerome limits himself to the Christological, sacramental, moral, and ascetic dimensions of deification. His understanding of deification stems from St. Paul's adoptive sonship. Those who believe in Christ and receive baptism obtain the "spirit of adoption," which gives them the first fruits of future promises, kinship with God, and participation in his life.

Ron Haflidson

## 9. "WE SHALL BE THAT SEVENTH DAY"

Deification in Augustine

In response to the persistent and pervasive view that Augustine did not believe in deification, recent scholars have marshaled overwhelming evidence to prove that he did. Such evidence is of two kinds: first, explicit evidence in which Augustine either uses the term *deificare* itself or describes human redemption with reference to our participation in and increasing likeness to God's nature; second, implicit evidence in which Augustine's understanding of some aspect of human redemption clearly implies our participation in and increasing likeness to God's nature.[1] Much attention has been given to the first kind of evidence, especially Augustine's use of the term *deificare*. While Augustine only uses the term eighteen times, which does seem minuscule compared to the amount he wrote, Norman Russell notes that Augustine uses *deifi-*

---

1. The authoritative guide on the subject is now David Meconi's *The One Christ: Saint Augustine's Theology of Deification* (Washington, D.C.: The Catholic University of America Press, 2013). One of the features that sets Meconi's study apart is that he situates Augustine's use of the term *deificare* within a comprehensive overview of Augustine's theology, which brings to light just how central deification was to his thinking. Key earlier articles, in chronological order, include Victorino Capanaga, "La deification en la soteriologia agustiniana," *Augustinus Magister* 2 (1954): 745–54; Gerald Bonner, "Augustine's Concept of Deification," *Journal of Theological Studies* 37 (1986): 369–86; Roland Teske, "Augustine's *Epistula* X: Another Look at 'Deificari in Otio,'" *Augustinianum* 32 (1992): 289–99; and Henry Chadwick, "Note sur la divinization chez saint Augustin," *Revue des sciences religieuses* 76, no. 2 (2002): 246–48. Also see below for other important treatments of Augustine on deification especially concerned with his relationship to the Eastern tradition.

*care* more than any other of his Latin patristic predecessors.² Further, attention should be paid not only to the number of times he uses it, but, as Augustine Casiday puts it, that he seems to do so "effortlessly."³ Thus Augustine can, for example, preach deification to his congregation as the substance of Christian hope: "We carry mortality about with us, we endure infirmity, we look forward to divinity. For God wishes not only to vivify us, but to deify us."⁴

In the first book-length study of Augustine's understanding of deification, David Meconi demonstrates that Augustine mostly uses *deificare* "(1) to explain both pagan and sacred scripture's (seemingly) polytheistic use of 'gods' and (2) to explain and even bolster other Christian metaphors for salvation."⁵ On the second point, Meconi explicates how Augustine uses *deificare* to complement four other metaphors for salvation: (1) "God's recapitulating all of creation in Christ," (2) "divine adoption [through Christ]," (3) "Christ's exchanging his humanity for humanity's divinity," and (4) "a 'new' humanity's exalted powers in Christ, human persons enjoying a new type of self in God (for example, deified eyes), a new way of interacting with others (for example, a new patience), and a new identification with God (for example, human dispositions in line with his own)."⁶ If Augustine can describe any of these as deification, even if he does so relatively rarely, then deification is not incidental to his theological concerns; instead he is evidently choosing how best to describe redemption according to the subject matter, context, and audience. As Meconi suggests, Augustine may have used *deificare* only sparingly because "it is a term already promoted by Augustine's opponents. Augustine is very suspicious of those who think that they can become equal to God without qualification, either in this life or in the next."⁷ Based on Meconi's study, then, we can conclude that Augustine's very explicit uses of deification indicate that an understanding of deification may also be present even when, for whatever reason, it is largely implicit. As proof of this, Meconi seeks and finds deification

---

2. Norman Russell, *The Doctrine of Deification in the Greek Patristic Tradition* (Oxford: Oxford University Press, 2005), 329. This observation is included within an appendix on Augustine on deification that offers a remarkably clear and concise introduction to the subject.

3. Augustine Casiday, "St. Augustine on deification: his homily on Psalm 81," *Sobornost* 23, no. 2 (2001): 24.

4. Augustine, *Sermon 23B*, in *Sermons*, trans. Edmund Hill (New York: New City Press, 1997), 11:37.

5. Meconi, *One Christ*, 127.

6. Ibid., 128.

7. Ibid., 129.

in Augustine's understanding of creation, redemption, the Holy Spirit, and the church.[8]

In this chapter, I will uncover the presence of deification in Augustine's eschatology, specifically in his commentaries on God's rest on the seventh day of creation (Gn 2:2), which he understands to foretell the eternal Sabbath rest of the saints. Such rest, I will argue, consists in full creaturely participation in God, that is, deification. I will briefly explore one result of that participation: deified knowledge, both in its earthly beginnings and its heavenly fulfillment. I shall trace out these themes in four texts—*Confessions* (written 397–401), *Letter 55* (401), *Literal Meaning of Genesis* (401–15) and *City of God* (413–27)[9]—that range over approximately three decades and include two of Augustine's undeniable masterpieces. The texts will often be treated out of chronological order, as my primary concern is what they share in common, rather than teasing out where there may be developments.

I take up this eschatological topic and approach for three reasons.[10] First, eschatology suggests itself as a focus because scholars have emphasized that Augustine tends to speak of deification primarily in eschatological terms,[11] yet little work has been done further examining how Augustine's eschatology reflects his belief in deification.[12] Representative of this view is Daniel Keating, who in his book on Cyril of Alexandria includes a comparison of Cyril and Augustine in which he concludes that they "present us with comparable and compatible accounts of our appropriation of the divine life."[13] By way of contrast, though, Keating writes that "the future eschatological pole ... re-

---

8. Ibid., chaps. 1, 2, 4, and 5, respectively.

9. For my dates I follow the chronology in *Augustine through the Ages: An Encyclopedia*, ed. Allan D. Fitzgerald (Grand Rapids, Mich.: Eerdmans, 2009), xliii–il.

10. For an overview of Augustine's explorations of Genesis, see Sabine MacCormack, "Augustine Reads Genesis," *Augustinian Studies* 39, no. 1 (2008): 5–47.

11. There also does seem to be some disagreement among scholars about whether to stress deification as entirely an eschatological reality or to highlight its beginnings in this life but its fulfillment in heaven. For an example of the former, see Bonner, "Augustine's Concept of Deification," 381; for the latter, see Meconi, *One Christ*, xx.

12. It appears Meconi may have initially intended to include a chapter on deification and heaven, as he mentions a sixth chapter on the subject in the introduction, though no such chapter made it into the book; see Meconi, *One Christ*, xx. It appears that J. C. Byeon's dissertation on Augustine on deification includes a discussion of eschatology; I was unable to acquire a copy of this dissertation in time to integrate his findings into this essay. See J. C. Byeon, "La deification hominis in sant' Agostino" (PhD diss., Rome Institutum Patristicum Augustinianum, 2008).

13. Daniel Keating, *The Appropriation of Divine Life in Cyril of Alexandria* (Oxford: Oxford University Press, 2004), 248.

ceives the greater accent in Augustine's thought."[14] This leads to a second (directly related) reason to explore deification in Augustine's theology: some have claimed that deification belongs primarily or even exclusively to Eastern Christianity, and its neglect or even absence in the West owes much to Augustine's influence.[15] Keating demonstrates that both Cyril and Augustine believed in deification, and instead he locates their difference in terms of eschatology. Thus a consideration of Augustine on deification and eschatology may also offer a more fruitful basis for subsequent comparison between Augustine and his Eastern brethren. Third, and finally, by exploring Augustine's eschatology through his interpretation of Genesis 2:2, I shall demonstrate the centrality of deification to an abiding passion of Augustine's life, the opening chapters of Genesis.

## Deification as Rest

From his earliest Genesis commentary onward,[16] Augustine interprets God's rest on the seventh day as a sign of the heavenly rest that the saints will enjoy for all eternity. Such an interpretation is authorized by scripture itself in two ways. First, the author of the Letter to the Hebrews himself interprets the Sabbath eschatologically: "So then, a sabbath rest still remains for the people of God; for those who enter God's rest also cease from their labors as God did from his. Let us therefore make every effort to enter that rest."[17] Second, with the description of God's rest, Genesis is using a figure of speech that is present throughout scripture (and in everyday speech) in which "cause is signified by effect."[18] Augustine cites how Paul in Romans describes the Holy Spirit as "groaning" in order to depict how the Spirit inspires Christians to groan in prayer to God,[19] and we might speak of a day as "happy" because its good

14. Ibid., 250.

15. Such characterizations seem to be rather recent in the history of the relationship between Eastern and Western traditions; see George Demacopoulos and Aristotle Papanikolaou, "Augustine and the Orthodox: 'The West' in the East," in *Orthodox Readings of Augustine*, ed. George Demacopoulos and Aristotle Papanikolaou (New York: St. Vladimir's Seminary Press, 2008), 11–40.

16. See Augustine, *On Genesis: A Refutation of the Manichees*, trans. Edmund Hill, in *On Genesis*, ed. John E. Rotelle (New York: New City Press, 2002), 1.34 (61–62). This text was written in 388–89.

17. Heb 4:9 (NRSV).

18. Augustine, *The City of God against the Pagans*, trans. R. W. Dyson (Cambridge: Cambridge University Press, 1998), 11.8 (459).

19. Augustine, *On Genesis*, 1.34 (61–62).

weather makes us happy, though common sense dictates that the Spirit does not groan and the day itself is not happy. When this hermeneutical principle is applied to God's rest on the seventh day, God does not rest after six days of hard work, but God causes human beings to rest at the end of time. Underlying this hermeneutical principle is a theological one: the saints' eternal rest, like all good things, comes to them as a result of God's activity in them. Such rest, though, does not denote the absence of activity; instead it refers to full creaturely participation in God's nature. In order to uncover this sense of rest, I shall begin with how Augustine applies the term to God, then to creatures, especially human beings. Having established that rest consists in creaturely participation in God, I shall conclude by exploring a particular result of that participation, as it begins on earth and is fulfilled in heaven: deified knowledge.

### Divine Rest

Without in any way wanting to deny that God acts—after all, creation and redemption depend on God acting—Augustine also affirms that God is eternally at rest. God eternally possesses the rest by nature that human beings will enjoy only by participation in God. How can God simultaneously act and rest? In *Confessions* 13, an important (if brief) commentary on the saints' Sabbath rest, God's simultaneous acting and resting come to the fore. Apart from God's activity, the saints would never come to their rest; and yet, God's acting does not share the character of human acting.[20] Whereas human beings will only come to rest "when our works are finished,"[21] God accomplishes all good works while remaining "in repose."[22] Augustine offers a brief explanation of this contrast in terms of the relation between divine and human nature and goodness. God is in "need [of] no other good" and so God is "eternally at rest, because you yourself are your rest."[23] We can surmise from this description of God, then, our first definitions of rest and restlessness: to be restless is to be in need of some good external to one's nature, which defines, as we will see, the existence of all God's creatures; for God to rest is to have no need outside God's nature, as God is self-sufficient good. Even when God is active, God's

---

20. Augustine, *Confessions* 13.37.52; trans. Maria Boulding (New York: New City Press, 1997), 306–7.
21. Ibid., 13.36.51 (306).
22. Ibid.
23. Ibid., 13.38.53 (307).

activity does not come from any need, and so Augustine can describe God as "ever working, ever resting."[24]

An expanded discussion of this sense of rest is given in a rare instance in which Augustine interprets God's rest on the seventh day literally in *Literal Meaning of Genesis*. Having foregrounded the primary meaning of God's Sabbath rest as the promise of eternal rest for believers,[25] Augustine then asks in what sense God literally rested after making all things; even though his preferred interpretation is the allegorical one, he also insists that scripture would not describe God as resting if there were not some literal truth to it.[26] He argues, then, that God rests on the seventh day to indicate that God is independently good of all God made; if God rested on a day in which he created something, that would indicate that God needed what God made: "he stands in need of no other good besides himself, seeing that he does not need the good which he made. This is his resting from all his works."[27] When taken literally, then, God's rest on the seventh day defines God's relation with creation: God is the independent origin of creation's goodness.

### Creaturely Restlessness and Rest

All created things, in contrast, are in need of goods that are not inherent to their nature in order to come to rest. Augustine offers a brief account of this, while discussing his interpretation of Sabbath rest, in *Letter 55*. All created things, from the souls of human beings to the air that makes up the atmosphere, desire rest. To rest does not involve ceasing from all activity; instead to rest is to come to the place where one's activity conforms to, indeed is an outworking of, one's nature as created and sustained by God.[28] To not fulfill one's purpose is to be at odds with one's own nature and the nature of creation as a whole, and such a creature, inevitably, will endure a state of restlessness. In Augustine's teleological cosmos, every creature has its place, and it is only in that place that it can fulfill its purpose. When a creature is in motion, then, it is striving for that place.[29] In bodies, Augustine believes, that motion occurs be-

---

24. Ibid., 13.37.52 (306).
25. Augustine, *The Literal Meaning of Genesis*, trans. Edmund Hill, in *On Genesis*, 4.16.9 (250).
26. Ibid., 4.10.20 (252).
27. Ibid., 4.16.27 (257).
28. Augustine, *Letter 55*, in *Letters 1–99*, trans. Roland Teske (New York: New City Press, 2001), 10.18 (224–25). *Letter 55* can serve, in many ways, as an unpacking of key themes in *Confessions* 13.
29. Joe Sachs's comment on Aristotle's *Physics* reflects something of the ancient tradition Augustine

cause of their weight, which is not an external force at work on things, as in a post-Newtonian universe, but is instead an internal inclination by which bodies tend toward their rightful places.

When applied to human beings, Augustine reinterprets ancient physics in terms of the nature of Christian love. And so the weight of souls is their love: "For, just as a body strives to move by its weight, either upward or downward, until it comes and rests in the place toward which it was striving ... so souls strive toward those things that they love in order that they may rest in them when they arrive."[30] This love of rest, though, does not lead inevitably to its attainment, as sin ensures that the soul's inclination towards its proper place is disordered. As a result, we confuse the ultimate good (God) with secondary goods (creatures); the secondary goods we seek to find rest in can vary from material goods, such as food or sex, to spiritual goods, such as relationships with our fellow human beings or ourselves. None of these secondary goods, though, can bring us rest, because none of them realizes what is most essential about our nature, that we are meant for God. Indeed, a dominant principle of Augustine's theology is that our relation to all secondary goods will ultimately be destructive for us and them apart from a relation to God as the primary good. As Augustine writes: "When the soul finds delight in God, it finds in him the true, certain, eternal rest that it was seeking in other things and was not finding there."[31] This rest, as I will detail further below, consists in creaturely participation in God.

The love that leads human souls to find their rest comes only by the gift of the Holy Spirit. Chad Gerber refers to this as Augustine's "order-pneumatology."[32] The Holy Spirit's nature and work is defined in terms of establishing and main-

---

is drawing on and transforming: "Place ... is an idea that presupposes an organized cosmos. We and all other beings have not just relative positions, but lives and activities that can only take place in an appropriate environment, which the cosmos not only makes room for, but sustains and nourishes." See Aristotle, *Physics: A Guided Study*, trans. Joe Sachs (New Brunswick, N.J.: Rutgers University Press, 1995), 106.

30. Augustine, *Letter* 55, 10.18 (225). Oliver O'Donovan offers an illuminating analysis of this cosmology in terms of Augustine's "cosmic love" in his *The Problem of Self-Love in Saint Augustine* (New Haven, Conn.: Yale University Press, 1980), 19–24.

31. Ibid.

32. Gerber's analysis of the development of this order-pneumatology is helpful background to the texts we consider. See Chad Tyler Gerber, *The Spirit of Augustine's Early Theology: Contextualizing Augustine's Pneumatology* (Burlington, Vt.: Ashgate, 2012), 156–59. For the development of Augustine's pneumatology beyond his early period, see Lewis Ayres, *Augustine and the Trinity* (Cambridge: Cambridge University Press, 2010). Meconi also provides a clear and concise overview of Augustine's pneumatology in relation to deification in *One Christ*, 135–74.

taining order in creation. Augustine believes God the Father brings all things into existence, the Son gives them their particular natures, and the Spirit maintains things in their nature and further empowers them to perfect that nature. This logic holds for both the order of creation and redemption.

In *Letter* 55, then, Augustine discerns the presence of the Holy Spirit in all seven days of creation and in the third commandment to observe the Sabbath. On the first six days of creation, God does the good works in us that qualify us for rest by his gift, the Holy Spirit, just as on the eternal Sabbath God will rest in us for all eternity by that same Spirit. The commandment to observe the Sabbath day does not refer to a day of bodily leisure, but instead it refers to the Holy Spirit "in whom that rest is given to us that we love everywhere, but do not find except in loving God."[33] Genuine observation of the Sabbath comes when our good works "have no other goal but the everlasting rest to come."[34]

## Rest as Participation

Human beings finally achieve rest by participation in God's nature, in other words, by deification.[35] The external good that fully realizes human nature is found only in union with God. In *Confessions* 13, the whole course of a Christian's life is explicated in terms of increasing participation in God's nature. This is clearest in a passage near the conclusion of *Confessions* 13, but it stands as a review of what has come before, especially Augustine's allegorical interpretation of the days of creation as stages in humanity's redemption. This crucial passage is worth quoting at length:

Once our heart had conceived by your Spirit we made a fresh start and began to act well, though at an earlier stage we had been impelled to wrongdoing and abandoned you; but you, O God undivided and good, have never ceased to act well. Some of our

---

33. *Letter* 55, 11.20 (224).
34. Ibid.
35. God's other spiritual creatures, the angels, also only fulfill their natures through participation in God. As Alexey Fokin writes, "Augustine states that angels are also *like* God not only in their immortality, possessed by nature, but also by contemplation of His nature, through participation in which they are blessed, and therefore may also be called gods (*dii*). Thus, Augustine ... recognizes that angels are *now* in a *deified state*, in what state righteous men will partake only *in future*. That is why Augustine identifies the concept of 'deification' (*deum fieri*) with that of 'equality to angels' (*aequalitas angelorum*)." See Fokin, "The Doctrine of Deification in Western Fathers of the Church: A Reconsideration," in *'Für Uns und für unser Heil': Soteriologie in Ost und West*, ed. Theresia Hainthaler, Franz Mali, Gregor Emmenegger, and Mante Lenkaityte Ostermann (Innsbruck: Tyrolia-Verlag, 2014), 208–20, at 216.

works are indeed good, thanks to your Gift, but they will not last forever, and when they are done we hope that we shall rest in your immense holiness.[36]

God is identified as having by nature what human beings receive from God. The first level of participation identified here occurs when by the Spirit the Christian turns from sin to acting well. In the second level, the passing nature of good works gives way to eternal rest in God's holiness. Human beings only become good and achieve rest by participation in God who is simply good and forever at rest. The eternal nature of that rest only comes by God's sanctification. The seventh day's lack of an evening symbolizes that when God rests in the saints it will be eternal.[37] That marks human beings' final fulfillment of their purpose in complete, creaturely union with God; they will find the rest that they seek when God transforms them to find their good in God.

Similarly, in *Literal Meaning of Genesis*, Augustine sketches human existence in terms of three levels of participation in God's goodness. First, he writes, "it is indeed a great thing for us to have derived our very being from [God]."[38] Existing in itself depends on participation in God's nature, and therefore existing all on its own is something good. Second, the ability to perform good works is a greater participation than mere existence, for it comes only by "our having been justified by him."[39] Salvation, then, is a second level of participation in God's nature. The third and final stage, though, is to participate fully in God's nature: "what we are meant to rest in, surely, is a certain unchangeable good, which is what the one who made us is for us."[40] Augustine explicitly draws out that if "we wished to be like God" in resting, we ought not to rest in ourselves, as we are not the ultimate good; rather, we ought to rest in God, "the unchangeable good." So even God's literal rest on the seventh day, then, serves to bolster Augustine's allegorical interpretation of Sabbath rest: "This therefore will be our supreme rest, wholly without pride and truly religious, that just as he rested from all his works, because he himself, not his works, is the good in which he finds bliss, so we too should be spurred on by the hope of resting one day in that same good."[41] Such rest serves as the

---

36. Augustine, *Confessions* 13.38.53 (307).
37. Ibid., 13.36.51 (306).
38. Augustine, *Literal Meaning* 4.17.29 (257–58).
39. Ibid.
40. Ibid.
41. Ibid.

culmination of our participation in God, begun in creation, continued in redemption, and completed in heaven.

## Becoming the Sabbath

While participation has certainly been at issue in the description of the saints' eschatological rest discussed thus far, Augustine has not explicitly referred to heavenly rest as becoming divine. In *City of God* 22, he does. With this great apologetic work, Augustine explicates Christianity in terms of its distinctive understanding of deification. In his discussion of Adam and Eve's sin, for example, Augustine writes that they "would have been better fitted to resemble gods if they had clung in obedience to the highest and true ground of their being, and not, in their pride, made themselves their own ground. For created gods are gods not in their own true nature, but by participation in God."[42] Deification sought apart from God, then, constitutes humanity's first sin. When Augustine comes to describe the eschatological rest of the saints, he includes a contrast between false and true forms of deification. This passage stands as the culmination of our examination of deification as rest:

> We ourselves shall become that seventh day, when we have been filled up and made new by His blessing and sanctification. Then shall we be still, and know that He is God; that He is what we ourselves desired to be when we fell away from Him and listened to the words of the tempter, "Ye shall be as gods," and so forsook God, Who would have made us as gods, not by forsaking Him, but by participating in Him. For what have we done without Him, other than perish in His wrath? But when we are restored by Him and perfected by His greater grace, we shall be still for all eternity, and know that He is God, being filled by Him when He shall be "all in all."[43]

Before turning to a more in-depth analysis of this passage, we can first note that Augustine describes the saints' existence as consisting in that participation in God which was available for Adam and Eve, but they rejected. In other words, the saints will attain the deification that Adam and Eve sought after by other, destructive, means.

Strikingly, in the first line of this passage, Augustine does not say the saints will enjoy the rest of God's Sabbath. Instead he says: "We ourselves shall become that seventh day."[44] In the passage in which Augustine most explic-

---

42. Augustine, *City of God* 14.13 (610).
43. Ibid., 22.30 (1181).
44. Ibid.

itly identifies the saints' rest as deification, he includes this provocative image of the saints *as* God's Sabbath. As we have seen already in our previous texts, Augustine's allegorical interpretation of the seventh day depends on identifying what God does on the Sabbath with what God does for Christians to bring them to eternal rest. Thus, this interpretation has always depended on a certain equivalence between the Sabbath and the saints. In *City of God* 22, however, by saying that the saints are not just *like* the Sabbath, but they *are* the Sabbath, Augustine intensifies the unity between the nature of the Sabbath and the saints. He does so in three ways.

First, as we have already seen, the seventh day and the saints both become what they are by God sanctifying them. God makes the seventh day holy and so sets it apart from the other six, just as God makes the saints holy and so distinguishes them from their sinful lives and from other human beings. And, as we have come to expect, the language of sanctification is dense with pneumatological significance.[45]

Second, the saints' existence is transformed by what defines the Sabbath: peace. Earlier in *City of God* 22, Augustine refers to the saints as "participants of [God's] peace" who will know "the perfection of peace in ourselves, among ourselves, and with God."[46] The language of participation here fits with Augustine's description of the saints as becoming gods. Further, he also explicates the nature of that heavenly peace in terms of the saints' threefold relationships with self, other, and God. Doing so recalls Augustine's description of Christians' earthly hope for an eternal peace of "perfectly ordered and perfectly harmonious fellowship in the enjoyment of God, and of one another in God."[47] Something of this "harmonious fellowship" is captured in the fact that Augustine uses the first-person plural to describe the saints: "*We ourselves* shall become that seventh day."[48] Human beings' inherently social nature is perfected in the communion of the saints. When peace is achieved by participation in God's nature, the saints come together to form a blessed unity, the *one* Sabbath in which God rests.

45. In *City of God* 11, Augustine argued that the Holy Spirit's title indicates what is distinct about its personhood: while both Father and Son may be said to be both "holy" and "spirit," the third person of the Trinity is the "substantial holiness consubstantial with the other two" (11.24 [481]). Augustine continues that a title for the Holy Spirit synonymous with holiness is goodness.
46. Ibid., 22.29 (1172).
47. Ibid., 19.13 (938).
48. Ibid., 14.13 (610); emphasis added.

The third and final reason that Augustine identifies the saints as the seventh day is because both the Sabbath and deified humanity are the culmination of God's work. Augustine will explicate this further several paragraphs later, immediately before the conclusion of *City of God*, when he writes: "After [the current] age, God will rest, as on the seventh day; and He will give us, who will be that seventh day, rest in Himself."[49] This sentence comes after Augustine has briefly reviewed how the seven days of creation correspond to seven divisions of salvation history, including the first age that stretches from Adam to the Flood, the fifth age which spans the life of Christ, and the sixth age after the earthly life of Christ in which we now find ourselves. Whereas Augustine reads the six other days as periods in which God acts to bring about redemption, the seventh day is the consummation and end of all that work. Thus, God's Sabbath cannot be marked by an age that has a beginning and end, defined by God acting in history to achieve God's purposes; instead, the eternal Sabbath is without end, as God's purposes have been achieved. The seventh age simply *is* that multitude of humanity who have been perfected by God's grace.[50]

If, as we have seen, rest refers primarily to humanity's fulfilling the purpose of its nature through participation in God, then such rest does not preclude activity. The question then arises, what activity will characterize the saints deified life? The answer, of course, is praise of God, but Augustine is concerned to show that such an activity could be restful. Earlier in *City of God* 22, when preparing to imagine details of the saints' heavenly existence, Augustine turns to what activity they will be engaged in, but then qualifies speaking of heaven-

---

49. Ibid., 22.30 (1182).

50. It is also important to note that in two of our texts, *Letter* 55 and *City of God* 22, Augustine includes an eighth day. Because Christ's resurrection was on the day *after* the Jewish Sabbath, Augustine, like others before him, would eventually conclude that it occurred on the equivalent of the eighth day of creation, the first day of the new creation. In *Letter* 55, Augustine argues that the saints' souls enter in the rest of the seventh day immediately upon their death, but they await the resurrection of their bodies on the eighth day. As Christ rose with his body, so too will his disciples. Augustine does not place a firm distinction between these two days because the eighth day "glorifies" the rest of the seventh day (13.23 [227]). In *City of God* 22 he mentions the eighth day briefly at the very conclusion of the work; the seventh day of creation will not have an evening because it continues into the eighth day. In other words, the eternal Sabbath rest of the seventh day and the resurrected bodies of the eighth day together form the new creation (22.30 [1182]). Indeed, it's notable that throughout *City of God* 22, as we have seen, Augustine considers the nature of the saints' resurrected bodies when discussing the eternal Sabbath, without mentioning the eighth day until the final paragraph of the work. Thus often in his treatment of the eternal Sabbath he assumes the eighth day. My analysis has followed him in this approach.

ly activity by saying "or, shall I rather say, repose and leisure."[51] To participate in God's nature is to no longer be in need of any good, and so "repose and leisure" are appropriate descriptors; and yet that same participation involves the unending praise of God's goodness. The ambiguity between rest and activity in *City of God* 22 is expressed elsewhere as a paradox. He describes the saints' praise as "the work of those who are at leisure,"[52] "the ineffable tranquillity of leisurely action,"[53] or simply as "leisurely work."[54] Praise of God comes not from any need, but from the complete satisfaction of all needs. And so it is an activity that simultaneously has the character of rest.[55] By their participation in God's nature, then, the saints' existence parallels the description of God we encountered in *Confessions* 13 as "ever working, ever resting."[56]

## Deified Knowledge

The saints' eternal praise of God is incited and sustained by a deified knowledge of God's goodness. Such knowledge is not confined to heavenly existence, but has its first glimmerings in this life. And so, before returning to *City of God* 22 to explore the saints' heavenly knowledge, we shall look to the deified knowledge of those on pilgrimage in this life, as evident in *Confessions* 13, *City of God* 11, and *Literal Interpretation*. Guiding my analysis will be Augustine's interpretation of another verse, God's declaration that the light was good (Gn 1:4). Augustine consistently reads this verse pneumatologically in

---

51. Ibid., 22.29 (1171).

52. Augustine, *Answer to Faustus, a Manichean*, trans. Roland Teske (New York: New City Press, 2007), 15.11 (197). I have altered the translation from "the work of those who are free of work" to capture the use of the word leisure (*otium*) present in the Latin.

53. Augustine, *Letter* 55, 9.17 (224).

54. Augustine, *Exposition of Psalm 147* in *Expositions of the Psalms*, ed. Boniface Ramsey (New York: New City Press, 2004), 20:445; and *Exposition of Psalm 46* in *Expositions of the Psalms*, ed. John E. Rotelle (New York: New City Press, 2002), 18:255.

55. Notably the phrase that recurs in Augustine's above descriptions of this activity is *otium* (leisure), which is paired with *deificare* in Augustine's earliest use of the term, when he refers to being "godlike in leisure" in *Letter* 10, written approximately 388–91. Much debate has arisen about how to interpret this phrase. See Roland Teske, "Augustine's *Epistula* X: Another Look at 'Deificari in Otio,'" *Augustinianum* 32 (1992): 289–99. If, as I argue, the saints' eschatological rest consists in deification, and that deification is associated with a certain kind of heavenly leisure, this suggests that there may be some continuity between Augustine's first use of the term *deificare* and his later understanding of rest. For an overview of Augustine's use of the term *otium*, see Dennis Trout, "Otium," in *Augustine Through the Ages* (ed. Fitzgerald), 618–19.

56. Augustine, *Confessions* 13.37.52 (306).

one of two complementary ways: the "good" refers either to the Spirit's work of perfecting creation (*City of God* 11, *Literal Interpretation*) or to a particular instance of that work, enabling human beings to know the goodness of what God has made (*Confessions* 13). The latter is an example of deified knowledge.

## Earthly Deified Knowledge

In *Confessions* 13, Augustine interprets the days of creation allegorically as a description of how God redeems human beings. I shall confine my treatment of the first six days of creation to the earthly climax: deified knowledge. For the sixth day, Augustine interprets the creation of humanity in the image of God as the restoration of that image in the spiritually mature believer. In his dense description of this re-creation, he interweaves God's declaration that God made humankind in God's image (Gn 1:26) with Paul's call for the Christian to undergo the transformation of his mind to discern the will of God (Rom 12:2). The repeated interweaving of portions of these two verses serves to indicate how the restoration of the image of God in human beings brings a transformation of their understanding.[57] Augustine begins his description of spiritual maturity thus: "A person thus made new considers your truth and understands it."[58] Such a person does not need to imitate others, he writes, but can discern how to act on his own.[59] He can now "contemplate the Trinity in Unity, the Unity that is Trinity."[60] Spiritually mature Christians, then, have insight into God's triune nature and how God is at work in creation redeeming all things.

Augustine's interpretation of Genesis 1:4 is reserved for after his interpretation of the renewal of the image of God (i.e., Gn 1:26). When he finally does comment on Genesis 1:4, he does not comment on it independently from God's other daily declarations on the goodness of what was made (Gn 1:10, 12, 18, 21, 25, 31); all these verses are discussed together so that they may be interpreted as a distinguishing feature of the Christian's spiritual maturity. As with the other interpretations of this verse, Augustine wants to be clear that God is not suddenly discovering that what God made is good. In the prayer-

---

57. Ibid., 13.22.32 (293–94).
58. Ibid.
59. Imitation of Christian exemplars is how authority functions to initiate Christians into virtue; this was required earlier in a Christian's spiritual development, prior to the sixth day; see 13.21.30 (292).
60. Ibid., 13.22.32 (293–94).

ful narration of *Confessions* 13, we see Augustine struggling to discover another way to interpret this verse so that it will not compromise God's omniscience. Augustine attributes the resolution to this challenge to God's inspiration, and so he articulates it as though God were speaking it to him: "What you see through my Spirit, I see, just as what you say through my Spirit, I say. You see these things in terms of time, but I do not see in time, nor when you say these things in temporal fashion do I speak in a way conditioned by time."[61] A true judgment about a created thing's goodness, then, is a seeing in the Spirit, which can also be described as the Spirit's seeing in us. We see at work here the same hermeneutical principle by which Augustine interprets God's rest on the seventh day: the cause is signified in the effect. God is said to see that what God has made is good because God makes human beings see that it is good. This text surely stands as an explicit affirmation of deification: "What you see through my Spirit, I see."[62] Even so, Augustine specifies that even this deified seeing occurs in time and so remains a creaturely knowledge.

But how does this deified knowledge compare to other human knowing of creation? First, Augustine suggests that by our deified knowledge we are attuned to God's purposes in creation, and so we judge created things according to a recognition of God's goodness only available by the Spirit. Augustine gives two examples of other inaccurate ways of perceiving creation. The first is to see creation as necessary, like the Manicheans who see creation as necessitated by a cosmic battle. To see creation in these terms is to judge creatures according to their utility.[63] The second is to see creation in strictly materialist terms, which regards creation as good because created things provide one pleasure. This perception of creation occurs whenever we find our own pleasure as the sole arbiter of value, apart from creatures' relation to God as their creator.[64]

For Christians, in contrast, their perception of creation is defined neither by utility nor by individual pleasure; instead, writes Augustine:

When such people see that these things are good, you are seeing that they are good; whatever created things please them for your sake, it is you who are pleasing them in these things; and anything that pleases us through your Spirit, pleases you in us.... If,

61. Ibid., 13.29.44 (302).
62. Ibid.
63. Ibid., 13.30.45 (302).
64. Ibid., 13.31.46 (303).

then, seeing something in God's Spirit, they perceive it to be good, it is evidently not they, but God, who sees that it is good.[65]

A deified knowledge of creation, then, is attuned to how created things' goodness brings God pleasure. The Spirit's work within the Christian makes the believer increasingly sensitive to the Spirit's work in creation as a whole.

The second way that deified knowledge contrasts with sinful knowledge of creation is that by participation in God the Christian is able to discern all that is good in creation as itself an expression of God's goodness. Thus creation's goodness becomes a mirror of God's goodness. Augustine writes:

> Different from both is the attitude of one who sees it as good in such a way that their God views its goodness through that person's human eyes. This means that God is loved in what he has made. But he could not be loved were it not through the Spirit he has given us, "because the love of God has been poured out into our hearts through the Holy Spirit bestowed upon us" (Romans 5:5). Through him we see that everything is good which in any degree has being, because it derives from him who has being in no degree at all, but is simply, "He is."[66]

He thus grounds this deified knowledge in the Spirit's nature and role. The recognition of God's goodness in creation is a particular aspect of the Christian's love of God and such love comes only by the Spirit's indwelling. It is this participation in God's own love that enables the Christian to recognize all existing things as themselves participating in God. Thus it is not only that the Christian is able to recognize creation's goodness, but also that the Christian recognizes that goodness as itself finding its origin and end in God's goodness.

*Confessions* 13 is unique in Augustine's interpretations of Genesis 1:4 because he applies the Spirit's perfection of creation specifically to the Christian's sanctification. While he does not do so in two later commentaries on this verse, *City of God* 11 and *Literal Meaning of Genesis*, the nature and role of the Spirit is still absolutely central and in continuity with *Confessions* 13. Further, I will argue that while the Trinitarian logic in these two later commentaries is essentially identical, differences in their structure will suggest a subtle reference to deified knowledge in *City of God* which aligns with *Confessions* 13.

In *City of God* 11, five chapters before he turns to Genesis 1:4, we encounter a refrain now familiar from *Confessions* 13, that judgments of created things

---

65. Ibid.
66. Ibid.

according to pleasure or necessity are too narrow; judgments by reason, in contrast, may discern the value that a created thing has "as part of the order of nature," in other words, according to its place in God's good creation.[67] When he turns to Genesis 1:4, we see that God's approval of light indicates that light conforms to its nature given it in Wisdom, the Son; thus, we have the inseparable activity of Father and Son in creation. Two chapters later, Augustine will return to God's declaration of the light's goodness and find present in it also a reference to the Spirit's activity. In particular, God's declaration indicates that God "made what He made not from any necessity, not because He had need of any benefit, but simply from His own goodness: that is, that it might be good.... And if this goodness is rightly understood to be the Holy Spirit, then, the whole Trinity is revealed to us in the works of God."[68] The Spirit's nature as goodness is contrasted with necessity; God creates out of God's gratuitous goodness, the Spirit at work making all things good. Augustine gives essentially the same interpretation of Genesis 1:4 in *Literal Meaning of Genesis*. Especially of note there is his description of the Holy Spirit as "a supreme and holy and just courtesy and a kind of love in his activity which comes not from any need on his part but from his generosity."[69] In this text, too, the Spirit as God's generosity is contrasted with necessity; God perfects what God has made out of the fullness of God's love, not out of any need.[70]

This discussion in *City of God* 11 is structured in such a way that Augustine subtly points to human beings' need for deified knowledge to discern the true goodness of created things. Comparing the identification of the triune persons in *City of God* 11 and *Literal Meaning of Genesis* uncovers how deified knowledge is at issue. In *Literal Meaning*, in several lines all three persons of the Trinity are immediately identified and their particular activities are defined; in *City of God* 11, Father and Son arrive first when he comments on a verse in chapter 21, but then the Spirit is not explicitly identified until chapter 24. In between chapters 21 and 24 we encounter a discussion of the false judgments about creation made by the Manicheans (chap. 22) and Origen and his

67. Augustine, *City of God* 11.16.
68. Ibid.
69. *Literal Meaning of Genesis* 1.5.11 (172–73).
70. Ibid. Robert Crouse argues that there is a relation between the comprehensive affirmation of creation's goodness that is central to Augustine's doctrine of creation and his Trinitarianism. See R. D. Crouse, "Augustinian Platonism in Early Medieval Theology," in *Augustine: From Rhetor to Theologian*, ed. Joanne McWilliam (Waterloo: Wilfrid Laurier University Press, 1992), 109–20, at 112.

followers (chap. 23). In short, then, in *City of God* 11 Augustine *delays* offering his full pneumatological reading of Genesis 1:4. Notably, given that the Holy Spirit will be described as God's goodness in opposition to necessity, the discussion of the Manicheans[71] and Origenists[72] turns on how they view creation in terms of necessity in their differing ways. When this discussion is followed by the Spirit's description as God's goodness who perfects all things according to divine Wisdom, the reader is invited to conclude that the Manicheans and Origenists are ignorant of the Spirit's work in creation because they have yet to be transformed by the Spirit's perfecting work. Augustine is, in other words, subtly inviting his readers to reflect on the need for participation in the Spirit—a deified knowledge—to accurately perceive the Spirit's good work in creation. As we saw, such a perception is depicted positively in *Confessions* 13, while the implications of its absence are embedded in the structure of *City of God* 11.

### Heavenly Deified Knowledge

We may now return to *City of God* 22 to consider the saints' heavenly deified knowledge. We saw that earthly deified knowledge consists in the recognition that all goodness comes from God and further the recognition of that goodness as gratuitous. The saints' heavenly knowledge fulfills what was begun on earth. So even though Augustine stresses that we cannot begin to imagine the glories of our resurrected life, even so he maintains that there will be some continuities with the first glimmerings of Christians' earthly sanctification. Indeed, how could it be otherwise, given that God begins to make us holy here and now? In *City of God* 22, the saints' participation in God's nature involves a transformation of their knowledge of God, self, other, and creation that sustains the eternal praise of God. For our purposes, I shall confine my analysis to two kinds of deified knowledge: knowledge of self and of creation.

The saints' self-knowledge involves a transformed memory of their earthly lives. They will remember the sins they committed, but that memory will be a theoretical knowledge, like a doctor's knowledge of sickness or a virtuous man's knowledge of vice, so such memory will not bring pain.[73] Memory

---

71. Augustine, *City of God* 11.22 (478).
72. Ibid., 11.23 (478–80).
73. Augustine, *City of God* 22.30 (1180–81).

of their sins is necessary so that they might know the character of their redemption as defined by God's unmerited generosity towards them in forgiving them.[74] Conversely, their memory of their good works will involve the recognition that "all our good works are His, and not our own, [so] that those works are credited to us for the attainment of Sabbath rest."[75] Their earthly good works are only genuinely good when they are recognized to have their origin in God. What is a bold affirmation of humanity's deification also comes with a clear articulation of how even as we are deified we will remain creatures: the saints' deified self-knowledge includes the knowledge of God as the ultimate source of all that is good and human beings as unworthy recipients of God's grace.[76]

The deified knowledge of creation involves knowledge of God as the source of good, and of the character of that goodness as gratuitous. When speculating about the unimaginable glory of resurrected bodies, Augustine applies a principle demonstrable from creation now: no created thing is merely functional, but always contributes to a creature's beauty in some way.[77] The importance of beauty in creation is further evident in the fact that some created things appear to have no function at all, and so exist only for beauty's sake, like men's beards.[78] From such observations, Augustine concludes that "necessity is a transitory thing; whereas the time is coming when we shall enjoy each other's beauty without any lust."[79] He includes two examples of this. First, he argues that even though childbirth will no longer be necessary, women will remain women, despite some who argue they will become men in heaven. Augustine believes their bodies will "be accommodated not to the old uses, but to a new beauty."[80] Second, we shall see the beauty of our internal organs,

---

74. Ibid. This description of heavenly memory is brief; it can helpfully be supplemented by Augustine's lengthier description of memory in *Confessions* 10. In that text he marveled at how we can remember being happy or sad without necessarily feeling happy or sad; indeed, he notes that while feeling sad we can remember being happy or vice versa. This capacity in our earthly lives described in *Confessions* 10 seems to serve as the basis for his understanding of heavenly memory in *City of God* 22. See *Confessions* 10.14.21 (192–93).

75. Augustine, *City of God* 22.30 (1180–81).

76. Note that the understanding of participation that was present in *Confessions* 13 and *Literal Meaning of Genesis* then becomes folded into the saints deified self-knowledge in *City of God* 22.

77. Augustine, *City of God* 22.24 (1163–64).

78. Ibid.

79. Ibid.

80. Ibid., 22.17 (1145).

which will further disclose the wondrous harmony of our bodies. Our internal organs are currently hidden from view in order that they can fulfill their function. When our bodies are resurrected, no such need will remain, and so we shall see our internal organs in all of their beauty and "those harmonies which are now hidden, will then be hidden no longer."[81] With both these examples, we see that the saints' heightened sensitivity to beauty is caused by the perfection of creation in two ways: first, resurrected bodies themselves will be more beautiful than their earthly counterparts; second, and most important for our purposes, the saints' total sanctification includes a dramatically increased perception of beauty. Thus, deified knowledge is not simply a result of what is known becoming perfected, but also the perfection of the knower. And as we saw in our discussion of earthly deified knowledge, this perfection of the knower may begin in this life by the transforming work of the Holy Spirit.

## Conclusion

Over the course of this chapter, we have seen that for Augustine the saints' eternal Sabbath rest consists in creaturely participation in God. Humanity's goodness is realized only through union with God, who is the eternal, self-sufficient good. Such an understanding of rest is at work throughout the four texts we considered, which range over three decades of Augustine's mature writings. While this understanding is consistently present in all four texts, the most explicit references to deification are made in *City of God* 22; even so, the characterizations of rest in *Confessions* 13, *Letter* 55, and *Literal Meaning of Genesis* reveal that deification is at issue, even when largely implicit. This further confirms the conclusions of other scholars that Augustine not only believed in deification, but it also suffused his theology. In particular, this study demonstrates that the saints' rest consists in deification, and rest is central to Augustine's eschatology and his interpretation of the opening chapters of Genesis, both major concerns of his theology. By considering one feature of deified humanity, our knowledge of God's goodness, I also established one way that Augustine sees continuity between the beginnings of our deification in this life and its fulfillment in the life to come. The Spirit's perfecting of creation includes inspiring the Christian to recognize God as the source of all

---

81. Ibid., 22.30 (1178).

that is good and the character of that goodness as gratuitous. Augustine, then, stands united with many other theologians of East and West in his hope that by God's grace human beings will become divine. To say he shares in this belief is not to deny his distinctiveness; indeed, as we have seen, his understanding of rest as deification reflects trademarks of his theology, including his teachings on nature, grace, and the Holy Spirit. A more fruitful avenue for comparison between Augustine and other major theologians no doubt lies in exploring how such trademarks of his theology distinguish his understanding of deification from them. Yet it is also worth underlining the common hope that Augustine shared and shares with Christians across traditions and spanning centuries.

Fr. David Meconi, SJ

## 10. BETWEEN EMPIRE AND *ECCLESIA*
### Deification in Peter Chrysologus

After his condemnation at the Synod of Constantinople in 448, the denounced archimandrite Eutyches (d. ca. 456) composed a treatise clarifying his views and pleading for episcopal support. He sent this now-lost treatise *not* to the great Leo, bishop of Rome, but to Peter, bishop of Ravenna, which was the latest home of the imperial family.[1] In the year 404, Emperor Honorius, shaken by the relatively unobstructed advancements of Alaric and his armies, moved the seat of the western Roman Empire to a more readily defendable location northeastward. Ravenna was nestled safely amidst marshes and narrow canals, and benefitted greatly from the natural backing of the Adriatic Sea. The pomp of Rome had given way to the practicality of Ravenna. Here, now, was a city suddenly full of imperial importance, soldiers of various stripes, and seafaring businessmen intent on making a profit.[2] Yet the rel-

---

1. For this letter, see George Ganss, 17:285–87. The sermons of Peter Chrysologus will be cited in the body of this essay with sermon number, English translation, and (where necessary) the Latin edition. All citations of Peter's sermons included in the body of this essay come from Fathers of the Church 17, 109, and 110. The first collection was translated and edited by George Ganss, SJ (Washington, D.C.: The Catholic University of America Press, 1953) and included random selections from sermons 1–170. The second collection was translated and edited by William B. Palardy (Washington, D.C.: The Catholic University of America Press, 2004) and included the sermons between 7 and 72 omitted by Ganss. The third set of sermons was also edited by Palardy (2005) and included the remaining sermons, 72A–179. These texts are cited below by volume number and page number. The critical editions of Peter's sermons are found in Corpus Christianorum: Series Latina (hereafter, CCL) 24, 24A, and 24B.

2. For a good history of Ravenna at this time, see Deborah Mauskopf Deliyannis, *Ravenna in Late Antiquity* (Cambridge: Cambridge University Press, 2010).

atively new prominence of Ravenna was reflected not only in the home of the emperor, but also in the city's bishop himself, who was *ex-officio* metropolitan over fourteen local *ecclesiae*. All good Catholics of the day knew that Ravenna was protected by its legendary first bishop and patron, Apollinaris, supposed disciple of St. Peter and martyr under Vespasian. Throughout most of the fifth century, then, Ravenna not only enjoyed immense economic prosperity, it also witnessed a robust Christianity's eclipse of a moribund paganism.

As the empire waned, the church waxed, and at the heart of these transformative decades stood Bishop Peter of Ravenna (ca. 380–ca. 450), known since the ninth century as the Golden Word, Chrysologus.[3] It is unfortunate that Peter is a woefully understudied figure of late antiquity, because he not only played a pivotal role in bolstering Ravenna's importance as both an imperial and an ecclesiastical center, but also bequeathed to the Latin West wonderfully rich and theologically dense sermons which provide insight into a people growing in understanding and acceptance of their new life in Christ.

The purpose of this essay is to contribute to the larger purpose of outlining particularly Western soteriologies of deification by showing how Christian divinization runs throughout Peter's preaching in three main ways: (1) in the "great exchange" of God's humanity for humanity's divinity as realized in God's own incarnation, (2) in the originally Pauline doctrine of divine adoption, and (3) in how he described salvation not as mere reconciliation but as humanity's participation in the divine nature. These three aspects show how the members of the mystical body of Christ are able, by virtue of their baptism, to enjoy the exchange of the Son's becoming human so that their humanity can be changed by the divine. The most intimate of unions exists between Christ and Christians, and Chrysologus's sermons are filled with deifying images in order to explain this transformative union.

Any study of Chrysologus must be a study of his preaching. In 1962 a Spanish Benedictine, Dom Alejandro Olivar, began to gather the 176 sermons attributed to Peter by the industrious ninth-century bishop of Ravenna,

---

3. The moniker "Chrysologus" first appears in Agnellus of Ravenna's *Pontifical Book of the Ravenna Church*, after 846 (that it was bestowed upon Peter by the Empress Gallia Placida upon hearing her new bishop preach for the first time, is regarded today as fictional). This is the most established history we have for the cultural context, the architecture, and the liturgical year of the Christian church in ancient Ravenna. See *Agnelli qui et Andreas Liber Pontificalis Ecclesiae Rauennatis*, ed. O. Holder-Egger, in *Scriptores Rerum Langobardicarum et Italicorum*, ed. G. Waitz (Hannover: Impensis Bibliopolii Hahniani, 1878).

Felix (the *Collectio Feliciana*). Of these, Olivar judged eight to be of another authorship, but discovered fifteen other homilies safely attributable to Peter, thereby settling upon the 183 sermons in today's critical edition. Each of these sermons is safely attributable to Peter, each is relatively short (with an average delivery time of approximately fifteen, perhaps twenty, minutes per homily),[4] and each is preached so as to catechize intellectually as well as exhort morally a Christian people. These sermons reveal the movement of the liturgical year as celebrated in Ravenna and in the surrounding areas. But, more importantly, through these expositions on scripture we are brought into the everyday realities of fifth-century Christians living in a bustling Roman civic and commercial center. Here followers of Jesus shared street and shop with followers of Jove, the old ways of *romanitas* strained to remain significant, and the security that Rome and her borders once gave was beginning to give way.

Most certainly born in or near the town of Imola, known to the ancient Romans as the Forum Cornelium (today outside of Bologna in north-central Italy), around 380, Peter excelled through the traditional Latin training, showing evidence of having mastered Ovid, Horace, and Virgil. While we can ascertain nothing particular of his early years, he became archbishop of Ravenna before the Council of Ephesus, probably around 429. He was bedside in 448 when Germanus of Auxerre died in Ravenna while on imperial business: Germanus had sought an appearance at court in order to petition the emperor for assistance with his people, the Armoricans, on whom the Gallic Alans—originally Iranian marauders—were waging war. At this same time, we know Peter wrote to Eutyches, the ousted bishop of Constantinople; but we hear nothing of him again after the mid-to-late 450s. The paucity of historical facts has forced pious tradition to set many dates of Peter's life, thus placing his death on December 3, 450.

In the midst of the mingling and change that was fifth-century Ravenna, Bishop Peter sought for strategies with which to lead his people out of the old ways and into the newness of Christ. As Hughes Oliphant Old has so enthusiastically noticed, Chrysologus's "sermons show an awareness of the problems of his day which does not commonly appear in the sermons of the patristic period. His solid knowledge of Scripture makes it possible for him to speak the Word of God to the situation in a way that is prophetic. Peter was above all a

---

4. For the codicology and transmission of this collection, see Palardy, 109:30n153.

pastoral preacher."[5] If so, the most common pastoral trope Peter used to draw his people into the beauty of the Gospel was originally Pauline—the Apostle's illustration of how the Son of God became poor so we might become rich (see 2 Cor 8:9 and Phil 2:6–8). The prevalence of this trope throughout Peter's sermons suggests a congregation who were quite familiar with riches, and yet also were a people longing to attain a new wealth and thus a new identity. Let us now turn to this "great exchange" in the sermons of Peter Chrysologus.

## The Great Exchange

Language of God the Son's becoming human so humans can become divine enjoyed a rich pedigree before reaching Chrysologus. As mentioned, St. Paul taught that in Christ's economic poverty lies the eternal wealth of Christians. But it would be Athanasius of Alexandria (d. 373) who would give this exchange formula its most legendary syntax: "God became man, so that man could become God."[6] Such exchange language is a common aspect of Christian divinization, stressing that humanity's salvation comes first from God's initiative and the Son's taking on humanity, thus enabling humans to participate in his own divinity and thereby in the life of the Trinity.

In his sermons, Peter relies on this way of expressing Christian salvation because it allows him to stress the divine enterprise of arranging humanity's entry into heaven by God's prior purchasing of all that is human. We hear many beautiful images of exchange. For example, preaching on Christ's desire to eat with sinners, we hear: "Life came to the feast, so that he might make those destined for death live with him; the Resurrection lay down, so that those who were lying down might rise from the tombs.... Divinity came to humanity, so that humanity might come to divinity" (*Sermon* 30.3; Palardy 109:127). But more often Peter uses these occasions to develop a deeper theology of exchange, expressed most often in a remunerative tone. One can easily imagine the bishop of Ravenna looking for ways to appeal to the lived experience of the affluent merchants and imperial powerbrokers, as well as the destitute and derelict before him at each liturgy.

---

5. Hugh Oliphant Old, *The Reading and Preaching of the Scriptures in the Worship of the Christian Church* (Grand Rapids, Mich.: Eerdmans, 1998), 2:423.

6. *De Incarnatione* §54: αὐτὸς γὰρ ἐνηνθρώπησεν, ἵνα ἡμεῖς θεοποιηθῶμεν (Patrologia Graeca [ed. Migne], 25:192).

Chrysologus easily intertwines the pastoral with the more theological, exhorting the prosperous of Ravenna to corporal works of mercy by first translating the sacrifice of Calvary into a divine transaction. Here we capture a glimpse of an *ecclesia* divided among those who were able to enjoy material riches, and those who had suffered quite obvious losses on many levels. For apart from the imperial official naturally present at Peter's preaching, there was also a people who, in the words of Peter Brown, "had to face a higher incidence of conjunctural poverty than did Leo. [Peter] preached in a region that had been exposed to frequent dislocations, such as Attila's terrible raid into northern Italy in 452."[7] To those who "had," Peter daringly points out how the rich man's pain is due *not* to his wealth as such, but due to his unwillingness to share what the Lord had first given him. That is, the eponymous Diues suffers torment not because he possessed riches, not because he wore purple (see *Sermon* 121.3), but because whatever he had received from the Lord's own largesse, he thought that such generosity was due to him (*qui non sibi data, sed reddita credidit, quaecumque domino largiente possedit*: *Sermon* 123.4; CCL 24A:739–40). Ingratitude and thirst for worldly honors often accompany each other in Peter's mind. But for those who have neither social status nor material comfort, his sermon can turn quickly.

We hear in the same exposition on Lazarus and Diues that the rich nonetheless still have a responsibility to the materially poor. Benevolence and beneficence are expected from those God blesses with riches: "this rich man is even more wicked [*plus inpius diues iste*], since he was not kind toward another, and, although he received good things, he did not receive good things for good deeds [*non pro bonis bona*], but in his unworthiness he received good things for bad deeds" (*Sermon* 123.4; Palardy 110:163; CCL 24A:740). This type of exhortation is found in all the homilies on Lazarus. We hear a bishop thus focused not only about the eternal securities of heaven, but even the necessities of this world as well.

What is most striking is the audacity Peter shows when illustrating what will happen to the rich who have no concern for the poor. In quite stark terms he does not shirk away from offending the many wealthy in Ravenna, stating

---

7. Peter Brown, *Through the Eye of a Needle: Wealth, the Fall of Rome, and the Making of Christianity, 350–550 AD* (Princeton, N.J.: Princeton University Press, 2012), 467; see my review, "Earthly Treasure Spiritually Refined," *Harvard Theological Review* 108, no. 4 (2015): 621–28.

that "the one who shuts his hand to the poor man requests alms from a fingertip, and he who shut off his vat of wine from giving even a drop, thirsts for a drop of water" (*Sermon* 66.3; Palardy 109:269). And just a few lines later, we see this unmatchable and rather intimidating warning in a very direct second-person singular, *Tu diues*:

You, rich man, formerly radiant, radiant in purple, now be covered with smoke, instead of scarlet be adorned with flames, instead of a soft bed endure hard torments, instead of elegant dishes feast on punishments, compensate for your wealth with poverty, let your intoxication quench your thirst, instead of fragrances a dab of decay will suffice, and you who had any pleasure at your beck and call, now be attended there by afflictions, since you brought this kind of reversal [*taliter tu mutasti*] on yourself by despising the poor man. (*Sermon* 66.4; Palardy 109:270; CCL 24A:396)

One wonders how many finely-clad senators Peter had squirming in their seats. Notice the "reversal" of the great exchange works both ways: in becoming poor, the incarnate Christ makes Christians rich; yet in remaining selfishly rich, even those who hear the word of God can become eternally poor.

This exchange comes to a fever pitch on Calvary where Christ "sells" his divinity in order to buy sinful humanity. Peter knew well how his hearers were people who understood that every gift involves some sort of expenditure, and convincingly points to the cross to show imperial Christians the ultimate cost of human redemption. Perhaps the maritime trading and the global alliances of Ravenna influenced Peter's most widely used images of the divine exchange, *consortium* and *commercium*, two originally mercantile terms.

Christ came so as to make a holy partnership between divinity and humanity. In fact, Chrysologus is so intent on making his soteriology unitive in nature that he makes this the end that clarifies all of Christ's other actions. Peter offers a myriad of examples: this is the reason Christ espoused himself to the church, the reason he partook of food so heartily with others, and the reason he intentionally came across as kind and appealing: "so as to join the human to the Divine, and make a partnership [*consortium*] with heaven out of fellowship on earth."[8] The same unitive and deifying connotation of *commercium* is also used more technically to explain the hypostatic union: it connotes a unifying exchange of perfect humanity and divinity in the Christ. It points

---

8. *Sermon* 31.3: "Christus ergo, qui tunc ecclesiam disponsabat, indulgebat se mensis, conuiuentibus non negabat; humanum, communem, blandum se pia caritate reddebat, donec diuinis humana coniungeret, et faceret de terrena societate caeleste consortium" (CCL 24:180).

us directly to the divinized humanity of the incarnate Word. Or as Chrysologus asks: "Who can approach the mystery of God, the virgin birth, the causes of events, the activity of the ages, the partnership between divinity and the flesh [*commercium diuinitatis et carnis*], the mystery that man and God are one God?"[9] In Christ humanity has been placed with God and God in humanity, earth has been elevated to heaven and heaven is now available to those on earth: *in terra caelum, in caelo terram; in deo hominem, in homine deum* (*Sermon* 160.2; CCL 24B:990). This is a wholly comprehensive condescension: in assuming created humanity to his own divine nature, the Son unites all aspects of the human condition into himself. Yet what is key to see for Peter is his insistence to his parishioners that this exchange was never meant to be limited to the incarnate Lord only, but that it can be appropriated and thus continued by all those who are willing to bring their humanity to God.

This is the entire point of the incarnation: God has come into the human condition to bring our nature into union with his own divinity (*ipsam naturam in caelestem commutet substantiam*: *Sermon* 45.5; CCL 24:253). Consequently, Peter must show how the divine life can now be appropriated by all human persons. He therefore chooses to rely on scriptural examples of how God entered the life of a creature and changed him or her forever. To demonstrate to those before him how the divine life can be lived even now, Peter draws from concrete examples of very familiar Christian faces.

First, of course, comes Mary the mother of God. At her *fiat*, the perfect exchange of divinity for humanity occurred and now she gives God "a dwelling that she may request in payment, and get as the price for use of her very womb peace for the earth, glory for heaven, salvation for the lost, life for the dead, for those on earth relationship with the saints—even union of God himself with mankind" (*cum carne commercium*: *Sermon* 147.6; Ganss 17:229; CCL 24B:848). Mary's "yes" exchanges worldly striving and strife for heavenly peace and possession. Furthermore, as we learn from a homily on the creed, such a labor as Mary's renders humanity holy and one with God without diminishing God's divinity.[10] Both Mary's "yes" as well as her very womb are represented by Chrysologus as the loci of recapitulation and exchange: whereas

---

9. *Sermon* 143.1: "Quis adtingit archanum dei, partum uirginis, rerum causas, saeculorum negotium, commercium diuinitatis et carnis, hominem deum que unum deum?" (CCL 24B:870–71).

10. *Sermon* 58.5: "Tali natiuitate consecrata est in deo humanitas, non tali dignatione minorata est in deo diuinitas" (CCL 24:327).

the first Eve was duped by a fallen angel, Mary assents to a "life-giving conversation" with a holy angel and now, so we hear, humanity has been released from its "deadly plan" with Satan and enters into a new relationship with the angel and the new Eve, a new *commercium* between heaven and earth has been established (see *Sermon* 74.5).

Like Mary, John the Baptist also shares in this new conversation with the enfleshed Word. Preached most likely on the Feast of the Martyrdom of John the Baptist, June 24, we hear (in *Sermon* 173) how the Son's coming in the flesh has inaugurated a new way of the divine's dwelling within the human. This is why on a feast in honor of John the Baptist, we hear Peter contend that, "just as those who belong to Christ rise in him, so too does Christ himself suffer in those who belong to him ... just as honor given to the head extends to the members, so too does the pain of the members result in hurting and injuring the head" (*Sermon* 173.5; Palardy 110:326). While Mary and John were the most familiar figures in the early church to show how this new life could be received by creatures, Peter looked for other faceless, nameless examples of God's transforming an otherwise normal human person.

Take, for example, where Peter (in *Sermon* 36) treats Mark 5:22–34 and the hemorrhaging woman's encounter with Christ. He describes how the Lord draws near to the infirmed and broken and seeks a way to exchange his divinity for our infirmities.[11] In order not to bring greater shame to a woman who has already suffered public shame too long, Christ draws respectfully and silently (*ad secretum*) near.[12] He comes to effect a *grande commercium*, offering his weakness for her strength. Yet this is a healing that achieves not only physical restoration but eternal salvation as well. How so? Peter makes it quite clear that in the person of Jesus Christ humanity is not only assumed to divinity, but that same divinity is extended to all who are willing to follow the Christ as Lord. In this way, servants are turned into sons and daughters. This is how Christ's "exchange" results in our own divine filiality, our adoption as his own

---

11. Consistent with other Latin Fathers, Peter constantly stresses how God calibrates his power to our weakness: e.g., *Sermon* 23.1: "Dat se tibi deus homo ut ferre potes, quia ut est tu non potes sustinere" (God gives himself to you as a man so that you can bear it, because you are unable to endure him as he is) (CCL 24:135).

12. *Sermon* 36.1: "Inter deum et mulierem furtiuae salutis agitur tam grande commercium, et dum publica petitio uiam facit rogatus, fidei cogitatio diuinum penetrat et peruenit ad secretum" (CCL 24:206). In more explicit fashion, Augustine also links this deifying touch of Christ with secrecy: "That God should make us into gods is to be understood in divine silence" (*Contra Adimantum* 93.2).

brothers and sisters. Let us now turn to that second aspect of deification for Peter, our divine adoption as children of our heavenly Father.

## Divine Adoption

In the early hours of Easter morning, the bishop of this newly baptized flock asks what it is they find more amazing: "that God has lowered himself to our level of servitude, or that God has carried us off to the dignity of his divinity?" (*Sermon* 72.3; Palardy 109:293). The divine exchange is presented as the entire reason for the Son's incarnation; this is why divinity comes into contact with the human person, to raise humans to the level of Christ, a child of the almighty Father. Preaching on the opening line, *pater noster qui es in cœlis*, Peter discerns the perfect relationship between divinity and humanity. In his sixth and final sermon on the Lord's Prayer (*Sermon* 72), Peter accordingly opens with the claim that calling God *Pater* is impossible without the prior condescension of the Son. This divine debasement is admittedly the only way our preacher is able to call upon God, so aware of how humanity's own servitude prevents

> any heavenly or terrestrial creature from even imagining: that so great an interchange [*commercium*] between heaven and earth, between flesh and God would suddenly be able to occur, that God would be turned into man [*ut deus in hominem*], that man would be turned into God [*homo in deum*], that the Lord would be turned into a servant [*dominus in seruum*], that the servant would be turned into a son [*seruus uerteretur in filium*], and that in an ineffable fashion divinity and humanity would become relatives once and for all. (*Sermon* 72.3; Palardy 109:293; CCL 24A:430)

As God is "turned into" a human, humans are "turned into" God. For Chrysologus, human deification involves this double "turn" (*uerteretur*) effected in the incarnation: God's turn downward is simultaneously humanity's heavenly exaltation. Peter wants to explain to the catechumens standing before him that their lives are about to change in the baptismal font. Here they will arise no longer natural humans only, but children of God: "This is why, O man, divinity comes into contact with you, why it is aflame now with such great love for you, why through the words you speak God adopts you as a son [or daughter]" (ibid.). In this way, divine adoption most often appears in the sermons of Chrysologus as a way to explain this fullness of the Christian life:

in exchanging his humanity for our divinity, Christ elevates us into his own filial relationship before the Father.

Preaching on Psalm 29:1 (*Afferte domino, filii dei*), Peter asks if these words are meant for the angels or for something even more mysterious. This great mystery is in fact not the presence of heavenly beings (*caelestes uirtutes*), but how God "is turning human beings into children of God and raising earthly flesh up to the heavenly nature" (*Sermon* 10.2; Palardy 109:53; CCL 24:68). God alone is powerful enough to transform earthly children into divinely adopted sons and daughters, and this is the only true provocation to proper Christian living. That is, Peter is pastorally very sensitive in first encouraging his congregation to accept their own belovedness and filiality before their heavenly Father and second, collectively exhorting them to change their lives to not only leave sin behind, but to become more like God himself: "Let us believe that we are the [children] of God, let us prove equal to our lineage, let us live for heaven, let us represent our Father by our resemblance so that we do not destroy with our vices what we have attained through grace" (*Sermon* 10.2; Palardy 109:53).

This leads us to a theme particular to Peter, namely, his emphasis on the psychological and spiritual anxiety that claiming such divine filiality can invoke. As "human frailty is powerless to discover how it has ever come to deserve such generous graces from God, such great promises and such bountiful gifts" (*Sermon* 68.1; Palardy 109:274), we are to find this more breathtaking than even the Christian doctrine of God's bringing all of creation out of nothing. One may not tremble upon learning how God constructed the cosmos out of nothing into a harmonious whole, but one cannot help but tremble (*expauit*) when realizing that servants have been made God's very own children (*Sermon* 68.1; CCL 24A:406). That is, the production of material and celestial bodies is ultimately nothing when compared to how God transforms a creature into his child, relating to one who had come from nothing as one who now partakes of everything.

Chrysologus is quite clear that such transformation into a brother or sister of Christ is nothing other than divine graciousness. It is nonetheless a grace that demands human cooperation. As Christ's identification with humanity is so unified, he is able even to extend his own name to creatures. Peter therefore contends that if one bears the name of Christian, one bears Christ, and so, he teaches how "the privilege of so great a name may be reinforced in you by your subsequent good deeds" (*Sermon* 68.4; Palardy 109:277; see *Sermon* 69.4). The Son extends his own filiality to those who could in no way expect or merit such a divine relationship (see *Sermon* 49.4 and 72.3). Peter found sermons on the *Our Father* a fitting occasion to expound this doctrine—all six of these contain elaborations on divine adoption (namely, *Sermon* 67–72). Moreover, each of these sections has strong admonitions that such filiality must be maintained through virtuous living. This is not the sort of relationship that a creature can take for granted, but must continually strive to appropriate this new reality in one's own way of life.

In a prebaptismal homily to the Easter catechumens, Chrysologus asks them what they find more amazing (*terribilius*): that the earth be transformed by the heavens or that the human person is changed by means of divinity (*homo deitate mutatur*). From this transformation, those who were once enslaved now enjoy "the rights of domination" (*iura dominationis*).[13] These "rights" thus enable the sanctified to enjoy the divine gifts of heaven, thereby transferring our allegiance from this world to the next: "He who gave himself to us as a Father, who adopted us as his [children], who made us the heirs of his goods, who raised us up in name and gave us his own honor and kingdom, he has directed that we should ask for our daily bread" (*Sermon* 67.2; Ganss 17:117; CCL 24A:403). Notice how Peter seemingly always looks for ways to stress the convergence of heavenly reward and earthly responsibility. If our Father is intent on feeding us each and every day, we should not fear approaching him in filial boldness, as Peter suggests that this is God's way of keeping us united to himself in gratitude and constant petition. The image of divine adoption is the most common soteriological metaphor Peter uses in his Easter homilies, reminding the newly baptized that God "recently allowed you to become his son. Therefore, so know that you are a son as not to become unaware of being a servant. So hear that you have been made into a likeness of Christ as to know yourself always as the servant of Christ" (*Sermon* 67.11; Ganss 17:119). Here Peter very subtly but very astutely distinguishes the dual filiality found

---

13. It is telling that Ganss simply assumes this phrase *homo deitate mutatur* is a matter of deification and overzealously translates it as such: "It is indeed more awesome that earth is transformed into a heaven, that man is changed by a deification" (*Sermon* 67; Ganss 17:115). This solecism actually supports an underlying assumption of this essay here, namely, that the reality of Christian deification is clearly evident in places where the term itself may be absent.

in other fifth-century Fathers.[14] There are two ways of being God's child: a son *in se* as well as sons and daughters who are simultaneously servants. The saints' divinity is therefore more of a matter of dependency than of determination. One may remain forever a "servant" (*subiectum*) but in Christ the elect are now elevated to resemble (*similitudinem*) the Father's eternal and perfect Son (*Sermon* 67.11; CCL 24A:405). That is, Jesus Christ is the one true Son, consubstantial with the Father, equal in full divinity; Christians, the Father's children not by nature but by grace, are substantially less than he and in no way inherently deserving of becoming his children. But this is the whole point of Peter's Easter expositions: those who have been made God's sons and daughters through grace never enjoy such a state autonomously but only in graced and transformative union with God.

So, lest Christians in imperial Ravenna wonder to which sovereign court they belong, Peter continually stresses how God's calling us into his own life demands that we embrace God as our only Father, our only defender and provider. This signals how so many of Chrysologus's comments about Christ's great exchange orbit the idiom of enslavement and true liberty, indentured servant and freeborn child. Perhaps Ravenna as the imperial arena of rights and freedoms, or perhaps Peter's association with the ever formidable Galla Placidia in particular, provided him with a living metaphor of how the Christian ought to relate to God the Father: "as soon as you confessed God as Father of his only Son, you yourself were adopted as a son [or daughter] of God, so that you may be an heir of heaven" (*Sermon* 68.3; Palardy 109:276; CCL 24A:408; see *Sermon* 71.1). As we have seen, Peter depicts baptism as the beginning of one's new life in Christ. In particular, when catechumens profess the Christian faith, these who were earthbound are now given a heavenly nature (*caelestem naturam*: *Sermon* 74.6; CCL 24A:455), these neophytes who were once enslaved are thus made free.

What is uniquely important to Chrysologus here is how Peter appeals to having a new lineage, the dignity of which surpasses any royal family on earth. Without a robust use of analogy, he never builds off the goodness that an earthly father or ruler provides his children but instead encourages his hearers to disown their own, presumably still pagan, families and present them-

---

14. Distinguishing between the Son's natural filiality and Christians' graced adoption was a required move for most of the Fathers; e.g., Augustine, *Homilies on the Gospel of John* 121.3.

selves for a new father and a new set of siblings (see *Sermon* 68.2). Here we see him standing in the center of Ravenna, with imperial connections surrounding him, and drawing off such admirable familiarity—urging those who hear him to become members of a new family, an eternal family. He exhorts them to imitate the Apostle Paul, who was given the Spirit to cry "Abba, Father" (Gal 4:6) and thereafter, "in the depths of his being, he was amazed that he was considered of such a thing" (*Sermon* 68.2; Palardy 109:275). Henceforth, Christians must live lives "corresponding to so great a lineage, and so that your conduct on earth may not defile what the heavenly nature has now bestowed and conferred" (*Sermon* 69.3; Palardy 109:283). Finally, Peter stresses how adoption into this new family has immediate consequences. The deified state is not something reserved *in patria*, but offers a new lifestyle and a new set of powers today, *in uia*: "*Hodie adoptionis est dies, hodie promissionis tempus est*" (*Sermon* 71.11; CCL 24A:428).

Consequently, Christians become coheirs with Christ even on their earthly pilgrimage. The second point to raise here is how divine adoption is continuously linked with being made an heir of the Father's riches, a coheir with one's brother, Jesus Christ. While this may seem a natural enough connection, Chrysologus intentionally stresses the divine heredity of the Christian people. Excluding none of the baptized, the Father accepts anyone who comes to him in Christ. In this way, Peter is able to forefront the equal dignity of all his congregation and all the human race:

> God the Father deems human beings worthy of being heirs [*haeredes*], God the Son does not disdain having his mere servants as coheirs [*deus filius non dedignatur seruulos cohaeredes*], God the Spirit welcomes flesh to partake of divinity; heaven is made the possession of earthlings, and those who had been consigned to the underworld administer justice in the celestial realm, as the Apostle attests when he says, "Or do you not know that we shall judge angels?" [1 Cor 6:3] (*Sermon* 71.2; Palardy 109:286; CCL 24A:424).

The deified elect are now above even the heavenly hosts, as they have been made coheirs of all that the Son is. This new life is never a matter of possession, but remains always and eternally one of participation. Let us now turn, then, to the third and final way Peter Chrysologus relies on a deifying soteriology throughout his sermons: participating in the divine nature.

## Participation in Divinity

Peter's theological anthropology hinges entirely on his strong assertion that the human person has been created to be a participant in God himself. This is the essential nature of the human person and the only true means of his ultimate flourishing, in that no person has been created simply to be measured by an earthly good or goal, but to become an eternal citizen of the heavenly court. This is why the Son "raised [*transtulit*] the nature of the flesh into one divine, when he brought his divinity down to human nature." Yet, what is more:

> At that time he made man co-heir [*cohaeredem*] with himself among the dwellers of heaven, when he made himself the sharer [*participem*] of the things of the earth. He took upon himself everything characteristic of man, even sin and death; then what love, what gift could he refuse man? Or can it be that he who made himself the sharer of man's adversity will not let man be his companion in prosperity. (*Sermon* 70.2; Ganss 17:119–20; CCL 24A:420)

Chrysologus is theologically very careful when he uses such deifying images as participation, stressing how humanity's godliness is always and only a *response* to the prior participation of God in humanity. Deification is clearly the result of divine grace; before humanity could ever participate in the divine nature, divinity had first to descend to participate in all things human. This is how our coheredity and Christian companionship is simultaneously effected and offered.

Similar to the first two metaphors of deification—the great exchange model and the divine adoption imagery—divine participation emphasizes the Son of God's initiative in bestowing a new life upon those who come to him. To highlight this intimacy of humanity's participation in the divine life, Peter employs the metaphor of spousal love, drawing from Paul's directives toward Christian husbands and wives in Romans 7:1–6. The bishop of Ravenna uses this opportunity to explain that the Apostle Paul is here speaking of ultimate union with Christ, and that any other excluding love in one's life is nothing other than spiritual adultery: "*adulteram ad Christi nititur reuocare consortium*" (*Sermon* 115.3; CCL 24A:700). In this *consortium*, this union with Christ, men and women are elevated above the old Law. This new espousal raises human persons out of slavishly following merely human precepts: those who have been so wed are now "partakers of a heavenly nature" and bring forth "fruit not unto the earth, but unto God; not unto death, but unto life; not unto the flesh, but unto God" (*Consortes caelestis naturae per christum, non terrae, sed deo; non morti, sed uitae, et deo fructum deferri, non carni*: *Sermon* 115.4; Ganss 17:192; CCL 24A:701). In union with the one true bridegroom Jesus, human persons participate in a life not naturally their own. Just as Christ had to take a nature not eternally his own in order to calibrate his infinite power to our fallen weakness, so we are elevated through union with another nature not concomitantly human. In this espousal to Christ, creatures are elevated and transformed, not only vivified but also deified, making possible their new agency and immortality.

Peter easily parlays images of Christ the bridegroom into nuptial metaphors of the church as bride, whose union with God makes the divine life of the baptized possible (see *Sermon* 57.13 and 60.14). Preaching in honor of Marcellinus's elevation to the newly-created Diocese of Voghenza (November 1, 431), for example, Bishop Peter wants to focus his people's attention on how Marcellinus is their "first born" (*primum*) son, the first bishop to go forth from their home. He uses the occasion, therefore, to stress the familial unity achieved by Christ's love for his bride the church. Peter relies on erotic imagery to claim that God's union (*coniunctio*) with creatures has been consummated on the marriage bed of the one who is both virgin and mother (*Ipsa quoque genetrix sponsa, mater et uirgo in ipso sponsi suo thalamo, in ipso coniunctionis suae cubiculo genuisse*).[15] Given this rather amatory and sensual language, Peter fittingly stresses the bodily virginity of Mary by next turning to the role of Joseph in this great mystery. The just man Joseph stands "as proof of her chastity, the guardian of her purity" (*Sermon* 175.4; Palardy 110:337). In this way, the church that is presented from the pulpit in Ravenna is not only a juridical body, active in birthing new dioceses across Italy, but the church is also the fruitful virgin who is protected by St. Joseph and not any temporal ruler, however strong. In this way the church is both an active political force and also the universal bride who bears all of God's children into ultimate identity and union, sanctified together with all the saints into one *ecclesia*.

Before this study comes to a close, we should notice how Peter's robust theory of deification never draws from the biblical precedents to "become

---

15. *Sermon* 175.4 (CCL 24B:1066).

gods" (Ps 81:6; Jn 10:34). He instead stresses relational terms like *cohaeredem* or *consortes*. While there is no question that Peter exhorted his people to participate in a nature not their own, to ask for the grace to be elevated above their own fallen humanity, he does so by emphasizing the dependency and concomitancy of becoming godly not apart from Christ but only with and in him.

Surely serving as the bishop of the city that boasted the imperial court affected how Peter chose to present the Christian life. We have seen how Peter is sensitive to the actual daily realities of his people's lives. Whereas other fifth-century bishops like Augustine who, worlds away from the imperial court down in the dusty plains of North Africa, have no problem exhorting his people to become "gods," the absence of terms and taxonomies being employed by Peter may suggest that he did not think the members of the Ravennate court were entirely free of thinking of their salvation as a matter of independent power and self-acclaimed might. We know one of the first emperors in Ravenna, Johannes (423–25), offended the church by demanding that accusations against clerics be heard not in an ecclesial but in a civil court, thereby submitting the power of the presbytery to the higher authority of the emperor.[16] But this was very minor in comparison to the hubris of Valentinian III (425–55) in whose reign Peter spent most of his.

Having come to the purple at an early age, named caesar at four and emperor at six, Valentinian proved to be puffed up with self-importance his entire life. While he showed some fiscal support to the church and even expelled Jewish soldiers from the Roman army so they would not negatively influence the Christians, Valentinian was far from a humble Catholic ruler. He brought pagan astrologers and diviners into the court, his pleasure-seeking went unrestrained, and the raping of his rivals' wives brought great shame to those around him. In fact, he was killed by assassins hired to do away with an emperor who knew no bounds. The eighteenth-century historian Edward Gibbon put it this way:

He faithfully imitated the hereditary weakness of his cousin and his two uncles, without inheriting the gentleness, the purity, the innocence, which alleviate in their characters the want of spirit and ability. Valentinian was less excusable, since he had passions

---

16. John Matthews, *Western Aristocracies and Imperial Court A.D. 364–425* (Oxford: Clarendon, 1990), 379.

without virtues: even his religion was questionable; and though he never deviated into the paths of heresy, he scandalised the pious Christians by his attachment to the profane arts of magic and divination.[17]

As such, Valentinian III certainly appeared to Peter as a possible candidate for bringing imperial apotheosis back to the emperor's cult; and this is perhaps why the bishop stayed away from calling Christians to become a *deus* or *dominus*. While such a theocratic structure had been made extinct with the Constantinian turn of the early fourth century, it is certainly possible that the stories and images of Rome's pagan past were attractive to ruling men like Valentinian and anyone who sought ultimate power apart from the church's cultic and moral expectations.

## Conclusion

This chapter has argued that Peter Chrysologus is a worthy figure in a study that examines the Latin Fathers' theology of deification. Throughout his pastorally sensitive and well-crafted homilies, Bishop Peter exhibits a triadic theology of deification: (1) in the "great exchange" of God's humanity for humanity's divinity, (2) in the doctrine of divine adoption, and (3) in humanity's participation in the divine nature. What makes these soteriological images particularly Bishop Peter's is how he presents an image of Christ alongside all the realities of Ravenna's imperial court, ever mindful of how deification language could have been more readily associated with the imperial cult and not the salvation of the average citizen. Chrysologus's special "awareness" of these realities, to use Oliphant Old's term, comes through his mediation of the rather complex doctrine of divinization to his congregation in Ravenna. Delicately poised between court and congregant, the bishop there had to exhort his flock to receive the divine life in such a way that they understood their true homeland without ever neglecting this present world. A new citizenry had to be formed that taught Christians to whom true allegiance was owed.

For Peter, one is saved not by moral exertion or ethical purity; Christian salvation is realized only as one is made a participant in the divine nature, a child of God and coheir of Jesus Christ. Perhaps in stressing this relational-

---

17. Edward Gibbon, *Decline and Fall of the Roman Empire*, ed. David Womersley (New York: Penguin, 1994), chap. 35 (3:355).

ity of union with Christ, Peter decided to stay away from calling Christians "gods," even though there is scriptural (e.g., Ps 81:2 and Jn 10:34) as well as theological precedent.[18] Instead, Peter characterized one's life in Christ as being brought into a new relationship with God and with one's neighbors, thereby most often preferring the term *filii*—sons and daughters—to describe creatures' lives in Christ. The baptized are thus adopted into the triune life of God not out of any goodness they could ever merit, but out of the love of the Father who longs to extend his heredity throughout all of time. In so doing, God deifies those to whom he comes, and those who are humble enough not to resist his grace. This transformation runs often tacitly but almost constantly throughout the powerful preaching of Peter Chrysologus.

18. For earlier uses of "gods" to describe the Christian life, see Russell, *The Doctrine of Deification*.

Daniel Keating

## 11. THE WONDERFUL EXCHANGE
### Deification in Leo the Great

We know little about the early life of Leo the Great.[1] He is reputed to be of Tuscan heritage, born in the last decade of the fourth century. The first we hear of Leo is in his role as the influential archdeacon of Pope Celestine, who in 430 entrusted Leo with the task of sorting out the controversy between Cyril of Alexandria and Nestorius. Leo recruited John Cassian to investigate the controversy and Cassian concluded that Nestorius was in error—a position that Leo himself adopted and defended many times in his writings. We also have Leo's own testimony that Cyril wrote to him directly in 431 to gain his support against Juvenal's attempt to promote the patriarchate of Jerusalem. A few years later, now serving Pope Sixtus III, Leo was engaged in a different controversy, actively resisting the Pelagian teaching of Julian of Eclanum. Leo succeeded Sixtus as pope in 440 and reigned until his death in 461.

Leo's extant writings consist of 123 letters and 97 homilies preached on the major feasts of the church calendar.[2] The letters and homilies, written in simple, elegant Latin prose, cover a wide range of theological and pastoral perspectives. But Leo is known primarily for his role in the Christological contro-

---

[1]. For background to Leo's life and ecclesiastical career, see Trevor Jalland, *The Life and Times of St. Leo the Great* (London: SPCK, 1941), and Susan Wessel, *Leo the Great and the Spiritual Rebuilding of a Universal Rome* (Leiden: Brill, 2008).

[2]. For a summary of Leo's extant corpus, see Bronwen Neil, *Leo the Great*, The Early Church Fathers (New York: Routledge, 2009), 13–15.

versies of his day, encapsulated in his letter to Patriarch Flavian in 448, known as his Tome. Leo strenuously rejected the results of the Council of Ephesus in 449 (dubbing it the "Robber Council") and called for another council to declare what he considered to be the true teaching about Christ. The Council of Chalcedon, held in 451, satisfied Leo's hopes in this regard by composing a statement of faith in the incarnation that fundamentally upheld Cyril's teaching but that also incorporated expressions from Leo's Tome concerning the fullness and completeness of Christ's human and divine natures. As I hope to show, it is especially Leo's teaching on the fullness of humanity and divinity in Christ, and the exchange to our advantage that he sees at the heart of Christ's work, that grounds his approach to deification.

## Deification in Leo?

Norman Russell sets the stage for this study by posing a general question about deification and the Western tradition: "Whether you can really graft *theosis* on to a Western theological approach remains to be seen."[3] It appears that Russell believes there are genuine accounts of deification in the West, but the question he raises expresses a wider concern about whether a doctrine of deification or divinization can exist within a Western theological approach, and if so, how to label these efforts.[4]

Even if we grant that deification can be found in the West, do we find it in Leo? In her seminal study of Leo, Susan Wessel concludes categorically that "divinization was not a possibility for Leo because he was committed to the idea that Christ was linked to humanity only through the complete integrity of his human nature."[5] With greater nuance, J. Mark Armitage allows that

---

3. Norman Russell, "Why Does Theosis Fascinate Western Christians?," *Sobornost* 34 (2012): 15. If the question is really whether one can graft *the later Byzantine account of theosis* onto a Western theological approach, this may be a more trenchant question. For a recent effort by a Western theologian to describe deification using the energy-essence distinction found in the Byzantine tradition, see David Fagerberg, "From Divinization to Evangelization: An Overview," in *Divinization: Becoming Icons of Christ through the Liturgy*, ed. Andrew Hofer (Chicago: Hillenbrand Books, 2015), 15–31.

4. For these concerns, see Gösta Hallonsten, "*Theosis* in Recent Research: A Renewal of Interest and a Need for Clarity," in *Partakers of the Divine Nature: The History and Development of Deification in the Christian Traditions*, ed. Michael J. Christensen and Jeffrey A. Wittung (Madison, Wis.: Fairleigh Dickenson University Press, 2007), 281–93, and Paul Gavrilyuk, "The Retrieval of Deification. How a Once-Despised Archaism Became an Ecumenical Desideratum," *Modern Theology* 25 (2009): 647–59.

5. Wessel, *Leo the Great*, 251.

Leo teaches a form of deification, but he distinguishes this from the variety found, for example, in Athanasius and concludes that "Leo's is not a theology of mystical inclusion and divinization—at least, not in the sense in which these are usually understood."[6]

In this chapter, I will offer a sketch that supports a theology of deification in Leo. Though Leo does not employ the technical terminology of deification, he does display many of the central features of a theology of deification found in other patristic authors such as Athanasius and Cyril of Alexandria. To claim this, though, is not to suggest that Leo's account is identical to that of his Eastern peers. Leo unfolds an account of our deification in Christ that follows his own understanding of the full transformation of our humanity in the incarnate Christ.

## The Formula of Exchange

The "formula of exchange" is, in a sense, both the entry point and the culmination of Leo's theology of deification. It is the bridge that connects his richly developed Christology with his account of human transformation in Christ, and at the same time points to the soteriological goal of that Christology. The "formula of exchange" refers to a form of a paradoxical expression that describes the eternal Son of God assuming our human condition in order to communicate to us his divine life and power. In short, this formula expresses, in a variety of ways, that the Word of God became what we are so that we could become what he is. It is modeled in the New Testament in 2 Corinthians 8:9: "For your sake he become poor, though being rich, so that by his poverty you may become rich."[7]

Leo offers many varieties of the exchange formula (I count at least twenty-five different instances). An initial set appears in his first round of sermons in the early days of his papacy (441–45); a second set emerges in both sermons and letters from the years surrounding and following the conflict with Eutyches and the Council of Chalcedon (448–54). This ample use of the "formula of exchange" from his early ministry right through the season of great

---

6. J. Mark Armitage, *A Twofold Solidarity: Leo the Great's Theology of Redemption* (Strathfield: St. Paul's Publications, 2005), 133.

7. Author's translation.

doctrinal conflict demonstrates that Leo held firmly to this formula even when his own account of Christ came under fire.[8] A selection of these statements of the exchange formula will enable us to see the contours of Leo's understanding of our salvation.

In his first set of sermons for Holy Week (in 441) Leo speaks of the mystery of Christ's birth, death, and resurrection as the context for our transformation: "This whole mystery (which both humanity and divinity have completed together) was a dispensation of mercy and an act of love.... Condescension by the divinity therefore becomes our advancement [*provectio*]."[9] He sees the celebration of the Christian Passover as the occasion for the faithful to embrace the "advancement" given to them in Christ: "Let us, then, embrace the wonderful mystery of the saving Passover, and be reformed into the image of the one who conformed himself to our deformity. Let us be raised to the one who made the dust of our lowliness into the body of his glory."[10] A year later he refers explicitly to the "wonderful exchange" at the heart of the Gospel message: "He had come into this world as the rich and merciful ambassador from heaven. He had entered the economy of salvation [*salutare commercium*] in a wonderful interchange [*commutatione mirabili*], receiving our state and giving us his own, giving honors for insults, health for pain, life for death."[11] In a sermon for Pentecost that same year, Leo speaks of "the elevation [*provectio*] of humanity by the Incarnation of the Word" and frames the exchange formula in one of its most common configurations: "I have united you to myself, and I have become the son of man [*filius hominis*] so that you can be sons of God [*filii Dei*]."[12]

Leo's emphasis on the full integrity of both the divine and human natures in Christ does not leave them cut off from one another but assumes that they are joined so that our humanity can be lifted up to Christ's divinity, as this selection from a Holy Week sermon in 443 displays: "Being at once like unto

---

8. For the value and importance of reading Leo's sermons and letters in a chronological fashion, see Bernard Green, *The Soteriology of Leo the Great* (Oxford: Oxford University Press, 2008).

9. *Sermon* 52.2, in *St. Leo the Great: Sermons*, trans. Jane P. Freeland and Agnes J. Conway, Fathers of the Church (hereafter, FOTC) 93 (Washington, D.C.: The Catholic University of American Press, 1996), 227. Unless otherwise noted, parenthetical page numbers for *Sermons* citations are taken from this volume.

10. *Sermon* 33.3 (232).

11. *Sermon* 54.4 (235).

12. *Sermon* 77.5 (344, translation adjusted).

us and equal with the Father, he lowered his divinity to the human state and lifted his humanity up to the divine [*divinitatem usque ad humana submisit humanitatem usque ad divina provexit*]."[13] In the Christmas sermons from the same year, Leo employs the "formula of exchange" to reveal the wonder of the incarnation: "Though whatever the Creator expends on the creature comes from one and same concern, nevertheless it would be less amazing that a human being should advance to divine things [*hominem ad divina proficere*] than that God should descend to human ones [*Deum ad humana descendere*]."[14] Though the emphasis here is on the descent of the Word in the incarnation, the logic of our ascending through "advance" to divine things is clearly present. The point of the incarnation is the communication of "divine things" (*divina*) to us: "His divinity conducted his power and goodness in such a way that he raised what was ours by taking it up and did not lose what was his own by sharing it."[15]

And it is here in the Christmas sermons that we see Leo's use of the text of 2 Peter 1:4. He employs this momentous passage to express just this "exchange" by which we come to share in the eternal life that is in Christ: "His humanity has not destroyed the equality which remains inviolable in the divinity, and the descent of the Creator to the creature is really the elevation of believers to eternal life.... Consequently, the Lord Jesus ... was made a man of our race, so that we might be able to become 'partakers of the divine nature' [2 Pt 1:4]."[16] Leo also cites 2 Peter 1:4 in an earlier Christmas homily: "Realize, O Christian, your dignity. Once made a 'partaker of the divine nature' [2 Pt 1:4], do not return to your former baseness of life." When did this change occur, according to Leo? "Through the sacrament of baptism you were made 'a temple of the Holy Spirit' [1 Cor 6:19]. Do not drive away such a dweller by your wicked actions."[17] For Leo, it is the indwelling Spirit given through baptism that inaugurates our participation in the divine nature and elevates us to eternal life.

Leo's ample use of variations on the "formula of exchange" continues in

---

13. *Sermon* 3.2 (22). Green, *The Soteriology of Leo the Great*, 144, defends Leo against holding a composite view of the incarnation: "The two natures are not components brought together; rather, one nature assumed and the other was assumed. It is a personal not a composite union."
14. *Sermon* 24.2 (93).
15. *Sermon* 24.3 (94).
16. *Sermon* 25.4–5 (102–3).
17. *Sermon* 21.3 (79).

the period of conflict that arose with the controversy concerning Eutyches beginning in 448. Leo voices the unequal exchange at the heart of Christ's work in his letter to the clergy and people of Constantinople in 449, following the so-called Robber Council in Ephesus. Despite his determined effort to maintain the genuinely human nature that Christ assumed (against what he perceived as Eutyches's denial of this), Leo upholds the "increase" given to our nature through Christ's assumption and redemption of that nature: "Abiding in the form of God, he united to himself the form of a slave, and the likeness of sinful flesh, whereby he did not lessen the divine by the human, but increased the human by the divine [*non minueret divina humanis sed augeret humana divinis*]."[18] In a Christmas sermon (December 451) delivered just weeks after the Council of Chalcedon concluded, Leo continues to display the incarnation of the Word as the inauguration of our share in divine things: "That supreme and eternal essence which condescended to save the human race has drawn [*transtulit*] us into its own glory, without ceasing to be what it was.... He grafted himself into us and us into himself in such a way that God's descent to human things [*ad humana*] became the elevation [*provectio*] of human beings to those divine [*ad divina*]."[19] The following Christmas (452) Leo uses striking language to speak of this exchange at the core of the incarnation: "Turning our attention to that ineffable condescension by which the Creator of human beings deigned to become himself a human being, may we be found in the nature of the one whom we adore in our own [*in ipsius nos inveniamur natura, quem adoramus in nostra*]."[20] The phrase, "that we may be found in his nature" probably means nothing other than what Leo understands 2 Peter 1:4 to communicate, that in Christ we become "partakers of the divine nature." To ward off any misunderstanding, Leo underlines that "this happened without any damage to his majesty, so that he might lift us up to his state rather than that he should decline into ours."[21]

As controversy increased following the Council of Chalcedon and Leo's account of Christ encountered sharp criticism in the East, Leo felt the need to clarify his view of Christ (as given in the Tome of 448) by underlining the

---

18. *Ep.* 59.3 (Nicene and Post-Nicene Fathers, ed. Schaff, Second Series [hereafter, NPNF-II], 12:59–60).
19. *Sermon* 27.1–2 (111–12, translation adjusted).
20. *Sermon* 28.1 (116).
21. Ibid.

unity of person in Christ. In this polemical context, he continues to boldly express the exchange that has occurred for us because of the Son's assumption of our nature. In a letter to the monks of Palestine (June 453), Leo writes: "He who was in the form of God took the form of a slave in such wise that Christ is one and the same in both forms: God bending himself to the weak things of man [*inclinante se Deo usque ad infirma hominis*], and man rising up to the high things of the Godhead [*et proficient homine usque ad summa Deitatis*]."[22] For Leo, the incarnation of the Word is not simply a divine strategy for rescuing human beings and *leaving them as they are*, but involves the advancement of the human race to the high things of the deity. What Leo means by this is partly specified elsewhere when he speaks about the regaining of the image and likeness of God through imitation, but it is plain that he portrays human salvation in terms of a sharing in the things of God. This becomes luminously clear in a homily given just months later during the September fast (in 453) in which Leo states perhaps most clearly in all his writings the exchange at the heart of human salvation: "He united humanity to himself in such a way that he remained God, unchangeable. He imparted divinity to man [*deitatem homini impertiens*] in such a way that he did not destroy, but enriched [*augeret*] him, by glorification [*glorificatione*]."[23]

In partial explanation of how Christ has imparted divinity to us and enriched our nature, Leo explains in a sermon for Holy Week in the year following (March 454) that Christ assumed our nature in order to *heal* it in himself: "He nevertheless took the reality of our weakness and excluded nothing of human infirmity from himself except participation in our sin. That way, he might bring his own nature to us and heals ours in himself.... As a result, the Lord rightly became 'the Way' [Jn 14:6] for us, since we cannot come to Christ except through Christ."[24] For Leo, this healing occurs through the exchange that lies at the heart of the incarnation and passion of Christ: "Divine power [*virtus divina*] joined itself to human frailty to this end, that God, while making what was ours his [*sua facit esse quae notra sunt*], might at the same time make what was his ours [*nostra faceret esse quae sua sunt*]."[25]

Leo's use of the "formula of exchange" in many varieties displays how cen-

22. *Ep.* 124.9 (NPNF-II 12:95).
23. *Sermon* 91.2 (384, translation adjusted).
24. *Sermon* 67.5–6 (294–95).
25. *Sermon* 68.1 (NPNF-II 12:180).

tral this was to his theological outlook. Yes, Leo was especially concerned to uphold the integrity and reality of the two natures in Christ and was allergic to any confession that called the ongoing integrity of the natures into question. But for Leo the entire point of the dual constitution of Christ is the assuming, healing, raising, and glorifying of our nature through our share in Christ. In Leo's own terms, this involves a participation in the divine nature; it means that what the Son is in his divinity is what we are raised to. The Son shares in what is ours so that we can share in what is his, in "divine things" (*divina*), in such a way that our nature is not changed but glorified.

## Participation in the Divine Nature

In an attempt to demarcate a "comprehensive doctrine" of deification, Gösta Hallonsten identifies the concept of participation as one of the constituent elements of deification.[26] Leo exemplifies the use of participation language in a way comparable to others of his day, including Augustine in the West and Cyril of Alexandria in the East. He employs a related set of terms to express this: as nouns, *communio*, *communicatio*, *participatio*, and *consors*; and as verbs, *communicare* and *participare*. All of these words appear in the Vulgate as Latin equivalents for the Greek words for "participation" found in the New Testament.[27]

Leo employs the concept of participation in three distinct senses. The first is to show the participation of human beings in a common nature: "We must love the mutual participation [*communio*] in the human nature of all people."[28] The second sense is a Christological application of the first sense. Christ fully participated in our nature by assuming it, by actually becoming a man: "The infirmity of the human mind, as it comes to accept the true humanity of Christ, cannot help but tremble on account of this participation [*communio*] with our nature."[29] The third sense of participation describes a contingent hu-

---

26. "*Theosis* in Recent Research," 286. Hallonsten more precisely identifies this as "the Platonic concept of participation." I would prefer to speak of this as a concept of participation, drawn from the Platonic tradition but deeply reconfigured and transformed by a specifically Christian doctrine of creation and further informed by participationist language in the New Testament.

27. For a survey of the vocabulary of participation in the New Testament, see Daniel A. Keating, *The Appropriation of Divine Life in Cyril of Alexandria* (Oxford: Oxford University Press, 2004), 148–50.

28. *Sermon* 41.3 (178, translation adjusted).

29. *Sermon* 38.2 (163).

man relationship to God, both in the sense of participation in *being* and of dynamic participation through *grace*. On the one hand, God is the source of all being; we exist by participating in the being of God.[30] On the other hand, we receive spiritual life through our participation in the grace of God.

Dynamic participation in God through grace—the sense crucial to a theology of deification—is employed by Leo to describe how God has come to dwell in us and transform us from within by his power. In a Christmas sermon (453), Leo speaks of our participation in Christ as the basis for our ongoing and freely chosen participation in his work and character: "We have been taken up through the New Covenant into a participation [*consortium*] with him.... Let those who are going to be co-heirs with Christ in glory be co-participants [*conparticipes*] in his lowliness as well."[31] Our participation in Christ makes us a new creation and serves as the ground for our ongoing growth into the likeness of Christ: "What is participation [*participatio*] with Christ for us except that we cease to be what we were? Or what is the likeness to the resurrection except the putting off of the old self?"[32]

While it is clear that Leo consistently speaks of our dynamic participation in Christ through grace, just what does he mean by this? Is it, in fact, a form of participation that entails what the Christian tradition normally understands by deification? We gain some insight into Leo's view from a sermon given on Palm Sunday (453). Speaking of faith as making us a sharer (*participes*) in Christ's nature (here plainly referring to his *divine* nature), Leo says that through a participation (*communionem*) in Christ's birth/origin (*generis*), the faithful have come to "the peace of divinity [*ad pacem deitatis*]" and are free "to glory in his power."[33] Just what he means by coming to the "peace of divinity" is unclear, but Leo points to a genuine share in Christ's own power by sharing in his nature.

Two sermons on the resurrection shed further light on what Leo means by our participation in Christ. In the first, Leo maintains that the resurrection did not bring an end to our nature but led to a new state and quality of our nature:

---

30. For this sense of participation in being, see Leo's letter against the Priscillianists, *Ep.* 15.6.
31. *Sermon* 29.3 (124–25, translation adjusted).
32. *Sermon* 50.1 (214, translation adjusted).
33. *Sermon* 64.3 (280, translation adjusted).

Our Lord's resurrection did not put an end to his flesh, but changed it. No, the substance [*substantia*] was not destroyed by an increase in power. Its state [*qualitas*] changed, but the nature [*natura*] did not give out. His body—which could be crucified—became impassible. His body—which could be killed—became immortal. What could be wounded became incorruptible.... Consequently, it both remains the same with respect to its essence [*per essentiam*] and does not remain the same with respect to its glory [*per gloriam*].[34]

What are the new qualities that Christ's resurrected body possesses? Leo points to impassibility, immortality, and incorruptibility—these are "divine" qualities that now characterize the human body of Christ and will be ours in the resurrection of our bodies. For Leo, this is rightly seen as "the exaltation [*provectione*] of our nature" because in Christ our nature has received its share in the divine qualities. Rowan Williams concludes that "communication of divine attributes" is one of the marks of the patristic doctrine of deification.[35] Leo shows that he holds to such a communication of divine attributes to our nature in a way that does not change human nature but elevates and glorifies it for life with God. This appears to be what Leo means by "imparting divinity" to the human race: we take on divine qualities and powers that enable us to live and act fully in the likeness of Christ. All this begins now but will only happen fully in the resurrection when we undergo the same transformation that Christ has already undergone for us.

In the second sermon on the resurrection, Leo depicts the result of Christ's work of redemption as more than mere restoration but not as a change in human nature, and he does so using explicitly participationist language:

> The merciful God wanted to help the creature ... in such a way that the restoration of its nature should not be outside of that nature, and that the second creation should advance beyond the dignity of its original state.... It was a great thing to have received a form [*formam*] from Christ [*a Christo*], but greater still to have its substance [*substantiam*] in Christ [*in Christo*].... As we must not doubt our participation [*consortio*] in his glory, so we must not doubt his participation [*communione*] in our nature.[36]

---

34. *Sermon* 71.4 (313).
35. Rowan Williams, "Deification," in *A Dictionary of Christian Spirituality*, ed. Gordon S. Wakefield (London: SCM Press, 1983), 106.
36. *Sermon* 72.2 (317).

Through the transformation Christ accomplished for our nature in himself, we already have a share in his own glory, but remain the human beings that we are.

To sum up Leo's concern: he is intent on upholding the full integrity of human and divine natures in Christ, but not to keep those natures hermetically sealed off from one another (either in Christ or with respect to our share in Christ). He wants to ensure that it is *our nature* that shares in the divine power and qualities that mark its glorification. All this now occurs *in Christ* in a new and profound way because he has taken our nature to himself in order to glorify it in himself and for us.

## The Image and Likeness of God

Gösta Hallonsten identifies a certain anthropology as a further mark of a comprehensive doctrine of deification: "Anthropology is the fundamental feature that marks the Eastern doctrine of deification and is thus the key to an accurate understanding of this doctrine."[37] He understands this anthropology to consist in a dynamic account of human nature, such that "human beings from the very beginning are endowed with an affinity and likeness that potentially draws them to God."[38] Hallonsten sees this as typically cast in terms of a dynamic growth from the image, given in creation and not lost in the Fall, to the likeness, regained in Christ and gradually attained in the believer through ascetic effort and participation in the life of the church. While this theological distinction between image and likeness is found in certain Church Fathers and marks the later Byzantine account of deification, it is notably not present in several of the leading proponents of deification among the *Greek* Fathers—Athanasius, Gregory of Nyssa, and Cyril of Alexandria—who treat "image" and "likeness" as synonyms.[39] In the West, Hilary, Ambrose, and Leo all follow this latter pattern whereby image and likeness are central terms for anthropology but are treated as equivalents. Nonetheless, there exists among them a "dynamic" anthropology, grounded in creation and fulfilled in Christ, that re-

---

37. Hallonsten, "*Theosis* in Recent Research," 286.
38. Ibid., 285.
39. Russell, *Fellow Workers*, 77–80, shows the equivalence of image and likeness in these three major figures from the East.

quires the full exercise of a human grace-filled response to bring about growth into the full image and likeness of Christ.

Leo himself consistently employs the terms "image" and "likeness" to indicate the basic constitution of the human race (following Gn 1:26–27),[40] but he also uses these terms to describe both the healing and *reconstitution* of our nature in Christ himself and our active cooperation as we grow into the likeness of Christ. The following exhortation from a Christmas sermon of 451 shows how Leo views human nature, created and redeemed, in terms of the image of God: "Wake up then, O friend, and acknowledge the dignity of your nature. Recall that you have been made 'according to the image of God.' This nature, although it had been corrupted in Adam, has nevertheless been refashioned [*reformata*] in Christ."[41] For Leo, Christ assumed our nature in order to restore it to the full image and likeness of God: "'God was in Christ, reconciling the world to himself'" (2 Cor 5:19), and the creator himself was bearing the humanity that was about to be restored to the image of its Maker."[42]

For Leo, this refashioning is not just a return to an original pristine state but advances the human race according to the purpose of God because our nature has now been taken up by the Son:

> Yet the merciful God wanted to help the creature "made in his own image" [Gn 1:27] through his only Son Jesus Christ—in such a way that the restoration [*reparatio*] of its nature should not be outside of that nature, and that the second creation should advance beyond the dignity of its original state. Happy the nature which has not fallen away from what God made, but happier still the one which remains in what God has remade. It was a great thing to have received a form from Christ, but greater still to have its substance in Christ.[43]

Leo speaks of the same "advance" gained in Christ in a Christmas sermon from 443: "Although he had given much to our human origin in making us to his image, the Lord put far more into our restoration [*reparationi nostrae*] when he accommodated himself to the 'form of a servant' [Phil 2:7]."[44]

Through his incarnation, passion, death, resurrection, and ascension Christ has accomplished the restoration and advancement of our nature in himself—

---

40. See *Sermon* 9.1 and 77.2; *Ep.* 15.1.
41. *Sermon* 27.6 (114).
42. *Sermon* 54.4 (234).
43. *Sermon* 72.2 (316).
44. *Sermon* 24.2 (93, translation adjusted).

this is the secure work that is the basis for our own growth into the likeness of Christ. But for Leo, the fact that Christ accomplished the full perfection of the image and likeness of God does not eliminate, but calls for and secures, our own full cooperation of this work in each one of us. We are not merely passive recipients of what Christ has done but active cooperators in the work.[45] "Human beings, made in the image and likeness of God, have nothing in the dignity of their nature so especially their own as that they can match the goodness of their Creator, who as he is a merciful donor of his own gifts, so he is a just creditor, willing for us to be participants [*consortes*] in his work."[46] This cooperation is not an independent work accomplished by human beings through their own power but is a gift of God that enables human beings to "mirror" what God has done: "How much more glorious is it for those born of God to mirror brightly the image of their Creator and to show in themselves the one who created them?"[47] And again, "In this way the Creator will appear in his own creature, and the image of God expressed through the paths of imitation, may shine in the mirror of the human heart."[48]

The metaphor of a mirror, in which our action is grounded in our being "in Christ" and is fueled by his grace, is a characteristic mark of Leo's teaching. As Wessel explains, the quality of divine mercy, expressed especially through almsgiving, is the preeminent sign of how we "mirror" the mercy that God has shown to us: "For Leo, [mercy] facilitated its unmediated knowledge of the self. It was the divine quality most amenable to imitation, the mirror ('speculum') by which ordinary human beings might examine their souls and determine how and whether they conformed to the image of God ('imago Dei')."[49]

Leo's most developed account of how we are refashioned to the image and likeness on a daily basis through our cooperative effort appears in a sermon given during the December fasting season. He begins by showing the

---

45. Wessel, *Leo the Great*, 144, recognizes this particular emphasis in Leo on the link between being made in the image and likeness and our free cooperation in our own renewal in Christ: "Following the example of the good works performed by Christ was the way in which humanity was expected to exercise virtuously the freedom that had been bestowed upon it. What made that demand well within the capacity of ordinary people was the deeply held conviction that humanity, as Leo and others conceived it, had been made in the image and likeness of God."

46. *Sermon* 20.2 (73).
47. *Sermon* 26.4 (108).
48. *Sermon* 95.7 (398–99).
49. *Leo the Great*, 147.

link between our creation in the image and likeness of God and the free cooperation called forth from us. It is *because* we are made in the likeness of God that we are called to imitation:

> We shall come to the realization that human beings have been formed according to the image of God precisely with a view that they might imitate their Designer. Our race has this dignity of nature, so long as the figure of divine goodness continues to be reflected in us as in a kind of mirror. Indeed, the Savior's grace re-fashions us to this image on a daily basis [*cotidie*]. What fell in the first Adam has been raised up in the second. But our being re-fashioned has no other cause than the mercy of God.[50]

The great dignity of our nature is that we are called to a freely chosen imitation of our creator, as a kind of mirror of the divine goodness. This refashioning occurs on a *daily basis*—it is a constant and progressive growth into the image and likeness of God. And the *cause* of this refashioning is the mercy of God. God himself makes this possible by the mercy that he has shown us in Christ.

Leo takes this one stage further by showing divine love as the primary cause of our refashioning. By receiving God's love and then putting that very love into practice, we are daily refashioned to the divine likeness: "It is by loving that God re-fashions us to his image. That he might find in us the image of this goodness, he gives us the very means by which we can perform the works that we do—by lighting the lamps of our minds and inflaming us with the fire of his love, so that we might love not only him but also whatever he loves."[51] Leo then draws attention to the three specific practices through which the image of God is renewed in us, each one a manifestation of the love of God: prayer, fasting, and almsgiving. It is especially by practicing these that we come to the fullness of the image and likeness and that we are made inseparable from the indwelling Holy Spirit: "Through all of them [prayer, fasting, almsgiving] at the same time, the image of God is renewed in us—provided we are always ready to praise him, concerned about our purification without respite, and constantly intent upon supporting our neighbor. This threefold observance, dearly beloved, encompasses the effects of all virtues. It brings us to the image and likeness of God and makes us insepara-

---

50. *Sermon* 12.1 (49).
51. Ibid. (50).

ble from the Holy Spirit."[52] Implicit in Leo's theology of image and likeness, I contend, is a theology of deification. The human race, made in the image and likeness of God, has now been remade and refashioned in Christ—but now to a higher and more advanced place because we are now not just "in Adam" but "in Christ." But what is the content of this difference? It is nothing other than real participation, through the assumed humanity, in the divine Son of God. We are now partakers of the divine nature through Christ (as Leo says in two of his sermons),[53] and his remaking and advancing of our nature in himself now becomes ours. What Leo demonstrates is a dynamic sense of image and likeness, grounded in our creation as free creatures, a freedom now released and empowered by being in Christ by the indwelling of the Spirit.[54] It is *because* Christ has fully restored the image and likeness of God that we are now enabled—and required—to cooperate in the task of bringing this image and likeness to completion. In sum, Leo displays a dynamic anthropology, rooted in creation, refashioned and brought to perfection in Christ, and now calling forth our full cooperation.

## Participation through *Sacramentum* and *Exemplum*

Drawing on a tradition found already in Hilary and Augustine, Leo employs the paired terms, *sacramentum* and *exemplum*, to describe and coordinate what Norman Russell has called the "realistic" and "ethical" aspects of our incorporation into Christ.[55] By *sacramentum* Leo means the action of Christ to redeem our nature in himself that we then share in "realistically" primarily through the gift of the Spirit and participation in the sacraments of

---

52. Ibid. (53).
53. *Sermon* 21.3 and 25.5.
54. For Leo's understanding of the role of the Spirit in the faithful in Leo, see Keating, *The Appropriation of Divine Life in Cyril of Alexandria*, 269–72: "Leo conceives of the Spirit as both the divine agent who effects our rebirth in baptism, and as the divine indweller who comes to live in the soul of the believer as the agent of ongoing sanctification" (270).
55. See Norman Russell, *The Doctrine of Deification in the Greek Patristic Tradition*, 1, 9, 14. See also his *Fellow Workers with God*, 23–27, where Russell shows that these two terms (realistic and ethical) encompass the two primary senses of deification found in the Fathers. The realistic sense refers to the transformation of our humanity through the incarnation and our participation in Christ through the sacramental life of the church; the ethical sense refers to the ascetic effort needed to attain likeness to God through imitation.

baptism and the eucharist. This is the "remedy" provided by Christ himself.[56] By *exemplum*, Leo means the pattern set forth by Christ himself that we are to imitate, an imitation necessarily grounded in being in Christ but also calling forth our full cooperation and effort.

In a sermon on the passion (in April 444), Leo displays the pairing of these terms in regard to the cross of Christ: "Now, indeed, the Cross of Christ (which represents the cost of saving mortals) contains both a mystery [*sacramentum*] and an example [*exemplum*]. Divine power has been fulfilled through the mystery, human devotion aroused by the example."[57] Later the same year Leo expounds how the two work together in the plan of God. Referring to how Christ undid the work of Adam, through his meekness and humility in the incarnation, the cross, and the resurrection, Leo writes: "These works of our Lord, dearly beloved, are useful to us, not only as a mystery [*sacramento*], but also as an example [*exemplo*] for our imitation—if only these remedies would be turned into instruction, and what has been bestowed by the mysteries would benefit the way people live."[58] The unique and irreplaceable work of Christ (*sacramentum*) not only brings us to new birth and new life in him but leaves us with an ethical task—the imitation of his lowliness and humility in our lives. Armitage contends that this ethical response is not mere imitation of an example but sweeps us up, through the reading of the sacred mystery in the liturgy, into the work that Christ himself accomplished for us, and so truly makes our imitation a real participation in Christ's work in us: "This *imitatio Christi*, however, is far more than just a response to an exemplum. As well as responding to the exemplum of Jesus, we are swept up into the sacramentum of Jesus' narrative, which we encounter in 'the narrative which is read to us from the gospel,' and so become part of the new creation."[59]

There is both a proper order and an internal link between Christ's work

---

56. *Sermon* 21.2 (79): "Were he not indeed true God, he could apply no remedy [*remedium*]. Were he not indeed true man, he could not show example [*exemplum*]." Green, *Soteriology in Leo the Great*, 119, sums up the meaning of *sacramentum* in Leo as "the saving acts of the Incarnate Word, the object of faith and cause of a loving response in the faithful."

57. *Sermon* 72.1 (316).

58. *Sermon* 25.6 (103–4).

59. Armitage, *A Twofold Solidarity*, 102. Green, *Soteriology of Leo the Great*, 114, also concludes that *exemplum* in Leo means more than mere "example": "*Exemplum* does not mean example but rather pattern or model or paradigm.... It thus means that, in his human nature, Christ is the embodiment of perfect manhood; but it must also mean that Christ is the prototype, the pattern, to which we shall be conformed."

as *sacramentum* and *exemplum*. His objective work for our salvation has primacy; receiving this is the first "act" of the Christian. But at the same time this one unique work is also an *exemplum*, and the second act of the Christian is the appropriate imitation of the pattern that he set: "Our Saviour, the Son of God, gave both a mystery [*sacramentum*] and an example [*exemplum*] to all who believe in him, so that they might attain to the one by being reborn, and arrive at the other by imitation."[60] In a sermon for the passion (454), Leo identifies this twofold aspect of Christ's one work as a "double remedy": "A double remedy has been prepared for us miserable people by the Almighty Physician, one of which is in the mystery [*in sacramento*], the other in his example [*in exemplo*]. Through the one, divine things [*divina*] are conferred; through the other, human response is required. As God is the author of justification, so human beings are debtors of devotion."[61]

For Leo, the one multifaceted work of the incarnate Son of God provides *at one and the same time* both the accomplishment of our salvation and the ground for our conscious and cooperative imitation of him. On the one hand, Christ uniquely accomplished the work of salvation, that is, the reclamation, restoration, and the advancement of our nature to "divine things." Our realistic appropriation of that unique work is the *sacramentum*—and the liturgy provides the privileged occasion for renewed participation in that mystery. On the other hand, this one work also supplies an example, a pattern, to be consciously adopted by the faithful. By our effort and struggle we share through imitation in this one work of Christ. For Leo, it is by receiving the *sacramentum* and cooperating in the *exemplum* that we grow progressively into the image and likeness of God. In Leo's hands, these two terms artfully capture and coordinate the two fundamental aspects of our deification in Christ.

In order to describe the inner working of how we cooperate with Christ and imitate his example, Leo makes frequent appeal to Philippians 2:12–13 ("Work out your own salvation with fear and trembling, for God is at work in you, both to will and to work for his good pleasure"). The paradoxical language of this verse captures for Leo the two truths we must maintain and coordinate. It is *God* who is at work in us even as *we* are called to be cooperators in this work. This verse deflects us from a Pelagian sense of self-sanctification

---

60. *Sermon* 63.4 (274).
61. *Sermon* 67.5 (294, translation adjusted).

while at the same time securing the necessity of our real and free cooperation in our own transformation into the image and likeness of God.

In an early sermon for Epiphany, Leo speaks of the need for us to cooperate with the grace that God gives: "When we consider, dearly beloved, the ineffable generosity of God in his gifts to us, we should be cooperators [*cooperatores*] with the grace of God 'working in us' [Phil 2:13]."[62] Some years later while in the midst of the Eutychian controversy, Leo returns to this text as signaling our collaboration with the work of God in us: "If we are of one mind with him (willing what he wills, disapproving of what he disapproves), he himself will bring us victory in all our battles. He who has given the 'will' will bestow also the ability [Phil 2:13]. In this way we can be cooperators [*cooperatores*] with his works."[63] In one instance, Leo links Philippians 2:13 specifically to having recourse to genuine divine power, enabling believers to be light in the world:

Who would not understand the divinity [*deitatem*] to be present where they behold a manifestation of true power. Indeed, without God there is no true power. Power does not hold any property of divinity [*deitatis*] unless it is invigorated by the Spirit of its Author. Since the Lord said to his disciples, "Without me you can do nothing," there is no doubt that a human being who does good has from God both the effect of his work as well as the beginnings of the intention to do it.[64]

While the text of Philippians 2:12–13 provides Leo with biblical language that expresses our active cooperation with the power of God at work in us, he often describes the same reality in different words. In a late sermon for the Feast of Pentecost, Leo refers to the indwelling Holy Spirit, referencing Romans 5:5, as the divine presence and power within us that enables us to carry out good works in a way genuinely pleasing to God.

Because even with great almsgiving it will be sterile unless it has come forth under the outpouring of the Holy Spirit. Since the Apostle says that no virtues "benefit him without love" [1 Cor 13:3], and, when the same one says that "the love of God is spread abroad through our hearts by the Holy Spirit who has been given to us" [Rom 5:5], we must beware lest we lose by pride the good things that we cannot do without his goodness.[65]

62. *Sermon* 35.3 (152).
63. *Sermon* 26.4 (108).
64. *Sermon* 38.3 (164). That Leo has Phil 2:13 plainly in view here is confirmed by his citing Phil 2:12–13 in its entirety in the very next sentence of the sermon.
65. *Sermon* 79.3 (348).

This divine indwelling through the Spirit is a constant theme throughout Leo's writings. In a sermon for Christmas, Leo cites 1 Corinthians 3:16 and concludes: "If we are 'the temple of God and the Spirit of God dwells in us,' what each believer has become in their heart exceeds the marvels of heaven."[66] Speaking of the whole church during the Lenten fast, Leo calls the faithful to sanctify the fast so that "we may be the eternal dwelling place of the Holy Spirit, who deigns to possess us washed from the stains of our sins, and to rule us forever."[67] Leo is not referring in these texts merely to a work of grace in the heart, but to the divine presence of the Spirit who lives in the heart and effectively leads believers to eternal life. In a remarkable text from a sermon given toward the end of his career, Leo expresses in poetic language the glory of the divine indwelling in human beings: "If the houses of kings and the courts of high officials are with reason honored with every adornment to make more noble residences for those whose services are greater, with how much labor should the 'home of divinity itself' [*ipsius Deitatis habitaculum*] be built and with how much honor it should be decorated!"[68]

In sum, Leo presents throughout his writings a coherent and scripturally-based account of our participation in Christ through the Spirit. Christ is both our *sacramentum* and *exemplum*: by being in Christ and having the Spirit dwell in our hearts we are brought to new life in God and are able to be active "cooperators" in the work of God both in us and through us. And Leo is clear that it is genuinely *divine* power at work in us that enables us to be cooperators with God. By virtue of this active cooperation, we become progressively conformed to the image and likeness of God. What we see here in Leo is a dynamic anthropology, Christologically and pneumatically grounded, that expresses both the realistic and ethical aspects of our deification.

## Conclusion: The Shape of Deification in Leo

As noted above, Susan Wessel concludes that "divinization was not a possibility for Leo because he was committed to the idea that Christ was linked

---

66. *Sermon* 27.6 (115).
67. *Sermon* 42.6 (185).
68. *Sermon* 48.1 (206). Leo appears to be making an allusion here to Eph 2:22 which speaks of us being "the dwelling place of God in the Spirit" (*in habitaculum Dei in Spiritu*).

to humanity only through the complete integrity of his human nature."[69] This is difficult to square with the view stated earlier in her study that, for Leo, "because the divine and human natures were so complete in their respective attributes, and so intertwined by the unity of their person, the implication was that the impassible divinity was paradoxically present in the humanity that suffered."[70] The intertwining of the two natures and the presence of the divinity in the humanity that suffered better expresses the nuance of Leo's thought.

Wessel skillfully shows Leo's determination to present a full humanity in complete union with the divinity in Christ, but she fails to take account of the rich language of exchange that runs like a thread throughout Leo's writings. Leo not only employs the text from 2 Peter 1:4 to express our participation in the divine nature,[71] but states this reality many times over in his own words, showing that he is not merely quoting this text but making theological use of it to describe our destiny in Christ. He speaks of the elevation and advancement of the human being to things divine,[72] of the Word lowering himself to our state so that we might share in his,[73] of the increase of what is human by the divine,[74] and of human participation in the Son's divine nature.[75] When Leo says that the Son "imparted divinity to man in such a way that he did not destroy, but enriched him, by glorification," he is expressing the heart and center of his doctrine of deification.[76]

For Leo, human nature is repaired, renewed, and fully glorified first in Christ himself, through his own divine power. Nowhere does Leo explain what he means by the "glorification" of human nature in Christ, but plainly when Christ imparts his divinity to our nature it becomes glorified without ceasing to be human nature. For Leo, the eternal Word was not changed by taking our human nature, but so exalted "the assumed nature that it remains glorified in him who glorifies it."[77] Even in the resurrection of Christ, his human

---

69. *Leo the Great*, 251.
70. Ibid., 229.
71. *Sermon* 21.3 and 25.5.
72. *Ep.* 124.9; *Sermon* 24.2 and 27.2.
73. *Sermon* 3.2, 28.1, 54.4, 71.2.
74. *Ep.* 59.3.
75. *Sermon* 64.3.
76. *Sermon* 91.2 (384, translation adjusted).
77. *Ep.* 35.2, in *St. Leo the Great: Letters*, trans. Edmund Hunt, FOTC 34 (Washington, D.C.: The Catholic University of America Press, 1957), 113.

nature "remains the same with respect to its essence and does not remain the same with respect to its glory."[78] The biblical language of glorification appears to function in Leo as a description of what he means by saying that in Christ our nature is not changed but elevated and filled with divine life and power.[79]

Crucially for Leo, Christ's humanity is not partitioned off from his divinity but actively partakes of divine life and power so that while remaining the nature that it is (i.e., human nature) it can be raised to the glory God intended. When we are joined to Christ, our humanity partakes of this same repair, renewal, and glorification, and we too as human beings share in the divine life and power that Christ possesses because of his full divinity. Like his older contemporary Cyril of Alexandria, Leo understands the indwelling of Christ and the Spirit in the believer (and in the church) to be the basis for this repairing, renewal, and glorification of human nature in the life of the believer. This was the purpose for which Christ came, that by becoming what we are he might enable us to become what he is. And this is accomplished by the divine presence within us, through our active cooperation and the full enlistment of our will.

J. Mark Armitage acknowledges a doctrine of deification in Leo, but contrasts this with what he sees present in Eastern writers such as Athanasius: "Where eastern writers like Athanasius speak of 'deification' (theosis), western writers such as Leo depict this process (at least by implication) more in terms of the idea that the Son enters *in solido* with us in order that we might enter *in solido* with him."[80] He appears to qualify this one-sidedness when he admits that for Leo, "the Son experienced all that it means to be human in order that we, in due course, might share in what it means to be divine."[81] But he still wishes to distinguish this Western form of deification from that found in the East: "But Leo's is not a theology of mystical inclusion and divinization—at least, not in the sense in which these are usually understood."[82]

Armitage rightly identifies an emphasis in Leo's thought—the full solidarity of Christ in our humanity—but underplays the full implication of this

---

78. *Sermon* 71.4 (313).

79. For the use of "glory" and "glorification" in Leo to describe the transformation of Christ's own humanity and our humanity in Christ, see *Ep.* 165.8 and *Sermon* 51.2; 53.3; 71.4, 6; 73.2; 74.4; 91.2.

80. Armitage, *A Twofold Solidarity*, 11.

81. Ibid., 133.

82. Ibid.

solidarity as found in Leo's frequent variations on the "formula of exchange." The point of this solidarity is that we might be united to Christ and experience the fruits of his divinity in our transformed and glorified humanity. And it remains unclear what Armitage means by "mystical inclusion and divinization." If he has in mind the cosmic-mystical theology of deification found, for example, in Maximus the Confessor, then certainly Leo's approach is distinct from this. But if he means the approach to deification found in Athanasius and Cyril, then I would argue that Leo's account is of this genus, even if he offers a specific form of it. Like his Alexandrian predecessors, Leo understands our share in the divine life in terms of an incarnational-sacramental participation.[83]

Why then, we might ask, does Leo shy away from the terminology of deification that would have been available to him through the writings of Augustine? While we cannot answer with certainty why Leo refrained from using deification terminology, three reasons may be surmised. First, the language of deification was not used widely in Western authorities to this point. Though Augustine uses this terminology sparingly, it is not found in Hilary, Ambrose, or Jerome—though in all three writers we can discern elements of a theology of deification and the use of 2 Peter 1:4 in a deification context. By employing biblical phrases and language drawn from the biblical sources, especially the language of glorification, Leo is expressing a theology of deification in a way consistent with the Western tradition before him. But by richly applying the "formula of exchange" within a highly developed Christology of the two natures, Leo advances the Western account of deification without using the technical terminology.

Second, Leo may have avoided the technical language of deification (in Latin, *deificare* and *deificatio*) because of the close links this language had with emperor worship. Living in Rome in the context of a strong connection to the empire, Leo may have judged that the language of deification was too closely linked with emperor worship, and so not suitable for speaking to the Christians in Rome.

Third, Leo may have shied away from the language of deification for the

---

83. See Russell, *Fellow Workers with God*, 47–54, for a helpful distinction between two broad versions of deification. The first takes its cue from Maximus and has a more cosmic mystical orientation; the second follows the lead of Athanasius and Cyril and is focused more on the incarnate Son and sacramental participation in him.

very reason that he found such fault with the theology of Eutyches. From the start Leo shows a determination to guard the full integrity of Christ's humanity, and this would only have been strengthened by what he saw happening in Eutyches—that is, a loss of the sense of Christ's full humanity by virtue of being swallowed up by his divinity. The terminology of deification may have seemed to Leo to give unhelpful support and encouragement to what he saw as a quasi-docetic approach to Christ.

But the maintenance of his use of the "formula of exchange" right through the Eutychian controversy shows that he did not withdraw from his conviction that Christ became fully what we are so that we might become what he is and might partake of the riches of his divine life and power. For Leo, through our realistic participation in Christ, especially through baptism and the eucharist,[84] we are joined to Christ and receive the full benefits of his redemption and the glorification of our nature. And through the full use of our graced capacities, willing what God wills, we grow stage by stage into the fullness of the divine image and likeness. In the present age, this attainment of the image and likeness is shown especially through our share in Christ's own humility and mercy—and notably Leo sees these as *divine* qualities that we imitate, following Christ in a human fashion. In the age to come, our share in the divine life for Leo will be revealed in a glorified humanity through the qualities of immortality and incorruptibility, and by our entire docility to the Spirit and our unhindered vision of God.[85]

---

84. In *Sermon* 63.7, Leo speaks of our participation in the eucharist as a means by which we "pass over" (*transeamus*) into what we have eaten, namely the body and blood of Christ, and participate therefore fully in the riches of Christ.

85. For Leo's statement of the vision of God in eternal life, when our human nature is fully transformed, see *Sermon* 95.8 (399).

Michael Wiitala

## 12. EVERY HAPPY MAN IS A GOD
*Deification in Boethius*

Boethius (ca. 480–526) is unique among the other figures considered in this volume in that his account of deification makes no explicit reference to Christ. This is no doubt due in part to the time and place in which he lived. The Roman aristocracy to which Boethius belonged was thoroughly Christianized.[1] Thus, unlike the authors considered in this volume that preceded him, it is likely that Boethius did not see a need to combat paganism or to sharply differentiate a uniquely Christian notion of deification from the Neo-Platonic notion of deification found in the pagan philosophers that influenced him.[2] Unlike later authors such as St. Gregory the Great, however, Boethius still lived in a properly Roman social context, was immersed in classical Greek and Roman literature and philosophy, and was profoundly influenced by Plato, Aristotle, and Neo-Platonism. The result is that Boethius developed a distinctly Neo-Platonic notion of deification that is nonetheless compatible with the orthodox Catholic Christianity he professed.[3]

---

1. John Marenbon, *Boethius* (Oxford: Oxford University Press, 2003), 157.
2. For an overview of the various scholarly answers to the question of Boethius's Christianity in the *Consolation* see ibid., 154–57.
3. See Henry Chadwick, *Boethius: The Consolations of Music, Logic, Theology, and Philosophy* (Oxford: Oxford University Press, 1981), 211. Although the character of Boethius's Christianity has sometimes been questioned by modern scholars, he has long been venerated as a martyr in northern Italy and was canonized by Pope Leo XIII in 1883. See Noel Harold Kaylor Jr., "Introduction: The Times, Life, and Work of Boethius," in *A Companion to Boethius in the Middle Ages*, ed. Noel Harold Kaylor Jr. and Philip

Boethius's account of deification is found in his most well-known work, the *Consolation of Philosophy*, which he wrote while imprisoned. Before his imprisonment, Boethius had been active in Roman politics and was eventually appointed by Theodoric to the prestigious position of master of the offices. Boethius's political enemies, however, accused him of conspiring against Theodoric. Although Boethius maintained that he was innocent of the charges, Theodoric had him imprisoned and eventually executed. Boethius portrays himself in the *Consolation* as someone whose spirit has been crushed by this calamity, in need of the medicine against despair that philosophy can offer. Boethius writes the *Consolation* as a dialogue between himself and Lady Philosophy, who consoles "Boethius" (the character) with poetry, rhetoric, and, most importantly, philosophical argument. The text alternates between prose and metered sections. The centerpiece of Lady Philosophy's argument is that God is happiness itself, goodness itself, and unity itself. On the basis of her identification of happiness and God, she concludes that the happiness human beings desire can only be attained through deification.[4] Although a number of claims Philosophy makes throughout the *Consolation* suggest that a virtuous life, contemplation, and prayer are all necessary for attaining happiness and deification, she does not indicate that they are sufficient for happiness and deification; nor does she specify what would be sufficient. The reason for her silence in this regard is presumably Boethius's orthodox Catholic belief that salvation, and therefore deification, is only attainable through Christ.[5] While Philosophy, as Boethius portrays her, can identify *that* happiness is only attainable through deification, she cannot on her own sufficiently identify *how* to achieve deification.[6]

---

Edward Phillips (Leiden: Brill, 2012), 5; Scott Goins and Barbara H. Wyman, "Introduction," in *The Consolation of Philosophy*, ed. Scott Goins and Barbara H. Wyman (San Francisco: Ignatius Press, 2012), xv.

4. Boethius, *Consolation of Philosophy* 3.10.22–25. Unless otherwise indicated, all translations of the *Consolation* are my own, in consultation with *Boethius: Theological Tractates. The Consolation of Philosophy*, trans. H. F. Stewart, E. K. Rand, and S. J. Tester, Loeb Classical Library 74 (Cambridge, Mass.: Harvard University Press, 1973); *The Consolation of Philosophy*, trans. P. G. Walsh (Oxford: Oxford University Press, 2000); and *Consolation of Philosophy*, trans. Joel C. Relihan (Indianapolis, Ind.: Hackett, 2001).

5. *Tractates and Consolation* (trans. Stewart), 67–71; see John Marenbon, "Boethius: From Antiquity to the Middle Ages," in *Medieval Philosophy*, ed. John Marenbon, Routledge History of Philosophy III (New York: Routledge, 1998), 23; John Magee, "Boethius," in *A Companion to Philosophy in the Middle Ages*, ed. Jorge J. E. Gracia and Timothy B. Noone (Oxford: Blackwell, 2003), 224; Marenbon, *Boethius*, 157.

6. Some scholars argue, incorrectly I think, that Lady Philosophy does not represent Boethius's

## Boethius's Ascent to God in the *Consolation*

Lady Philosophy's account of deification is found in the central book of the *Consolation*, book 3. This is significant because the *Consolation* has the same four-stage ascent-descent structure found in most of Plato's dialogues and in the poem of Parmenides.[7] Works arranged according to this structure (1) begin at the level of human opinion, (2) move to disclose the limitations of human opinion, (3) reveal the divine truth that transcends human opinion, and (4) finally return to the level of human opinion with the insight gained in stage (3) as a guide.[8] This ascent-descent structure is given literary expression in Plato's Allegory of the Cave. The philosopher-to-be begins chained in the cave, aware of nothing but the shadows on the wall, which represent human opinion. The philosopher-to-be is then unchained and sees the fire and the puppets that produce the shadows. This experience begins to disclose the limitations of human opinion. After the philosopher-to-be leaves the cave and his eyes have adjusted, he can finally look at the objects outside and the sun, which represent the forms and the good itself—the divine truth that transcends human opinion. Our now-philosopher, however, must return to the cave, bringing his insights from above to help those still imprisoned by the limitations of human opinion.

This ascent-descent structure is clear in the *Consolation*.[9] The discussion

---

own views, and that the purpose of the *Consolation* is to show that the sort of consolation (pagan) philosophy can offer is inadequate—one can only find consolation elsewhere, namely, in Christ. See for example, Joel C. Relihan, *The Prisoner's Philosophy: Life and Death in Boethius's* Consolation (Notre Dame, Ind.: University of Notre Dame Press, 2007) and *Ancient Menippean Satire* (Baltimore, Md.: Johns Hopkins University Press, 1993), 187–94; John D. Jones, "Does Philosophy Console? Boethius and Christian Faith," *Proceedings of the American Catholic Philosophical Association* 57 (1983): 78–87; John Marenbon, "Rationality and Happiness: Interpreting Boethius's *Consolation of Philosophy*," in *Rationality and Happiness: From the Ancients to the Early Medievals*, ed. Jiyuan Yu and Jorge J. E. Gracia (Rochester, N.Y.: University of Rochester Press, 2003), 175–97; and John R. Fortin, "The Nature of Consolation in *The Consolation of Philosophy*," *American Catholic Philosophical Quarterly* 78, no. 2 (2004): 293–307. Against this view see Chadwick, *Boethius*, 248–49; Magee, "Boethius," 224.

7. See Mitchell Miller, "Platonic Mimesis," in *Contextualizing Classics: Ideology, Performance, Dialogue*, ed. Thomas Falkner (Lanham, Md.: Rowman and Littlefield, 1999), 253–66; Jonathan Ketchum, "The Structure of the Plato Dialogue" (PhD diss., State University of New York at Buffalo, 1980). It is worth noting that Parmenides and Plato are the two philosophers Boethius has Lady Philosophy mention by name as her argument reaches its high point at the end of book 3 (see *Consolation* 3.9.32, 3.11m.15, 3.12.1, 3.12.37–38).

8. Miller, "Platonic Mimesis," 259.

9. See John Magee, "The Good and Morality: *Consolatio* 2–4," in *The Cambridge Companion to*

between "Boethius" and Lady Philosophy in book 1 occurs on the level of human opinion—stage one. "Boethius" laments his fall from power and his loss of political freedom. In book 2, "Boethius" continues his complaints against fortune. Lady Philosophy, however, responds by attempting to show him that his opinions concerning happiness and concerning good and bad fortune are incoherent. Thus the second stage of the ascent-descent structure begins in book 2, as Philosophy starts to show the limitations of human opinion. She continues in this way through most of book 3. In 3.9, however, she brings "Boethius" to the third stage, as she commences the ascent to the "divine truth"—the nature of God himself in this case. In 3.10–12, she enables "Boethius" to understand God in his simplicity as true happiness itself, goodness itself, and unity itself. Then, as book 3 closes, she speaks to "Boethius" in verse about Orpheus's descent to the underworld for Eurydice, warning "Boethius" not to lose the insight he has attained by returning to the opinions he had before. "Boethius" must be careful to descend back into the Hades of human opinion without losing the object of his love—God. This turn at the end of book 3 points to the descent back down to the level of human opinion that occurs in books 4 and 5—the fourth stage.[10] The worries that "Boethius" raised about fortune from book 2 are in book 4 reintroduced in a new way and definitively resolved in light of insights gained in 3.9–12. Finally, in contrast to the discussion of the loss of political freedom in book 1, Philosophy in book 5—again, drawing on the insights gained in book 3—shows "Boethius" what true freedom is and dispels his doubts concerning the compatibility of human freedom and divine providence.[11]

Given that Lady Philosophy introduces and explains the nature of deification—that is, of being made gods (*deos fieri*)[12]—during stage three of the ascent-descent structure, some consideration of the transition from stage two to three is necessary in order to properly understand the notion of deification she develops. The nature of true happiness (*beatitudo*) is the bridge between the second and third stage of the inquiry. "Boethius" thinks that his fall from

---

*Boethius*, ed. John Marenbon (Cambridge: Cambridge University Press, 2009), 181–84; Robert McMahon, *Understanding the Medieval Meditative Ascent: Augustine, Anselm, Boethius, and Dante* (Washington, D.C.: The Catholic University of America Press, 2006), esp. 211–25; Stephen Blackwood, *The Consolation of Boethius as Poetic Liturgy* (Oxford: Oxford University Press, 2015), esp. 189–94.

10. Magee, "The Good and Morality," 182.
11. Ibid., 183.
12. *Consolation* 3.10.24.

power and imprisonment entail unhappiness. Philosophy seeks to demonstrate that this is not the case. She argues that his fall and imprisonment only seem to him to entail unhappiness because he has false opinions concerning what happiness is. Hence, in book 2 and in the first part of book 3, Philosophy argues that what people generally regard as happiness is in fact not happiness at all.

In the first part of book 3, "Boethius" and Philosophy consider the goods that people typically identify with happiness. Philosophy identifies five such goods: wealth, honors, worldly power, fame, and pleasures.[13] Philosophy argues, however, that people do not seek these goods for their own sake, but rather as means to attain five corresponding more fundamental goods: self-sufficiency, due respect, power as such, acclamation, and delight. Those who seek wealth do so in order to become self-sufficient. Self-sufficiency, then, is the good they really seek. They only think that wealth is good because they think it can bring self-sufficiency. Likewise, those who seek honors really desire due respect; those who seek worldly power really want power as such; those who seek fame are searching for acclamation; and those who seek pleasures want delight.[14] Philosophy argues in 3.2–8, however, that one cannot gain true self-sufficiency, due respect, power, acclamation, and delight by means of wealth, honors, worldly power, fame, and pleasures. Therefore the happiness people seek, concludes Philosophy, is not identical to wealth, honors, and so on. Rather, the happiness people seek seems to be identical to self-sufficiency, due respect, power, acclamation, and delight.

Having shown that the sort of happiness most people attempt to gain is not the true happiness they desire, Philosophy begins in 3.9 to show what true happiness is. Given that the happiness people seek seems to be identical to self-sufficiency, due respect, power, acclamation, and delight, Philosophy asks "Boethius" to consider the nature of these goods more carefully. She begins by pointing out that happiness is not identical to self-sufficiency, due respect, power, acclamation, and delight if they are had in isolation from one another. The reason that each of these five fundamental goods in isolation from one another cannot be identical to true happiness, Philosophy explains, is that it is impossible to possess any one of these goods without also possessing all

13. Ibid., 3.2.12.
14. See esp. ibid., 3.2.19.

the others. One cannot be fully self-sufficient unless one possesses all power; and one cannot possess all power without being fully self-sufficient.[15] Likewise, one cannot truly enjoy delight unless there is no fear of losing it.[16] Yet unless one were self-sufficient and all-powerful, one's delight could at least in principle be lost. Conversely, if one were self-sufficient and all-powerful, one would always necessarily be in a state of delight, as one would not be self-sufficient unless all one's desires were always fulfilled.[17] Furthermore, Philosophy argues, that which is fully self-sufficient, all-powerful, and full of delight would also be that to which respect was most due.[18] Similarly, that to which respect was most due would have to be fully self-sufficient, all-powerful, and full of delight, as anything without those attributes would be less worthy of respect than that with those attributes. Finally, that which is fully self-sufficient, all-powerful, and full of delight would also possess all the acclamation it needed, as otherwise it would not be self-sufficient.[19] Philosophy concludes, therefore, that although self-sufficiency, due respect, power, acclamation, and delight differ in name, they in no way differ in substance.[20] In other words, what it is to be self-sufficient, what it is to be worthy of respect, what it is to be powerful, what it is to be worthy of acclamation, and what it is to be delighted do not differ in substance. Rather they compose a simple unity that Philosophy will in 3.10 identify as God himself.[21]

## Being Made a God in *Consolation* 3.10.1–25

With the nature of true happiness identified as the simple unity of true and complete self-sufficiency, due respect, power, acclamation, and delight, Lady Philosophy moves in 3.10.1–20 to identify true happiness with God. Then in 3.10.22–25 she argues that attaining happiness is identical with being made a god *via* participation in God. In what follows, I offer an analysis of Philosophy's argument in 3.10.1–25. The argument in 3.10.1–25 is compact and

15. Ibid., 3.9.5–6.
16. See ibid., 2.4.25–27.
17. Ibid., 3.9.13–14.
18. Ibid., 3.9.7–8.
19. Ibid., 3.9.9–11.
20. Ibid., 3.9.15.
21. For a less favorable assessment of the notion of happiness that Philosophy develops in 3.9, see Marenbon, "Rationality and Happiness," 182–84.

elliptical.[22] After all, Philosophy is simply reminding "Boethius" the character of arguments with which he was familiar prior to his present calamity.[23] Her claims, therefore, leave both "Boethius" and the reader of the *Consolation* to supply unstated premises and inferences. Hence, in my analysis of the argument of 3.10.1–25, I attempt to supply whatever implicit premises and inference are necessary to make sense of the text.[24] I divide the argument into four parts. In the first part, Philosophy argues that given there are incomplete goods and incomplete happiness, there is necessarily a complete good and true happiness (3.10.1–6). In the second, she argues that the complete good and true happiness are in God (3.10.7–10). In the third, she argues that God is true happiness itself (3.10.11–21). In the fourth, she argues that truly happy people are divine (3.10.22–25). I consider each part in turn.

### The Complete Good and True Happiness (3.10.1–6)

Lady Philosophy's argument in 3.10.1–25 depends on a distinction she makes between the *perfectum bonum* and an *imperfectum bonum*. Although *perfectum* is often translated as "perfect" and *imperfectum* as "imperfect," I will translate the two as "complete" and "incomplete" respectively, as that is the sense of *perfectum* required by the argument.[25] This distinction between what is completely good and what is incompletely good is best understood as an instance of the more basic Platonic distinction—with its origins in *Republic* V (476e–480a)—between what is completely *x* and what both is and is not *x* (incompletely *x*). A brief example can clarify the distinction. Consider a hammer. A hammer is useful in some ways and not useful in others. For instance, it is useful for the task of pounding nails, but is not useful for the task of trimming one's hair. According to the Platonic analysis, in relation to the task of pounding nails the hammer participates in the form useful, but in relation to the task of trimming one's hair it does not participate in the form useful. The form useful itself simply is what it is to be useful. Thus, if we reword things

---

22. This has led some scholars to conclude that Philosophy's arguments in this section are hopelessly implausible. See, for example, ibid., 182–92; Relihan, *Menippean Satire*, 187; Relihan, *The Prisoner's Philosophy*, xi, 1, 4–5, 17, 21, 48.

23. *Consolation* 3.12.1; see 3.11m.

24. For alternative formulations of the argument see Marenbon, *Boethius*, 108–12; Siobhan Nash-Marshall, "God, Simplicity, and the *Consolatio Philosophiae*," *American Catholic Philosophical Quarterly* 78, no. 2 (2004): 225–46; Magee, "The Good and Morality," 195–97.

25. See especially *deminutis inconsummatisque* at 3.10.5 and *integris* at 3.10.5 and 3.10.9.

so as to drop the term "participation," we get the following. For the task of pounding nails, a hammer is what it is to be useful. For the task of trimming hair, in contrast, a hammer is not what it is to be useful. The hammer, then, both *is* what it is to be useful and *is not* what it is to be useful. Hence, the hammer is useful, but its usefulness is incomplete. The form useful itself, however, is completely useful. The form useful *is* what it is to be useful. Yet, unlike the hammer—which both *is* and *is not* what it is to be useful—it is not the case that what it is to be useful *is not* what it is to be useful. Usefulness itself *is* usefulness itself and there is no sense in which it is not usefulness itself. In short, what it is to be useful is completely what it is to be useful.

In the argument of *Consolation* 3.10, the complete good should be understood along these lines. The complete good is the good itself: what it is to be good. All entities other than the complete good are incomplete goods, because they are good in some ways but not in others. To put it differently, all entities other than what it is to be good both are and are not what it is to be good.[26]

Philosophy's argument in 3.10.1–6 attempts to establish that the complete good is and that true happiness is.[27] Consider true happiness. Human beings desire to possess true happiness. In other words, they desire to be what it is to be happy. Given that this desire is not a desire for nothing, it is a desire for something—namely true happiness. Hence, true happiness is something. Therefore, true happiness is. In this Platonic context, to claim that "true hap-

---

26. Boethius discusses this claim in some detail in his *Quomodo Substantiae* (*Tractates and Consolation*, trans. Stewart, 38–51).

27. I translate the Latin verbs *esse* and *exsistere* here and throughout using the English verb "to be" rather than "to exist." The verb *exsistere* could also be translated in the *Consolation* as "to appear," e.g., "In this I think we first have to inquire whether any good of this kind, as you have just defined it, is able to appear in the nature of things [*in rerum natura possit exsistere*].... But it cannot be denied that this complete good certainly does appear [*exsistat*], and is, as it were, a sort of fount of all goods" (*Consolation* 3.10.2–3). Translating *exsistere* as "to exist," as most translators of the *Consolation* do, is misleading. Recent scholarship on the Ancient Greek verb *einai* (to be) as it is used in Greek and Roman philosophy has shown that, for Platonic philosophy in particular, the study of being is first and foremost a study of intelligibility and predication, and only secondarily, if at all, a study of "what exists" in the sense that has in modern and contemporary metaphysics. For Boethius as well, *esse* (by which he translates *einai*), and with it *exsistere*, are tied to intelligibility and predication, such that the inference "*x* is *F*, therefore *x* is" is a valid inference. See Charles Kahn, "Why Existence Does Not Emerge as a Distinct Concept in Greek Philosophy," *Archiv Für Geschichte Der Philosophie* 58, no. 4 (1976): 323–34, *The Verb "Be" in Ancient Greek* (Indianapolis, Ind.: Hackett, 2003), and *Essays on Being* (Oxford: Oxford University Press, 2009); Lesley Brown, "Being in the *Sophist:* A Syntactical Enquiry," *Oxford Studies in Ancient Philosophy* 4 (1986): 49–70, and "The Verb 'To Be' in Greek Philosophy," in *Language*, ed. Stephen Everson, Companions to Ancient Thought 3 (Cambridge: Cambridge University Press, 1994).

piness is" is neither to affirm nor to deny that there is a being somewhere in the universe who is truly happy.[28] Rather it is to claim that happiness is something intelligible—something about which true and false predications can be made.[29] If human beings desire true happiness, then true happiness must be something intelligible. If it were not intelligible, it could not be desired or conceptualized at all.

Philosophy's argument that there is a complete good can be formulated in the following way:

1. That which is incompletely $x$ cannot be unless that which is completely $x$ is (premise).[30]
2. There are things that are in some respects not good (premise).[31]
3. Therefore, incomplete goods are (from 2).[32]
4. Therefore, that which is completely good is (from 1–3).[33]

Premise 1 is a basic Platonic principle claiming that there is an asymmetric relationship of dependence between that which is completely $x$ and that which is incompletely $x$. Consider the hammer again. To say that a hammer is good in relation to $y$ is, on this Platonic analysis, to say that, in relation to $y$, the hammer is what it is to be good. Consequently, if what it is to be good were unintelligible, it would be impossible for the hammer to be what it is to be good in relation to $y$. The hammer cannot be good, in other words, unless what it is to be good is something intelligible; whereas what it is to be good would be something intelligible even if there were no good hammers. The goodness in things other than the complete good depends on the complete good; whereas the complete good does not depend on the goodness in other things. Accordingly, the complete good is the source (*fons*) of the goodness in other things.[34] Therefore, given that there are things that are incompletely good, the complete good is (= 4).

---

28. The claim does imply that God is truly happy, but God, on this account, is the simple unity of every perfection, including happiness itself, not one among the many individual beings that exist in the universe.
29. See note 27 above.
30. *Consolation* 3.10.4.
31. Ibid., 3.10.6.
32. Ibid.
33. Ibid.
34. Ibid., 3.10.3.

### The Complete Good and True Happiness Are in God (3.10.7–10)

Having established that the complete good and true happiness are, Philosophy turns to showing that the complete good and true happiness are in God. The argument in 3.10.7–10 can be formulated as follows:

5. The term "God" (*deus*) indicates that which is the source and ruler of all things (*princeps*) (terminological stipulation).[35]

6. That which is completely good is in God (from 6a–6j).[36]

    6a. Assume that that which is completely good is not in God (for *reductio*).

    6b. Then that which is completely good is in some entity different from God (6a).

    6c. God is the source of all things (= 5).

    6d. That which is completely $x$ is the source of $x$ in things that are incompletely $x$ (premise).

    6e. That which is completely good is the source of the good in things that are incompletely good (from 4 and 6d).

    6f. The source of the good in things that are incompletely good is in some entity different from God (from 6b and 6e).

    6g. Therefore, that entity different from God is the source of the good in things that are incompletely good (from 6f).

    6h. Therefore, God is not the source of all things (from 6g).

    6i. But 6c and 6h contradict one another.

    6j. Therefore, the assumption stated in 6a is false.

7. The complete good is the highest good (premise).[37]

8. The highest good is true happiness (premise).[38]

9. Therefore, true happiness is in God (from 6–8).[39]

The *reductio* in 6a–6j establishes that the complete good is in God. Lines 7–8 state two further premises: the complete good is the highest good (= 7); and the highest good is true happiness (= 8). To say that the complete good is

---

35. Ibid., 3.10.7 and 3.12.8.
36. Ibid., 3.10.9.
37. Ibid., 3.10.10.
38. Ibid., 3.10.10, 3.2.3, 3.2.11.
39. Ibid., 3.10.10.

the highest good (*summum bonum*) is to say that what it is to be good is the highest good. What it is to be good is the highest good in the sense that all good things other than what it is to be good depend on what it is to be good for their goodness. In other words, what it is to be good is the highest good in the sense that it is ontologically prior to all other goods—it is that which explains why all other goods are good.

Philosophy established premise 8—that the highest good is true happiness—in *Consolation* 3.2.[40] There she argued that the highest good is true happiness because true happiness is that for the sake of which human beings seek whatever else they seek. True happiness, therefore, is the highest good in relation to the other goods that human beings seek. But is true happiness the highest good as such? In other words, is true happiness what it is to be good? Philosophy answers this question affirmatively. Given that human beings have a rational nature, they seek whatever they seek because they think it is good as such. As Philosophy makes explicit in 3.10.28–42, the good itself—what it is to be good—is that for the sake of which human beings seek whatever they seek. Thus, according to Philosophy, the highest good is both true happiness and the good itself. Given that what it is to be good is in God, given that what it is to be good is the highest good, and given that the highest good is true happiness, true happiness is in God (= 9).

### God Is True Happiness Itself (3.10.11–17)

In the third portion of the argument, Philosophy moves from the claim that true happiness is in God to the claim that God is identical to true happiness. The argument can be formulated as follows.[41]

10. The highest good is not in God through something external to God (from 10a–10f).[42]

    10a. Assume that the highest good is in God through something external to God (for *reductio*).

    10b. Then something other than God is the source of the highest good that is in God (from 10a).

---

40. See esp. ibid., 3.2.3 and 3.2.11.

41. In addition to the argument that I present here, in 3.10.18–20 Lady Philosophy offers another argument in which she derives the same conclusion from the premise that there cannot be two highest goods.

42. Ibid., 3.10.13.

10c. Then God is not the source of all things (from 10b).

10d. But God is the source of all things (= 5).

10e. But 10c and 10d contradict one another.

10f. Therefore, the assumption stated in 10a is false.

11. God cannot be different in substance from the highest good (from 11a–11l).[43]

11a. Assume that God is different in substance from the highest good (for *reductio*).

11b. Then God and the highest good are in principle different substances (from 11a).

11c. But God and the highest good are united such that the highest good is in God (from 6–9).

11d. If two or more substances are united, there must be something other than them that explains their unity (premise).

11e. Then something other than God and the highest good explains why the substance of the highest good and the substance of God have been united such that the highest good is in God (from 11b–d).

11f. That which explains why two or more substances are united is the source of their unity (premise).

11g. That which explains why the substance of the highest good and the substance of God have been united is the source of their unity (from 11e–f).

11h. The source of the unity of God and the highest good is something other than God (from 11e and 11g).

11i. Therefore, God is not the source of all things (from 11h).

11j. But God is the source of all things (= 5).

11k. But 11i and 11j contradict one another.

11l. Therefore, the assumption stated in 11a is false.

12. Therefore, the substance of God and the substance of the highest good are identical (from 10–11).[44]

13. Therefore, the substance of God and the substance of true happiness are identical (from 8 and 12).

14. In other words, God is true happiness itself (= 13).[45]

---

43. Ibid., 3.10.14 and 3.10.16.
44. Ibid., 3.10.16.
45. Ibid., 3.10.17.

Philosophy begins by asking "Boethius" to consider the sense in which the highest good is in God.[46] She then identifies three different ways in which someone might imagine that the highest good is in God. The first is that the highest good is in God through something external to God. For instance, one might think that God received the highest good from some other being. The second is that although God does not receive the highest good through something external to himself, he is nevertheless in principle different in substance from the highest good. In other words, the nature of God is such that it is possible for him not to possess the highest good. The third is that God and the highest good are identical in substance.

Given that God is the source and ruler of all things, the first and second ways of imagining how the highest good is in God are impossible. If, as the first option would have it, God received the highest good through something other than himself, then that other thing would be the source of the highest good for God. If something other than God were the source of the good in God, however, then God would not be the source of all things. Yet by "God" we simply mean the source of all things. As a result, if option one were true, the source of all things would not be the source of all things, which is absurd. If, as the second option would have it, God and the highest good were two different substances that only happened to be united such that the highest good is in God, then something other than God would have to explain why they were united. That which explained why they were united, however, would be the source of their unity. If, however, something other than God explained his unity with the highest good, then God would not be the source of his unity with the highest good. As a result, God would not be the source of all things, and therefore the source of all things would not be the source of all things, which is absurd. Thus, Philosophy concludes that God and the highest good are identical in substance. Furthermore, given that the highest good is true happiness, God and true happiness are identical in substance. In other words, God is what it is to be truly happy (= 14).

### All Truly Happy People Are Gods (3.10.20–25)

Given the Platonic metaphysical framework Boethius is using, God is divinity itself—what it is to be divine. If God were not divinity itself, divinity

---

46. Ibid., 3.10.8.

would be attributed to him due to his participation in divinity itself. But then divinity itself would be the source of God's divinity. Hence God would not be the source of all things, which is absurd. Given that God is divinity itself and God is happiness itself, happiness itself is divinity itself. With the identity of divinity itself and happiness itself in place (3.10.20), Lady Philosophy offers a corollary to her preceding argument in which she contends that all those who are truly happy are gods through participation in God. This corollary is the heart of Boethius's account of deification and worth quoting in full:

Since people are made happy [*beati*] by the acquisition [*adeptione*] of happiness [*beatitudinis*], but true happiness is divinity itself [*ipsa divinitas*], it is obvious that they are made happy by the acquisition of divinity. Yet as they are made just by the acquisition of justice, and wise by the acquisition of wisdom, so it is necessary, by the same reasoning, that those who have acquired divinity are made gods [*divinitatem adeptos deos fieri*]. Therefore, every happy person is a god [*Omnis igitur beatus deus*]. But God, to be sure, is by nature one; yet nothing prevents there being as many gods as you like by participation [*Sed natura quidem unus; participatione vero nihil prohibet esse quam plurimos*].[47]

The Platonic account of participation in form is on full display in this passage. People are made happy by the acquisition of happiness, just by the acquisition of justice, wise by the acquisition of wisdom, and gods by the acquisition of divinity. Philosophy makes clear at the end of the passage that participation in form—in what it is to be $x$—is the sort of "acquisition" (*adeptio*) she has in mind.[48] People are made happy by participation in what it is to be happy and made gods by participation in what it is to be divine. Because, as Philosophy has already established, what it is to be happy is identical in substance to what it is to be divine, and because God is what it is to be divine, people are made happy by participation in God and are made gods by participation in true happiness. Thus, insofar as a human being is truly happy, to that extent he is divine. This in no way detracts from God's unity, as God is the simple unity of true happiness itself, divinity itself, and every other perfection. This is clear in light of the Platonic account of what is completely $x$ and what is incompletely $x$ that I offered earlier.[49] Something other than God can,

---

47. Ibid., 3.10.23–25.
48. See M. V. Dougherty, "The Problem of *Humana Natura* in the *Consolatio Philosophiae* of Boethius," *American Catholic Philosophical Quarterly* 78, no. 2 (2004): esp. 283–84.
49. See "The Complete Good and True Happiness" above.

in some respects, be what it is to be divine. Yet in other respects it will not be what it is to be divine. God himself, however, is what it is to be divine in such a way that there is no sense in which he is not what it is to be divine.

## The Simple Unity of Divine Nature: *Consolation* 3.10–12

Having argued that every truly happy person is a god by participation in God himself and that God is the good itself, happiness itself, and divinity itself, Philosophy turns in 3.10.28–42, 3.11, and 3.12 to clarifying how the good itself, happiness itself, and divinity itself are in fact the same simple substance. Her account of God's simplicity here is essential to understanding her notion of deification properly. Without it, her explanation of deification would seem to imply that all existing things are divine. Philosophy argues in 3.11 that God is unity itself. She further argues that because each thing only has being insofar as it is one thing, each thing only has being insofar as it participates in unity itself. Given that to participate in unity is to participate in God, and given that to participate in God is to be divine, it would seem that Philosophy's account entails that everything is divine insofar as it has being. Such an account of deification, however, is at odds with Boethius's own statement of Catholic doctrine in *On the Catholic Faith* and suggests a notion of deification radically different from that found in other Church Fathers.[50] In order to see how Philosophy's account of deification does not entail that all things are divine insofar as they have being, a brief consideration of her account of the unity of God's substance in 3.10–12 is necessary. Her argument proceeds in three stages. In the first, 3.10.28–42, she articulates how true happiness and the good are the same substance. In the second, 3.11, she argues that the good and unity are the same substance. In the third, 3.12, she shows how unity and divinity are the same substance.

---

50. *Tractates and Consolation* (trans. Stewart), 57. "The divine nature then ... determined of himself to fashion the world, and brought it into being when it was absolutely naught, nor did he produce it from his own substance, lest it should be thought divine by nature."

## True Happiness and the Good Itself Are Identical in Substance (3.10.28–42)

The first stage begins with Philosophy asking "Boethius" about the sort of unity happiness has. Happiness seems to be many things: for instance, self-sufficiency, due respect, power, acclamation, and delight. Yet happiness is one thing insofar as it is considered as that for the sake of which we do all that we do. Philosophy points out that each of the many things that seem to compose happiness is sought for the sake of the good. Self-sufficiency, due respect, power, acclamation, and delight are such that each is complete only in relation to the good itself. What it is to be good sets the limits to power, for instance, that make power something good rather than something bad. Without those limits set by the good, power becomes something bad for its possessor—think, for example, of someone who uses his power to do things that are harmful to himself. Similarly, what it is to be good sets limits to self-sufficiency without which self-sufficiency would be bad for its possessor—think, for example, of someone who in attempting to gain independence from others cuts off the possibility of friendship. Self-sufficiency, due respect, power, acclamation, and delight—the different things that seem to compose happiness—are such that each is only complete and only good in relation to the good itself—that for the sake of which whatever is sought is sought. Therefore, concludes Philosophy, "the good is the sum and cause [*summa atque causa*] of all things that are to be sought."[51] Furthermore, she argues that "those things that are not good by nature, provided they seem good, are sought as if they were really good."[52] "That is why," she continues, "goodness is rightly believed to be the sum, the center-point, and the cause of all the things sought after."[53]

By pointing out that the good itself is that for the sake of which not only good things are sought, but that for the sake of which anything that seems good from any possible perspective is sought, Philosophy is able to show that happiness itself—defined as that for the sake of which human beings, or all rational beings, seek whatever they seek—is identical in substance to the good itself—defined as that for the sake of which whatever is sought by any be-

---

51. *Consolation* 3.10.37.
52. Ibid., 3.10.38.
53. Ibid.

ing whatsoever is sought.[54] Human beings, due to their rational nature, have the capacity to understand the perspective from which anything that any being seeks is sought. People can understand, for example, why jellyfish seek to spend their lives in the ocean. Understanding why jellyfish seek to spend their lives in the ocean involves recognizing that if jellyfish were rational beings, they would seek to be in the ocean as if that were constitutive of their happiness. What this demonstrates is that in seeking happiness, human beings seek the good itself. Thus, Philosophy concludes that the substance of happiness and the substance of the good itself are identical.[55] What it is to be happy and what it is to be good are the same substance considered from different inquiries. Happiness is that substance considered from an inquiry into the question of what human beings seek, whereas the good is that substance considered from an inquiry into what all things seek.

### The Good Itself and Unity Itself Are Identical in Substance (3.11)

Having shown that happiness itself and the good itself are the same substance, in 3.11 Philosophy argues that the good itself is unity itself. The good is that which all things seek. What all things seek, however, turns out to be unity, because each thing strives to be one.

Rational beings strive to be one by seeking the things that seem to them to bring happiness. The things that seem to bring happiness are only in fact constitutive of happiness, however, if they are united as one, because happiness is one thing. Self-sufficiency, due respect, power, acclamation, and delight are only constitutive of happiness if each is identical in substance to all the others.[56] The simple unity of complete self-sufficiency, due respect, power, acclamation, and delight is the unity that human beings *qua* their rational nature seek.[57]

Philosophy, however, goes on to argue that not only rational beings, but all things strive after unity. On the account she develops, all animals, plants, and even inanimate objects "seek" or "desire" unity. While there are many ways in which beings of each of these classes desire unity, Philosophy focuses

54. See ibid., 3.11.38.
55. Ibid., 3.10.42.
56. Ibid., 3.9.15.
57. Ibid., 3.11.5–7.

primarily, although not exclusively, on the way each entity desires unity insofar as it desires to maintain its own existence. Animals desire to maintain their own lives and to do the things they naturally do. In this way, each animal desires to be one.[58] The death of an animal is its dissolution as the kind of thing it is. A horse, for example, is no longer one horse once it dies. The flesh and bones that were unified as its body when alive, at death become a corpse—an aggregate of flesh and bones rather than a vitally unified whole. A horse, by desiring to live and to do the things that horses do, desires to be one thing: namely, this horse.

Something similar holds for plants. Each kind of plant strives to grow, develop, and reproduce itself. This "striving," "seeking," or "desiring" in the case of a plant does not involve awareness or perception, yet there is in plants still a vital drive to grow and reproduce. This vital drive is a drive for unity.[59] An acorn, if left unhindered and allowed the proper nourishment, will develop into one kind of thing—an oak tree—and that is the "goal" in terms of which its activities are intelligible.

Finally, even inanimate objects "desire" or "strive after" their own unity in the sense that they maintain their own properties and their own existence as the things they are. "Things that are hard, like stones," explains Philosophy, "cohere in their parts most unyieldingly and resist being easily disintegrated, while liquids, like air or water, do yield quite easily to things that divide them."[60] Inanimate objects have what we would today call various physical properties, by which we can count and categorize them—which is to say, by which we identify their unity. Today, we might say that inanimate objects "obey" laws of chemistry and/or physics. Instead of using obedience to law as her primary metaphor here, Philosophy uses desire. Both are metaphors for the same thing: the way that objects conform to the various structures according to which they can be counted and categorized—the structures that constitute them as one thing rather than another.

Whether the beings under consideration are rational, animal, plant, inanimate, or any combination of these, each is what it is due to its desire for and conformity to the structure it possesses. Thus, each being is in whatever way it

58. Ibid., 3.11.10–16.
59. Ibid., 3.11.18–24.
60. Ibid., 3.11.28–29.

is due to the good itself, because the good itself is that which all things desire; or to put it another way, the good itself is the norm to which each thing conforms insofar as it has the structure it does. Furthermore, given that the structure each being possesses is that which constitutes it as one thing, each being is the sort of being it is due to its unity. Each being is the sort of thing it is only insofar as it is in some way what it is to be one—whether what it is to be one as a horse, what it is to be one as a toe, what it is to be one as a tree, what it is to be one as a rock, etc. Unity itself, then, is the source, sustainer, and goal of all things. Insofar as it is considered as the goal of all things, unity itself is the good itself.

### The Good Itself, Unity Itself, and Divinity Itself Are Identical in Substance (3.12)

As we saw above, Philosophy argues in 3.10.1–25 that God is identical in substance to happiness itself and the good itself. How exactly happiness itself, the good itself, and divinity itself are identical in substance, however, is at 3.10.25 still in need of clarification. Philosophy begins the needed clarification in 3.10.28–42, showing how happiness itself and the good itself are identical in substance. Yet it is not until 3.12 that she clarifies how exactly happiness itself and the good itself are identical to divinity itself. The bridge that Philosophy uses to move from the good itself to divinity itself is unity itself. Hence, after showing in 3.11 how the good itself and unity itself are identical in substance, Philosophy goes on in 3.12 to show how the good itself and unity itself are identical to divinity itself.

"Boethius" and Philosophy understand divinity itself as the source and ruler of all things.[61] That is to say, what it is to be divine is to be the source and ruler of all things. So the question is whether what it is to be good and what it is to be one are identical in substance to the source and ruler of all things. Given Philosophy's account of unity in 3.11, the answer we find in 3.12 is not surprising. Philosophy characterizes unity itself in 3.11 as the source, sustainer, and goal of all things insofar as they have being. Unity itself, then, is the source of everything that is. Given that unity itself is also the sustainer and goal of all things, unity itself is their ruler. Unity itself rules all things by

---

61. See ibid., 3.10.7 and 3.12.8.

being their good.[62] It governs them, in other words, by their own striving for it.[63] Each thing does whatever it does for the sake of achieving some sort of unity. Therefore, unity explains why each thing does whatever it does. To rule over something is to explain why that thing does what it does. Therefore, unity itself—what it is to be one—is identical in substance to divinity itself, the source and ruler of all things.

### Divinity, Deification, and the Simple Unity of God's Nature

Philosophy's task in 3.10.28–3.12 is to show that what it is to be truly happy, what it is to be good, and what it is to be divine are in fact the same simple substance considered in different ways. What it is to be truly happy is this simple substance considered with reference to what human beings desire—or perhaps with reference to what all rational creatures desire. What it is to be good, in contrast, is this simple substance considered with reference to what is desirable as such, instead of only with reference to what is desirable for human beings. In other words, what it is to be good is this simple substance considered as that which all things desire.[64] Philosophy argues in 3.11, however, that all things—including even inanimate objects—"desire" or "seek" unity. Hence, the same simple substance that with reference to what is desirable for human beings appeared as true happiness, and with reference to what is desirable as such appeared as the good, now appears in the more metaphysically oriented inquiry of 3.11 as unity itself. Finally, in 3.12, Philosophy shows how this same simple substance is divinity itself—what it is to be divine. What it is to be divine is to be the source and ruler of all things.[65] Given that anything only has being inasmuch as it is one thing and that whatever anything does it only does because it "desires" what it is to be good, the simple substance that in 3.11 appeared as what it is to be good and what it is to be one, now appears in 3.12 as what it is to be divine—as the source of being for all things and that which rules all things by being what explains why all things do what they do. Although what it is to be truly happy, what it is to be good, what it is to be one, and what it is to be divine have different definitions, each is the same substance considered from a different line of inquiry. If we follow Boethius in

---

62. Ibid., 3.12.14.
63. Ibid., 3.12.17.
64. Ibid., 3.11.38.
65. See ibid., 3.10.7 and 3.12.8.

calling that simple substance "God," we can say that what it is to be truly happy is God considered from an inquiry into that which human beings, or perhaps all rational creatures, desire; what it is to be good is God considered from an inquiry into that which all things desire; what it is to be one is God considered from an inquiry into what makes each thing what it is; and what it is to be divine is God considered from an inquiry into the source and ruler of all things.

Given this way of understanding the simplicity of God's nature, Philosophy's account of deification does not entail that all things are divine. Although all things participate in God considered as the good itself and as unity itself, all do not participate in God considered as divinity itself. The simple substance that is God is unity itself, the good itself, and divinity itself in relation to all things. It is only happiness itself, however, in relation to human or rational beings.[66] Although God's substance is divinity itself in relation to all things—as he is the source and ruler of all things—only rational beings can participate in his divinity, because only they can, due to their rationality and freedom, participate in his ruling.[67] Moreover, rational and free beings can only participate in divinity itself insofar as they are truly happy and truly free.[68] Thus, although all things participate in God's substance considered as goodness and unity, only rational beings can participate in God's substance considered as happiness and divinity.

## Conclusion

Boethius's account of deification makes no explicit reference to Christ. The argument of the *Consolation* claims that deification is achieved by attaining the goodness and unity proper to a human being as a rational creature, but does not specify in detail how one should go about attaining this goodness and unity. While the fact that Boethius fails to specify precisely how to attain deification has led some contemporary commentators to criticize his account in 3.10–12, perhaps this lack of specification is a virtue.[69] Boethius states in

---

66. See Aristotle, *Nicomachean Ethics* X.8, 1178b24–25.
67. *Consolation* 5.2.
68. Ibid., 3.10.23–25, 5.2.8.
69. See note 22 above.

*On the Catholic Faith* that salvation is only attainable through Christ.[70] This presumably entails that deification is only attainable through Christ. Thus, as Boethius sees it, although Philosophy can define what deification is and identify it as the goal of human life, she cannot herself bestow divinity on human beings. Philosophy can show *that* deification and happiness are identical, but cannot fully explain *how* to attain them. Can human beings achieve the goodness and unity proper to their rational nature apart from Christ? As a Catholic, Boethius would give a negative answer. This question, however, is neither raised nor addressed in the *Consolation*. Thus, although Boethius's account of deification in the *Consolation* is not specifically Christian, it is nonetheless compatible with his Catholic Christianity.[71]

---

70. *Tractates and Consolation* (trans. Stewart), 67–71.
71. See Chadwick, *Boethius*, 211 and 248–49.

Fr. Luke Dysinger, OSB

# 13. BEHOLDING CHRIST IN THE OTHER AND IN THE SELF

*Deification in Benedict of Nursia and Gregory the Great*

## "Deification" in the Late Patristic West

The words "divinization," "deification," and *theosis* have increasingly appeared in theological texts by Christians who have traditionally regarded these terms with skepticism or even frank disapproval. As a result of the rediscovery of Eastern Christianity by Western Christians, articles have appeared, written by Lutheran, reformed, evangelical, and Baptist theologians, who point to elements in their respective traditions that they regard as analogous or equivalent to the eastern Christian doctrine of *theosis*.[1] While this approach may reflect both ecumenical zeal and a desire to enrich the systematic and spiritual theology of the Christian West, it can also be criticized as having the potential for diluting or even completely obscuring what is meant by "divinization" or *theosis*. In attempting to discern the presence of this concept in one's own spiritual tradition, there can arise a tendency to define "divinization" so broad-

---

1. Roland Chia, "Salvation as Justification and Deification," *Scottish Journal of Theology* 64, no. 2 (2011): 125–39; Paul Gavrilyuk, "The Retrieval of Deification: How a Once-Despised Archaism Became an Ecumenical Desideratum," *Modern Theology* 25, no. 4 (October 2009): 647–59; Roger Olsen, "Deification in Contemporary Theology," *Theology Today* 64 (2007): 186–200; K. P. Wesche, "The Doctrine of Deification: A Call to Worship," *Theology Today* 65 (2008): 169–79; Simo Peura and Antti Raunio (eds.), *Luther und Theosis: Vergöttlichung als Thema der abendländischen Theologie* (Helsinki: Luther-Agricola-Gesellschaft, 1990), 1–232.

ly as to deprive the term of any real content. Roger Olsen has noted that it is "confusing to find 'deification' being used of something that has for a very long time been called 'sanctification,' or 'union with Christ,' or 'communion with God,' or even 'being filled with God.'"[2] He argues that a more robust definition of *theosis* should take into account Gregory Palamas's distinction between the essence and the energies of God: that is, between the transcendent and ultimately unknowable divine nature on the one hand, and the divine power to heal and refashion the soul in God's image on the other.[3] Olsen cites the Orthodox theologian John Zizioulas in arguing that a doctrine of *theosis* without such a distinction inevitably leads to either "a near-pantheistic identity of the redeemed person with God or belief that deification is merely a metaphor and not real participation in God."[4] In an article written in 2009, Paul Gavrilyuk recommends that in addition to the Palamite energies/essence distinction any serious definition of *theosis* should also include "synergistic anthropology [and] sacramental realism."[5]

These are important observations. However, as my purpose here is to consider early Western sources on deification, it should be borne in mind that Gregory Palamas wrote in Greek in the early fourteenth century, and that it is hardly reasonable to expect his conclusions or theological precision to be obvious in much earlier Latin sources that employ a very different theological vocabulary. Nevertheless, the Palamite distinction could be considered a useful touchstone, if not a *sine qua non* for the concept of *theosis*; and to it a second Palamite insight could be added, namely the interrelationship between *theosis* and *theoria*, between deification and contemplation. Palamas wrote in defense of hesychasts, practitioners of the Jesus Prayer, who described an experience of interior divine light during their contemplative exercise. He defended the hesychasts against charges of blasphemy and heresy, explaining that what they beheld within their innermost self, their *nous*, was the "Taboric light" seen by the disciples at the transfiguration, and that this light represents the divine energies, rather than God's essence. For Palamas this contemplation of divine light was both evidence of *theosis* and one of its several sources.[6] As will be de-

2. Olsen, "Deification in Contemporary Theology," 192–93.
3. Ibid., 199.
4. Ibid., 191.
5. Gavrilyuk, "Retrieval of Deification," 655.
6. Gregory Palamas, *The Triads, Defense of the Holy Hesychasts*, ed. and trans. Nicholas Gendle

scribed, comparable if not identical themes are found in the *Rule of Benedict* and the writings of Pope Gregory the Great.

## Benedict and Gregory the Great

"Benedict" is the name traditionally given to the author of what has come to be known as the *Rule of Benedict*, a sixth-century reworking of earlier monastic legislation that during the succeeding three centuries first accompanied then gradually supplanted other rules and combinations of rules to become the dominant monastic rule in the Christian West. The traditional identification of the author of this rule with the founder of Monte Cassino and the "Benedict" who is the subject of book 2 of Gregory the Great's *Dialogues* is less certain today than it was in the past,[7] and almost no biographical data concerning its author can be deduced from the text of the Rule. What is now almost universally agreed is that, especially in the first seven chapters of his rule, Benedict relies heavily on the anonymous, early sixth-century *Rule of the Master* as well as the earlier monastic legislation of which the Master made use. As we possess no other texts from Benedict's pen than his Rule, we would know nothing whatever of his life were it not for Gregory's *Dialogues*. Sometime after the year 600 Pope Gregory the Great assembled four books of *Dialogues*, a compilation of local hagiography intended to encourage and edify, interspersed with Gregory's often theologically sophisticated commentary and pastoral exhortation. The second book of this work is devoted entirely to the life of Benedict, although as a work of hagiography the historical circumstances of Benedict's life have clearly been subordinated to Gregory's theological and pastoral purposes. The question whether Gregory the Great was, indeed, the author of the *Dialogues* has been vigorously raised in recent times, partic-

---

(Mahwah, N.J.: Paulist Press, 1983), 32. These themes recur throughout Palamas's writings, most clearly and concisely in *Triads* 1.3.5, 1.3.23, 1.3.27, 2.3.9, 3.1.34, 3.3.13.

7. Thus, for example, in a recent article M. O. de Simone presumes and defends Gregory's familiarity with Benedict's Rule: M. O. de Simone, "Another Look at Benedict in Gregory's *Dialogues*," *Cistercian Studies* 49, no. 3 (2014): 327. Diem, on the other hand, not only denies that Gregory knew Benedict's Rule, but suggests that apart from the traditional identification there is no reason to date the Rule earlier than the 630s, i.e., after Gregory's time. Albrecht Diem, "Inventing the Holy Rule: Some Observations on the History of Monastic Normative Observance in the Early Medieval West," in *Western Monasticism ante litteram: The Spaces of Early Monastic Observance*, ed. Hendrik Dey and Elizabeth Fentress (Turnhout: Brepols, 2011), 72–75.

ularly by Francis Clark,[8] who noted among other characteristics that the author of the *Dialogues* relies heavily on reported miracles and visions, and that the literary style of this work appears deliberately adapted to a more rustic audience than Gregory's other writings. Nevertheless, present scholarly consensus generally favors Gregorian authorship.[9] Unlike the *Rule of Benedict*, which remained unknown in the Christian East, the *Dialogues* were translated into Greek, probably by Pope Zacharias around the year 700. This assured Gregory's Benedict a place in Eastern hagiography and earned Gregory himself esteem in the Greek church with the cognomen *Gregorios Dialogos*. Thanks to the labors of Jean Neufville and Fr. Adelbert De Vogüé, excellent critical editions of Benedict's Rule and Gregory's *Dialogues* are available in the series Sources Chrétiennes, and will constitute the principal sources to be considered here.

## *The Rule of St. Benedict*

There is one instance in *The Rule of St. Benedict* of a Latin term associated with the doctrine of deification. In the ninth verse of the prologue, Benedict offers a poetic couplet taken directly from the *Rule of the Master*.[10] Benedict invites his readers to arise from spiritual sloth and:

> Open our eyes to the deifying light [*apertis oculis nostris ad deificum lumen*] and attune our ears to hear the divine voice [*attonitis auribus audiamus, divina ... uox*] that admonishes us, daily crying out: *Today if you hear his voice, harden not your hearts* [Ps 95:7–8]. And again, *You who have ears to hear, hear what the Spirit says to the churches* [Rv 2:7].[11]

The translation of *deificum lumen* in this passage as "deifying light," although accepted by some scholars and commentators, is debatable.[12] Some

---

8. Francis Clark, *The Pseudo-Gregorian Dialogues* (Leiden: Brill, 1987).

9. Paul Mayvaert, "The Authentic Dialogues of Gregory the Great," *Sacris erudiri* 43 (2004): 55–130; Adalbert de Vogüé, "Is Gregory the Great the author of the *Dialogues*?," *The American Benedictine Review* 56 (2005): 309–14; Matthew Dal Santo, "The Shadow of a Doubt? A Note on the *Dialogues* and *Registrum Epistolarum* of Pope Gregory the Great (590–604)," *The Journal of Ecclesiastical History* 61, no. 1 (2010): 3–17.

10. *The Rule of the Master* (hereafter, *RM*), Theme Sequence 5.

11. *Rule of Benedict* (hereafter, *RB*) Prol. 9–11; see Timothy Fry et al., *The Rule of St. Benedict* (Collegeville, Minn.: Liturgical Press, 1980), 80 and 158 (hereafter, Fry).

12. Blair and Delatte/McCann have "deifying light." Hunter Blair, *The Rule of St. Benedict* (Fort

translators render it "divine light" or some variant thereof, emphasizing the light's origin in God, rather than its transforming effect on the one who contemplates.[13] However, the translation "deifying light," which at least hints at a doctrine of *theosis*, can be defended. The use of *deificus* in the sense of "deifying," rather than simply "divine," occurs in Latin texts employed by both Benedict and the Master, most notably in the first Latin version of the *Life of Anthony* where it is used numerous times in the sense of "rendering God-like."[14]

Benedict's call to "open our eyes to the deifying light" is in this context part of an invitation to attend to the transforming presence of God in scripture.[15] It initiates an exegesis of Psalms 14 and 33 as well as a catena of biblical citations. Two biblical verses are cited here as instances of the divinizing light and divine voice: Psalm 95:7–8, the warning not to "harden the heart" on hearing the divine voice, recited daily at the beginning of Vigils (or "Matins") the first office of the day; and Revelation 2:7, the magisterial voice of Christ commanding the hearer to listen to what the Spirit says to the churches. Benedict's citation of these verses emphasizes the importance of listening

---

Augustus: Sandy and Co., 1906), 5; Paul Delatte, *Commentary on the Rule of St. Benedict*, trans. Justin McCann (London: Burns and Oates, 1921), 7. Puzicha translates *ad deificum lumen* as "auf dem göttlichen Licht," but comments that this implies "das vergöttlichende Licht" (the divinizing light). Michaela Putzicha, *Kommentar zur Benediktusregel* (St. Ottilien: EOS Verlag, 2002), 51. Similarly, Kardong translates the term as "divine light" but admits somewhat grudgingly that "it is not impossible that the term refers to deification." See Terence Kardong, *Benedict's Rule: A Translation and Commentary* (Collegeville, Minn.: Liturgical Press, 1996), 3 and 11.

13. Fry has "light that comes from God" (159). Similarly, de Vogüé renders it as "lumière de Dieu," noting that it is a metaphor for the sacred scripture, the *divina vox*. *La Règle de saint Benoît*, ed. and trans. Adalbert de Vogüé, Sources Chrétiennes (hereafter, SC) 181 (Paris: Cerf, 1987), 1:415n9.

14. It appears to have been the anonymous Latin version of the *Life of Anthony* that was available to the Master and Benedict. Vincent Desprez, "Saint Anthony and the Origins of Anchoretism II," *American Benedictine Review* 43, no. 2 (1992): 160n100. The translator of the anonymous Latin version of Athanasius's *Life of Anthony* employs *deificus* very frequently when there is no basis for doing so in the Greek original, often as a way of describing Anthony's virtue and ascetical practice. Ludovicus Lorié, *Spiritual Terminology in the Latin Translations of the Vita Antonii: With Reference to Fourth and Fifth Century Monastic Literature* (Nijmegen: Dekker and Van De Vegt N.V., 1961), 73–74 and 84. Lois Gandt, "A Philological and Theological Analysis of the Ancient Latin Translations of the "Vita Antonii" (PhD diss., Fordham University, 2008), 122–24, 249, 253–54. In the Greek original of the *Life of Anthony*, θεοποιέω, "to deify," is used only once (chap. 76) and in a pejorative sense, referring to idolatry: "making god[s] of creatures" (θεοποιῆσαι τὰ ποιήματα). *Athanase D'Alexandrie, Vie d'Antoine*, ed. and trans. G. Bartelink, SC 400 (Paris: Cerf, 1994), 330.

15. Delatte notes (*Commentary*, 8) and de Vogüé emphasizes that both the *deificum lumen* and the *divina vox* of Prol. 9–10 refer to scripture, cited here and throughout the prologue (de Vogüé, *La Règle*, 1:415n9). This identity between scripture and the "divine light" and "divine voice" is also the basis for the practice of psalmody and daily *lectio divina*. See de Vogüé, *La Règle*, 7:184–240 and 338–50.

to the voice of God as it is heard in proclaimed biblical texts. These verses and the emphasis on sacred scripture they reveal are reminders that in the *Rule of Benedict* the experience of contemplation, the ability to perceive God's presence and hidden purposes beneath surface appearance, is very often invoked using the analogy of hearing, rather than the traditional and more frequent metaphor of seeing. The first word of Benedict's Rule is *obsculta*, "listen"; and unlike the *Rule of the Master* on which he depends, Benedict primarily understands the voice to which we listen as that of Christ, rather than of the abbot or "master." The conviction that psalmody and meditation on scripture can lead to contemplation had been gaining considerable traction since the time of Origen, and Benedict's Eastern contemporary Dionysius the Areopagite would describe in detail the deifying power of scripture, especially when read or chanted in the liturgical assembly.[16] In the Christian West a similar emphasis on scripture as divinizing is found in Ambrose and especially in Cassian,[17] whose *Conferences* Benedict recommends in chapter 73, the concluding chapter of his Rule.

Another point of relevance in regard to a possible theology of divinization in Benedict's Rule is his recurring emphasis on cenobitic rather than eremitical monasticism. He inherited from Jerome and Cassian a tradition that the life of the hermit is superior to that of the cenobite; and although he repeats this conventional wisdom with his own modifications in chapter 2, it is significant that nowhere in his Rule does Benedict explain how a monk can

---

16. According to Dionysius the chanting of scripture, especially psalmody, has the power, "for those capable of being divinized" (τοῖς πρὸς θέωσιν ἐπιτηδείοις ὑφηγήσατο), to "harmonize the habits of our souls and [...] establish unity of mind and feeling with things Divine, with [our]selves and with one another" (τὰς ψυχικὰς ἡμῶν ἕξεις ἐναρμονίως [...] τὴν πρὸς τὰ θεῖα καὶ ἑαυτοὺς καὶ ἀλλήλους ὁμοφροσύνην). Dionysius the Areopagite, *Ecclesiastical Hierarchies* 3.3.4–5; in *De Coelesti Hierarchia, de Ecclesiastica Hierarchia, de Mystica Theologia, & Epistulae*, ed. Günter Heil and Adolf Ritter, Corpus Dionysiacum II (Berlin: de Gruyter, 1991), 83–84.

17. Ambrose considered the soul that hears and believes scripture as analogous to the Virgin Mary at the Annunciation. In commenting on Lk 1:44–45 he notes that such a soul, like Mary, "incarnates" and "bears" the divine Word: "Every soul that believes—that soul both conceives and gives birth to the Word of God. [...] For every soul can receive the Word of God" (quaecumque enim crediderit anima et concipit et generat Dei Verbum ... secundum fidem tamen omnium fructus est Christus. [...] Omnis enim anima accipit Dei Verbum). Ambrose, *Expositio Evangelii secundum Lucam*, ed. M. Adriaen, Corpus Christianorum: Series Latina (hereafter, CCL) 14 (Tournhout: Brepols, 1957), 42.361–67. For Cassian the biblical text is the source of "fiery" (imageless, wordless) prayer (*Conf.* 9.15, 9.25–27, 10.11) and "contemplation of things divine" (contemplatio rerum divinarum) (*Conf.* 14.1.3 and 14.8.1–7). John Cassian, *Conferences (Conlationes XXIIII)*, ed. M. Petschenig, Corpus Scriptorium Ecclesiasticorum Latinorum (hereafter, CSEL) 13 (Vienna, 1886), 262–64, 272–74, 286–332, 398–99, 404–7.

become a hermit. He mentions the hermit life as a theoretical goal, but offers no practical steps by which it may be attained.[18] Indeed, his Rule is explicitly intended for those who "persevere in [Christ's] teaching in the monastery until death."[19] And it is within the community, serving one another, that the monks learn the contemplative art of perceiving Christ in each another and rendering fitting honor to one another as Christ-bearers. First, the monks learn to "see" Christ in the abbot, "who is believed to hold the place of Christ in the monastery."[20] But Christ must also be contemplated aurally and perhaps paradoxically in the voice of the youngest newcomers to the monastery, through whose counsel God often (*saepe*) indicates what is best for the community to do.[21] Guests, too, are to be contemplated as Christ-bearers: on arrival and departure they "are to be received as Christ" and venerated with a bow or prostration, "because Christ is to be adored in them just as he is received in them."[22] Similarly, monks visiting from another monastery may be the unexpected bearers of a prophetic message from Christ.[23] Finally, the sick are "truly to be served as Christ Himself [...] out of honor for God."[24]

For Benedict the monastic community is not only a setting where monks learn the contemplative art of seeing Christ in one another and in guests: it is also a context where the innermost self, the heart, is changed. That the community is a locus of contemplative transformation is particularly clear at the

---

18. *RB* 1.3–4. Benedict inherited this traditional praise of the hermit life from *RM* 1.3–4. The trope of the hermit's supposed spiritual superiority to the cenobite was inspired by the *Life of Anthony*, the *Sayings* and *Lives* of the Desert Fathers and the *Institutes* and *Conferences* of Cassian. Rather than overtly contradicting this received wisdom, Benedict subtly calls it into question by failing even to mention hermits elsewhere in his Rule, and by recommending to his readers the *Rule of Basil* whose author extolls the cenobium and explicitly rebukes hermits. After reminding his readers that Christ washed the feet of his disciples, Basil asks, "Whose feet, therefore, will you wash? To whom will you minister? In comparison with whom will you be the lowest, if you live alone?" (Tu ergo cujus pedes lavabis ... cum solus vivas?), in Basil of Caesarea, *Rule* (Latin version of Rufinus) Q.3.35–36, ed. Klaus Zelzer, CSEL 86 (Vienna: Hoelder-Pichler-Tempsky, 1985), 31.

19. *RB* Prol. 50: "in eius doctrinam usque ad mortem in monasterio perseverantes" (Fry, 166).

20. *RB* 2.24: "Christi enim agere vices in monasterio creditor" (Fry, 174).

21. *RB* 3.3: "all should be called to council because it is often to the younger that the Lord reveals what is best" (quia saepe iuniori Dominus revelat quod melius est) (Fry, 178–80).

22. *RB* 53.1.7: "Omnes supervenientes hospites tamquam Christus suscipiantur [...] Christus in eis adoretur qui et suscipitur" (Fry, 254–56).

23. *RB* 61.4: "if [a visiting monk] reasonably and with humble charity criticizes or suggests something, the abbot should prudently consider whether the Lord may not have sent him for this very reason" (pro hoc ipsud eum Dominus direxerit) (Fry, 274).

24. *RB* 36.1.4: "sicut revera Christo ita eis serviatur [...] in honorem Dei sibi servire" (Fry, 234).

end of the prologue where Benedict modifies the Master's definition of the monastery as a "school of the Lord's service" (*dominici schola servitii*).[25] Unlike the Master, Benedict's *schola* includes "nothing harsh, nothing burdensome," but only the strictness necessary to amend vice and safeguard love.[26] The word *schola* can be understood here as a place intended for both communal instruction and learning a skill or trade; but it also carries the implication of the English idiom "a school of fish," suggesting a community that moves together with a common purpose, toward a common goal.[27]

The result of attending to the divinizing light and divine voice is, according to both Benedict and the Master, a transformed heart that, in the words of Psalm 119:32, is widened, expanded by "running" the path of Christian obedience, an ascetical "way of salvation" that necessarily seems narrow (*angusto*) at the beginning. The narrow "restrictiveness" (*restrictio*) of the school of the Lord's service, however, serves only to preserve fairness, heal from vice, and preserve love (*caritas*).[28] In his commentary on Psalm 119, Ambrose had stressed that the Christian's heart must be widened to allow the indwelling of the triune God.[29] Benedict appears to echo this sentiment, noting that the widened heart becomes the habitation of "inexpressibly sweet love" (*dilectio*): "Truly as we advance in this way of life and faith, our hearts open wide, and we run with inexpressibly sweet love on the path of God's commandments."[30]

If it is possible to speak of a doctrine of divinization in Benedict's Rule, then it is both in the conclusion to the prologue and also in chapter 72 that he

---

25. *RB* Prol. 45 (Fry, 164).

26. *RB* Prol. 46–47: "nihil asperum nihil grave nos constituturos speramus; sed et si quid paululum restrictius, dictante aequitatis ratione, propter emendationem vitiorum vel conservationem caritatis processerit" (Fry, 164).

27. Both meanings are discussed in detail in Fry 165 (note to Prol. 45) and 365–66. The term *schola* also occurs in Cassian, *Conf.* 3.1, 18.16, 19.2. It is tempting to speculate whether the notion of a musical *schola*, a group of singers whose blended voices lead the community in chanted prayer, might not also be in play; however, the equation of *schola* with "cantors" does not appear in the literature of the West until the eighth century.

28. *RB* Prol. 47–48: "sed et si quid paululum restrictius, dictante aequitatis ratione, propter emendationem vitiorum vel conservationem caritatis processerit, non ilico pavore perterritus refugias viam salutis quae non est nisi angusto initio incipienda" (Fry, 164).

29. Ambrose, *Commentary on Psalm 118*, serm. 4 (*Daleth*), 27, in CSEL 62 (Vienna: Akademie der Wissenschaften, 1913), 80–81; this passage can be found in English in *Commentary of Ambrose on Psalm 118* (Daleth), 27, trans. Íde Ní Riain (Dublin: Halcyon Press, 1998), 52.

30. *RB* Prol. 49: "Processu vero conversationis et fidei, dilatato corde inenarrabili dilectionis dulcedine curritur via mandatorum Dei" (Fry, 164–66).

portrays most clearly the effects of such divinization: namely a heart opened wide by the practice of asceticism, able to behold, even to venerate Christ who is perceived both within the depths of the monk's own heart and also in the other members of the monastic community with whom one journeys, "running" as it were toward eternal life. Chapter 72 is the penultimate chapter and concluding summary of Benedict's Rule. It serves a literary purpose analogous to Athanasius's portrayal of Anthony the Great in chapter 14 of the *Life of Anthony*. Athanasius depicts the monk Anthony emerging from twenty years of solitary asceticism, a living exemplar of restored primordial integrity and the form that divinization could take in a teacher and spiritual guide. Anthony is "like an initiate in sacred mysteries [μεμυσταγωγημένος], filled with God [θεοφορούμενος]." Having achieved perfect inner balance (ὅλος ἴσος) he now lives in accordance with nature (κατὰ φύσιν). Anthony further exemplifies the monastic virtues through compassionate attentiveness to the spiritual struggles of those who seek his counsel.[31] In chapter 72 of his Rule, Benedict offers a similar idealized portrait of the transforming power of monastic practice. This chapter on the "good zeal which monks ought to have" gives concrete form to the prologue's image of the "widened heart," but it also expands on practical themes Benedict had introduced earlier in chapter 7, the "Ladder of Humility." It will thus be helpful to briefly summarize Benedict's important modification of texts on humility he inherited from the earlier monastic tradition.

Numerous commentators have observed that chapter 72 of Benedict's Rule effectively "takes up where Chapter 7 on humility leaves off."[32] Benedict's ladder of humility is taken almost word-for-word from the *Rule of the Master*, whose author had transformed John Cassian's twelve "signs [*indiciis*] of humility" (*Institutes* 4:28) into twelve steps or rungs (*gradus*) of a ladder of humili-

---

31. Athanasius, *Life of Anthony* 14.7, 18–19: "μεμυσταγωγημένος καὶ θεοφορούμενος [...] ὅλος ἦν ἴσος, ὡς ὑπὸ τοῦ λόγου κυβερνώμενος, καὶ ἐν τῷ κατὰ φύσιν ἐστώς." *Athanase D'Alexandrie, Vie d'Antoine*, ed. G. J. M. Bartelink, SC 400 (Paris: Cerf, 1994), 128. The Latin *Vita Prima* renders Anthony's ascetical practice (ἀσκούμενος) during his twenty years in seclusion in the abandoned fort as *deifico uacans* ("Viginti itaque annos prope sic transiuit solus studio deifico uacans"). H. Hoppenbrouwers, *La plus ancienne version latine de la vie de S. Antoine*, Latinitas Christianorum primæva 14 (Nijmegen: Dekker and Van de Vegt, 1960), 96.

32. Aquinata Böckmann, *Perspectives on the Rule of St. Benedict* (Collegeville, Minn.: Liturgical Press, 2005), 52–53. Kardong discusses Böckmann's observations on the relationship between *RB* 7 and 72 together with those of André Borias and other commentators. Kardong, *Benedict's Rule*, 600–601.

ty (*Rule* 10). These steps include mortification of desires, obedience, gentleness, patience, and taciturnity. In all three—Cassian, the Master, and Benedict—they culminate in a yet higher step: namely, love (*caritas/amor*). However, Benedict is not content to make love simply the goal or the spiritual consequence of humility: he recognizes that it is a necessary means and aid to ascent of the "ladder" and thus unlike Cassian and the Master, he inserts *amor Dei* already at the third step, insisting that Christian obedience be undertaken "for the love of God."[33] And whereas for Cassian and the Master the ladder or signs of humility culminate in love "of virtue for its own sake,"[34] Benedict insists that it is not simply "love," but rather "love of God," and indeed "love of Christ" that casts out the fear that had characterized the lower rungs of the ladder.[35]

How this love of Christ is practically manifested is the subject of chapter 72. Here in the penultimate chapter of his Rule, Benedict describes the characteristics of a community that "runs together" toward God with "hearts expanded in love." Chapter 72 offers clear examples of what it means to honor, even to venerate, the presence of Christ in other members of the community through mundane acts of compassion and obedience. Benedict begins with the traditional and ancient contrast between two ways or paths, one leading toward, the other away from God. He describes two kinds of "zeal" (*zelus*): "an evil zeal of bitterness which separates from God and leads to hell," and "a good zeal which separates from vices and leads to God and to life everlasting." The exercise of this good zeal has at its core Paul's injunction in Romans 12:10 (= *RB* 72.4): "Let them outdo one another in showing honor" (*ut honore se invicem praeveniant*). Thus, the only permissible competition in the monastery is to become the best at perceiving and honoring Christ in one's confreres. This takes concrete form in ordinary encounters throughout the day, especially encounters that reveal limitations and brokenness, and tempt the monk to imagine that the "other" is the problem: "Let them most patiently endure one another's infirmities, whether of body or of character" (*sive corporum, sive mo-*

---

33. *RB* 7.34: "Tertius humilitatis gradus est, ut quis pro Dei amore omni obedientia se subdat majori" (Fry, 196).

34. Cassian, *Institutes* 4.39.3 has "sed amore ipsius boni et delectatione uirtutum," in John Cassian, *De institutis coenobiorum et de octo principalium vitiorum remediis*, in *Jean Cassien Institutions Cénobitiques*, ed. and trans. Jean-Claude Guy, SC 109 (Paris: Cerf, 1965), 180. In *RM* 10.90 the ladder of humility culminates "sed amore ipsius consuetudinis bonae et delectatione uirtutum"; see de Vogüé, *La Règle*, 1:438.

35. *RB* 7.67–69: "monachus mox ad caritatem Dei perveniet [...] non iam timore gehennae sed amore Christi, et consuetudine ipsa bona et delectatione virtutum" (Fry, 200–202).

*rum patientissime tolerent*).³⁶ The motif of competition in revering the God who is contemplated in the confrere is echoed in the injunctions: "Let them compete in showing obedience to one another [*oboedientiam sibi certatim impendant*]. None should follow what he judges useful for himself, but rather what is better for another."³⁷

By doing this, the community is to grow in every imaginable form of love. Benedict rings the changes of the Latin words for "love" (*caritas, amor, diligere*) as he continues: "They should practice fraternal charity [*caritas*] with purity; offering to God reverence of love [*amor*], loving [*diligere*] their abbot with sincere and humble affection [*caritas*]."³⁸ His conclusion echoes the imagery he employed at the end of the prologue: namely, that of a community, now transformed by acquiring the practical skills of loving one another, moving together toward their heavenly goal: "preferring nothing whatever to Christ, and may he bring us all together [*pariter*] to life everlasting."³⁹

This penultimate phrase, "preferring nothing whatever to Christ," appears to be a deliberate echo of both the earliest Latin version of the *Life of Anthony* and the *Treatise on the Lord's Prayer* by Cyprian of Carthage.⁴⁰ The final sentence is a reminder of Benedict's emphasis on the significance of the community in monastic observance. It is precisely within the community that the brethren learn to honor, to venerate, Christ. And none goes alone to God: rather, the monks are brought together—*pariter*—to everlasting life.

## Gregory the Great

In the writings of Gregory the Great, there are several instances, chiefly in his *Homilies on the Gospels*, where he employs vocabulary redolent of a theology of divinization. However, it would be fair to say that in these texts the im-

---

36. *RB* 72.5 (Fry, 294).
37. *RB* 72.6–7 (Fry, 294).
38. *RB* 72.8–10 (Fry, 294).
39. *RB* 72.11–12 (Fry, 294).
40. Cyprian, *On the Lord's Prayer* 15.11: "Prefer nothing whatever to Christ, because He did not prefer anything to us" (Christo nihil omnino praeponere, quia nec nobis quicquam ille praeposuit). *De Dominica oratione*, ed. William Hartel, CSEL 3.1 (Vienna, 1868), 277–78. Benedict appears to have used chaps. 4–5 of the same treatise in composing chaps. 19–20 of his Rule. The Latin *Vita Prima* of the *Life of Anthony* has "omnibus dicens nihil debere praeponere ipsos horum quae sunt in mundo dilectionis Christi" (14.21–23). Hoppenbrouwers, *La plus ancienne version latine*, 198.

agery of divinization tantalizes rather than satisfying the reader. His purpose is to exhort and illustrate by way of contrast, to highlight the gulf between God and humankind by emphasizing the divine condescension in raising up fallen humanity, rather than to describe the nature of the transformed soul. Thus in a homily for the Feast of Pentecost he contrasts the incarnation when "God became human by nature [*naturaliter*] with the Feast of the Holy Spirit," with when "human beings become gods by adoption" (*per adoptionem dii*).[41] A few sentences later in the same homily he makes an almost Palamite distinction between our utter incapacity to see God in Himself (*in se videre*) and the contrasting possibility of seeing God in his servants (*in servis suis*). In a homily on the healing of the blind man near Jericho Gregory explains: "When divinity upholds our broken human flesh, the human race receives back light that it had lost. And so from God's human suffering comes human elevation to divinity."[42] This reference to light lost by the human race suggests where we must look for a fuller explication of Gregory's theology of *divinization*: namely, in his doctrine of contemplation. As Bernard McGinn has noted, for Gregory "the fall, first and foremost, was loss of the ability to contemplate."[43] According to Gregory, Adam "fell into the misery of that blindness and banishment we all endure to this very day: for his sin resulted in the inability to see those joys of heaven which he had previously contemplated. [...] after his fall he lost that [inner] light of the mind [*lumen mentis*], which he had abundantly enjoyed before."[44] Gregory considered the restoration of this capacity for contemplation to be a foretaste of our eschatological destiny. This restored power enables us to contemplate and to be transformed by the divine light that renews and strengthens us, widening our hearts so that we can perceive others, ourselves, and indeed the whole creation as refulgent with God's glory.

These themes of divinizing light and the heart expanded by love are de-

---

41. Gregory, *Homily 30 on the Gospels* (on Jn 14:23–27), "In illa Deus naturaliter factus est homo, in ista homines facti sunt per adoptionem dii," in *Gregorius Magnus Homiliae in Evangelia*, ed. Raymond Étaix, CCL 141 (Turnhout: Brepols, 1999), 266.

42. Gregory, *Homily 2 on the Gospels* (on Lk 18:31–43): "quia dum divinitas defectum nostrae carnis suscepit, humanum genus lumen, quod amiserat, recepit. Unde enim Deus humana patitur, inde homo ad divina sublevatur" (13).

43. Bernard McGinn, *The Growth of Mysticism* (New York: Crossroad, 1994), 51.

44. Gregory, *Dialogues* 4.1.1: "in hujus caecitatis atque exsilii quam patimur venit aerumnam, quia peccando extra semetipsum fusus, jam illa coelestis patriae gaudia, quae prius contemplabatur, videre non potuit. [...] postquam huc cecidit, ab illo quo implebatur mentis lumine recessit." In *Les Dialogues de Grégoire le Grand*, ed. Adalbert De Vogüé and Paul Antin, SC 265 (Paris: Cerf, 1980), 3:18.

picted most clearly toward the end of Gregory's biography of St. Benedict, which comprises the whole second book of his *Dialogues*. This biography dates from more than fifty years after Benedict's Rule, and was based according to Gregory on the reminiscences of refugee-monks who fled from Benedict's monastery of Monte Cassino to Rome when their abbey was destroyed by the Lombards in roughly 580. It should be borne in mind that although Gregory praises Benedict's Rule for its *discretio*, it cannot be demonstrated from Gregory's writings that he knew or had ever read Benedict's Rule closely, as he never quotes from it; nor do Gregory's descriptions of his own monastic foundations suggest any uniquely "Benedictine" influence. Nevertheless, it is in the second Book of the *Dialogues*, in his description of the last months of Benedict's life, that Gregory provides his most vivid description of how the innermost self, the human *mens* or *nous* can be transformed, widened, so as to contemplate divine light illuminating the whole of creation.

In his critical edition and commentary on the *Dialogues*, as well as in subsequent articles, Adalbert de Vogüé emphasized the careful, intentional literary construction of the whole of book 2 of the *Dialogues*, but especially of chapters 33–38 which conclude the book.[45] These chapters take the form of a literary "triptych" with three progressively illuminating "panels" that depict the transformation of Benedict from a spiritually powerful ascetic and miracle-worker into a contemplative whose "widened heart" can behold both the ascent of saints into heaven and the whole universe scintillating within in a ray of divine light. Before describing each panel in detail, it will be helpful to summarize the content of the whole triptych. The first panel, chapters 33 and 34, describes the meeting of Benedict and his sister Scholastica, who by means of "holy conversation" and prayer is able to demonstrate to her reluctant and increasingly indignant brother that love is superior to ascetical legalism. Benedict's chastened heart is thus enabled to behold in vision the ascent of his sister's soul into heaven. The second panel, chapter 35, parallels the first. This time Benedict meets and shares "sweet words of life" with a fellow abbot, and afterwards contemplates not only the ascent of another soul into heaven, but the whole of creation scintillating in a ray of divine light. The final panel, chapters 36 and 37, includes a brief encomium of Benedict and a description of

---

45. Adalbert de Vogüé, *Les Dialogues*, SC 260 (Paris: Cerf, 1979), 2:230–49, and "The Meeting of Benedict and Scholastica: An Interpretation," trans. J. B. Hasbrouck, *Cistercian Studies* 18 (1983): 167–83.

his death, followed by a vision seen by two of his monks, of the shining path on which Benedict's soul had ascended into heaven.

De Vogüé has emphasized that these chapters offer a hagiographic portrait of conversion and transformation. Throughout the first thirty-two chapters of the *Dialogues*, Benedict is depicted as a powerful spiritual warrior, fighting and overcoming vices within and demonic powers without. His ascetic rigor culminates in the powers of prophecy and miracles: these early chapters present him as the archetypal monastic practitioner and lawgiver. But chapter 36 marks an abrupt change. Gregory begins by reminding his readers that St. Paul once "willed something he was powerless to obtain," *quod voluit obtinere non valuit*, and then he applies the *quod voluit ... non valuit* to Benedict, describing the final meeting between him and his sister, the nun Scholastica.[46] Following their festive meal and "sacred conversation [*sacra conloquia*] on the spiritual life,"[47] Benedict's almost frenzied desire to obey monastic custom by returning to the monastery before nightfall is frustrated by his sister, whose prayers summon a thunderstorm and force Benedict to remain.[48] Gregory explains that she proved the "more powerful" (*plus potuit*) because "hers was the greater love" (*quae amplius amavit*).[49] De Vogüé considers this an allusion to Luke 7:44, where Jesus rebukes Simon the Pharisee, comparing him unfavorably with the sinful woman "who loved much" (*dilexit multum*). This, of course, casts Benedict in the role of the Pharisee; but Gregory suggests that this frustration of Benedict's will was also an occasion of conversion and spiritual growth, because after being forced to stay they both enjoyed "sharing with each other to their hearts' content holy conversation on the spiritual life." Gregory implies that this forced *sacra spiritalis vitae conloquia* facilitated Benedict's transformation into a contemplative. For Gregory the experience of looking inward and enduring painful self-discovery, the act of going into and "abiding with one's self" (*habitare secum*) is an essential preparation for contemplation;[50] and, indeed, Gregory had already described this as part of Benedict's earlier ascesis in chapter 3 of book 2.[51]

---

46. Gregory, *Dialogues* 2.33.1–2 (230).
47. Ibid., 2.33.2–4 (232).
48. Ibid., 2.33.3–4 (232).
49. Ibid., 2.33.5 (234).
50. McGinn, *The Growth of Mysticism*, 48–50 and 56–57.
51. Gregory, *Dialogues* 2.3.5–9 (143; notably, 143n5 contains a detailed bibliography of Gregory's use of *habitare secum*).

The result of this encounter between brother and sister is Benedict's first celestial vision: that of Scholastica's soul "penetrating the secret recesses of heaven."[52] In pagan hagiography the vision of a revered figure's heavenly ascent had become a traditional feature of the imperial cult, providing either a pretext or a later confirmation of the Roman Senate's declaration of a not-unexpected imperial apotheosis.[53] In Christian literature this tradition, modeled perhaps on Elisha's vision of Elijah's ascent (2 Kgs 2:11–12) or on the pseudepigraphal Book of Enoch (chaps. 14–18) appears in the *Martyrdom of Perpetua and Felicity* (1.3 and 4.7) and, more relevant here, in the *Life of Anthony* (60). In these cherished accounts, the vision confirms both the holiness of the ascending saint and the spiritual authority of the seer. Another well-known Christian text with strong parallels to this narrative is the conversation of Augustine and his mother Monica in Ostia, described in book 9 of Augustine's *Confessions*.[54] As in Gregory's narrative, Augustine's conversation concludes with the contemplation of heavenly mysteries and the suggestion of an imminent death. And in Gregory's account Benedict's vision not only confirms his sister's holiness, it is a sign of his own ongoing transformation that will shortly be explored by Gregory using the image of the "widened heart." It is significant that this vision follows, not the solitary ascetical struggle frequent in monastic hagiography and apophthegmata, but what can only be described as a communal interaction, an event less typical of the hermitage than of the cenobium: namely, an extended spiritual conversation during a meal attended by a variety of individuals from different monastic communities. In both the *Institutes* and *Conferences*, John Cassian had praised such gatherings as he experienced them in late fourth-century Egypt, thus subtly encouraging their implementation in the communities he helped form in early fifth-century Gaul. Benedict's own Rule and the monastic sources on which he depends specifically describe and legislate for such gatherings.

The meeting of Benedict and Abbot Servandus in chapter 35 introduc-

---

52. Ibid., 2.34.1.

53. Seutonius describes both Julius Caesar's own prophetic vision (*De Vita Caesarum* 1.81.3) and the celestial omen seen by many and interpreted as "the soul of Caesar which had been taken up to heaven" (1.88). Suetonius, *De Vita Caesarum*, trans. John Rolf as *The Lives of the Caesars* (London: Loeb, Macmillan, 1914), book 1, 108–9.

54. Augustine, *Confessions* 9.8–11. De Vogüé discusses the parallels in detail in *Gregory the Great: The Life of Saint Benedict*, trans. Hilary Costello and Eoin De Bhaldraithe (Petersham: St. Bede, 1993), 157–62.

es the second, central panel of Gregory's literary triptych, containing what Bernard McGinn has called "perhaps the most famous nonbiblical vision of the early Middle Ages."[55] This vision is reminiscent of both Cicero's famous Dream of Scipio (10–16)[56] and, to a lesser extent, Augustine's Neo-Platonic ecstasy during his meeting with Monica in Ostia. Gregory's description of the setting and events preceding the vision closely parallel the meeting with Scholastica in the preceding chapter, though the cenobitic context is even more distinctly highlighted. Abbot Servandus brought with him members of his monastery in Campania, and during the night the two abbots stay in a tower above their monks, as if symbolically standing guard or keeping watch. Through their holy conversation the two abbots "mutually imbue one another with the sweet words of life,"[57] permitting them a hint of eschatological fulfillment: "at least [a] taste of the joys of the heavenly banquet—the delightful banquet of their heavenly homeland which they were not yet able to enjoy perfectly, but for which they longed."[58] Following this mutually sanctifying exchange the abbots retire to their separate tower rooms, and Benedict keeps vigil, praying at the tower window above his sleeping community.

In the vision that follows, Gregory creates a verbal portrait of the flowering, the opening out of the human capacity for contemplation. As Benedict prays, he beholds "an outpouring of light from above which swept away the darkness of night, shining with such splendor that it surpassed the light of day, illuminating the darkness as it shined."[59] It is thus a vision of light triumphant over darkness; but it is more than that: "the whole world was gathered beneath a single sunbeam [*omnis mundus ... sub uno solis radio collectus*] and brought before his eyes." And finally, as in his earlier vision of Scholastica's ascent, Benedict beholds "the soul of Germanus the bishop of Capua in a sphere of fire, being carried by the angels to heaven."[60]

Gregory explains the significance of this vision in some detail. When the soul beholds "even a little" of God's light the deepest part of the self is unbound and expands. He employs different nouns and verbs to describe this

55. McGinn, *The Growth of Mysticism*, 71.
56. Cicero, *Republic* 6.9–26 (esp. 6.10–16).
57. Gregory, *Dialogues*, 2.35.1: "dulcia sibi invicem vitae verba transfunderent" (236).
58. Ibid.: "et suavem cibum caelestis patriae, quia adhuc perfecte gaudendo non poterant, saltem suspirando gustarent."
59. Ibid., 2.35.2.
60. Ibid., 2.35.2–3 (236–38).

divine expansion of the innermost self. The interior place that opens out in contemplation is, alternately, the soul (*anima*), the mind (*mens*), the bosom (*sinus*). To describe the effect upon it of the divine light Gregory says that it is unbound (*laxatur*), it expands (*ampliator*), it opens wide, dilates (*dilatatus*).[61] Thus transformed by contemplation it "stands above the world" rising "even above itself" and in looking out or down on the world, perceives how narrow (*angusta*) all created things are in comparison with the divine light. This vision entails awareness not only of the divine radiance, but also of the soul's own luminescence: "Corresponding to the light gleaming before his exterior eyes was an interior light within the mind."[62] Thus the heart unbound by contemplation perceives not only creation in the light of God, but also the nature of the transformed heart, an "interior light within" (*lux interior in mente*) causing the contemplative's own mind to shine with reflected glory.[63] The *lumen mentis* lost through Adam's fall has been, at least temporarily, restored.[64]

In the third panel of his literary triptych, Gregory praises Benedict using the language and imagery of light, portraying both Benedict's life and Rule of as worthy objects of contemplation. Benedict "shone [*claruit*] in the world by his many miracles, and was no less than brilliant [*fulsit*] in his words of teaching." His Rule for monks is "remarkable in discretion and brilliant [*luculentam*] in language."[65] Shining lights are again seen in the vision that accompanies Benedict's heavenly ascent. Benedict dies while praying, fortified by the eucharist and supported in the arms of his disciples.[66] Shortly thereafter, the third and final vision Gregory relates is seen not by Benedict, but by his monks. Two different members of Benedict's community mystically behold "a path strewn with carpets and innumerable bright lights, stretching toward the

61. Ibid., 2.35.6 (240).
62. Ibid., 2.35.7 (240).
63. Ibid.: "In illa ergo luce, quae exterioribus oculis fulsit, lux interior in mente fuit."
64. Gregory employs language and imagery identical to this in his explorations of the nature of contemplation in the *Moralia*, and in his *Homilies on the Gospels* and *Homilies on Ezekiel*. Butler notes that in these texts Gregory frequently calls the divine light "uncircumscribed" (*incircumscriptum*), suggesting that divinization consists in the human heart becoming increasingly capable of perceiving God. However, the distinction between creator and created remains, and contemplation is always partial and limited. Cuthbert Butler, *Western Mysticism: The Teaching of SS. Augustine, Gregory and Bernard on Contemplation and the Contemplative Life*, 2nd ed. (London: E. P. Button and Co., 1926), 77–80.
65. Gregory, *Dialogues*, 2.36.1: "In mundo claruit, doctrinae quoque verbo non mediocriter fulsit. Nam scripsit monachorum regulam discretione praecipuam, sermone luculentam" (242).
66. Ibid., 2.37.2.

East, extending from his cell, reaching into heaven." Although they do not see their master, a heavenly voice assures them that "This is the path on which the Lord's beloved Benedict ascended to heaven."[67] Here, as frequently throughout his *Life of Benedict*, Gregory alludes to the Elijah cycle in the Books of Kings.[68] Elisha, the disciple of Elijah, was confirmed in his status as the prophet's successor by a vision of his master's ascent into heaven in a horse-drawn fiery chariot (2 Kgs 2:10–12). In Gregory's account, Benedict's monks do not see the actual ascent of their abbot: they are informed of it by the heavenly voice. What they behold is, rather the light-strewn path, that road or pathway their abbot had bequeathed to them in the form of the Rule that Gregory had so richly praised in the preceding chapter.

## Conclusion

In the introduction to this chapter, reference was made to the contributions of Gregory Palamas, the great theologian of *theosis* and defender of contemplatives. It is fitting to observe that this pillar of the Eastern church particularly emphasized (in his theological treatise the *Triads*, also known as the *Defense of the Holy Hesychasts*) the significance of St. Benedict's contemplative experience. Palamas writes: "Another saint, one of the most perfect, saw everything that exists as if contained beneath one ray of this noetic sun."[69] There can be no doubt that it is Benedict to whom Palamas refers, known through the Pope Zacharias's Greek translation of the *Dialogues* of "Gregorios Dialogos." The reference to "the whole universe in a single ray of [the] sun" is unique and specific.[70] For Palamas, Benedict is "one of the most perfect" of those who experience *theosis* through *theoria*. Moreover, Palamas interprets Gregory's explication of Benedict's vision as a clear example of his essence/energies dis-

---

67. Ibid., 2.37.3: "Viderunt namque quia strata palliis atque innumeris corusca lampadibus uia recto orientis tramite ab eius cella in caelum usque tendebatur.... Haec est uia, qua dilectus Domino caelum Benedictus ascendit" (244).

68. Olivier Rousseau, "Saint Benoît et le prophète Élisée," *Revue Monastique* 144 (1956): 103–14.

69. Gregory Palamas, *Triads* 1.3.22.2–4: "Πάντα δὲ τὰ ὄντα, ὥσπερ ὑπὸ μίαν τινὰ περιεχόμενα ἀκτῖνα τοῦ νοητοῦ ἡλίου τούτου, τῶν τελεωτέρων τις ἕτερος ἑώρακεν ἁγίων." *Grégoire Palamas, Défense des saints hésychastes*, ed. and trans. John Meyendorff, Spicilegium Sacrum Lovaniense études et documents 30 (Louvain: Université catholique de Louvain, 1959) 157.9–11.

70. Emmanuel Lanne, "L'interprétation palamite de la vision de S. Benoît," *Le millénaire du Mont-Athos 963–1963*, Études et mélanges II (Venice: Fondazione Giorgio Cini, Éditions de Chevtogne, 1964), 21–47.

tinction. "By this contemplation and by his supra-intelligible union with this light, he did not learn what it is by nature, but he learned that it really exists, is supernatural and superessential, different from all things; that its being is absolute and unique, and that it mysteriously comprehends all in itself."[71]

Although the Christian East thus reveres the monks Benedict and "Gregorios Dialogos" as paradigms of *theosis*, the matter is more subtle in the West. In both the *Rule of Benedict* and the writings of Gregory the Great there is what may be described as an understated but real doctrine of divinization. For both these monks this doctrine is intimately associated with their understanding of contemplation. For Benedict, the divinizing light and divine voice of scripture envelop the monk throughout the day during the divine office and in private *lectio divina* and prayer. By following Benedict's "little Rule for beginners" (*RB* 73) the monk learns to honor and venerate Christ in the abbot, in guests, in the sick, and eventually in all of the brethren, who "run with widening hearts in the sweetness of love" not as separate individuals but *pariter*—together—toward the heavenly kingdom. For Gregory the Great, the light of divine contemplation encompasses both the vision of the world illuminated by God and the divine light hidden within the depths of the soul. Both were lost in Adam's fall, but are restored to those who undertake the way of *askesis* and learn the "greater love."

---

71. Gregory Palamas, *Triads* 1.3.22.6–9: "ἀπὸ τῆς θεωρίας ταύτης καὶ τῆς πρὸς αὐτὸ ὑπὲρ νοῦν ἑνώσεως, οὐχ ὅπερ ἐστὶν αὐτὸ τὴν φύσιν, ἀλλ' ὅτι ἐστὶν ὡς ἀληθῶς, καὶ ὑπερφυὲς καὶ ὑπερούσιόν ἐστιν, ἄλλο τι παρὰ τὰ ὄντα πάντα ὄν, ὃν δὲ κυρίως τε καὶ μόνον καὶ πᾶν ὂν ἀπορρήτως ἐν ἑαυτῷ συνειληφός" (157.13–17).

*Norman Russell*

## 14. A COMMON CHRISTIAN TRADITION
*Deification in the Greek and Latin Fathers*

The preceding chapters of this book should have dispelled any doubt as to whether the notion of deification belongs properly to the Latin tradition. Jared Ortiz and Brian Dunkle are surely right in agreeing with John Scotus Eriugena that even if the term *deificatio* is not found in the Latin Fathers (until Eriugena himself introduced it in the ninth century), its *intellectus*, or meaning, is widely diffused in their writings.[1] It may also be noted that in the Greek tradition itself the *intellectus* of deification is not confined solely to texts where the technical terms are used. Furthermore, the Latin Fathers should be compared with their Greek contemporaries and not judged by the standard of the fully developed Greek teaching of the later Byzantine Empire.[2] In the fourteenth century Gregory Palamas distinguished between God in his inaccessible transcendence (the divine "essence") and God in his accessible immanence (the divine "energies") in order to defend the experiential participation in God in this life through sharing in the divine energies against those who

---

1. Eriugena, *Periphyseon* 5, 1015C.
2. Gösta Hallonsten makes a similar point in his influential article, "Theosis in Recent Research," in *Partakers of the Divine Nature: The History and Development of Deification in the Christian Traditions*, ed. Michael J. Christensen and Jeffery A. Wittung (Madison, Wis.: Farleigh Dickinson University Press, 2007), 281–93: "Current research on deification in the Latin tradition tends to choose St. Gregory Palamas as its preferential point of reference for comparison between East and West.... Yet it could very well be asked if Palamas is the most adequate point of reference" (284). Clearly, he is not the most adequate point of reference in an inquiry restricted to the early centuries.

would defer such participation to the life to come. Palamas accordingly sets deification within a specific doctrine of religious experience. The Greek Fathers of the classic patristic age had a broader agenda. I will not repeat here the detailed surveys I have attempted elsewhere,[3] but will simply summarize what seem to me the chief characteristics of the Greek approach to deification up to the mid-fifth century.

The first characteristic is that deification is *Christologically driven*. It is not just the product of philosophical reflection on the nature of spiritual ascent, but grew out of an understanding of Christ as both the agent and the pattern of our development as Christians. And as theological precision grew about how the human is related to the divine in the person of Christ, so the deification of the believer was understood increasingly in terms of participation through Christ in the life of the Trinity. The second characteristic is its *ecclesial nature*. Once the "gods" of Psalm 81(82) are taken to be the baptized, it is an easy step to make deification equivalent to adoption in Christ and then later to understand the eucharist in terms of the deified flesh of Christ communicating the divine attributes of immortality and incorruption to the ecclesial community. The third characteristic is its *eschatological orientation*. Deification—sharing in the immortality and incorruption that belong properly to God alone—is the goal of human life. Its inauguration, however, is not postponed to the eschaton, for the soul's (and even the body's) participation in divine glory can begin in this life. Finally, the fourth characteristic is the way in which certain *Platonic themes* have been appropriated. The concept of participation, the ascent of the soul to the supreme good, and the attainment of likeness to God through moral discipline and ascetical practice all owe something to contemporary Platonism. These four characteristics are mutually interdependent.[4] Deification is the appropriation of divine life through participation

---

3. Norman Russell, *The Doctrine of Deification in the Greek Patristic Tradition* (Oxford: Oxford University Press, 2004), and *Fellow Workers with God: Orthodox Thinking on Theosis* (Crestwood, N.Y.: St Vladimir's Seminary Press, 2009). For a concise overview, see Daniel A. Keating, "Deification in the Greek Fathers," in *Called to Be Children of God: The Catholic Doctrine of Human Deification*, ed. David Meconi and Carl E. Olson (San Francisco: Ignatius Press, 2016), 40–58.

4. For a searching analysis of various modern attempts to establish a taxonomy of patristic approaches to deification (in which my own earlier work is criticised perceptively and subjected to a "friendly amendment," which I gratefully accept), see Daniel A. Keating, "Typologies of Deification," *International Journal of Systematic Theology* 17 (2015): 267–83. Keating himself proposes three "core elements": (1) a grounding in the scriptures as a whole; (2) an embeddedness in the church's experience of

in the incarnate Word in whom human nature has been divinized through its assumption by the Word, a participation that is accomplished sacramentally with the necessary support of the moral life. When we turn to the Latin tradition, we find these characteristics well represented in a broad range of authors.

### The Christological Basis of Deification

The similarity of the theological patterning that we find in the Greek and the Latin Fathers—not to mention the Greek and Latin liturgies—is the fundamental point they have in common. Salvation was brought about by the incarnate Word, who not only remedied the effects of the Fall but raised humanity to a new level of existence characterized by communion with the Father and participation in immortality. This ontological transformation of human nature is expressed by the "exchange formula," which we first find enunciated by Irenaeus: the Son of God "became what we are in order to make us what he is himself."[5] And "what he is himself" is by nature incorruptible and immortal. The Word accepted the limitation of created existence; human nature received the boundlessness of divine existence. The pattern established by Irenaeus became normative for all who came after him.

The first Latin author to make more than a passing reference to the "exchange formula" was Novatian, writing in the mid-third century. Novatian uses the mercantile language of lending and borrowing (*feneror* and *mutuor*), which, as the concept of exchange implies, is not all one-way. Through the kenosis of the incarnation, the divine Word becomes capable of human experiences without undergoing any change of nature. "The divine nature of Christ," as James Papandrea says, "can *experience* suffering because of the *kenosis*, yet without *actually* suffering in a way that would compromise divine impassibility. The suffering of the divine nature is, in a sense, loaned and borrowed from the human nature."[6] Conversely, the immortality of the human nature is loaned and borrowed from the divine nature. The human nature lends the divine nature *fragilitas*; the divine nature in return lends the human nature *immortalitas*. It is this Christological linking of *kenosis* with *theosis*—to use the

---

faith; and (3) a reliance on the concept of participation. These seem to me roughly coterminous with the four "chief characteristics" I offer here.

5. Irenaeus, *Against Heresies* 5, Praefatio.

6. James A. Papandrea, "Loaning and Borrowing: Deification in Novatian," 104.

term that Gregory of Nazianzus later coined specifically as a counterpart to *kenosis*—that makes our own deification possible.

In the fourth century, Hilary of Poitiers extends the use of Novatian's mercantile imagery. Christ assumed the *fragilitas* of the human body in order to buy it back (*ad redemptionem*).[7] This sets us on the path of the forensic model of salvation which was developed further by Ambrose and came to dominate soteriological thinking in the West in the early Middle Ages.[8] Brian Dunkle, however, draws attention to a less familiar side of Ambrose's treatment of the *admirabile commercium*, arguing that "for Ambrose the work of the Incarnation is not only a process of atonement for sin, a redemption from a fallen state, but rather a conferral of what is beyond the human condition."[9] In Ambrose's own words, Christ "offered himself *according to* our nature that he might accomplish a work *beyond* our nature."[10] This aligns him closely with the Greek tradition, which emphasizes the transformation of human nature in Christ as the fundamental purpose of the divine economy of the incarnation.

The transformation of our nature in Christ is also taken up by Gregory of Elvira, who uses typological techniques of exegesis learned from Origen to interpret the "deification" of Adam in Genesis 3:22 ("See, the man has become like one of us") as indicating the communication, through the incarnation of the Word, of divine life and immortality to the human race as a whole represented in Adam. It was precisely in view of the incarnation that Adam was created in the first place in the image and likeness of God. This provides the theological basis for the exchange formula: "Adam became like God, because Christ became like Adam," Adam being already, despite the Fall—which required a "time of condemnation" to be fulfilled—oriented in his nature toward the divine.[11]

In the fifth century, the exchange formula is particularly prominent in Pope Leo the Great. In Daniel Keating's words, it is "both the entry point

---

7. Janet Sidaway, "Making Man Manifest: Deification in Hilary of Poitiers," 121.
8. See Ambrose, *Ep.* 72.8.
9. Fr. Brian Dunkle, SJ, "Beyond Carnal Cogitations: Deification in Ambrose of Milan," 150.
10. Ambrose, *Incarn.* 6.54: "Secundum naturam igitur se obtulit nostrum, ut ultra nostrum operaretur naturam." Cited in Dunkle, "Beyond Carnal Cogitations," 150; emphasis added.
11. Gregory of Elvira, *Fragm. In Gen. 3:22*, cited and translated in Alexey Fokin, "The Doctrine of Deification in Western Fathers of the Church," in *Für Uns und für unser Heil: Soteriologie in Ost und West*, ed. Theresa Hainthaler et al. (Innsbruck: Tyrolia Verlag, 2014), 209–10.

and the culmination of Leo's theology of deification."[12] Leo envisages the advancement (*provectio*) of humanity, by means of this exchange, to the very perfection of the Godhead (*ad summa Deitatis*).[13] Leo's contemporary, Peter Chrysologus, however, returns emphatically to the commercial aspects of the exchange formula. David Meconi draws our attention to the frequency with which Chrysologus uses the mercantile terms *consortium* and *commercium* in his sermons.[14] In an image that for modern readers might suggest the kind of financial transaction associated with surrogate motherhood, the mother of God leases her womb to God as a dwelling that she may request in payment salvation for the lost.[15] "The exchange comes to a fever pitch on Calvary," says Meconi, "where Christ 'sells' his divinity in order to buy sinful humanity."[16] The Greek Fathers were not averse to using mercantile imagery—Gregory of Nazianzus, for example, discusses whether Christ's ransom (the λύτρον of our ἀπολύτρωσις) was paid to the Father or to the devil[17]—but they never adopted it with the enthusiasm of a Peter Chrysologus.

## The Ecclesial Nature of Deification

The second striking similarity between the Greek and the Latin Fathers is in their narrative of how the divine life transmitted by the Word of God to the humanity assumed by him is appropriated by the believer. Such appropriation is effected primarily through participation in the liturgical life of the ecclesial body. Baptism, as Ortiz emphasizes, "brings about a radical identification with Christ."[18] The eucharist develops and consolidates the believer's union with Christ. "Be what you see, and receive what you are," says Augustine in one of his sermons.[19] The eucharist makes the participant an *alter Christus*. The language is bolder than that which we find in Augustine's Greek contemporaries. Cyr-

---

12. Daniel L. Keating, "The Wonderful Exchange: Deification in Leo the Great," 210.
13. Leo, *Ep.* 124.9, cited in Keating, "The Wonderful Exchange," 213–14. Souter's *Glossary of Later Latin* (s.v. *summus*) gives *ad summa* as the Latin equivalent of πέρας.
14. Fr. David Vincent Meconi, SJ, "Between Empire and *Ecclesia*: Deification in Peter Chrysologus," 195.
15. Peter Chrysologus, *Sermon* 147.6; cited in Meconi, "Between Empire and *Ecclesia*," 196.
16. Meconi, "Between Empire and *Ecclesia*," 195.
17. Gregory of Nazianzus, *Oration* 45.22.
18. Jared Ortiz, "Making Worshipers into Gods: Deification in the Latin Liturgy," 15.
19. *Sermon* 272; cited in Ortiz, "Making Worshipers into Gods," 23.

il of Alexandria, for example, teaches that "the Son does not change the least thing belonging to the created order into the nature of his own deity,"[20] but that through the eucharist we partake of immortality and incorruption because the Holy Spirit, "the provider of immortality," becomes active within us.[21]

In his preaching Augustine uses rhetorical techniques designed to move his audience to action. But in his more reflective writing he can analyse the stages of spiritual ascent with as much subtlety as any Greek author. Jared Ortiz has recently made a convincing case for interpreting the two accounts of spiritual ascent in books 7 and 9 of the *Confessions* as a deliberate contrast drawn by Augustine between the philosophical ascent and the ecclesial.[22] The first relies on Platonic teaching. Through contemplating what exists in the mutable visible world, the mind ascends to a truth that is unchangeable and authentic. The culmination of this ascent for Augustine was a flash of understanding, a glimpse of eternal life attained through a fleeting transcendence of the bodily senses.[23] The second ascent was experienced by him in the company of his uneducated mother, Monica, who "represents the Church in all the simplicity of her faith."[24] This ecclesial ascent is accomplished not in solitude through intellectual effort, but communally through love. In contrast to the first ascent it has, as Ortiz points out, a salvific character.[25] Like the first ascent, it is described as a climbing step by step beyond all corporeal objects, but its culmination is "the region of inexhaustible abundance," where God feeds "Israel eternally with truth for food."[26] The eucharistic allusion is unmistakeable. Augustine's perspective here is both eucharistic and eschatological. Perfect existence may be entered upon in this life but will only be fully attained on the seventh day of the new creation: in Augustine's words, "We ourselves shall become that seventh day, when we have been filled up and made new by His blessing and sanctification."[27]

---

20. Cyril of Alexandria, *C. Nest.* 3.2 (cited in Russell, *Doctrine of Deification*, 202).

21. Cyril of Alexandria, *In Jo.* 3.6.324c, 4.2.362b, 4.2.365c (cited in Russell, ibid.).

22. Jared Ortiz, *"You Made Us for Yourself": Creation in St. Augustine's* Confessions (Minneapolis, Minn.: Fortress Press, 2016), 85–96 and 151–57.

23. Augustine, *Confessions* 7.27.24.

24. Ortiz, *"You Made Us for Yourself,"* 154.

25. Ibid., 157.

26. Augustine, *Confessions* 9.9.24; in *Confessions*, trans. Henry Chadwick (Oxford: Oxford University Press, 1991), 171.

27. Augustine, *City of God* 22; cited in Ron Haflidson, "We Shall Be That Seventh Day: Deification in Augustine," 178.

## The Eschatological Orientation of Deification

There is a division among the Fathers between those who treat deification as deferred until the resurrection and those who see it as already inaugurated in this life.[28] For some of the latter, the eschatological exaltation of the believer who participates in the new humanity transformed by Christ is prefigured in the Gospel accounts of the transfiguration. This aspect of the transfiguration as anthropophany is less prominent among patristic writers than the aspect of theophany. In his *Commentary on Matthew*, however, Hilary of Poitiers, the first Latin Father to discuss deification in terms of the transfiguration, sees the radiance reflected on the face of Moses as a foretaste of "the glory of the resurrection ... ordained for human bodies."[29] The same emphasis is found in the *De Trinitate*, where Hilary presents Christ as revealing in the transfiguration the glory of the resurrected body. Interestingly, this is also the perspective we find in John the Deacon, who in a passage quoted by Ortiz associates the white garments of the newly baptized with the dazzling white clothes of Christ on Mount Tabor and interprets them as signifying "the mystery of the risen Church."[30] In the Greek tradition we have to wait until Andrew of Crete at the end of the seventh century before we find an equally clear statement of the transfiguration as anthropophany, as a revelation of the deified humanity of Christ and therefore—once we have been conformed to Christ—of our own humanity as well. The feast that we celebrate, says St. Andrew in a homily for August 6, is "the deification of our own nature, its transformation to a better condition, its rapture and ascent from natural realities to those which are above nature."[31]

Yet the aspect of anthropophany is far from absent in the earlier tradition. Cyril of Alexandria, in his own homily on the transfiguration, connects Luke's account of the episode on Mount Tabor (Lk 9:28–36) with the immediately preceding passage that calls for anyone who wants to follow Christ to take up his cross.[32] In Luke's Gospel the apostles' experience of Christ's trans-

---

28. The former group includes theologians in the Antiochene tradition such as John Chrysostom, who was much appreciated in the West, and Theodore of Mopsuestia, who was translated by the Pelagian bishop, Julian of Eclanum.
29. *In Mt.* 17.2.14; cited in Sidaway, "Making Man Manifest," 124–25.
30. John the Deacon, *Letter* 6; cited in Ortiz, "Making Worshipers into Gods," 19.
31. Andrew of Crete, *Homily* 7.1, trans. McGuckin; cited in Russell, *Fellow Workers*, 97.
32. Cyril of Alexandria, *Various Homilies* 9.

figuration follows upon their reception of the teaching that "whoever wishes to save his life will lose it, but whoever shall lose his life for my sake shall find it" (Lk 9:23). It is the acceptance of suffering for Christ's sake that will lead to heavenly glory for them. Moreover, an ecclesial dimension is also implied. The manifestation of Christ's glory was not to a single apostle but to a group of three. Participation in Christ's transfiguration, with its attendant hope of glory, was from the beginning not a private mystical experience but something accomplished within the ecclesial body.

Parallel to this, however, there is another approach connected with spiritual ascent. The privatization—or rather, interiorization—of the transfiguration begins with the Macarian homilies[33] and comes to be fully articulated by Maximus the Confessor. The *gnostikoi*, the spiritually advanced who have become like the Apostles Peter, James, and John, prefigure within themselves the transfiguration of the Word that transforms and deifies them so that they come to "reflect with unveiled face the glory of the Lord" (2 Cor 3:18). Even in this life they begin to contemplate the eschatological glory of the eighth day.[34] The aspect of anthropophany, which we first find in Hilary, is thus interiorized in the Greek tradition and appropriated as a personal participation in divine glory.

## Platonic Themes

Even though most Latin authors did not have the direct access to Plato that the Greeks enjoyed,[35] they often handle Platonic themes with considerable skill. They tend, however, to use them in a way that is personal to each writer, rather than, as with the Greeks, drawing on a common Christian Platonizing tradition going back to Philo and Clement of Alexandria. Augustine, for example, respected the "Platonists" for showing what the human mind could achieve in attaining knowledge about God, but in his mature work he

---

33. See Russell, *Doctrine of Deification*, 244–45. Macarius gives an exegesis of Ezekiel's vision of the *merkabah* influenced by the transfiguration.

34. Maximus the Confessor, *Cap. Theol.* 1.97; see Russell, *Doctrine of Deification*, 292–93.

35. The only part of Plato himself available until the twelfth century was Calcidius's translation of the first part of the *Timaeus*, made in the early fourth century. In the mid-century Marius Victorinus translated Porphyry and perhaps some of Plotinus. He incorporated aspects of Platonic thought in his rather idiosyncratic reflections on the Trinity, but these were based on his study of pagan Neo-Platonism rather than on the Christian Platonism of Alexandria.

distinguishes clearly between the intellectual work of professional philosophers and the "true philosophy" of the Christian faith, whose truths are inaccessible to merely human reflection. Philosophy can tell us *how* to achieve ultimate fulfillment but only revelation can tell us *what* that fulfillment really is. Boethius provides a striking example of such separation of philosophy from theological reflection in his discussion of the attainment of happiness and goodness without specific reference to Christ.[36] These attributes belong perfectly to God alone. They are not merely attributes, however, because what God is *is* supreme happiness and goodness. Therefore by sharing in them, human beings become gods (*deos fieri*) by participation.[37] There is nothing in Boethius, as Michael Wiitala says, that is incompatible with Catholic Christianity.[38] But in the Greek tradition "genuine philosophizing," as Gregory of Nazianzus calls it, is almost always focused specifically on the contemplation of the Trinity, a contemplation that enables the mind to transcend the duality of material existence and become "akin to God ... so far as is permissible for human nature."[39]

Most theologians were not philosophers like Gregory or Boethius. They preferred to use biblical terms to express "the divine ascent,"[40] terms such as "image" and "likeness" (Gn 1:26) and "partakers of the divine nature" (2 Pt 1:4). Not all the Greek Fathers distinguish between image and likeness. Those who do, like Basil the Great and Diadochus of Photice (both of them theologians particularly valued in the monastic tradition), identify the image with humanity's rational faculty, which includes some kind of kinship with the divine, and the likeness with the supreme moral beauty to which human beings can ascend by contemplation and ascetic effort. Others, like Athanasius and Cyril of Alexandria, do not distinguish between image and likeness. For these Fathers both image and likeness are exemplified in Christ. Through sanctifica-

---

36. Michael Wiitala, "Every Happy Man Is a God: Deification in Boethius," 240–43.

37. Henry Chadwick, *Boethius: The Consolations of Music, Logic, Theology and Philosophy* (Oxford: Oxford University Press, 1981), 211 and 236.

38. Wiitala, "Every Happy Man Is a God," 252.

39. Gregory of Nazianzus, *Orat.* 21.2. To become "like God so far as possible" had been defined by Plato as the goal of human life (*Theaetetus* 176b). See also Maximus the Confessor's comment on Gregory of Nazianzus, *Orat.* 21.2, in *Ambiguum* 10, in Patrologia Graeca (ed. Migne) (hereafter, PG), 91:1113B–C. Maximus asserts that such philosophizing is not attained by intellectual effort alone but reciprocates God's love and is thus a divine power.

40. Gregory of Nazianzus, *Orat.* 3.1.

tion in the life of the Christian community the believer can recover in Christ what was lost by the Fall and through him advance beyond that to share in the divine attributes of immortality and incorruption that belong to the Father. In the Latin theologians (even those familiar with learned Greek monasticism) no distinction is made between the image and likeness.[41] They follow a broader ecclesiastical tradition that sees the image and likeness restored through the adoption of baptism.

Discussions of the appropriation of divine life in the Latin Fathers sometimes revolve around 2 Peter 1:4, "partakers of the divine nature" (with θείας κοινωνοὶ φύσεως rendered as *divinae consortes naturae*). In Origen, who is the first Christian writer to quote the text, such "partaking" has an ontological dimension: through Christ the believer acquires the divine attributes of goodness, immortality, and incorruption. This was soon taken to imply a sacramental context for, as Athanasius was to say, we partake of the divine nature by partaking of Christ, which makes us temples of the living God (1 Cor 3:16; 2 Cor 6:16).[42] Although Athanasius's dogmatic works were not translated into Latin, his interpretation became established in the West, largely, it would seem, through Ambrose. Like Origen and Athanasius, Ambrose cites 2 Peter 1:4 in a sacramental context to emphasize how the baptized Christian shares through Christ in a divinity which has its origin in the Father: "Because our Lord Jesus Christ himself is partaker both of divinity and of the body, you too, who receive his flesh, participate through that very food in his divine substance."[43] This teaching, as Dunkle points out, was for the more advanced Christian, not for the beginner.[44] That is perhaps why among the Latin Fathers, as among the Greeks, there is a relative scarcity of references to 2 Peter 1:4 until the first half of the fifth century, when it is used very frequently by both Cyril of Alexandria and Leo the Great. For Leo, 2 Peter 1:4, as Keating demonstrates, fills out the human side of the exchange formula. To partake of

---

41. This includes Pelagius, who sees the image and likeness as consisting in the freedom to choose (*To Demetrias* 2.2 and 3.1).

42. Athanasius, *Contra Arianos* 1.16, in *Orations of St. Athanasius Against the Arians*, ed. W. Bright (Oxford: Clarendon Press, 1873), 17.

43. Ambrose, *De Sacramentis* 6.14 (Corpus Scriptorium Ecclesiasticorum Latinorum [hereafter, CSEL] 73.73); cited and translated in Dunkle, "Beyond Carnal Cogitations," 143-44.

44. Dunkle, "Beyond Carnal Cogitations," 144. More precisely, Dunkle says: "Thus Ambrose's most remarkable reference to 2 Peter supports my main argument that the tropes of deification appear in Ambrose's works aimed at educated Christians, *except when* Ambrose wants to emphasize the singular wonder of the sacraments."

the divine nature is to realize the dignity of our human nature by accepting baptism and thus inaugurating our passage to eternal life.[45] This is a perspective very similar to that of Cyril, who defines "the divine nature" of 2 Peter 1:4 as "God the Word together with the flesh."[46] To partake of the divine nature is to participate through baptism and the eucharist in the new humanity exalted and transformed by Christ. By the end of the century Pope Gelasius is able to take it for granted that 2 Peter 1:4 has a sacramental reference: by the sacraments of the body and blood of Christ (a *divina res*) we are made "partakers of the divine nature."[47] Perhaps because *consortes* has a range of associations different from those of κοινωνοί, the sacramental interpretation is not the only one we find in the fifth century. Peter Chrysologus, for example, builds on the nuptial connotations of *consortes* to highlight, as Meconi shows, the "intimacy of humanity's participation in the divine life.... In this espousal to Christ, creatures are elevated and transformed, not only vivified but also deified, making possible their new agency and immortality."[48]

### The Technical Terms of Deification

As was first observed by Eriugena, *deificatio* never became naturalized in Latin theological literature in the way that θεοποίησις and later θέωσις were readily accepted as useful theological terms by many—not all—Greek writers. Augustine is an exception, although considering the bulk of his writings, his use of *deificare* is sparse and easily overlooked.[49] The adjective *deificus*, on the other hand, is used freely by Latin writers, but usually in a weak sense simply to mean "spiritual" or "divine."[50] By contrast, Christian authors writing

---

45. Keating, "The Wonderful Exchange," 213.
46. Cyril, *In Jo.* 6.1, 653d (cited in Russell, *Fellow Workers*, 67).
47. Ortiz, "Making Worshipers into Gods," 25.
48. Meconi, "Between Empire and *Ecclesia*," 203–4.
49. On Augustine's use of *deificare* see Meconi, *The One Christ: St. Augustine's Theology of Deification* (Washington, D.C.: The Catholic University of America Press, 2013), 126–34. Meconi concludes that "deification for Augustine is a strictly Christian term" (127).
50. Cyprian, for example, speaks of *deifica disciplina* (*De zelo et livore* 15; *Ep.* 52.2.1 and 67.9.1) and of a *spiritalis et deifica sanctitas* (*Ep.* 75.7.4). In some translated texts we even find *deificus* introduced where it is not present in the original Greek. In chap. 7 (ll. 11, 22, 43–44) of the anonymous Latin translation of the *Life of Anthony*, for example, we find *virtus deifica* and *studium deificum* where the Greek has, respectively, simply σπουδή and ἄσκησις. *Vita di Antonio*, ed. G. J. M. Bartelink, with an introduction by Christine Mohrmann (Milan: Fondazione Lorenzo Valla, 1991), 20–22.

in Greek were able to appropriate deification terms—and indeed coin their own—from the second century onwards in a manner that was not only free of pagan associations but was able to express the ultimate goal of salvation with considerable rhetorical power.[51]

The unwillingness of many of the Latin writers we have been considering to use the technical language of deification is a puzzling feature that several of the contributors to this volume have addressed. Brian Dunkle notes that Ambrose omits deification terms even when he comes across them in the Greek sources he is using.[52] Vít Hušek is surprised that despite "his vast knowledge of Greek literature, his fondness for analyzing Hebrew and Greek words, and his affection for comparing Greek and Latin translations, Jerome never uses any of the Greek expressions for deification."[53] Peter Chrysologus and Pope Leo the Great, although not Hellenists like Ambrose and Jerome, also attract comment for their avoidance of the technical terms of deification.[54] Meconi and Keating suggest that in the case of both Peter and Leo the possible association of deification language with the cult of the emperor may have been a factor inhibiting its use. While this is plausible in view of the status of Ravenna and Rome as imperial capitals, it should not be pressed too far. The Latin term for the deification of a deceased emperor was *consecratio* (not *deificatio*), and such an emperor became a *divus* (not a *deus*). To take an example from the Greek world, Athanasius was familiar with the concept of *consecratio* but this did not inhibit him from adopting deification language very readily, especially in connection with the "exchange formula."[55] We need to look for other, perhaps stronger, reasons for the reticence of Western writers in this respect.

These other reasons are not ignored by Dunkle and Keating. First, both Ambrose and Leo were conscious practitioners of a pure Latin style. There was very little precedent for the use of the technical terms of deification in Latin theological writing. Circumlocutions in correct Latin, it is probably safe to assume, would have seemed more appropriate to both of them. Secondly,

---

51. On the Greek terms, see Russell, *The Doctrine of Deification*, 333–44.
52. Dunkle, "Beyond Carnal Cogitations," 137–38.
53. Vít Hušek, "Rebirth into a New Man: Deification in Jerome," 153. J. N. D. Kelly, drawing on P. Courcelle, points out that Jerome's knowledge of Greek classical literature was not firsthand; see *Jerome: His Life, Writings and Correspondence* (London: Duckworth, 1975), 14.
54. Meconi, "Between Empire and *Ecclesia*," 204–5; Keating, "The Wonderful Exchange," 229–30.
55. Athanasius, *C. Gentes* 9; see *De Incarn.* 54. On the attitude of the Greek Fathers to the ruler cult, see Russell, *Doctrine of Deification*, 23–26 and 168–69.

Dunkle has noticed that Ambrose avoids deification terms in his catechetical material but uses them in texts intended for more advanced Christians.[56] Not unreasonably, Ambrose may have regarded deification as a misleading concept for catechumens. Thirdly, in Leo's case there is also a plausible doctrinal reason for the avoidance of deification terms. Leo was asked to adjudicate the case of Eutyches, the Constantinopolitan archimandrite who held that after the incarnation the human and divine elements in Christ formed a single nature because the human had been totally divinized by the divine. Leo was quite clear that the human and the divine in Christ remained two distinct but inseparable natures. "The terminology of deification," as Keating suggests, "may have seemed to Leo to give unhelpful support and encouragement to what he saw as a quasi-docetic approach to Christ."[57] Leo's older contemporary, Cyril of Alexandria, provides a parallel example from a Greek perspective. After his controversy with Nestorius, Cyril never uses the technical terms of deification, preferring instead to speak of perfected Christians as "partakers of the divine nature" (2 Pt 1:4). He may actually have begun to prefer the biblical expression even before Nestorius ridiculed Alexandrian Christology as an "apotheosis" of Christ's flesh, but Nestorius's position can only have confirmed his choice. Cyril was sensitive to any charge of Apollinarianism, and Apollinarius, in his polemics against an adoptionist Christology, had made much of the ability of the deified body of Christ to deify the Christian believer.[58] Cyril's example demonstrates that an unwillingness to use the technical language of deification does not necessarily imply the rejection of its teaching.

Jerome presents an interesting case of the avoidance of deification language that was to have far-reaching consequences for the reception of the Origenian perspective on deification in the Latin-speaking world. As Hušek points out, Jerome was highly conservative both theologically and linguistically. Moreover, perhaps initially for personal reasons (his dispute with John of Jerusalem over the uncanonical ordination of his brother Paulinian), he joined the anti-Origenist camp of John's enemy, Epiphanius of Salamis. Jerome's mindset was anti-speculative. He could speak of Christians becoming "gods" not by nature but by grace through the adoptive sonship conferred by

---

56. Dunkle, "Beyond Carnal Cogitations," 144.
57. Keating, "The Wonderful Exchange," 230.
58. For a fuller discussion, see Russell, *Doctrine of Deification*, 192–93.

Christ. He could appeal to 2 Peter 1:4 but only to deny any ontological implication: "We are privileged to partake of His substance not in the realm of nature but in the realm of grace."[59] Participation in the divine is the equivalent of angelification, but in a moral not an ontological sense. The exciting new developments that were then taking place in the Evagrian version of Origenian spirituality are ignored by Jerome. But it was these (through John Cassian) that were to have an important influence on deification in the West from the fifth century until Eriugena's translations of Dionysius the Areopagite and Maximus the Confessor became available in the ninth century.

## The Availability of Translations

Early Christianity was, of course, Greek-speaking. Latin Christian literature only began to emerge at the end of the second and beginning of the third century in North Africa with the acts and narratives of martyrs who suffered at Carthage and with the theological works of Tertullian and Cyprian. The martyrdom narratives movingly describe, with the minimum of theological reflection, the transformatory union with Christ which the martyrs achieved through their witness.[60] This genre, as Thomas Heffernan observes, "does not employ the philosophical language of Justin or Irenaeus."[61] But such language does come to be employed by Tertullian and Cyprian. Tertullian clearly made use of Irenaeus, very likely—even though he was fluent in Greek—in the early Latin translation which is the only version in which Irenaeus's text has come down to us.[62] Cyprian, too, must have read Irenaeus, for in the pamphlet he wrote while still a catechumen, *That Idols Are Not Gods*, he reproduces Irenaeus's exchange formula: "What man is, Christ wished to be, so that man also

---

59. Jerome, *Adv. Jov.* 2.29; cited in Hušek, "Rebirth into a New Man," 160.

60. See Blandina, suspended from a stake in the amphitheater of Lyon, who "seemed to be hanging in the shape of a cross," so that the other martyrs "saw in the form of their sister him who was crucified for them" (Eusebius, *Hist. Eccl.* V.1.41; trans. K. Lake).

61. Thomas Heffernan, "Dying to Become Gods: Deification in the *Passion of Perpetua and Felicity*," 30.

62. Wigan Harvey, whose edition of Irenaeus is still of value, argues that Tertullian wrote his *Contra Valentinianum* with the Latin version of *Against Heresies* before him: "when the translator trips, Tertullian also stumbles; and too many minute peculiarities of nomenclature and style are found to agree in both, to be the result of accident. Cyprian possibly [*Ep. ad Pompetum* (*de Cerdone*)], and Augustine certainly [*C. Julian. Pelag.* 1.3.7], copied this version." W. Wigan Harvey, *Sancti Irenaei Episcopi Lugdenensis Libros quinque adversus Haereses* (Cambridge: Typis Academicis, 1857), 1:clxiv.

might be able to be what Christ is."[63] The same formula lies behind Novatian's statement that the Word (or Son) of God descended so that the Son of Man (taking our human nature with him) could ascend.[64] The early Latin tradition of theological reflection on deification clearly reflects Irenaeus and indeed appears to rely specifically on Irenaeus in Latin translation.

After Irenaeus, Greek thinking on deification underwent its most significant development in Alexandria, to such a degree that many have considered deification an Alexandrian *theologoumenon*. The key role was played by Clement and Origen, who devised the technical vocabulary (Irenaeus having only spoken of human beings becoming gods), and enriched the concept of deification by drawing on Hellenistic philosophy (chiefly Stoic and Platonic) and employing sophisticated techniques of biblical exegesis learned from Philo. In the East Origen lies behind all subsequent reflection on deification, not only with regard to the Alexandrians and the Cappadocians, but also with regard to Dionysius and Maximus the Confessor. In the West Origen had his admirers too, but only a handful, like Hilary or Ambrose, could read him in Greek. The majority of readers had to wait until the end of the century before a substantial number of translated works began to circulate in the West, largely as a result of the labors of Jerome and Rufinus. These works, however, were of limited use for disseminating an understanding of Greek thinking on deification. The demand in the West was for commentaries on books of the Old Testament. Yet two of the most important texts for Origen's discussions of deification are his commentaries on Matthew and John. The condemnation of Origen by an Alexandrian synod in 399, which was confirmed by a Roman synod in the following year, left Rufinus as the sole translator of Origen. He produced some magnificent translations before his death in 410 of Origen's exegetical works, but the commentaries on Matthew and John were not among them.

Both Jerome and Rufinus learned Greek after they had embraced monasticism. Their choice of texts was usually governed by considerations of their practical usefulness to men and women pursuing the ascetic life rather than their theological insight. Exceptions to the rule include Jerome's translation

---

63. Cyprian, *Quod idola dii non sint* 11; cited in Benjamin Safranski, "After the Fashion of God: Deification in Cyprian," 79.

64. Novatian, *De Trinitate* 13.4–5; cited in Papandrea, "Loaning and Borrowing," 108.

between 387 and 390 of a work *On the Holy Spirit* attributed to Didymus of Alexandria, which he undertook as part of an unedifying attempt to convict Ambrose of plagiarism, Rufinus's translation of nine of Gregory of Nazianzus's *Orations* made in 399 or 400 at the request of his friend and patron, the Roman nobleman Apronianus, and the rival translations by both men of Origen's *On First Principles*, published in 398 and 399. Jerome's rendering of Didymus's work makes no mention of deification.[65] Rufinus could hardly avoid the topic when translating Gregory, but in those of the *Orations* that touch on deification he tends to tone down the language.[66] It is perhaps largely for this reason that Gregory's *Orations*, which were later commented on extensively by Maximus and became a fundamental text for the Byzantine understanding of deification, made almost no contribution to the Western tradition on the topic.[67]

These two translations of Origen's *On First Principles* were based on opposing principles, Rufinus being anxious to make Origen conform to fourth-century orthodoxy, whereas Jerome wanted to highlight Origen's *un*orthodoxy in the buildup to his condemnation in 399. In *On First Principles*, Origen has nothing to say directly about deification. At the end of book 3, however, he states, in Rufinus's translation, that when God becomes "all in all" (1 Cor 15:28), it necessarily follows that those "who have become capable of receiving God" will assume even in their bodily nature "that supreme condi-

65. The Latin text of the *De Spiritu Sancto* (the original Greek has not survived) is in PG 39:1033–87 (= Patrologia Latina [ed. Migne], 23:103–54). The *De Trinitate*, also attributed to Didymus, which does survive in Greek, argues explicitly for the divinity of the Holy Spirit from the Spirit's power to deify through baptism. The *De Spiritu Sancto*, however, concerns itself with the role of the Spirit only in the ascetic life: "Anyone who transcends the life of the flesh and puts to death the works of the flesh by the Spirit will live a blessed and eternal life, having been enrolled among the sons of God [vivet beata aeternaque vita relatus in filios Dei]." *De Spiritu Sancto* 42 (PG 39:1070B).

66. The translated *Orations* are numbers 2, 6, 16, 17, 26, 27, 38, 39, and 40, ed. A. Engelbrecht, CSEL 46 (Vienna: Kaiserliche Akademie der Wissenschaften, 1910). In *Oration* 2 (the *Apologeticus*), for example, θεὸν ποιῆσαι is modified in translation to become *filium dei facere* (2.22); θεὸν ἐσόμενον καὶ θεοποιήσοντα is rendered as *ut ex hominibus in deorum numerum transeant* (2.73). I am grateful to Jared Ortiz for furnishing me with the Latin text.

67. It was not just Gregory of Nazianzus's *Orations*, however, that failed to make the impact they merited. Jean Gribomont comments: "How the work of the Cappadocians, and of Gregory of Nyssa in particular, remained outside the mainstream of Western thought in regard to its more significant manifestations remains unclear. Its exceptional importance was immediately recognized, but there seem to have been factors which held it in check." Among these factors Gribomont reckons the "paralyzing" of Rufinus "by the opposition of his enemies"; see "The Translations: Jerome and Rufinus," in *Patrology*, ed. Angelo di Berardino (Allen, Tex.: Christian Classics, n.d.), 4:210.

tion to which nothing can be added."⁶⁸ This phrase is highlighted by Jerome in the covering letter to his own translation of *On First Principles*: "And God shall be all in all, so that the whole of bodily nature may be resolved into that divine substance which is superior to all others, namely, into the divine nature, than which nothing can be better."⁶⁹ It is not clear whether the comment introduced by "namely" is a gloss by Jerome or an expansion by Origen himself discreetly suppressed by Rufinus. Origen sees the divine, the angelic, and the human as forming a continuum. Human beings, who possess a potential divinity in virtue of their creation by God, can realize that divinity by moving up through the continuum by prayer and the practice of the virtues. Jerome takes the statement that even our bodily nature will be resolved into the divine substance to imply that ultimately the believer will be absorbed, body and soul, into God (a heretical position adopted by the sixth-century Origenists known as "Isochrists"). In book 4 of *On First Principles*, Origen goes on to discuss what participation in God means. The very concept of participation entails two terms, one of which is the participant and the other the participated-in. The notion of absorption is therefore excluded. But this was a subtlety not appreciated by Jerome.

## The Role of Monasticism

Jerome and Rufinus were not, of course, the only Latin interpreters of the Greek tradition working within the monastic sphere. There was also John Cassian, their perfectly bilingual younger contemporary, who after serving a monastic apprenticeship in Egypt came to exercise enormous influence in the West through his *Institutes* and *Conferences*. Deification is mentioned specifically by Cassian only in a Christological context in a late work refuting Nestorius: "that which [Christ] was, namely, man and god, was made wholly god."⁷⁰

---

68. *De Principiis* 3.6.9; in *Origen On First Principles*, trans. G. W. Butterworth (Gloucester, Mass.: Peter Smith, 1973), 254.

69. *Ep.* 124 *ad Avitum* 14; Butterworth, *Origen*, 254–55. The translation itself has not survived: "By an irony of fate, regretted by modern scholars, the copyists placed Jerome's version on the index and preserved the edifying adaptation of the text of Rufinus" (Gribomont, "The Translations," 230).

70. *De Incarnatione* 5.7, ed. M. Petschenig, CSEL 17 (Vienna: Kaiserliche Akademie der Wissenschaften, 1888), 310: "quidquid erat, scilicet homo et deus, factum est totum deus." The deification of the humanity of Christ was a tenet of Alexandrian Christology, but stated baldly in this way without the qualifications that Cyril brings to it (e.g., *In Jo.* 4.2, 363b), it sounds distinctly Apollinarian.

Until Maximus the Confessor, monastic writers did not discuss spiritual ascent in the technical language of deification.[71] As a disciple of Evagrius Ponticus, Cassian takes μακαριότης (which he translates as *beatitudo*) as the summit of the Christian life. By passing through a hierarchy of contemplations, the monk strives to imitate the angelic life and even in this temporal existence to begin to experience the eschatological beatitude that awaits him.[72]

Also of importance was the early Latin translation of Athanasius's *Life of Anthony*.[73] The only direct mention of deification in this text is a version of the exchange formula. Anthony is represented as engaging in a disputation with two Greek philosophers. The stories of the pagan gods, he says, are full of dissolute and immoral details, whereas the Word of God "for the salvation and benefit of the human race assumed a human body and by sharing a human birth enabled us to share in that nature which is divine and rational."[74] The fruits of this sharing, in Anthony's case, were fully manifest. When he emerged from his cell after twenty years of solitude, years "occupied in spiritual ascesis" (*studio deifico vacans*), he appeared filled with the divine Spirit (*divinitate divinitus plenus*).[75] The radiance of his face marked him out in monastic assemblies.[76] This radiance was valued not as a personal achievement setting him apart on a spiritual pedestal but as a mark of his serenity and his availability to others. Benedict of Nursia and the "Master" whom Benedict incorporates into his Rule build on Cassian and the Latin *Life of Anthony*, as Luke Dysinger has emphasized, to present the goal of community life as the transformation of the heart so that the indwelling Christ may be perceived

---

71. The Macarian writings do speak of the ascetical life as leading to eschatological fulfillment in terms of deification, but this is attained through participation in the Holy Spirit, not through contemplation, or *theōria*. Dionysius the Areopagite's discussions of deification are mostly to be found in the *Ecclesiastical Hierarchy*, where they are centered on the work of Christ and the efficacy of the sacraments. His account in the *Mystical Theology* of humanity's ascent to God though a process of purification, illumination, and perfection makes no use of the language of deification.

72. For a good account of the ascent to beatitude by a "continuum of contemplations" see Columba Stewart, *Cassian the Monk* (Oxford: Oxford University Press, 1998), 47–57. Stewart emphasizes that "Spiritual knowledge is not esoteric gnosis but the ability to see more deeply into the biblical material that constitutes a monk's daily prayer" (51).

73. There were two Latin translations of the *Life of Anthony*, one a very free rendering by Jerome's friend, Evagrius Scholasticus, the other an anonymous (and earlier) translation that follows the Greek text faithfully. The latter survives only in a single manuscript of central Italian provenance.

74. *Vita Ant.* 74.4 (Bartelink, 140–42).

75. Ibid., 14.2 (36).

76. Ibid., 67.4 (132).

and venerated "both within the depths of the monk's own heart and also in the other members of the monastic community."[77]

## Theological Disputes

Cassian did not go unchallenged as a theorist of the monastic life. *Conference* 13 on the relationship between human effort and dependence on God's will, published in Marseilles in 426, aroused the hostility of a fanatical partisan of Augustine's doctrine of grace, Prosper of Aquitaine.[78] By allowing some scope for human effort, Cassian appeared to Prosper to be infected by Pelagianism. The Pelagian controversy had recently added a further dimension to the reception of deification in the West. Pelagius and his followers denied that Adam's fall had so perverted human nature that it was impossible to lead a life without sin. God's grace, they held, responds to the decision to live in accordance with Christ, but the initial decision belongs to the human will. Christians are therefore in control of their own destiny. By embracing the ascetical life they can attain salvation by training themselves to avoid sin. To the Pelagians, Augustine's teaching on grace smacked of fatalism. Calestius, Pelagius's more radical associate, had argued that to become a son of God means to be free from sin, and to support this he had appealed to 2 Peter 1:4, for "from what Peter says, that we are 'partakers of the divine nature,' it must follow that the soul has the power of being without sin, just in the way that God himself has."[79] He was nevertheless condemned at Carthage in 411 for teaching a doctrine of *impeccantia*, or the "impeccability" of man. The appropriation of 2 Peter 1:4 by Caelestius may have made Augustine, the Pelagians' chief opponent, wary of the text. It is telling that even though Augustine relies on the concept of participation for his account of salvation, he never appeals to 2 Peter 1:4.

Despite his hostility to Augustine's views on predestination, Cassian was no Pelagian. In his work against Nestorius he not implausibly links Pelagianism with Nestorianism. An anthropology in which the human soul pos-

---

77. Fr. Luke Dysinger, OSB, "Beholding Christ in the Other and in the Self: Deification in Benedict of Nursia and Gregory the Great," 261.
78. The "Semi-Pelagian controversy" was to last for many decades. For a comprehensive study see Ralph W. Mathisen, *Ecclesiastical Factionalism and Religious Controversy in Fifth-Century Gaul* (Washington, D.C.: The Catholic University of America Press, 1989).
79. Augustine, *De gestis Pelagii* 65. Augustine cites Marius Mercator's Latin translation of the acts of Diospolis.

sesses the natural capacity to orient itself toward the good may reasonably be seen as the counterpart of a Christology in which Christ's human nature can be the subject of its own distinct actions. Yet Cassian could not allow the human will to be totally quiescent. The Origenian ascent to God required ascetical effort, the rigorous training of the mind and the will as the appropriate human response to the Father's invitation to us to participate dynamically through the Son and the Spirit in the goodness, immortality, and incorruption that are his alone. It is not surprising that Cassian's writings were soon translated into Greek and have always remained much appreciated in the Christian East.

## Conclusions

A comparison of the Greek and Latin approaches to deification up to the time of Gregory the Great reveals a strong common tradition. Deification is the raising of the Christian to a new level of being by faith in Christ and participation in the ecclesial body. Keating is right to have said, in comparing Cyril of Alexandria with the Western Fathers, that "in terms of the patristic heritage, the differences appear to be ones in emphasis, not sharp distinctions in kind."[80] The differences that undeniably do exist are not connected with the presence or absence of the technical language of deification. Several Fathers on both sides of the linguistic divide speak of human fulfillment in terms of deification without the use of *deificare* or θεοποιέω. These are Fathers who, for various reasons, prefer to use biblical expressions, particularly 2 Peter 1:4, "partakers of the divine nature."[81] For them the "divine nature" is the deified humanity of Christ, the Holy Spirit renewing believers inwardly so that "in Christ" they may transcend the limitations of the created state.[82] Nor are the differences to do with whether the Fathers belonged to the Greek or Latin cultural spheres, except in so far as the term *deificare* might have carried associations of the imperial cult for those who wrote in Latin. The differences

---

80. Daniel A. Keating, *The Appropriation of Divine Life in Cyril of Alexandria* (Oxford: Oxford University Press, 2004), 291.

81. Notably Ambrose, Leo the Great, and Cyril of Alexandria in his later works. On the use of 2 Pt 1:4 by the first two, see the chapters by Brian Dunkle and Daniel Keating in the present volume.

82. On the Greek uses of the verse, see Norman Russell, "'Partakers of the Divine Nature' (2 Peter 1:4) in the Byzantine Tradition," in *ΚΑΘΗΓΗΤΡΙΑ: Essays Presented to Joan Hussey for Her 80th Birthday*, ed. Julian Chrysostomides (Camberley: Porphyrogenitus, 1988), 51–67.

seem in large part to be due to differences in the reception of the Origenian tradition.

All the Greek Fathers after Origen who discuss redemption in terms of deification are, at least in this respect, his heirs. It was Origen who trimmed away Clement's more exotic utterances and presented deification as the product of Christian discipleship, namely, the attainment of immortality through a dynamic participation in the Son through the Holy Spirit. In the West, Hilary and Ambrose studied Origen's writings in the original Greek. Others, such as Gregory of Elvira, relied on translations supplied by Jerome and Rufinus. Even Augustine himself wrote to Jerome asking him for translations of biblical commentaries by Greek authors, especially Origen.[83] Origen was widely regarded as the greatest biblical scholar the church had produced. The acceptance of his approach in the West, however, was not without certain reservations, even before Jerome mounted his attack on him. Ambrose, as Brian Dunkle has shown, preferred to speak of the process of deification in terms of the passage from nature to grace.[84] In the Greek Origenian tradition that culminated in Maximus the Confessor, nature had from the beginning an innate aspiration toward deification as its true *telos*.[85]

The Latin voices bring their own experience to the church's teaching on deification. The apparent thinness of the Latin tradition in comparison with the Greek that some scholars have noticed owes something to the scarceness of translations but more to the kind of audience the Latin authors were addressing. The readers or hearers of many of the texts we have been considering were the *simpliciores* rather than the spiritually advanced (Eriugena seems to have been right on that score).[86] The sermons of Augustine or the catechetical addresses of Ambrose were addressed to beginners. There *was* a learned readership in the Western provinces of the Empire, but just when the riches of Origen's approach to deification might have been made available to Western readers, his texts began to come under suspicion for doctrinal error. Jerome,

---

83. Augustine, *Ep.* 28.2. The Divjak letters have also shown that it is no longer possible to treat Augustine as a thinker working in isolation from his Greek contemporaries.

84. Dunkle, "Beyond Carnal Cogitations," 147–51.

85. Paul M. Blowers, *Maximus the Confessor: Jesus Christ and the Transfiguration of the Word* (Oxford: Oxford University Press, 2016), 5.

86. Eriugena, *Periphyseon* 5, 1015C: "I am not sure for the reason for this reticence: perhaps it is because the meaning of this word Theosis ... seemed too profound for those who cannot rise above carnal speculations" (trans. O'Meara); see Dunkle, "Beyond Carnal Cogitations," 134.

who had spent much time in the East and had read widely in Origen, had no feeling for him at all. Like most of his fellow Latins, it is the ecclesial dimension of deification that most appeals to him. As Vít Hušek shows, Jerome links deification—or rather, "becoming gods"—with adoptive sonship, a participation in divine life that is not merely a figure of speech but a reality bestowed as a gift not possessed by right.[87] Like Ambrose and Leo, Jerome refers to our becoming "partakers of divine nature," "not in the realm of nature but in the realm of grace" (*non naturae esse, sed gratiae*).[88] To be sure, the sacramental dimension is supported by the ascetical. Participation in the divine life is manifested in the maintenance of virginity,[89] and virginity is assimilation to angelic splendor. But Jerome, the sworn enemy of Origen's defender, Rufinus, has nothing to say about the ascent of the soul to God through the practice of Christian *philosophia*.

In both the Eastern and Western traditions, deification is Christologically based, ecclesiologically expressed, and eschatologically oriented. The differences of emphasis are due mainly to the different ways in which Origen's heritage was received, either directly or through writers influenced by him. Despite his condemnation by an ecumenical council in 553, he remained a common Father who never ceased to be studied eagerly, particularly in monastic circles, in both the Greek East and the Latin West. If Irenaeus was the first to enunciate the exchange formula and to speak of the baptized as gods, it was Origen who taught the church at large how Christian discipleship could lead even in this world to sharing in the divine life.

---

87. Hušek, "Rebirth into a New Man," 158–59.
88. Jerome, *Adv. Iov.* 2. 29; cited in Hušek, "Rebirth into a New Man," 160.
89. Jerome, *Adv. Iov.* 1. 39; cited in ibid.

# SELECTED BIBLIOGRAPHY

Adkin, Neil. *Jerome on Virginity: A Commentary on the Libellus de virginitate servanda (Letter 22)*. Cambridge: Francis Cairns, 2003.
The Ante-Nicene Fathers: Translations of the Writings of the Fathers Down to A.D. 325. Edited by Alexander Roberts, James Donaldson, and A. Cleveland Coxe. 9 volumes. Grand Rapids, Mich.: Eerdmans, 1951–57.
Armitage, J. Mark. *A Twofold Solidarity: Leo the Great's Theology of Redemption*. Strathfield: St. Paul's Publications, 2005.
Ayres, Lewis. *Nicaea and Its Legacy*. Oxford: Oxford University Press, 2004.
———. *Augustine and the Trinity*. Cambridge: Cambridge University Press, 2010.
———. "The Holy Spirit as the 'Undiminished Giver': Didymus the Blind's *De Spiritu Sancto* and the Development of Nicene Pneumatology." In *The Holy Spirit in the Fathers of the Church: The Proceedings of the Seventh International Patristic Conference*, edited by D. Vincent Toomey and Janet E. Rutherford, 57–72. Dublin: Four Courts, 2010.
Bagnall, R. S., and B. W. Frier. *The Demography of Ancient Egypt*. Cambridge: Cambridge University Press, 2006.
Bardy, Gustave. "Divinisation." In *Dictionnaire de Spiritualité*, edited by M. Viller et al., and continued by C. Baumgartner et al., 1390–98. Paris: Beauchesne, 1957.
Barnes, T. D. *Constantius and Athanasius: Theology and Politics in the Constantinian Empire*. Cambridge, Mass.: Harvard University Press, 1981.
———. *Tertullian: A Historical and Literary Study*. Oxford: Clarendon Press, 1985.
———. *Early Christian Hagiography and Roman History*. Tübingen: Mohr Siebeck, 2010.
———. *Constantine: Dynasty, Religion and Power in the Later Roman Empire*. Oxford: Wiley-Blackwell, 2011.
Beckwith, Carl L. *Hilary of Poitiers on the Trinity*. Oxford: Oxford University Press, 2008.
Berger, Adolf. *Encyclopedic Dictionary of Roman Law*. Philadelphia: The Lawbook Exchange, 1953.
Blackwood, Stephen. *The Consolation of Boethius as Poetic Liturgy*. Oxford: Oxford University Press, 2015.
Böckmann, Aquinata. *Perspectives on the Rule of St. Benedict: Expanding Our Hearts in

*Christ*. Translated by M. Handl and M. Burkhard. Collegeville, Minn.: Liturgical Press, 2005.

Boersma, Gerald. "Participation in Christ: Psalm 118 in Ambrose and Augustine." *Augustinianum* 54 (2014): 173–97.

——. *Augustine's Early Theology of Image: A Study in the Development of Pro-Nicene Theology*. Oxford: Oxford University Press, 2016.

Bonato, Antonio. "Incidenze della Grazia in Sant'Ambrogio." In *Dizionario di spiritualità biblicopatristica: i grandi temi della S. scrittura per la "lectio divina,"* edited by Salvatore Alberto Panimolle and Franco Bolgiani, 270–321. Rome: Borla, 1992.

Bonner, Gerald. "Augustine's Concept of Deification." *JTS* 37 (1986): 369–86.

Borias, André. "S. Benoît au fil des ans." *Collectanea Cisterciensia* 50, no. 18 (1988): 218–38.

Bouyer, Louis. *The History of Christian Spirituality*, vol. 1: *The Spirituality of the New Testament and the Fathers*. Translated by Mary P. Ryan. New York: Burns and Oates, 1963.

Bouyer, Louis, J. Leclercq, and F. Vandenbroucke. *The History of Christian Spirituality*, vol. 2: *The Spirituality of the Middle Ages*. Translated by the Benedictines of Holme Eden Abbey, Carlisle. New York: Burns and Oates, 1968.

Bowersock, Glen. "From Emperor to Bishop: The Self-Conscious Transformation of Political Power in the Fourth Century A.D." *Classical Philology* 81 (1986): 298–307.

Bradshaw, Paul, and Maxwell E. Johnson. *The Eucharistic Liturgies: Their Evolution and Interpretation*. Collegeville, Minn.: Liturgical Press, 2012.

Brakke, David. *Athanasius and the Politics of Asceticism*. Oxford: Clarendon Press, 1995.

Bray, Gerald. *Holiness and the Will of God: Perspectives on the Theology of Tertullian*. London: Marshall, Morgan, and Scott, 1979.

Bremmer, Jan, and Marco Formisano. *Perpetua's Passion: Multidisciplinary Approaches to the Passio Perpetuae et Felicitatis*. Oxford: Oxford University Press, 2013.

——. "Perpetua u. Felicitas." In *Reallexikon für Antike und Christentum* XXVII, cols. 178–90. Stuttgart: Anton Hiersemann, 2016.

Brown, Lesley. "Being in the Sophist: A Syntactical Enquiry." *Oxford Studies in Ancient Philosophy* 4 (1986): 49–70.

——. "The Verb 'To Be' in Greek Philosophy." In *Language*, edited by Stephen Everson. Companions to Ancient Thought 3. Cambridge: Cambridge University Press, 1994.

Brown, Peter. *Through the Eye of a Needle: Wealth, the Fall of Rome, and the Making of Christianity, 350–550 AD*. Princeton, N.J.: Princeton University Press, 2012.

Burns, Paul C. *The Christology in Hilary of Poitiers' Commentary on Matthew*. Rome: Institutum Patristicum Augustinianum, 1981.

——. *A Model for the Christian Life*. Washington, D.C.: The Catholic University of America Press, 2012.

Butler, Cuthbert. *Western Mysticism: The Teaching of SS. Augustine, Gregory and Bernard on Contemplation and the Contemplative Life*. Second edition. London: E. P. Button, 1926.

Cain, Andrew. *The Letters of Jerome: Asceticism, Biblical Exegesis, and the Construction of Christian Authority in Late Antiquity*. Oxford: Oxford University Press, 2009.

Capanaga, Victorino. "La deification en la soteriologia agustiniana." *Augustinus Magister* 2 (1954): 745–54.

Capone, Alessandro. "Folia uero in uerbis sunt: parola divina e lingua umana nei *Tractatus in Psalmos* attribuiti a Gerolamo." *Adamantius* 19 (2013): 437–56.

Cardman, Francine. "Tertullian on Doctrine and the Development of Discipline." *Studia Patristica* 16 (1985): 136–42.

Chadwick, Henry. *Boethius: The Consolations of Music, Logic, Theology, and Philosophy*. Oxford: Oxford University Press, 1981.

———. "Note sur la divinization chez saint Augustin." *Revue des sciences religieuses* 76, no. 2 (2002): 246–48.

Chadwick, Owen. "Benedict." In *The Study of Spirituality*, edited by Cheslyn Jones, Geoffrey Wainright, and Edward Yarnold, 148–56. Oxford: Oxford University Press, 1986.

Charlier, A. "L'Église corps du Christ chez saint Hilaire de Poitiers." *Ephemerides Theologicae Lovanienses* 41 (1965): 451–77.

Chia, Roland. "Salvation as Justification and Deification." *Scottish Journal of Theology* 64, no. 2 (2011): 125–39.

Church, F. Forrester. "Sex and Salvation in Tertullian." *Harvard Theological Review* 68, no. 2 (1975): 83–101.

Clark, Francis. *The Pseudo-Gregorian Dialogues*. 2 vols. Studies in the History of Christian Thought 37–38. Leiden: E. J. Brill, 1987.

Colish, Marcia. *Ambrose's Patriarchs: Ethics for the Common Man*. Notre Dame, Ind.: University of Notre Dame Press, 2005.

Congar, Yves. "La déification dans la traditions de l'Orient." *La vie spirituel, Supplément* 44 (1935): 91–107.

Crouse, R. D. "Augustinian Platonism in Early Medieval Theology." In *Augustine: From Rhetor to Theologian*, edited by Joanne McWilliam. Waterloo: Wilfrid Laurier University Press, 1992.

Daley, Brian E. *The Hope of the Early Church: A Handbook of Patristic Eschatology*. Grand Rapids, Mich.: Baker Academic, 2002.

———. "'One Thing and Another': The Persons in God and the Person of Christ in Patristic Theology." *Pro Ecclesia* 15, no. 1 (2006): 17–46.

Danielou, Jean. *Bible and Liturgy*. Notre Dame, Ind.: University of Notre Dame Press, 2002.

Dassmann, Ernst. *Die Frömmigkeit des Kirchenvaters Ambrosius von Mailand: Quellen und Entfaltung*. Münster: Aschendorff, 1965.

Davidson, Ivor. "Review of Marcia Colish, *Ambrose's Patriarchs: Ethics for the Common Man*." *Scottish Journal of Theology* 63 (2010): 235–37.

Dawson, Christopher. *Religion and the Rise of the Western Culture*. New York: Sheed and Ward, 1950.

De Clercq, Victor. "The Expectation of the Second Coming of Christ in Tertullian." *Studia Patristica* 11 (1972): 146–51.

de Simone, M. O. "Another Look at Benedict in Gregory's Dialogues." *Cistercian Studies* 49, no. 3 (2014): 299–346.

de Vogüé, Adalbert. "La rencontre de Benoit et de Scholastique. Essai d'interpretation." *Revue d'histoire de la spiritualite* 48 (1972): 257–73. Translated by J. B. Hasbrouck as "The Meeting of Benedict and Scholastica: An Interpretation." *Cistercian Studies* 18 (1983): 167–83.

———. "Benoît, modèle de vie spirituelle d'après le Deuxième Livre des Dialogues de saint Grégoire." *Collectanea Cisterciensia* 38 (1976): 147–57.

———. *Community and Abbot in the Rule of Saint Benedict*. 2 vols. Cistercian Studies 5.1–5.2. Kalamazoo, Mich.: Cistercian Publications, 1988.

———. "L'Auteur du Commentaire des Rois attribué à saint Grégoire: un moine de Cava." *Revue Bénédictine* 106 (1996): 319–31.

———. "Le Glossa Ordinaria et le Commentaire des Rois attribué à saint Grégoire le Grand." *Revue Bénédictine* 108 (1998): 58–60.

———. "Is Gregory the Great the author of the *Dialogues*?" *The American Benedictine Review* 56 (2005): 309–14.

Decret, Francois. *Le christianisme en Afrique du Nord ancienne*. Paris: Seuil, 1966.

Dehandschutter, B. *Polycarpiana: Studies on Martyrdom and Persecution in Early Christianity*. Edited by J. Leemans. Leuven: Peeters, 2007.

Demacopoulos, George, and Aristotle Papanikolaou. "Augustine and the Orthodox: 'The West' in the East." In *Orthodox Readings of Augustine*, edited by George Demacopoulos and Aristotle Papanikolaou, 11–40. New York: St. Vladimir's Seminary Press, 2008.

Den Boeft, Jan. "Delight and Imagination: Ambrose's Hymns." *VC* 62 (2008): 425–40.

Desprez, Vincent. "Saint Anthony and the Origins of Anchoretism II." *American Benedictine Review* 43, no. 2 (1992): 141–72.

Diem, Albrecht. "Inventing the Holy Rule: Some Observations on the History of Monastic Normative Observance in the Early Medieval West." In *Western Monasticism* ante litteram: *The Spaces of Early Monastic Observance*, edited by Hendrik Dey and Elizabeth Fentress, 53–84. Turnhout: Brepols, 2011.

Dougherty, M. V. "The Problem of *Humana Natura* in the *Consolatio Philosophiae* of Boethius." *American Catholic Philosophical Quarterly* 78, no. 2 (2004): 273–92.

Drewery, Benjamin. *Origen and the Doctrine of Grace*. London: Epworth Press, 1960.

Driscoll, Jeremy. "The Transfiguration in Hilary of Poitiers' *Commentarius in Matthaeum*." *Augustinianum* 24 (1984): 395–420.

Dunkle, Brian, SJ. *Enchantment and Creed in the Hymns of Ambrose of Milan*. Oxford: Oxford University Press, 2016.

Dunn, Geoffrey D. "Two Goats, Two Advents and Tertullian's *Adversus Iudaeos*." *Augustinianum* 39 (1999): 245–64.

———. "A Survey of Tertullian's Soteriology." *Sacris Erudiri* 42 (2003): 61–86.

———. *Tertullian*. The Early Church Fathers. New York: Routledge, 2004.

———. *Tertullian's* Adversus Iudaeos: *A Rhetorical Analysis*. Washington, D.C.: The Catholic University of America Press, 2008.

Eckmann, Augustyn. "Deification of Man in St. Ambrose's Writings." In *Being or Good?*

*Metamorphoses of Neoplatonism*, edited by Agnieszka Kijewska, 199–210. Lublin: Wydawnictwo KUL, 2004.

Elliott, Dyan. "Tertullian, the Angelic Life, and the Bride of Christ." In *Gender and Christianity in Medieval Europe: New Perspectives*, edited by Lisa M. Bitel and Felice Lifshitz, 15–33. Philadelphia: University of Pennsylvania Press, 2010.

Elm, Susanna. "Gregory of Nazianzus: Mediation between Individual and Community." In *Group Identity and Religious Individuality in Late Antiquity*, edited by Jörg Rüpke and Éric Rebillard, 89–107. Washington, D.C.: The Catholic University of America Press, 2015.

Fagerberg, David. "From Divinization to Evangelization: An Overview." In *Divinization: Becoming Icons of Christ Through the Liturgy*, edited by Andrew Hofer, 15–31. Chicago: Hillenbrand Books, 2015.

Fahey, Michael. *Cyprian and the Bible: a Study in Third-Century Exegesis*. Tübingen: J. C. B. Mohr, 1971.

Finlan, Stephen, and Vladimir Kharlamov, eds. *Theosis: Deification in Christian Theology*. Eugene, Ore.: Pickwick, 2006.

Fitzgerald, Allan. *Conversion Through Penance in the Italian Church of the Fourth and Fifth Centuries: New Approaches to the Experience of Conversion from Sin*. Lewiston, Penn.: Edwin Mellen Press, 1988.

———, ed. *Augustine Through the Ages: An Encyclopedia*. Grand Rapids, Mich.: Eerdmans, 2009.

Fokin, Alexey. "The Doctrine of Deification in Western Fathers of the Church: A Reconsideration." In *Für Uns und für unser Heil: Soteriologie in Ost und West*, edited by Theresia Hainthaler et al., 207–20. Innsbruck-Wien: Tyrolia Verlag, 2014.

Fortin, John R. "The Nature of Consolation in *The Consolation of Philosophy*." *American Catholic Philosophical Quarterly* 78, no. 2 (2004): 293–307.

Foster, Paul. "The Epistles of Ignatius of Antioch (Part I)." *The Expository Times* 117, no. 12 (2006): 487–95.

Frede, Hermann, ed. *Epistulae ad Thessalonicenses, Timotheum, Titum, Philemonem, Hebraeos*. In *Vetus Latina: Die Reste der Altlateinischen Bibel* 25.1. Freiburg: Herder, 1975–91.

Frisius, Mark A. *Tertullian's Use of the Pastoral Epistles, Hebrews, James, 1 and 2 Peter, and Jude*. New York: Peter Lang, 2001.

Gandt, Lois. "A Philological and Theological Analysis of the Ancient Latin Translations of the *Vita Antonii*." PhD diss., Fordham University, 2008.

Gavrilyuk, Paul. *The Suffering of the Impassible God: The Dialectics of Patristic Thought*. Oxford: Oxford University Press, 2004.

———. "The Retrieval of Deification: How a Once-Despised Archaism Became an Ecumenical Desideratum." *Modern Theology* 25 (2009): 647–59.

Gerber, Chad Tyler. *The Spirit of Augustine's Early Theology: Contextualizing Augustine's Pneumatology*. Burlington, Vt.: Ashgate, 2012.

Gibbon, Edward. *Decline and Fall of the Roman Empire*, vol. 3. Edited by David Womersley. New York: Penguin, 1994.

Gil-Tamayo, Juan Antonio. "De unitate Patris et Filii et Spiritus sancti plebs adunata (*De oratione dominica*, 23). La unidad trinitaria como fundamento de la unidad eclesial en Tertuliano y Cipriano de Cartago." *Scripta Theologica* 43 (2011): 9–29.

Gioia, Luigi. *The Theological Epistemology of Augustine's* De Trinitate. Oxford: Oxford University Press, 2008.

Goins, Scott, and Barbara H. Wyman, eds. *The Consolation of Philosophy*. San Francisco: Ignatius Press, 2012.

Gonzalez, Eliezer. "Anthropologies of Continuity: The Body and Soul in Tertullian, Perpetua, and Early Christianity." *Journal of Early Christian Studies* 21, no. 4 (2013): 479–502.

———. *The Fate of the Dead in the "Passion of Perpetua and Felicitas" and the Works of Tertullian: Ideologies of the Afterlife in Early Third-Century North Africa and Tertullian*. Tübingen: Mohr Siebeck, 2014.

González, Justo L. *A History of Christian Thought*, vol. 1: *From the Beginning to the Council of Chalcedon*. Nashville, Tenn.: Abingdon Press, 1987.

Gradel, I. *Emperor Worship and Roman Religion*. Oxford: Clarendon Press, 2002.

Graumann, Thomas. Christus interpres: *Die Einheit von Auslegung und Verkündigung in der Lukaserklärung des Ambrosius von Mailand*. Berlin: Walter de Gruyter, 1994.

Green, Bernard. *The Soteriology of Leo the Great*. Oxford: Oxford University Press, 2008.

Habermehl, P. *Perpetua und der Ägypter oder Bilder des Bösen im frühen afrikanischen Christentum*. Second edition. Berlin: Walter de Gruyter, 2004.

Hagendahl, Harald. *Latin Fathers and the Classics*. Göteberg: Göteberg Elanders, 1958.

Hägglund, Bengt. *History of Theology*. Translated by Gene J. Lund. St. Louis, Mo.: Concordia, 2007.

Hahn, Viktor. *Das Wahre Gesetz: Eine Untersuchung der Auffassung des Ambrosius von Mailand vom Verhältnis der beiden Testamente*. Münster: Aschendorff, 1968.

Hallonsten, Gösta. "*Theosis* in Recent Research: A Renewal of Interest and a Need for Clarity." In *Partakers of the Divine Nature: The History and Development of Deification in the Christian Traditions*, edited by Michael J. Christensen and Jeffrey A. Wittung, 281–93. Madison, N.J.: Fairleigh Dickinson University Press, 2007.

Hamalis, Perry T., and Aristotle Papanikolaou. "Toward a Godly Mode of Being: Virtue as Embodied Deification." *Studies in Christian Ethics* 26, no. 3 (2013): 271–80.

Hanson, R. P. C. *The Search for the Christian Doctrine of God*. Edinburgh: T and T Clark, 1988.

Harnack, Adolf von. *History of Dogma*, vol. 3. Translated by James Millar. London: Williams and Norgate, 1897.

Heffernan, Thomas J., and Thomas E. Burman, eds. *Scripture and Pluralism: Reading the Bible in the Religiously Plural Worlds of the Middle Ages and Renaissance*. Leiden: Brill, 2005.

Heine, Ronald. *The Commentaries of Origen and Jerome on St. Paul's Epistle to the Ephesians*. Oxford: Oxford University Press, 2002.

Hilary of Poitiers. *Commentarius in Matthaeum: Sur Matthieu*. Introduction, critical text, translation by Jean Doignon. Vol. 1: 1–13. SC 254. Paris 1978. Vol. 2: 14–33. SC 258. Paris, 1979.

———. *De Trinitate libri duodecim*. Edited by P. Smulders. CCL 62, 62A. Turnhout, 1979, 1980.

Holder-Egger, O., ed. *Agnelli qui et Andreas Liber Pontificalis Ecclesiae Rauennatis*. In *Scriptores Rerum Langobardicarum et Italicorum*, edited by G. Waitz. Hannover: Impensis Bibliopolii Hahniani, 1878.

Homes Dudden, F. *The Life and Times of St. Ambrose*. Oxford: Clarendon Press, 1934.

Howgego, Christopher. *Ancient History from Coins*. London: Routledge, 1995.

Hušek, Vít. "'Perfection Appropriate to the Fragile Human Condition': Jerome and Pelagius on the Perfection of Christian Life." *Studia Patristica* 67 (2013): 385–92.

Irwin, E. "Gender, Status, and Identity in a North African Martyrdom." In *Gli Imperatori Severi: Storia Archeologia Religione*, edited by E. del Covolo and G. Rinaldi, 252–60. Roma: LAS, 1999.

Jalland, Trevor. *The Life and Times of St. Leo the Great*. London: SPCK, 1941.

Jeanes, Gordon P. *The Day Has Come! Easter and Baptism in Zeno of Verona*. Collegeville, Minn.: Liturgical Press, 1995.

Jensen, Michael P. *Martyrdom and Identity: The Self on Trial*. London: T and T Clark, 2010.

Jensen, Robin. *Baptismal Imagery in Early Christianity: Ritual, Visual, and Theological Dimensions*. Grand Rapids, Mich.: Baker, 2012.

Johnson, Maxwell E. *The Rites of Christian Initiation: Their Evolution and Interpretation*. Collegeville, Minn.: Liturgical Press, 2007.

Johnston, David. *Roman Law in Context*. Cambridge: Cambridge University Press, 1999.

Jones, Cheslyn, ed. *The Study of Spirituality*. Oxford University Press, 1986.

Jones, John D. "Does Philosophy Console? Boethius and Christian Faith." *Proceedings of the American Catholic Philosophical Association* 57 (1983): 78–87.

Kahn, Charles. "Why Existence Does Not Emerge as a Distinct Concept in Greek Philosophy." *Archiv Für Geschichte Der Philosophie* 58, no. 4 (1976): 323–34.

———. *The Verb "Be" in Ancient Greek*. Indianapolis, Ind.: Hackett, 2003.

———. *Essays on Being*. Oxford: Oxford University Press, 2009.

Kalantzis, George. "Is There Room for Two? Cyril's Single Subjectivity and the Prosopic Union." *St. Vladimir's Theological Quarterly* 52, no. 1 (2008): 95–110.

Kaylor, Noel Harold, Jr., and Philip Edward Phillips, eds. *A Companion to Boethius in the Middle Ages*. Leiden: Brill, 2012.

Keating, Daniel A. *The Appropriation of Divine Life in Cyril of Alexandria*. Oxford: Oxford University Press, 2004.

———. *Deification and Grace*. Naples, Fla.: Sapientia Press, 2007.

———. "Typologies of Deification." *International Journal of Systematic Theology* 17, no. 3 (July 2015): 274–75.

Kelly, J. N. D. *Early Christian Doctrines*. Peabody, Mass.: Hendrickson, 2004.

Ketchum, Jonathan. "The Structure of the Plato Dialogue." PhD diss., State University of New York at Buffalo, 1980.

Kilmartin, Edward J. *The Eucharist in the West: History and Theology*. Edited by Robert J. Daly. Collegeville, Minn.: Liturgical Press, 1998.
Kloos, Kari. *Christ, Creation and the Vision of God: Augustine's Transformation of Early Christian Theophany Interpretation*. Leiden: Brill, 2011.
Ladner, Gerhart B. *The Idea of Reform: Its Impact on Christian Thought and Action in the Age of the Fathers*. Cambridge, Mass.: Harvard University Press, 1959.
Lanne, Emmanuel. "L'interprétation palamite de la vision de S. Benoit." In *Le millénaire du Mont-Athos 963–1963*, 21–47. Études et mélanges 11. Venice: Éditions de Chevtogne, Fondazione Giorgio Cini, 1964.
Leemans, J. *Martyrdom and Persecution in Late Antique Christianity*. Leuven: Peeters, 2010.
Lehtipuu, Outi. "'Flesh and Blood Cannot Inherit the Kingdom of God': The Transformation of the Flesh in the Early Christian Debates Concerning Resurrection." In *Metamorphoses: Resurrection, Body and Transformative Practices in Early Christianity*, edited by Turid Karlsen Seim and Jorunn Økland, 147–68. Berlin: Walter de Gruyter, 2009.
Liebeschuetz, J. H. W. G. *Ambrose of Milan: Political Letters and Speeches*. Liverpool: Liverpool University Press, 2005.
Lienhard, Joseph. *Contra Marcellum: Marcellus of Ancyra and Fourth Century Theology*. Washington, D.C.: The Catholic University of America Press, 1999.
López, Eduardo Toraño. *La teología de la Gracia en Ambrosio de Milan*. Madrid: Facultad de Teología "San Dámaso," 2006.
Lorié, Ludovicus T. A. *Spiritual Terminology in the Latin Translations of the Vita Antonii: With Reference to Fourth and Fifth Century Monastic Literature*. Nijmegen: Dekker and Van De Vegt, 1961.
Louth, Andrew. "The Place of *Theosis* in Orthodox Theology." In *Partakers of the Divine Nature*, edited by Michael J. Christensen and Jeffrey A. Wittung, 32–45. Grand Rapids, Mich.: Baker Academic Press, 2008.
———. "Gregory the Great in the Byzantine Tradition." In *A Companion to Gregory the Great*, edited by B. Neil, 343–58. Leiden: Brill, 2013.
Lukken, G. M. *Original Sin in the Roman Liturgy: Research into the Theology of Original Sin in the Roman Sacramentaria and the Early Baptismal Liturgy*. Leiden: Brill, 1973.
MacCormack, Sabine. "Augustine Reads Genesis." *Augustinian Studies* 39, no. 1 (2008): 5–47.
Madec, Goulven. "Jean Scot et les Pères latins: Hilaire, Ambroise, Jérôme et Grégoire le Grand." In *Jean Scot et ses auteurs: Annotations érigéniennes*, edited by Goulven Madec. Paris: Études augustiniennes, 1988.
Madeo, Angelo. *La dottrina soteriologica di S. Ambrogio*. Bergamo: Cattaneo, 1943.
Maes, Baziel. *La loi naturelle selon Ambroise de Milan*. Rome: Gregorianum, 1967.
Magee, John. "Boethius." In *A Companion to Philosophy in the Middle Ages*, edited by Jorge J. E. Gracia and Timothy B. Noone, 217–26. Oxford: Blackwell Publishing, 2003.
———. "The Good and Morality: *Consolatio* 2–4." In *The Cambridge Companion to Boethius*, edited by John Marenbon, 181–206. Cambridge: Cambridge University Press, 2009.

———. "Boethius." In *The Cambridge History of Philosophy in Late Antiquity*, edited by Lloyd P. Gerson. Cambridge: Cambridge University Press, 2010.

Marenbon, John. "Boethius: From Antiquity to the Middle Ages." In *Medieval Philosophy*, edited by John Marenbon, 11–28. Routledge History of Philosophy 3. New York: Routledge, 1998.

———. *Boethius*. Oxford: Oxford University Press, 2003.

———. "Rationality and Happiness: Interpreting Boethius's *Consolation of Philosophy*." In *Rationality and Happiness: From the Ancients to the Early Medievals*, edited by Jiyuan Yu and Jorge J. E. Gracia, 175–97. Rochester, N.Y.: University of Rochester Press, 2003.

———, ed. *The Cambridge Companion to Boethius*. Cambridge: Cambridge University Press, 2009.

Markschies, Christoph. *Ambrosius von Mailand und die Trinitätstheologie: kirchen- und theologiegeschichtliche Studien zu Antiarianismus und Neunizänismus bei Ambrosius und im lateinischen Westen (364–381 n. Chr.)*. Tübingen: Mohr, 1995.

Matthews, John. *Western Aristocracies and Imperial Court AD 364–425*. Oxford: Clarendon, 1990.

Mauskopf Deliyannis, Deborah. *Ravenna in Late Antiquity*. Cambridge: Cambridge University Press, 2010.

Mayvaert, Paul. "The Authentic Dialogues of Gregory the Great." *Sacris erudiri* 43 (2004): 55–130.

McCruden, Kevin B. "Monarchy and Economy in Tertullian's *Adversus Praxeam*." *Scottish Journal of Theology* 55, no. 3 (2002): 325–37.

McGinn, Bernard. *The Growth of Mysticism*. New York: Crossroads, 1994.

McGowan, Andrew. "Tertullian and the 'Heretical' Origins of the 'Orthodox' Trinity." *Journal of Early Christian Studies* 14, no. 4 (2006): 437–57.

McGuckin, John. *The Westminster Handbook to Patristic Theology*. Louisville, Ky.: Westminster John Knox, 2004.

McKechnie, Paul. "St. Perpetua and Roman Education in AD 200." *L'antiqué classique* 63 (1994): 279–91.

McLynn, Neil. *Ambrose of Milan: Church and Court in a Christian Capital*. Berkeley: University of California Press, 1994.

McMahon, Robert. *Understanding the Medieval Meditative Ascent: Augustine, Anselm, Boethius, and Dante*. Washington, D.C.: The Catholic University of America Press, 2006.

Meconi, David Vincent. *The One Christ: St. Augustine's Theology of Deification*. Washington, D.C.: The Catholic University of America Press, 2013.

———. "Earthly Treasure Spiritually Refined." *Harvard Theological Review* 108, no. 4 (2015): 621–28.

Mersch, Émile. *The Whole Christ*. Translated by John R. Kelly. Milwaukee, Wis.: Bruce, 1938.

Middletown, Paul. *Radical Martyrdom and Cosmic Conflict in Early Christianity*. London: T and T Clark, 2006.

Migne, Jacques-Paul, ed. Patrologia Cursus Completus. Series Graeca. 161 volumes. Paris: Excudebat Migne, 1856–66.

———, ed. *Patrologia Cursus Completus. Series Latina*. 221 volumes. Paris: Excudebat Migne, 1844–64.

Miller, Mitchell. "Platonic Mimesis." In *Contextualizing Classics: Ideology, Performance, Dialogue*, edited by Thomas Falkner, 253–66. Lanham, Md.: Rowman and Littlefield, 1999.

Minns, Denis. *Irenaeus: An Introduction*. London: T and T Clark, 2010.

Mohrmann, Christine. "Le style oral du 'De Sacramentis' de Saint Ambroise." *VC* 6 (1952): 168–77.

Moingt, Joseph. "La Théologie Trinitaire de St Hilaire." In *Hilaire et son temps*, Actes du Colloque de Poitiers, 159–73. Paris: Études Augustiniennes, 1969.

Moss, Candida. *The Other Christs: Imitating Jesus in Ancient Christian Ideologies of Martyrdom*. Oxford: Oxford University Press, 2010.

———. *Ancient Christian Martyrdom: Diverse Practices, Theologies, and Traditions*. New Haven, Conn.: Yale University Press, 2012.

Mosser, Carl. "The Earliest Patristic Interpretations of Psalm 82, Jewish Antecedents, and the Origin of Christian Deification." *JTS* 56, no. 1 (April 2005): 30–74.

———. "An Exotic Flower? Calvin and the Patristic Doctrine of Deification." In *Reformation Faith: Exegesis and Theology in the Protestant Reformations*, edited by Michael Parsons, 38–56. Eugene, Ore.: Wipf and Stock, 2014.

Nash-Marshall, Siobhan. "God, Simplicity, and the *Consolatio Philosophiae*." *American Catholic Philosophical Quarterly* 78, no. 2 (2004): 225–46.

Neil, B., ed. *A Companion to Gregory the Great*. Leiden: Brill, 2013.

*Nicene and Post-Nicene Fathers*. Edited by Philip Schaff. 24 volumes in 2 series. Peabody, Mass.: Hendrickson Publishers, 1995.

Nispel, Mark D. "Christian Deification and the Early *Testimonia*." *VC* 53 (1999): 298–99 and 301.

O'Donovan, Oliver. *The Problem of Self-Love in Saint Augustine*. New Haven, Conn.: Yale University Press, 1980.

Oepke, A. "μεσίτες." In *Theological Dictionary of the New Testament*, edited by Gerhard Kittel, translated by Geoffrey Bromiley, 598–624. Grand Rapids, Mich.: Eerdmans, 1967.

Oliphant Old, Hugh. *The Reading and Preaching of the Scriptures in the Worship of the Christian Church*, vol. 2: *The Patristic Age*. Grand Rapids, Mich.: Eerdmans, 1998.

Olsen, Roger. "Deification in Contemporary Theology." *Theology Today* 64 (2007): 186–200.

Oroz Reta, José. "De l'illumination à la deification de l'âme selon saint Augustin." *Studia Patristica* 27 (1993): 364–82.

Ortiz, Jared. "Deification in the Latin Fathers." In *Called to Be Children of God: The Catholic Theology of Human Deification*, edited by Fr. David Meconi, SJ, and Carl E. Olson, 59–80. San Francisco: Ignatius Press, 2016.

———. *"You Made Us for Yourself": Creation in St. Augustine's Confessions*. Minneapolis, Minn.: Fortress Press, 2016.

Osborn, Eric. *Tertullian: First Theologian of the West*. Cambridge: Cambridge University Press, 1999.

Otten, Willemien. "The Texture of Tradition: The Role of the Church Fathers in Carolingian Theology." In *The Reception of the Church Fathers in the West*, edited by Irena Backus, 1:31–44. Leiden: Brill, 1997.

———. "Tertullian's Rhetoric of Redemption: Flesh and Embodiment in *De carne Christi* and *De resurrectione mortuorum*." *Studia Patristica* 70 (2013): 331–48.

Palanque, Jean-Remy. "Le Gaule chrétienne au temps de Saint Hilaire." In *Hilaire et son temps*, Actes du Colloque de Poitiers, 11–17. Paris: Études Augustiniennes, 1969.

Palazzo, Eric. *A History of Liturgical Books from the Beginning to the Thirteenth Century*. Collegeville, Minn.: Liturgical Press, 1998.

Papandrea, James L. *The Trinitarian Theology of Novatian of Rome: A Study in Third-Century Orthodoxy*. Lewiston, Penn.: Edwin Mellen Press, 2008.

———. *Novatian of Rome and the Culmination of Pre-Nicene Orthodoxy*. Princeton Theological Monograph Series 175. Eugene, Ore.: Pickwick, 2011.

———. *Reading the Early Church Fathers: From the Didache to Nicaea*. Mahwah, N.J.: Paulist Press, 2012.

Parsons, S. E. *Ancient Apologetic Exegesis*. Eugene, Ore.: Wipf and Stock, 2015.

Pasini, Cesare. *Ambrogio di Milano: Azione e pensiero di un vescovo*. Milan: Edizioni San Paolo, 1996.

Pearson, Birger. *Ancient Gnosticism: Traditions and Literature*. Minneapolis, Minn.: Fortress Press, 2007.

Pelikan, Jaroslav. "The Eschatology of Tertullian." *Church History* 21, no. 2 (1952): 108–22.

Pelland, Gilles. *Notes to* La Trinité. SC 462. Paris: Éditions du Cerf, 2001.

Penner, T. *In Praise of Christian Origins: Stephen and the Hellenists in the Lukan Apologetic Historiography*. London: T and T Clark, 2004.

Perrone, Lorenzo. "Riscoprire Origene oggi: prime impressioni sulla raccolta di omelie sui Salmi nel *Codex Monacensis Graecus* 314." *Adamantius* 18 (2012): 41–58.

———. "*Codex Monacensis Graecus* 314: 29 Psalmenhomilien des Origenes." In Origenes, *Die neuen Psalmenhomilien: Eine kritische Edition des Codex Monacensis Monacensis Graecus 314*, 1–72. Berlin: De Gruyter, 2015.

Petersen, Anders Klostergaard. "Attaining Divine Perfection through Different Forms of Imitation." *Numen* 60 (2013): 7–38.

Peura, Simo, and Antti Raunio, eds. *Luther und Theosis: Vergöttlichung als Thema der abendländischen Theologie*. Schriften der Luther-Agricola Gesellschaft A 25; Veröffentlichungen der Luther- Akademie Ratzeburg 15. Helsinki: Luther-Agricola-Gesellschaft, 1990.

Philips, Gérard. "La grâce chez les orientaux." *Ephemerides Theologicae Lovanienses* 48 (1972): 37–50.

Pizzolato, Luigi. *La dottrina esegetica di sant'Ambrogio*. Milan: Vita e Pensiero, 1978.

Poirier, Michel. "'Christus pauper factus est' chez saint'Ambroise." *Rivista di storia e letteratura religiosa* 15 (1979): 250–57.

Porter, Lawrence B. "On Keeping 'Persons' in the Trinity: A Linguistic Approach to Trinitarian Thought." *Theological Studies* 41, no. 3 (1980): 530–48.

Radler, Charlotte. "The Dirty Physician: Necessary Dishonor and Fleshly Solidarity in Tertullian's Writings." *VC* 63 (2009): 345–68.

Rahner, Hugo. "Die Gottesgeburt: Die Lehre der Kirchenväter von der Geburt Christi im Herzen des Gläubigen." *ZKT* 59 (1935): 333–418.

Rankin, David I. "Tertullian and the Crucified God." *Pacifica* 10 (1997): 298–309.

———. "Was Tertullian a Jurist?" *Studia Patristica* 31 (1997): 335–42.

Relihan, Joel C. *Ancient Menippean Satire*. Baltimore, Md.: Johns Hopkins University Press, 1993.

———. *The Prisoner's Philosophy: Life and Death in Boethius's Consolation*. Notre Dame, Ind.: University of Notre Dame Press, 2007.

Rousseau, O. "Saint Benoît et le prophète Élisée." *Revue Monastique* (Maredsous) 144 (1956): 103–14.

Russell, Norman. *The Doctrine of Deification in the Greek Patristic Tradition*. Oxford: Oxford University Press, 2004.

———. *Fellow Workers with God: Orthodox Thinking of Theosis*. Crestwood, N.Y.: St. Vladimir's Seminary Press, 2009.

———. "Why Does *Theosis* Fascinate Western Christians?" *Sobornost* 34 (2012): 5–15.

Safranski, Benjamin B. "St. Cyprian of Carthage and the College of Bishops." PhD diss., The Catholic University of America, 2015.

Santo, Matthew Dal. "The Shadow of a Doubt? A Note on the *Dialogues* and *Registrum Epistolarum* of Pope Gregory the Great (590–604)." *The Journal of Ecclesiastical History* 61, no. 1 (2010): 3–17.

Savon, Hervé. *Saint Ambroise devant l'exegese de Philon le Juif*. 2 vols. Paris: Études augustiniennes, 1977.

Scully, Ellen. *Physicalist Soteriology in Hilary of Poitiers*. Leiden: Brill, 2015.

Shaw, B. "The Passion of Perpetua." *Past and Present* 139 (1993): 3–45.

Sheridan, James. "The Altar of Victory: Paganism's Last Battle." *L'antiquité classique* 35 (1966): 186–206.

Sidaway, Janet. *The Human Factor: Deification in Hilary of Poitiers' De Trinitate*. Studia Patristica Supplement 6. Leuven: Peeters, 2016.

Sider, Robert D. "Structure and Design in the '*De Resurrectione Mortuorum*' of Tertullian." *VC* 23, no. 3 (1969): 177–96.

———. *Ancient Rhetoric and the Art of Tertullian*. Oxford Theological Monographs. Oxford: Oxford University Press, 1971.

Smith, J. Warren. *Christian Grace and Pagan Virtue: The Theological Foundation of Ambrose's Ethics*. Oxford: Oxford University Press, 2010.

Smulders, Pierre. *La doctrine trinitaire de S. Hilaire de Poitiers*. Rome: Universitatis Gregorianae, 1944.

Sowers, B. "*Pudor et Dedecus*: Rhetoric of Honor and Shame in Perpetua's *Passion*." *Journal of Early Christian Studies* 23, no. 3 (2015): 363–88.

Starr, James M. *Sharers in Divine Nature: 2 Peter 1:4 in its Hellenistic Context*. Stockholm: Almqvist and Wiksell International, 2000.

Stewart-Sykes, Alistair. "Manumission and Baptism in Tertullian's Africa: A Search for the Origin of Confirmation." *Studia Liturgica* 31 (2001): 129–49.
Tabbernee, William. *Fake Prophecy and Polluted Sacraments: Ecclesiastical and Imperial Reactions to Montanism*. Leiden: Brill, 2007.
———. "The World to Come: Tertullian's Christian Eschatology." In *Tertullian and Paul*, edited by Todd D. Still and David E. Wilhite, 259–77. New York: Bloomsbury, 2013.
Thomassen, Einar. *The Spiritual Seed: The Church of the Valentinians*. Leiden: Brill, 2008.
Toom, Tarmo. "Hilary of Poitiers' *De Trinitate* and the Name(s) of God." *VC* 65 (2010): 456–79.
Townsend, Luke Davis. "Deification in Aquinas: A *Supplementum* to *The Ground of Union*." *JTS* 66 (2015): 204–34.
Trevett, Christine. *Montanism: Gender, Authority and the New Prophecy*. Cambridge: Cambridge University Press, 1996.
van de Beek, Abraham. "Cyprian on Baptism." In *Cyprian of Carthage: Studies in His Life, Language and Thought*, edited by Henk Bakker, Paul van Geest, and Hans van Loon, 143–64. Leuven: Peeters, 2010.
van Henten, J. W. *The Maccabean Martyrs as Saviours of the Jewish People*. Supplement to the *Journal for the Study of Judaism* 57. Leiden: Brill, 1997.
———. "Martyrdom, Jesus' Passion and Barbarism." *Biblical Interpretation* 17, no. 1 (2009): 239–64.
van Loon, Hans. "Cyprian's Christology and the Authenticity of *Quod idola dii non sint*." In *Cyprian of Carthage: Studies in His Life, Language and Thought*, edited by Henk Bakker, Paul van Geest, and Hans van Loon, 127–42. Leuven: Peeters, 2010.
Visonà, Giuseppe. *Cronologia Ambrosiana/Bibliografia Ambrosiana (1900–2000)*. Milan: Biblioteca Ambrosiana, 2004.
Von Campenhausen, Hans. *Ambrosius von Mailand als Kirchenpolitiker*. Berlin: De Gruyter, 1929.
Wallace, A. J., and R. D. Rusk. *Moral Transformation: The Original Christian Paradigm of Salvation*. New Zealand: Bridgehead, 2011.
Weinandy, Thomas G. *Does God Change?* Still River, Mass.: St. Bede's Publications, 1985.
Wesche, K. P. "The Doctrine of Deification: A Call to Worship." *Theology Today* 65 (2008): 169–79.
Wessel, Susan. *Leo the Great and the Spiritual Rebuilding of a Universal Rome*. Leiden: Brill, 2008.
Weston, Frank. *The One Christ: An Enquiry into the Manner of the Incarnation*. Second edition. London: Longmans Green, 1914.
Whitaker, E. C., and Maxwell E. Johnson. *Documents of the Baptismal Liturgy: Revised and Expanded Edition*. Collegeville, Minn.: Liturgical Press, 2003.
Wickham, Lionel. "Le livre 11 et l'apothéose de l'homme-Dieu." In *Dieu Trinité d'hier à demain avec Hilaire de Poitiers*, edited by Dominique Bertrand, 241–51. Paris: Éditions du Cerf, 2010.

Widdicombe, Peter. *The Fatherhood of God from Origen to Athanasius*. Second edition. Oxford: Oxford University Press, 2000.

Wild, Philip. *The Divinization of Man according to Hilary of Poitiers*. Mundelein, Ill.: St. Mary of the Lake Seminary, 1950.

Williams, D. H. "Monarchianism and Photinus of Sirmium as the Persistent Heretical Face of the Fourth Century." *Harvard Theological Review* 99 (2006): 187–206.

Williams, Daniel. *Ambrose of Milan and the End of the Nicene-Arian Conflicts*. New York: Clarendon, 1995.

Williams, Jarvis J. *Christ Died for Our Sins: Representation and Substitution in* Romans *and Their Jewish Martyrological Background*. Eugene, Ore.: Pickwick, 2015.

Williams, Rowan. "Deification." In *A Dictionary of Christian Spirituality*, edited by Gordon S. Wakefield, 106–8. London: SCM Press, 1983.

Wright, Frederick Adam. *Jerome: Selected Letters*. Loeb Classical Library 262. Cambridge, Mass.: Harvard University Press, 1933.

Yarnold, Edward. "*Videmus duplicem statum*: The Visibility of the Two Natures of Christ in Tertullian's *Adversus Praxean*." *Studia Patristica* 19 (1989): 286–90.

———. *The Awe-Inspiring Rites of Initiation*. Collegeville, Minn.: Liturgical Press, 1994.

Zimmerman, Reinhard. *The Law of Obligations*. Oxford: Oxford University Press, 1996.

# CONTRIBUTORS

*Fr. Brian Dunkle, SJ,* is assistant professor of historical theology at Boston College School of Theology and Ministry and author of *Enchantment and Creed in the Hymns of Ambrose of Milan* (Oxford University Press, 2016).

*Fr. Luke Dysinger, OSB,* is professor of church history and moral theology at St. John's Seminary in Camarillo, California. He is author of numerous books and articles on Evagrius Ponticus, monasticism, and Christian spirituality.

*Mark A. Frisius* is professor of theology at Olivet Nazarene University and author of *Tertullian's Use of the Pastoral Epistles, Hebrews, James, 1 and 2 Peter, and Jude* (Peter Lang, 2011).

*Ron Haflidson* is a tutor at St. John's College in Annapolis, Maryland, and author of a forthcoming study of Augustine's moral theology entitled *On Solitude, Conscience, Love and Our Inner and Outer Lives* (Bloomsbury).

*Thomas Heffernan* is the Curry Professor and director of the Humanities Center at the University of Tennessee. His most recent book is *The Passion of Perpetua and Felicity* (Oxford University Press, 2012).

*Vít Hušek* is lecturer in theology at Palacký University Olomouc, Czech Republic. He is author of *Symbol in the Philosophy of Paul Ricoeur* (Trinitas, 2004) and numerous articles in Czech and English on the Latin Fathers.

*Daniel Keating* is professor of theology at Sacred Heart Major Seminary in Detroit and author of *The Appropriation of Divine Life in Cyril of Alexandria* (Oxford University Press, 2004), *Deification and Grace* (The Catholic University of America Press, 2007), *First and Second Peter, Jude* (Baker Academic, 2011), and co-author of *James and 1–3 John* (Baker Academic, 2016).

# CONTRIBUTORS

*Fr. David Meconi, SJ,* is associate professor of theological studies at Saint Louis University. He is author of *The One Christ: St. Augustine's Theology of Deification* (The Catholic University of America Press, 2013) and co-editor of *Called to Be the Children of God: The Catholic Theology of Human Deification* (Ignatius Press, 2016).

*Jared Ortiz* is associate professor of religion at Hope College and author of *You Made Us for Yourself: Creation in St Augustine's Confessions* (Fortress Press, 2016).

*James L. Papandrea* is professor of church history and historical theology at Garrett-Evangelical Theological Seminary and author of several books on early Christianity and historical theology. Most recently he translated the works of Novatian in the Corpus Christianorum in Translation Series, and published *The Earliest Christologies: Five Images of Christ in the Postapostolic Age* (IVP Academic, 2016).

*Norman Russell* is an honorary research fellow of St. Stephen's House, Oxford, and the author of *The Doctrine of Deification in the Greek Patristic Tradition* (Oxford University Press, 2004).

*Benjamin Safranski* is lecturer in theology at the Franciscan University of Steubenville. He is author of *St. Cyprian of Carthage and the College of Bishops* (Lexington Press / Fortress Academic, 2018).

*Janet Sidaway* is a visiting research fellow in the Department of Theology and Religious Studies at King's College, London. She is the author of *The Human Factor: 'Deification' as Transformation in the Theology of Hilary of Poitiers* (Studia Patristica Supplement 6, 2016), and is currently researching Western interpretations of the transfiguration.

*Michael Wiitala* is assistant college lecturer of philosophy at Cleveland State University. He has written numerous articles on Plato, Neo-Platonism, and Christian medieval philosophy, which have appeared in *Proceedings of the American Catholic Philosophical Association, Apeiron, Epoché, Philosophy Today, International Philosophical Quarterly*, and the *British Journal for the History of Philosophy*.

# INDEX

Adam, 12, 13, 17, 66, 68–69, 95, 123, 149, 219, 222–23, 275; Christ as new, 12, 20, 64, 221; fall of, 59, 68n74, 105n46, 178, 264, 269, 271, 290
adoption, 5, 6, 7, 19–21, 40, 76, 88, 91, 96, 117, 134, 142, 145, 154–58, 163, 166–68, 170, 191, 197–202, 206–7, 264, 273, 281, 284, 293
adoptionism, 97–98, 104, 108, 117, 284
almsgiving, 5, 89–92, 195, 220, 221, 225
angelification, 6, 18n17, 55, 59, 73–74, 141, 147, 161–63, 165, 167–68, 285
angels, 19, 48, 73–74, 161–63, 176n35, 199, 202, 268
anointing, 10, 19–22, 23, 29
ark of the covenant, 27, 218
ascent, 8, 38–43, 48, 110, 168, 234–36, 262, 265–70, 273, 277–79, 280, 289, 291, 293
asceticism, 6, 7, 8, 28–29, 88, 134, 136, 140, 141, 144, 147, 152–54, 159, 162, 167, 218, 222n55, 257n14, 260, 261, 265–67, 273, 280, 286, 287n65, 289n71, 270, 291, 293

baptism, 4, 5, 9, 10, 12–19, 22, 23, 26–27, 28–29, 38, 41, 66, 74, 76, 77–80, 83–84, 85–88, 89–90, 118, 129–31, 138, 143, 151, 157–58, 167, 168, 191, 201, 212, 222–23, 230, 276, 281–82, 287n65
baptisteries, 9, 14, 15, 16, 17, 198
body: Christ's physical, 107–8, 112, 114, 121–22, 123–25, 141–44, 148, 211, 217, 281, 284, 289; human, 13, 15, 20, 22, 24–26, 45, 56, 61, 66, 67, 76, 78, 85, 86, 90, 107, 124–25, 127, 141, 154, 158, 162, 180n50, 187–88, 217, 262, 273, 275, 278, 288

body of Christ: church as, 17, 23, 28, 51, 82, 90, 112, 117, 191, 276, 279; eucharist as, 23–26, 27, 129, 230n84, 282; Gospel as, 27

Christmas, 11, 18, 212, 213, 216, 219, 226
church, 13, 17, 19, 22, 23n68, 47, 61, 77, 80, 81–83, 84, 90, 93, 136, 144, 163, 164, 166, 195, 204, 218, 277, 278. *See also* body of Christ
*communicatio idiomatum*, 5, 70, 72, 94, 96–107, 110, 273, 275
confirmation. *See* anointing
contemplation, 7–8, 77, 79, 176n35, 182, 232, 254, 257–59, 263, 264–71, 277, 279, 280, 289

death, 13, 14, 32, 36–38, 39, 45, 47, 48, 49, 51n44, 52, 57, 67, 68, 91n68, 108, 118, 123, 124, 158, 180n50, 193, 203, 211, 248, 259
demons, 14, 46, 73n87, 266
devil, 13–14, 21, 36, 46, 52, 88n58, 91n68, 137, 276
divine nature, 5, 7, 10, 11, 16, 17, 20–22, 62, 68–69, 71, 96, 102–7, 110, 121, 148, 191, 196, 202, 203, 215–18, 227, 245, 254, 274, 288. *See also* 2 Peter 1:4

Easter, 16, 17, 80, 198, 200–201
ecstasy, 53, 268
eighth day, 16–17, 180n50, 279
essence and energies, 209n3, 254, 270, 272
eucharist, 11, 19, 23–26, 27, 41, 80–81, 83, 112, 118, 129–31, 151, 223, 230, 269, 273, 276–77, 282. *See also* body of Christ

evil, 32, 40, 52, 68, 164, 166, 262
exchange formula, 5, 6, 7, 11n6, 65, 71, 72, 84n38, 86, 89–90, 91, 92, 95, 116–19, 134, 140–42, 150, 157, 159, 191, 193–98, 201, 203, 210–15, 227, 229, 274–76, 281, 283, 285, 289, 293; *admirabile commercium*, 11–12, 28, 30, 72n86, 91, 114, 275
exorcism, 13–14, 21, 23, 43

faith, 32–33, 36–38, 42, 51, 82, 89, 95, 113, 129, 130, 155, 166, 201, 216, 223n56, 260, 277, 291
Fall, 18, 59, 60n34, 68n75, 73, 105n46, 218, 264, 269, 271, 274, 275, 281, 290. *See also* Adam
fasting, 28–29, 129, 162, 221, 226
flesh. *See* body
forgiveness, 16, 17, 49, 77, 90–91, 93, 122, 157
frailty, 11–12, 24, 66n64, 71, 72, 101, 105–7, 121, 142, 165n62, 197, 199, 204, 214, 274, 275
freedom, 21, 52, 60, 68, 84n38, 90, 106n48, 148, 154, 163–67, 201, 216, 220–22, 225, 234, 251

garden. *See* paradise
Genesis *3*. *See* Fall; gods
glorification, 7, 26, 27, 87, 89, 104n40, 105, 112–14, 126–28, 154, 180n50, 214–15, 217–18, 227–30
glory, 6, 8, 11, 12, 19, 22, 79, 84n38, 86–87, 92, 111–14, 121–25, 127–30, 146, 154, 158, 159, 162, 164, 167, 187, 196, 211, 213, 216–18, 226, 228, 264, 269, 273, 278–79
gods: becoming, 9, 29, 61n41, 138–39, 149, 155–57, 158, 166–68, 176n35, 178–79, 197n12, 205, 234, 243–44, 264, 280, 284, 286, 293; in Genesis *3*, 68, 149, 178; in Psalm *82* (LXX, *81*), 58, 76, 95, 149, 155–57, 167, 207, 273

happiness, 7, 26, 27, 187n74, 232–45, 246–47, 249–51, 264, 280
healing, 5, 11–12, 17, 31, 36, 43–45, 197, 211, 214–15, 219, 254, 260, 264
heart, 20, 80, 81, 85–86, 146, 164, 176, 184, 220, 225–26, 256–62, 264–70, 289–90
holiness, 21, 72, 94, 108, 137, 141, 145, 156, 162, 177, 179, 185, 186, 195–96, 267
humility, 20, 64n56, 89, 107, 207, 223, 230, 261–62

illumination, 6, 8, 22, 47, 49, 51, 78, 82, 86, 181, 185, 225, 254, 256–57, 260, 264–65, 268–71, 289n71
image of God, 6, 28, 57, 66, 75, 84–85, 88–89, 93, 106n48, 114, 123, 132, 134, 138, 143, 145–47, 149–50, 165, 182, 214, 218–22, 224–26, 230, 275, 280–81. *See also* likeness
imitation, 5, 32, 50–51, 55, 57, 59–61, 66, 74, 75–76, 86, 89–93, 140, 157, 182, 202, 214, 220–24, 230, 289
immortality, 18, 48, 67, 84n38, 90–92, 95–96, 103, 105, 107–9, 141, 176n35, 204, 217, 230, 273–75, 277, 281–82, 291–92
incorruption, 5, 26, 31, 36, 59, 67, 73–74, 96, 107n53, 110, 217, 230, 273, 274, 277, 281, 291

kenosis, 6, 13, 102, 104, 106–7, 110, 120–21, 128, 157, 167, 274–75
kingship, 19–20, 91n68, 156, 201, 226
knowledge: spiritual, 6, 16, 21, 22n61, 27, 114, 123, 129, 155, 171, 173, 178–79, 181–88, 200, 220, 254, 279. *See also* illumination

light. *See also* illumination
likeness, 8, 11, 14, 17, 22–23, 27, 56–57, 60–61, 86–88, 146–47, 158–59, 161–62, 169, 200, 216–22, 273, 280–81. *See also* image of God
love, 85, 91, 95, 175–76, 184–85, 198–99, 203–4, 215, 221, 225, 260, 262–66, 271, 277

marriage, 15, 22, 101, 160–62, 166, 204
mediator, 43–45, 62–63, 67n69, 79, 118
mind, 78–79, 81, 85, 215, 221, 225, 258n16, 264, 269, 277, 280, 291. *See also* illumination; knowledge

obedience, 55, 57, 59–61, 74, 105n46, 178, 260, 262–63, 266

paradise, 10, 17, 20, 27, 38n19, 40, 48
peace, 26, 46, 52, 87–88, 179, 196, 216
perfection: bodily, 5, 55, 65, 71, 73–74, 188; spiritual, 22, 55, 71, 74, 95, 111–14, 122–28, 145, 156, 159–60, 165n62, 167, 178–80, 182, 184–86, 188, 220, 222, 237, 244, 261, 270, 276, 277, 284, 289n71
poverty: material, 89–91, 140, 194–95; spiritual, 21, 90, 95, 140, 193, 210

priesthood, 11, 19–20
Promised Land, 10, 26
Psalm *82* (LXX, *81*). *See* gods
purity, 15n23, 20, 44, 64, 66, 73, 78, 89, 157, 204, 205, 263

rebirth, 5, 6, 15–16, 17, 37, 76, 78n11, 84, 87–88, 91, 118, 158, 166–67, 222n54, 224
reformation, 11, 18, 211, 219
remaking, 18, 24, 36, 74n93, 182, 219–22, 254
renewal, 8, 16, 17, 24, 66, 86, 89, 220n45, 221, 227–28, 264, 291
restoration, 10, 12, 14, 16–18, 20–21, 44, 55, 60–61, 64–69, 71, 74, 78, 84, 90, 92, 105n46, 137n24, 178, 182, 197, 217, 219, 222, 224, 261, 264, 269, 271, 281

sacrifice, 20, 23, 29, 33, 41, 50–53, 76n4, 91n68, 194
slavery, 19, 21, 90, 106n48, 107, 163–64, 167, 200–201, 213. *See also* adoption

transfiguration, 6, 19, 26, 28, 29, 70, 114, 124–25, 127, 158, 254, 278–79
2 Peter *1:4*, 15, 24, 25, 26, 59n27, 95, 108–9, 138, 142–44, 161, 212, 213, 280–82, 284, 290, 291, 293. *See also* divine nature

virginity, 6, 12, 15, 88–89, 141, 154, 160–63, 165–67, 204, 293
virtue, 9, 11, 88, 94, 137, 141, 151, 166, 182n60, 221, 225, 261–62, 288

*Also in the series*
## CUA STUDIES IN EARLY CHRISTIANITY

**GENERAL EDITOR**
Philip Rousseau

*The Bible and Early Trinitarian Theology*
Christopher A. Beeley and
Mark E. Weedman, editors

*Group Identity and Religious Individuality
in Late Antiquity*
Éric Rebillard and Jörg Rüpke, editors

*Breaking the Mind: New Studies
in the Syriac "Book of Steps"*
Kristian S. Heal and Robert A. Kitchen, editors

*Re-Reading Gregory of Nazianzus:
Essays on History, Theology, and Culture*
Christopher A. Beeley, editor

*To Train His Soul in Books:
Syriac Asceticism in Early Christianity*
Robin Darling Young and
Monica J. Blanchard, editors

*Deification in the Latin Patristic Tradition* was designed in Garamond by
Kachergis Book Design of Pittsboro, North Carolina. It was printed on 60-pound
Maple Eggshell Cream and bound by Maple Press of York, Pennsylvania.